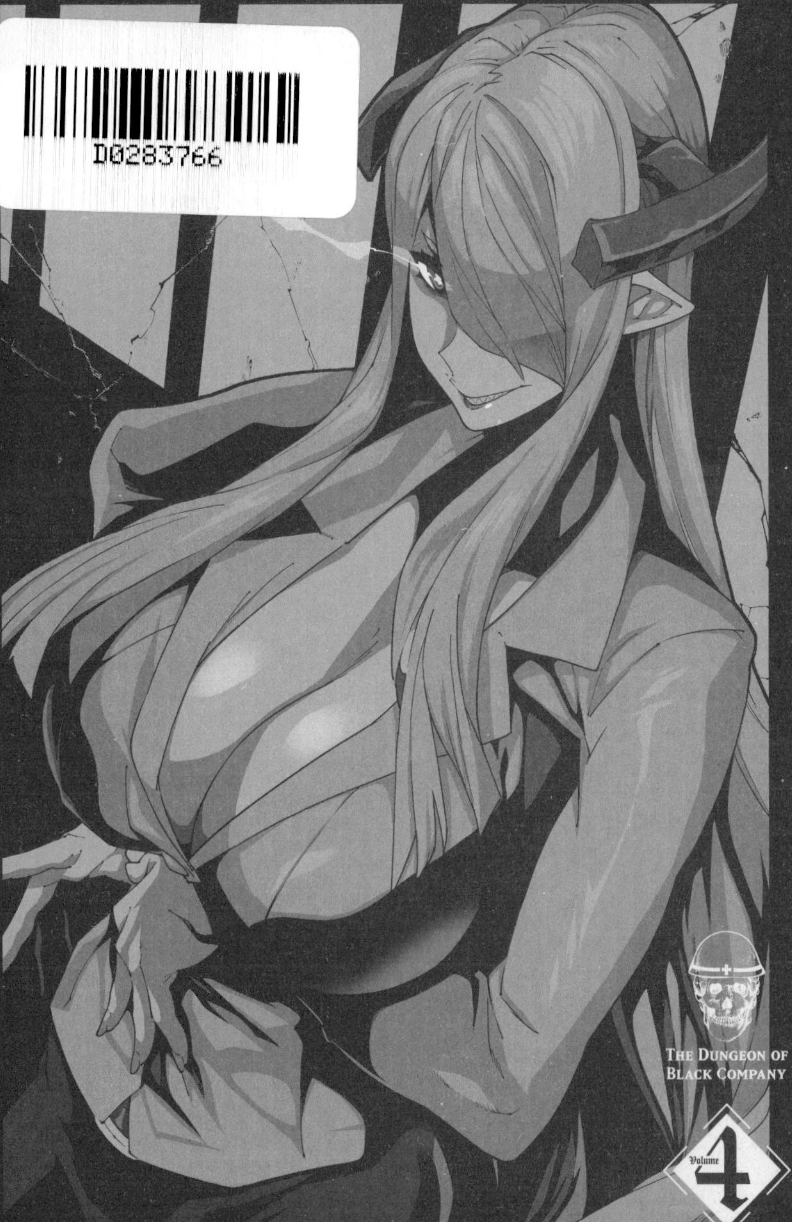
THE DUNGEON OF
BLACK COMPANY
Volume
4

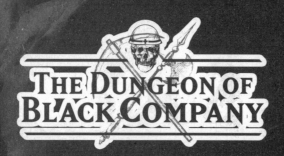

THE DUNGEON OF BLACK COMPANY

CHARACTER

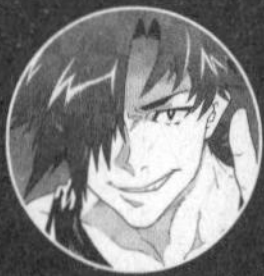

NINOMIYA KINJI
A man that was somehow, for some reason, transported to another world and forced to work at a ruthless company. A conceited man who will use any cunning or underhanded means.

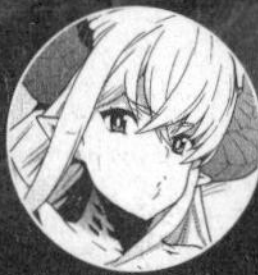

RIM
A monster girl with an insatiable appetite. So long as Ninomiya keeps her fed, she follows him. The most powerful good-for-nothing.

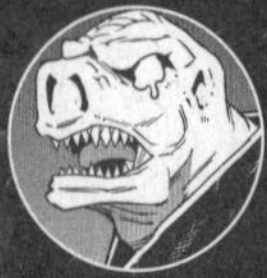

WANIBE
A lizardman who suffers from a severe lack of backbone. Having roomed with Ninomiya in the past, he's been used by him time and time again.

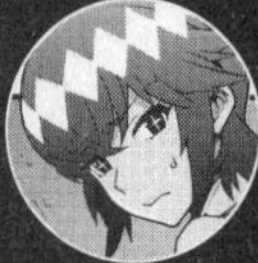

SHIA
A workaholic who rose from the ranks of mere livestock to attain the title of Hero. She has proven herself quite useful.

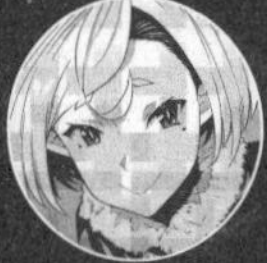

RANGA
An effeminite male mage. He followed Ninomiya from a messed-up future in order to knock some sense into his ancestor from current times.

STORY

Ninomiya Kinji was summoned from another world and forced into indentured servitude as corporate livestock. After paying off his debts and gaining Wanibe, Shia, and Rim as companions, he wound up getting transported through another portal, this time to the future. There, he learned that if the ruthless Raiza'ha Mining Company is not stopped, the world will fall into ruin. Armed with this knowledge, he returns to his companions in the present day, one new tag-along in tow...

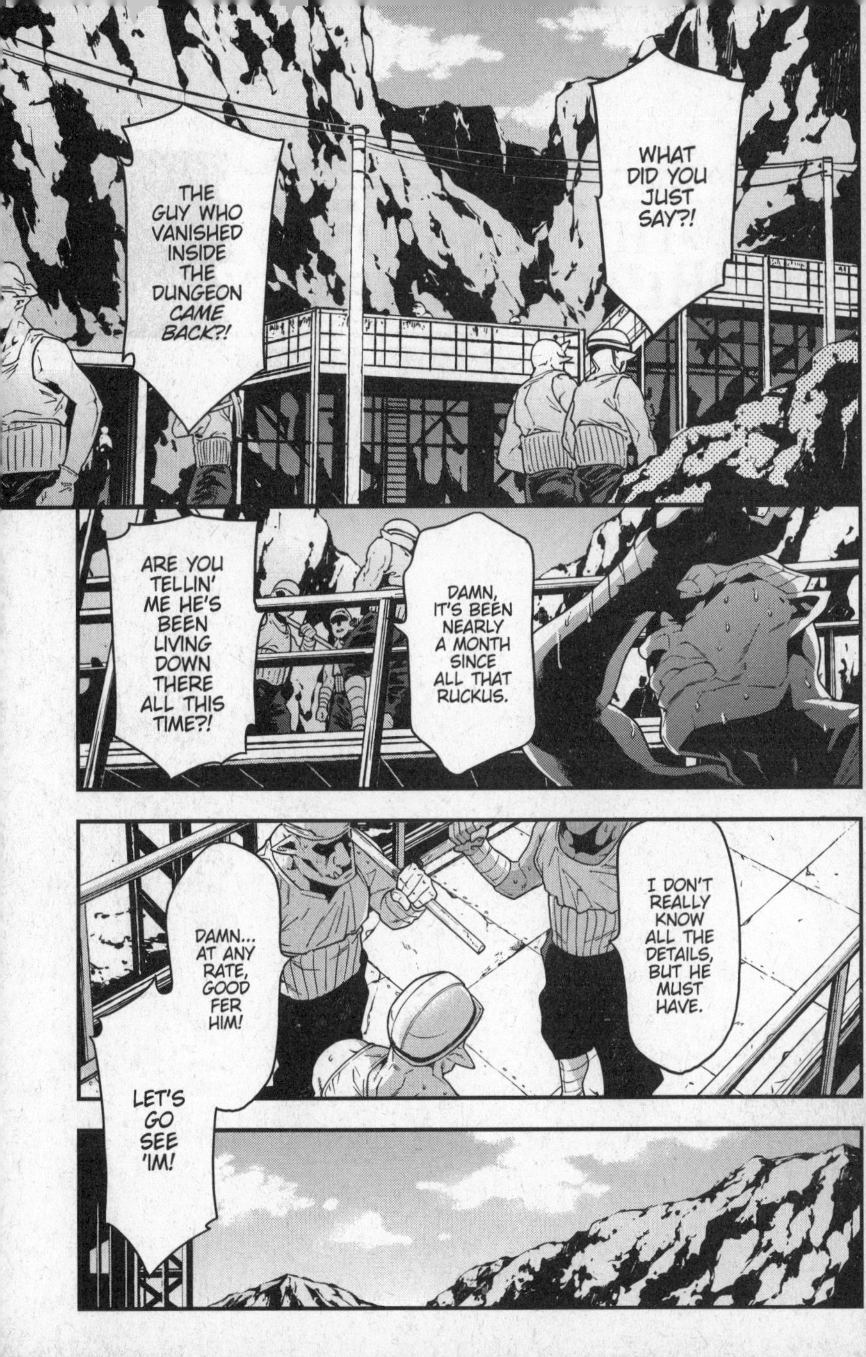
WHAT DID YOU JUST SAY?!
THE GUY WHO VANISHED INSIDE THE DUNGEON CAME BACK?!
DAMN, IT'S BEEN NEARLY A MONTH SINCE ALL THAT RUCKUS.
ARE YOU TELLIN' ME HE'S BEEN LIVING DOWN THERE ALL THIS TIME?!
I DON'T REALLY KNOW ALL THE DETAILS, BUT HE MUST HAVE.
DAMN... AT ANY RATE, GOOD FER HIM!
LET'S GO SEE 'IM!

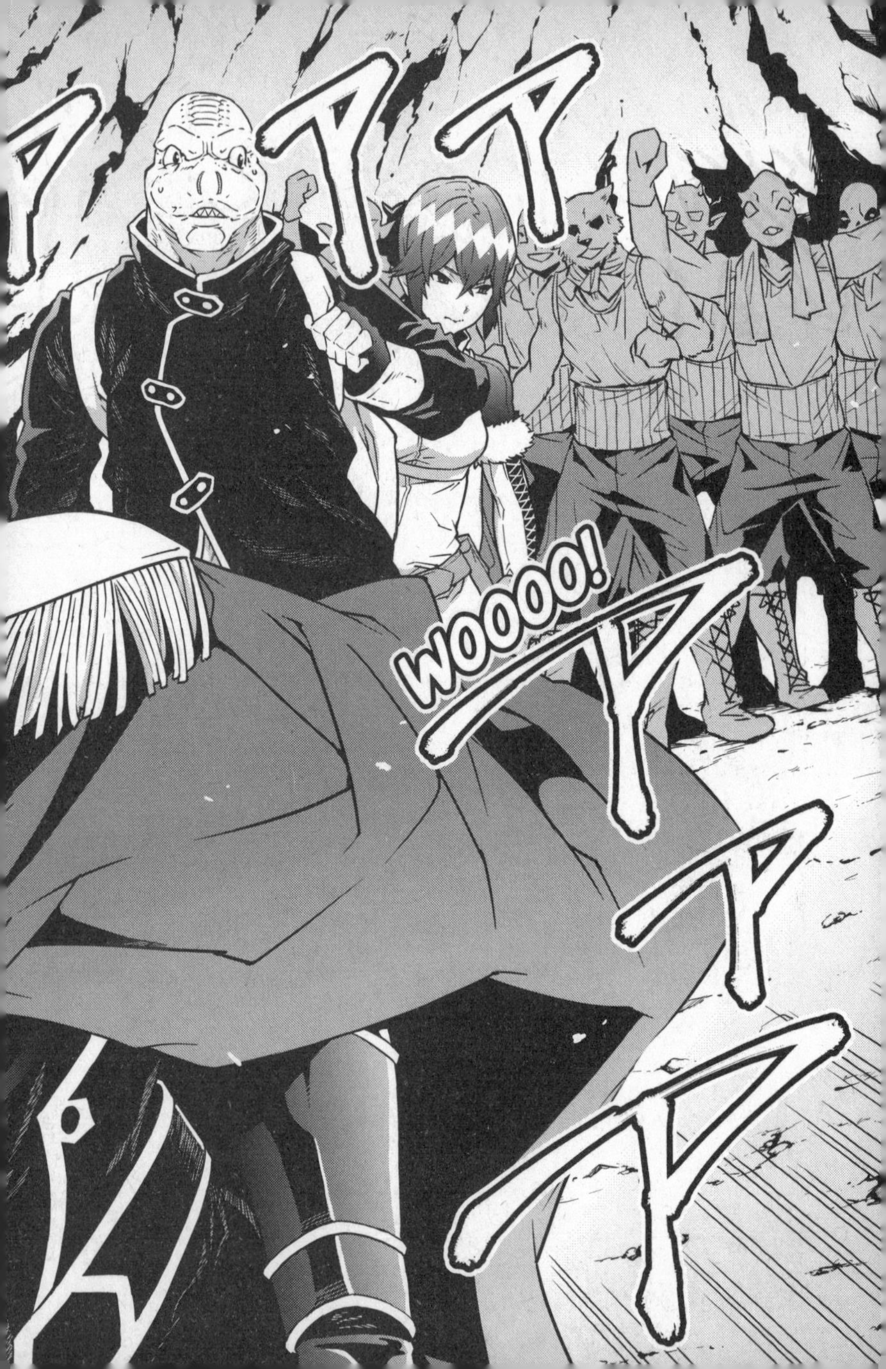
WOOOO!

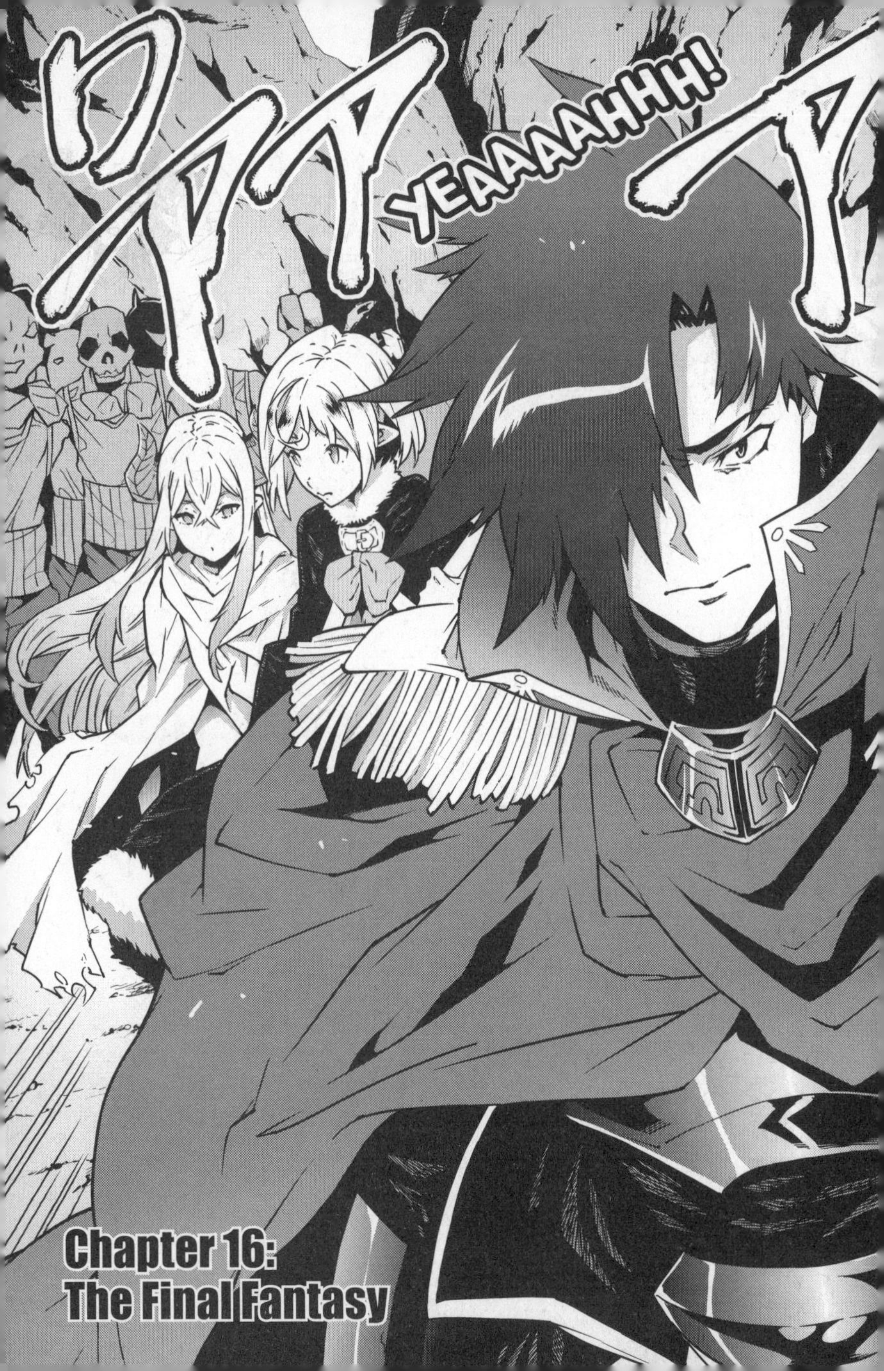
YEAAAAHHH!
Chapter 16:
The Final Fantasy

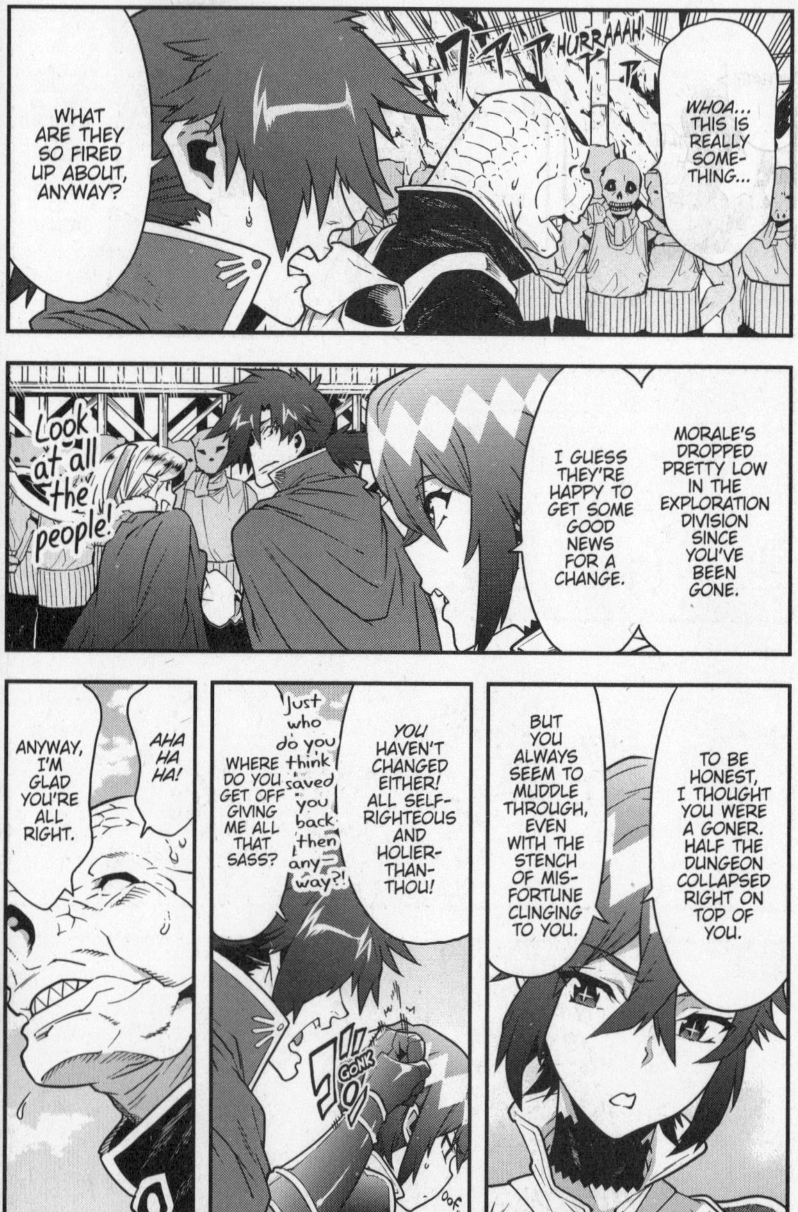
WHOA... THIS IS REALLY SOME-THING...
HURRAAAH!
WHAT ARE THEY SO FIRED UP ABOUT, ANYWAY?
MORALE'S DROPPED PRETTY LOW IN THE EXPLORATION DIVISION SINCE YOU'VE BEEN GONE.
I GUESS THEY'RE HAPPY TO GET SOME GOOD NEWS FOR A CHANGE.
Look at all the people!
TO BE HONEST, I THOUGHT YOU WERE A GONER. HALF THE DUNGEON COLLAPSED RIGHT ON TOP OF YOU.
BUT YOU ALWAYS SEEM TO MUDDLE THROUGH, EVEN WITH THE STENCH OF MIS-FORTUNE CLINGING TO YOU.
oof...
YOU HAVEN'T CHANGED EITHER! ALL SELF-RIGHTEOUS AND HOLIER-THAN-THOU!
Just who do you think saved you back then anyway?!
WHERE DO YOU GET OFF GIVING ME ALL THAT SASS?
GONK
AHA HA HA!
ANYWAY, I'M GLAD YOU'RE ALL RIGHT.

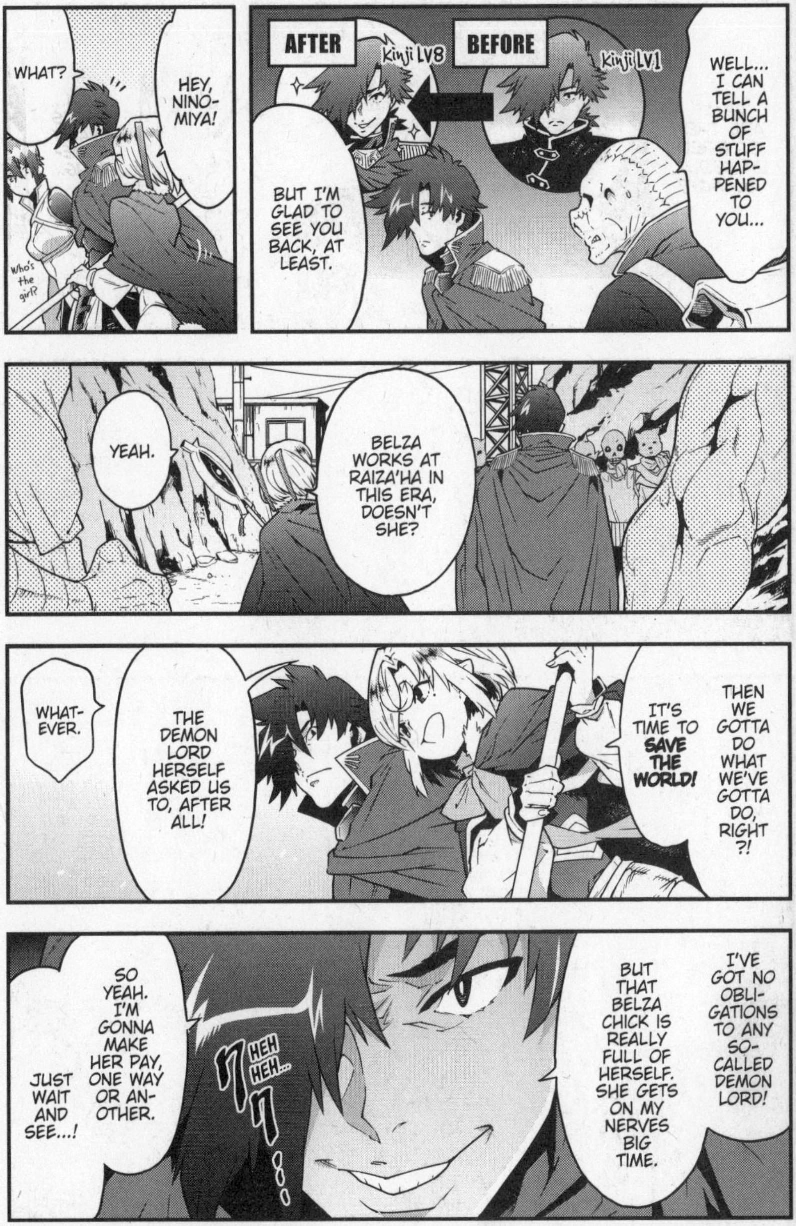
WELL... I CAN TELL A BUNCH OF STUFF HAPPENED TO YOU...
BEFORE
Kinji LV1
AFTER
Kinji LV8
BUT I'M GLAD TO SEE YOU BACK, AT LEAST.
HEY, NINO-MIYA!
WHAT?
Who's the girl?
BELZA WORKS AT RAIZA'HA IN THIS ERA, DOESN'T SHE?
YEAH.
THEN WE GOTTA DO WHAT WE'VE GOTTA DO, RIGHT?!
IT'S TIME TO SAVE THE WORLD!
THE DEMON LORD HERSELF ASKED US TO, AFTER ALL!
WHAT-EVER.
I'VE GOT NO OBLI-GATIONS TO ANY SO-CALLED DEMON LORD!
BUT THAT BELZA CHICK IS REALLY FULL OF HERSELF. SHE GETS ON MY NERVES BIG TIME.
HEH HEH...
SO YEAH. I'M GONNA MAKE HER PAY, ONE WAY OR AN-OTHER.
JUST WAIT AND SEE...!

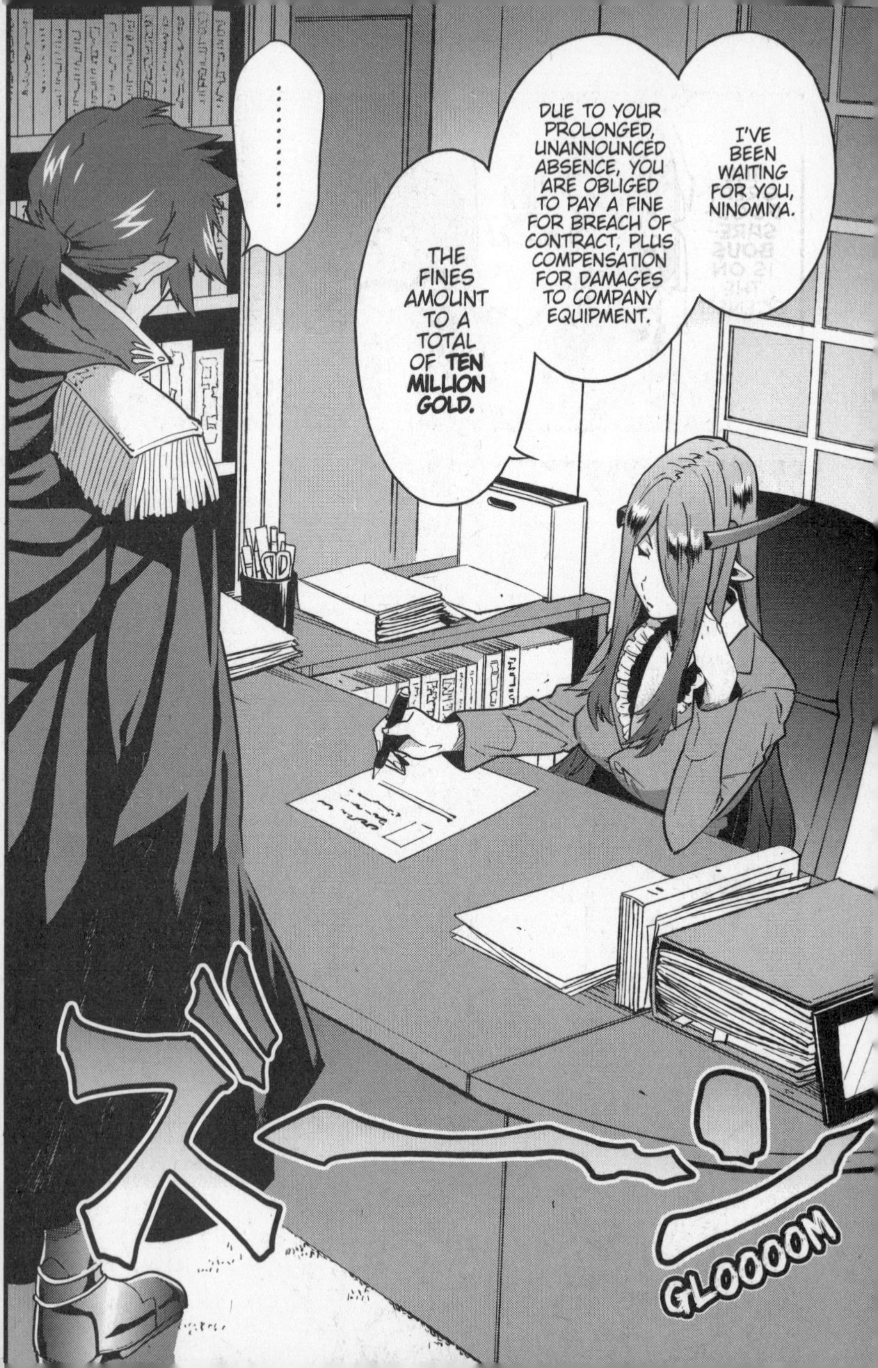
I'VE BEEN WAITING FOR YOU, NINOMIYA.
DUE TO YOUR PROLONGED, UNANNOUNCED ABSENCE, YOU ARE OBLIGED TO PAY A FINE FOR BREACH OF CONTRACT, PLUS COMPENSATION FOR DAMAGES TO COMPANY EQUIPMENT.
THE FINES AMOUNT TO A TOTAL OF **TEN MILLION GOLD.**
......
GLOOOOM

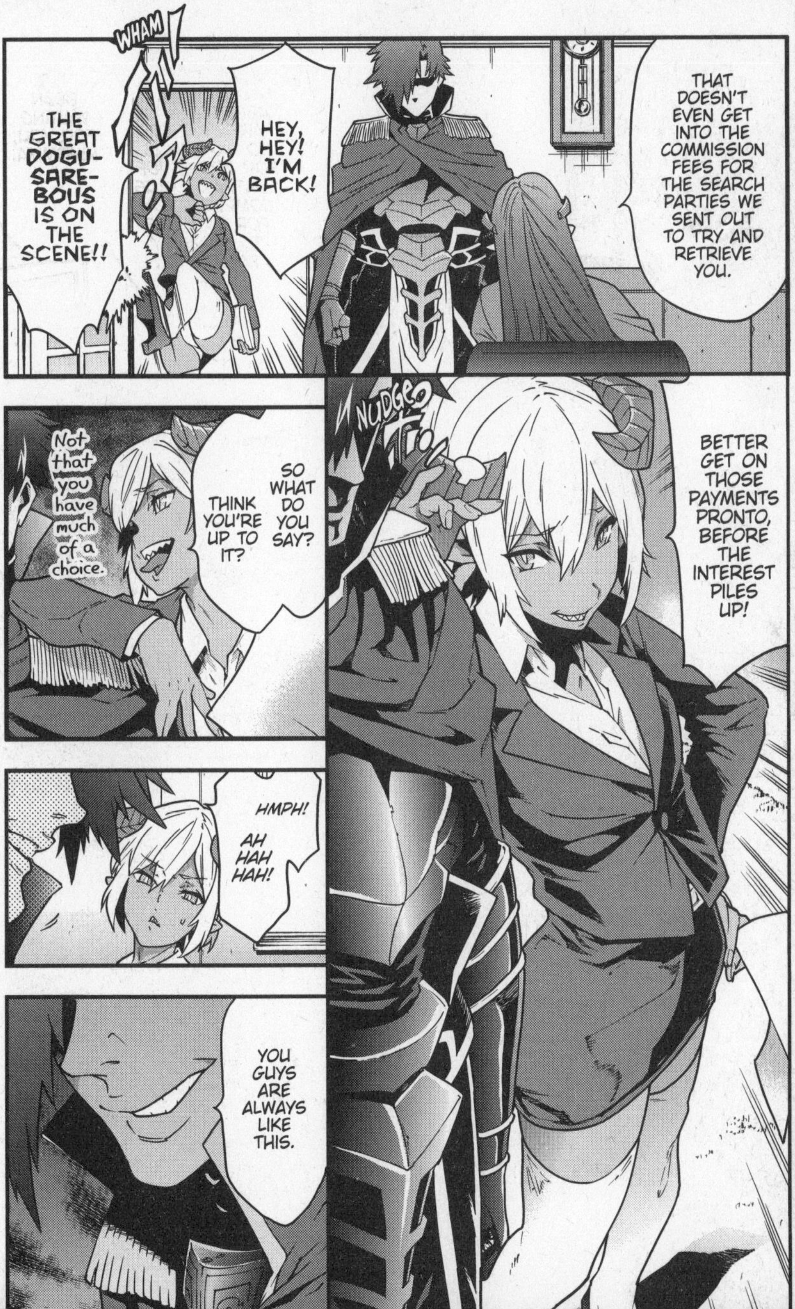
THAT DOESN'T EVEN GET INTO THE COMMISSION FEES FOR THE SEARCH PARTIES WE SENT OUT TO TRY AND RETRIEVE YOU.
HEY, HEY! I'M BACK!
THE GREAT DOGU-SAREBOUS IS ON THE SCENE!!
WHAM
BETTER GET ON THOSE PAYMENTS PRONTO, BEFORE THE INTEREST PILES UP!
NUDGE
SO WHAT DO YOU SAY?
THINK YOU'RE UP TO IT?
Not that you have much of a choice.
HMPH!
AH HAH HAH!
YOU GUYS ARE ALWAYS LIKE THIS.

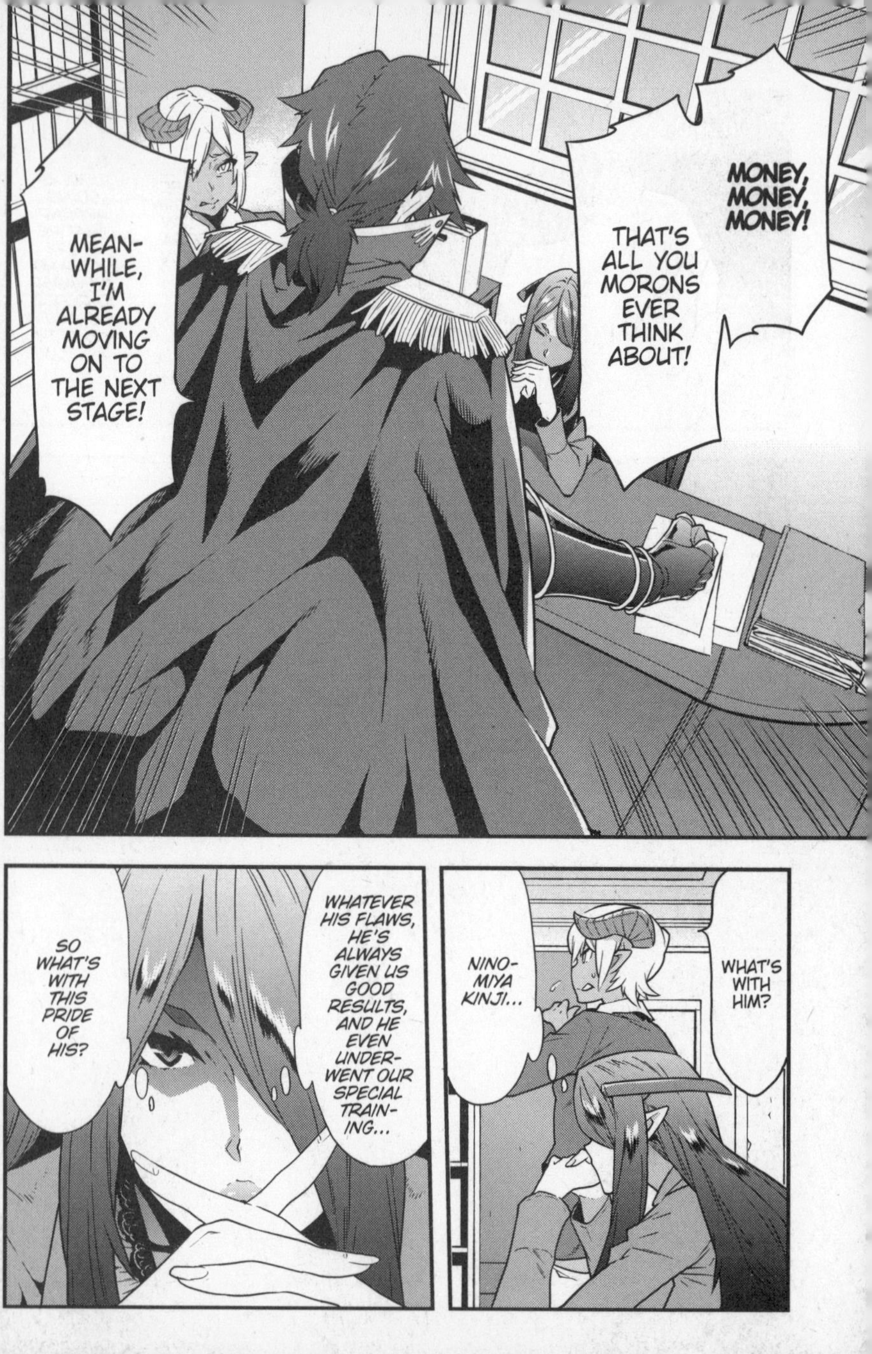
MONEY, MONEY, MONEY!
THAT'S ALL YOU MORONS EVER THINK ABOUT!
MEAN-WHILE, I'M ALREADY MOVING ON TO THE NEXT STAGE!
WHAT'S WITH HIM?
NINO-MIYA KINJI...
WHATEVER HIS FLAWS, HE'S ALWAYS GIVEN US GOOD RESULTS, AND HE EVEN UNDER-WENT OUR SPECIAL TRAIN-ING...
SO WHAT'S WITH THIS PRIDE OF HIS?

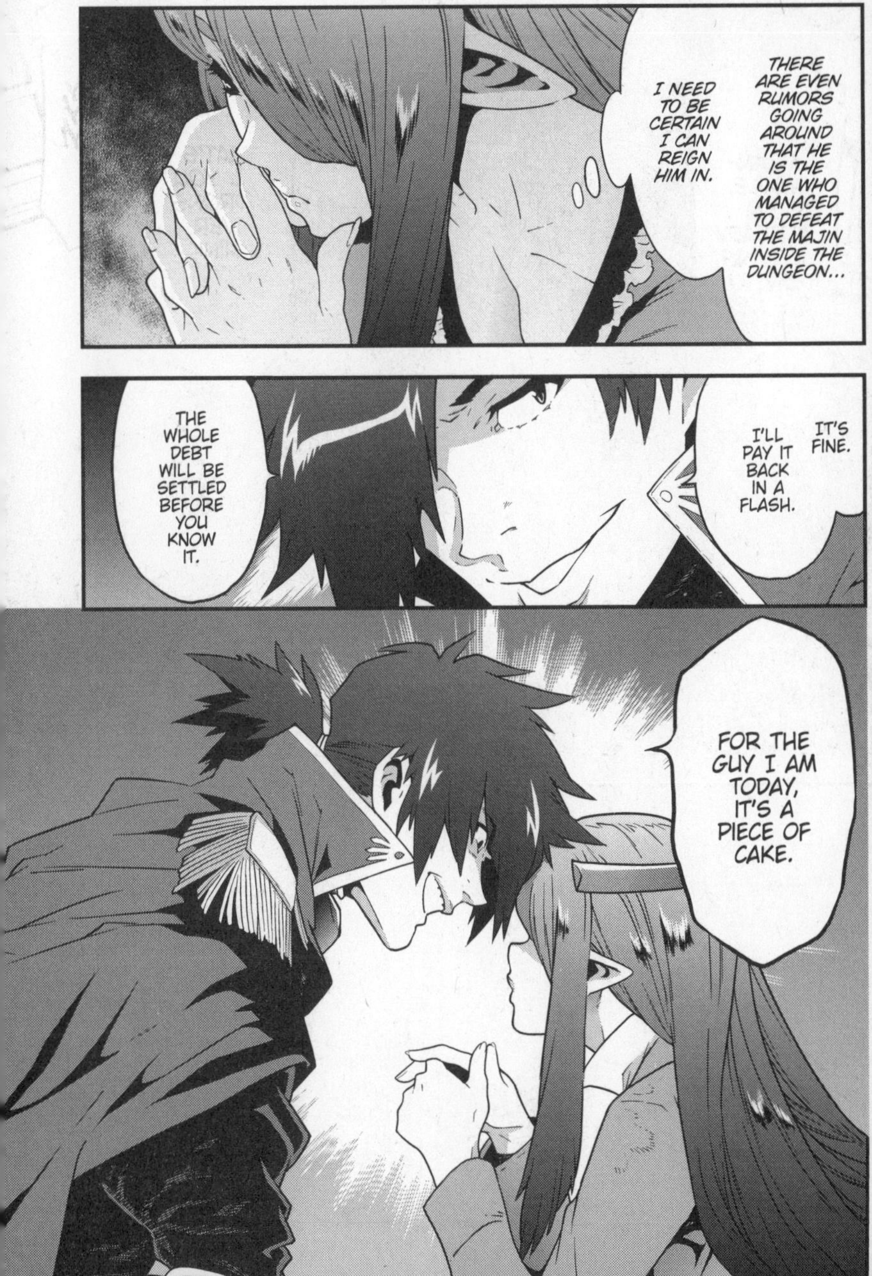
THERE ARE EVEN RUMORS GOING AROUND THAT HE IS THE ONE WHO MANAGED TO DEFEAT THE MAJIN INSIDE THE DUNGEON...
I NEED TO BE CERTAIN I CAN REIGN HIM IN.
IT'S FINE.
I'LL PAY IT BACK IN A FLASH.
THE WHOLE DEBT WILL BE SETTLED BEFORE YOU KNOW IT.
FOR THE GUY I AM TODAY, IT'S A PIECE OF CAKE.

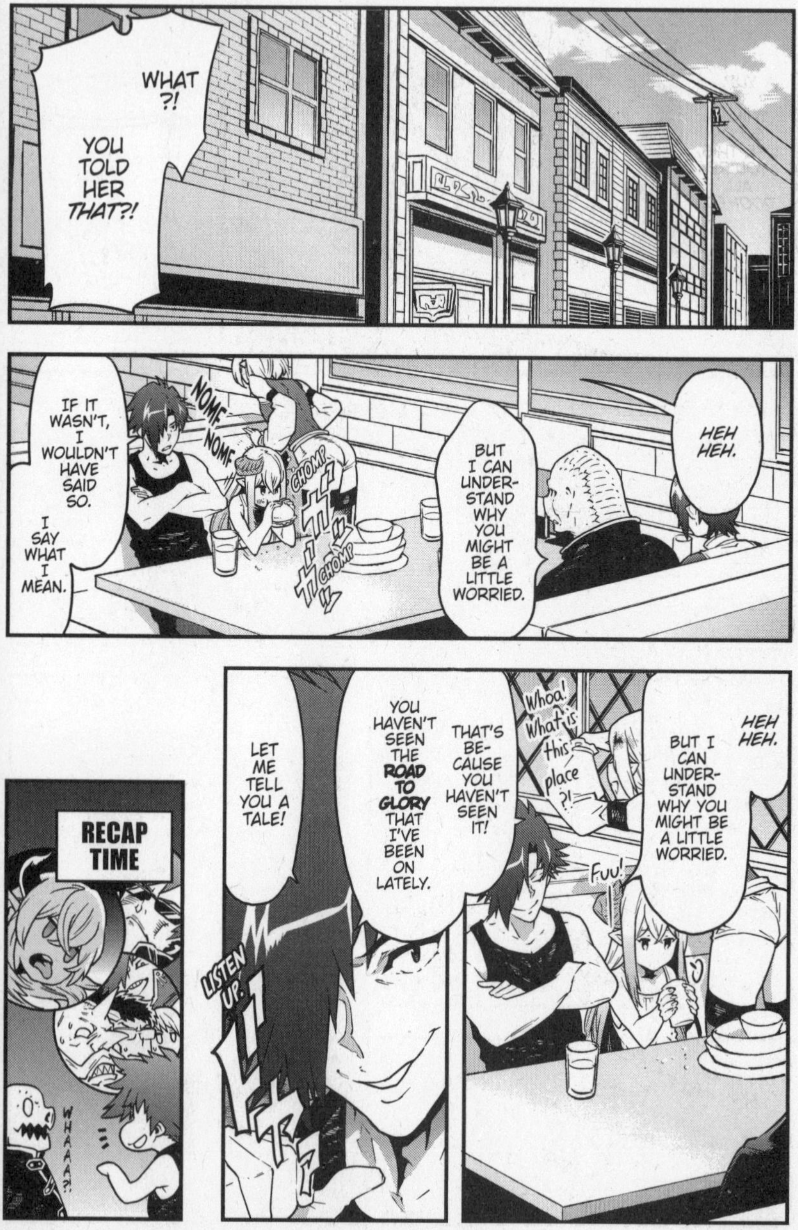
WHAT?!
YOU TOLD HER *THAT?!*
HEH HEH.
BUT I CAN UNDERSTAND WHY YOU MIGHT BE A LITTLE WORRIED.
CHOMP
CHOMP
NOMF NOMF
IF IT WASN'T, I WOULDN'T HAVE SAID SO.
I SAY WHAT I MEAN.
HEH HEH.
BUT I CAN UNDERSTAND WHY YOU MIGHT BE A LITTLE WORRIED.
Whoa! What is this place?!
Fuu!
THAT'S BECAUSE YOU HAVEN'T SEEN IT!
YOU HAVEN'T SEEN THE **ROAD TO GLORY** THAT I'VE BEEN ON LATELY.
LET ME TELL YOU A TALE!
LISTEN UP.
RECAP TIME
WHAAAA?!

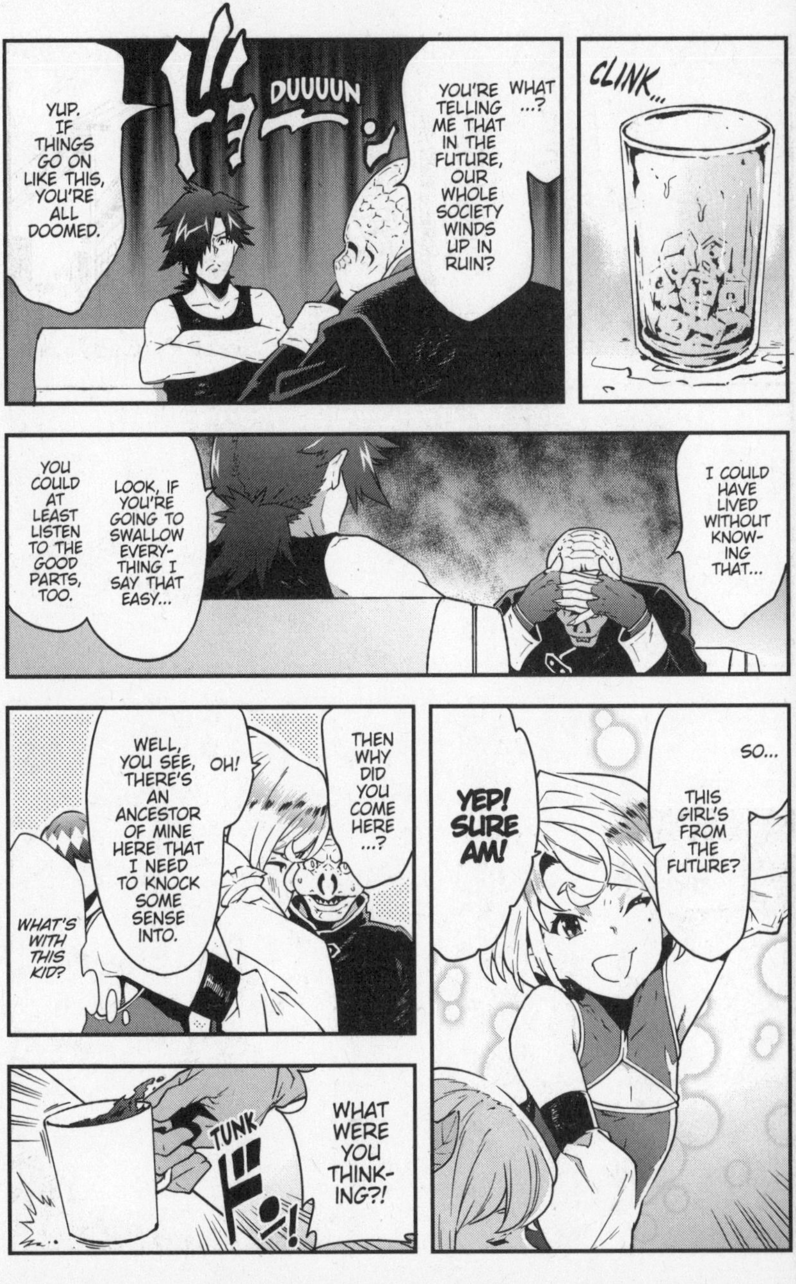
CLINK...
WHAT ...?
YOU'RE TELLING ME THAT IN THE FUTURE, OUR WHOLE SOCIETY WINDS UP IN RUIN?
DUUUUN
YUP. IF THINGS GO ON LIKE THIS, YOU'RE ALL DOOMED.
I COULD HAVE LIVED WITHOUT KNOWING THAT...
LOOK, IF YOU'RE GOING TO SWALLOW EVERYTHING I SAY THAT EASY...
YOU COULD AT LEAST LISTEN TO THE GOOD PARTS, TOO.
SO...
THIS GIRL'S FROM THE FUTURE?
YEP! SURE AM!
THEN WHY DID YOU COME HERE ...?
OH!
WELL, YOU SEE, THERE'S AN ANCESTOR OF MINE HERE THAT I NEED TO KNOCK SOME SENSE INTO.
WHAT'S WITH THIS KID?
WHAT WERE YOU THINKING?!
TUNK

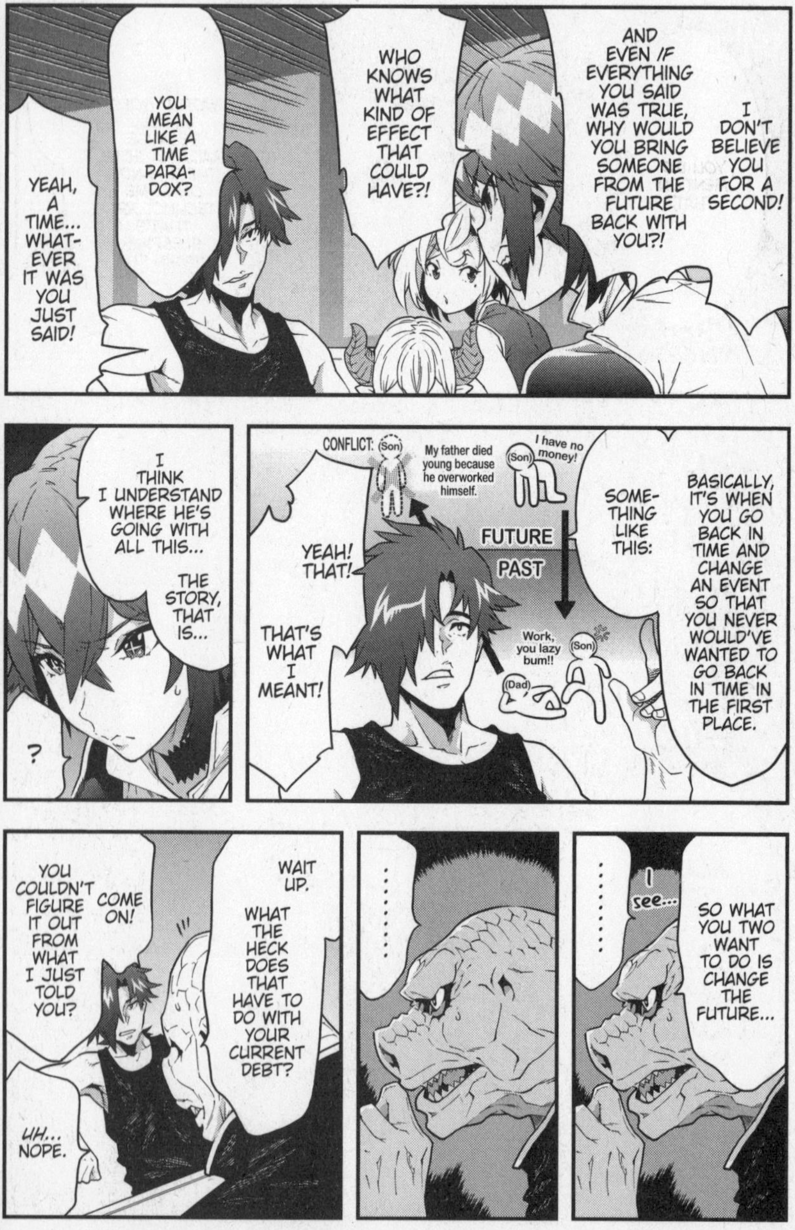
I DON'T BELIEVE YOU FOR A SECOND!
AND EVEN IF EVERYTHING YOU SAID WAS TRUE, WHY WOULD YOU BRING SOMEONE FROM THE FUTURE BACK WITH YOU?!
WHO KNOWS WHAT KIND OF EFFECT THAT COULD HAVE?!
YOU MEAN LIKE A TIME PARA-DOX?
YEAH, A TIME... WHAT-EVER IT WAS YOU JUST SAID!
BASICALLY, IT'S WHEN YOU GO BACK IN TIME AND CHANGE AN EVENT SO THAT YOU NEVER WOULD'VE WANTED TO GO BACK IN TIME IN THE FIRST PLACE.
SOME-THING LIKE THIS:
(Son) I have no money!
FUTURE
PAST
Work, you lazy bum!! (Son)
(Dad)
CONFLICT: (Son) My father died young because he overworked himself.
YEAH! THAT!
THAT'S WHAT I MEANT!
I THINK I UNDERSTAND WHERE HE'S GOING WITH ALL THIS...
THE STORY, THAT IS...
?
SO WHAT YOU TWO WANT TO DO IS CHANGE THE FUTURE...
I see...
......
......
WAIT UP.
WHAT THE HECK DOES THAT HAVE TO DO WITH YOUR CURRENT DEBT?
COME ON!
YOU COULDN'T FIGURE IT OUT FROM WHAT I JUST TOLD YOU?
UH... NOPE.

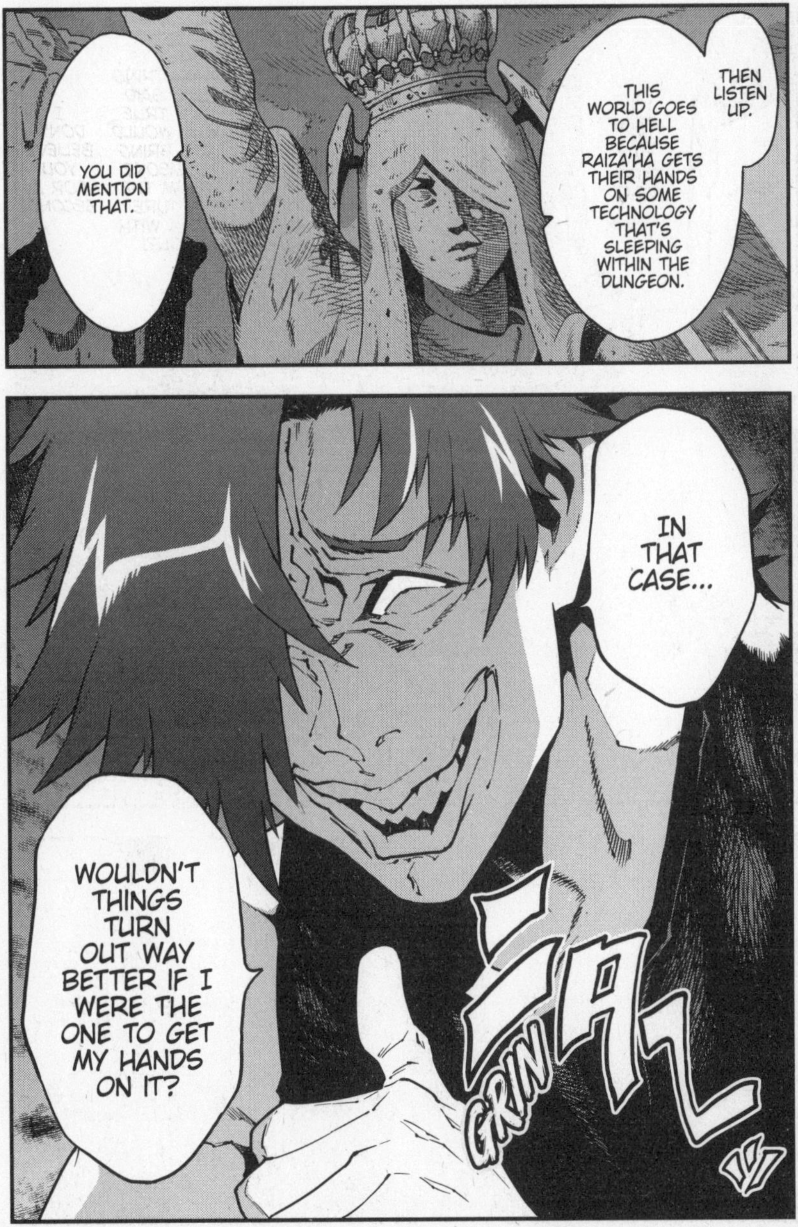
THEN LISTEN UP.
THIS WORLD GOES TO HELL BECAUSE RAIZA'HA GETS THEIR HANDS ON SOME TECHNOLOGY THAT'S SLEEPING WITHIN THE DUNGEON.
YOU DID MENTION THAT.
IN THAT CASE...
WOULDN'T THINGS TURN OUT WAY BETTER IF I WERE THE ONE TO GET MY HANDS ON IT?
GRIN

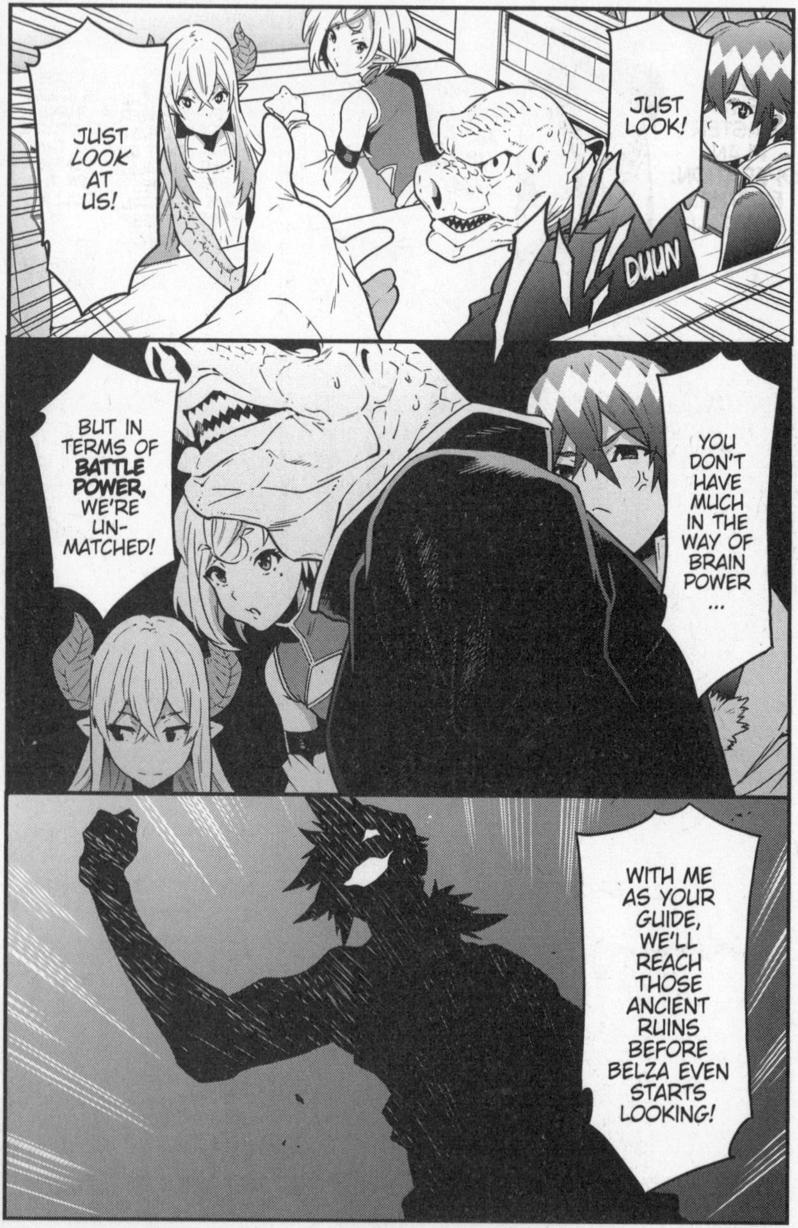
JUST LOOK!
JUST LOOK AT US!
DUUN
YOU DON'T HAVE MUCH IN THE WAY OF BRAIN POWER...
BUT IN TERMS OF **BATTLE POWER,** WE'RE UN-MATCHED!
WITH ME AS YOUR GUIDE, WE'LL REACH THOSE ANCIENT RUINS BEFORE BELZA EVEN STARTS LOOKING!

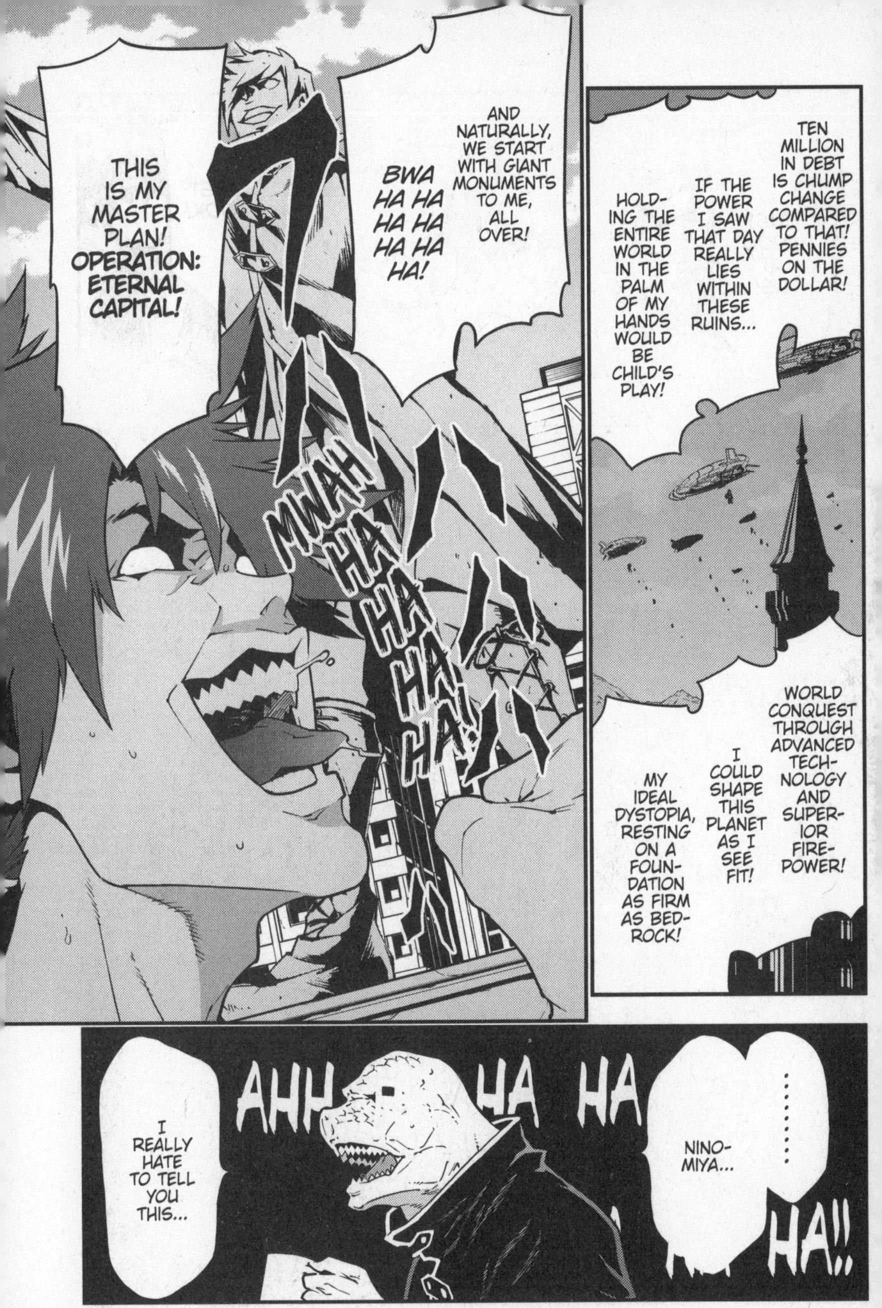
TEN MILLION IN DEBT IS CHUMP CHANGE COMPARED TO THAT! PENNIES ON THE DOLLAR!
IF THE POWER I SAW THAT DAY REALLY LIES WITHIN THESE RUINS...
HOLDING THE ENTIRE WORLD IN THE PALM OF MY HANDS WOULD BE CHILD'S PLAY!
WORLD CONQUEST THROUGH ADVANCED TECH-NOLOGY AND SUPER-IOR FIRE-POWER!
I COULD SHAPE THIS PLANET AS I SEE FIT!
MY IDEAL DYSTOPIA, RESTING ON A FOUN-DATION AS FIRM AS BED-ROCK!
AND NATURALLY, WE START WITH GIANT MONUMENTS TO ME, ALL OVER!
BWA HA HA HA HA HA HA HA!
THIS IS MY MASTER PLAN! OPERATION: ETERNAL CAPITAL!
MWAH HA HA HA HA HA!
....
NINO-MIYA...
AHH HA HA HA!!
I REALLY HATE TO TELL YOU THIS...

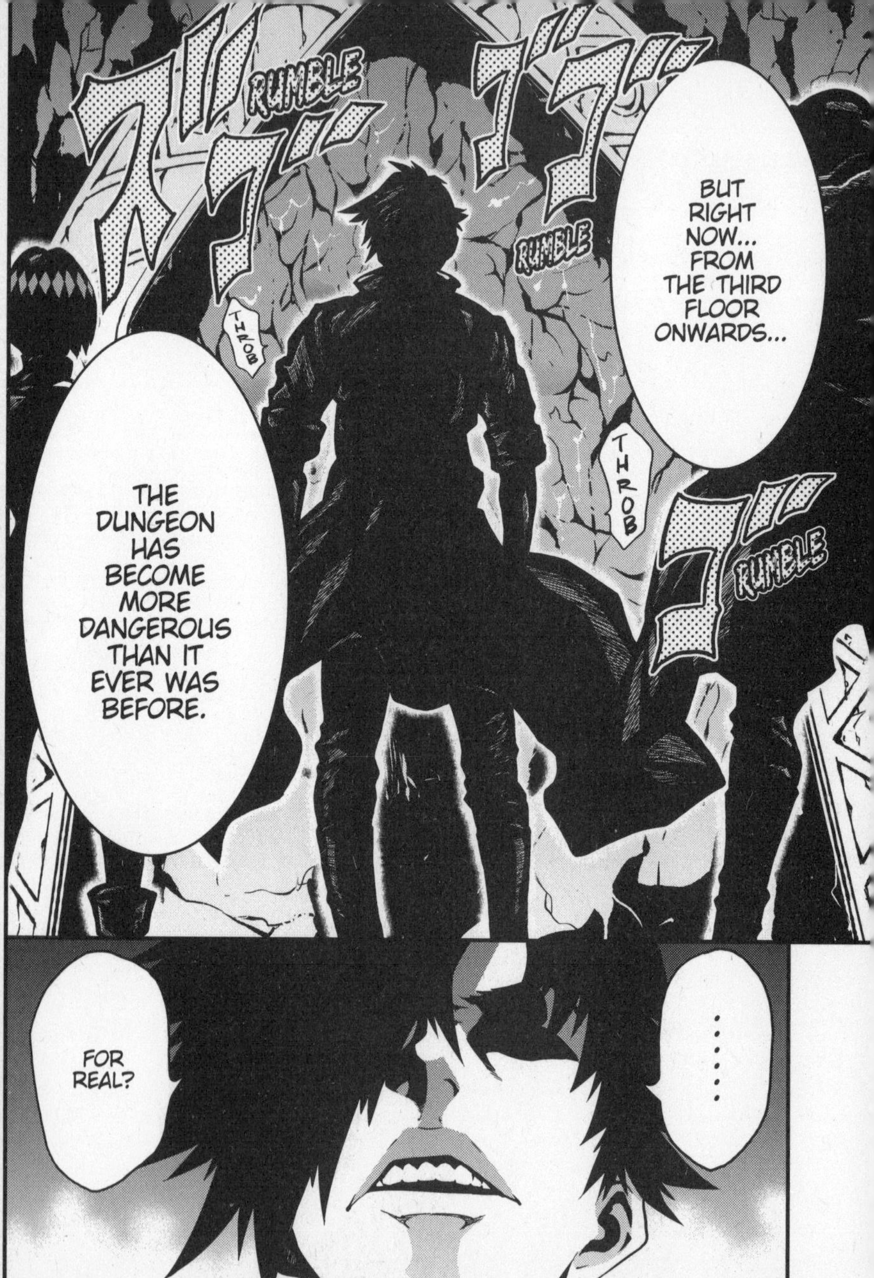
RUMBLE
BUT RIGHT NOW... FROM THE THIRD FLOOR ONWARDS...
RUMBLE
THROB
RUMBLE
THROB
THE DUNGEON HAS BECOME MORE DANGEROUS THAN IT EVER WAS BEFORE.
......
FOR REAL?

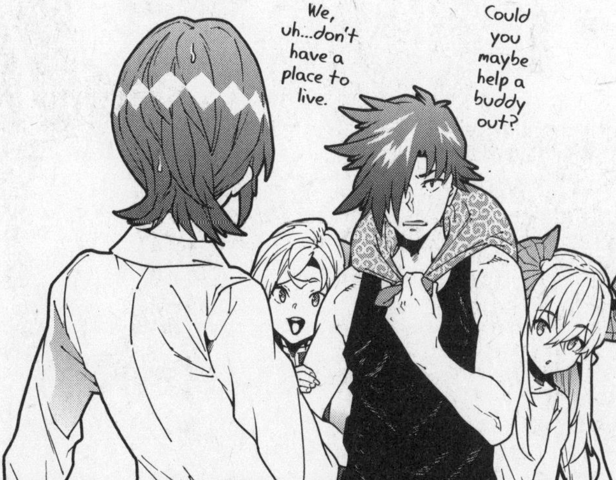
Could you maybe help a buddy out?
We, uh...don't have a place to live.

THE DUNGEON OF
BLACK COMPANY

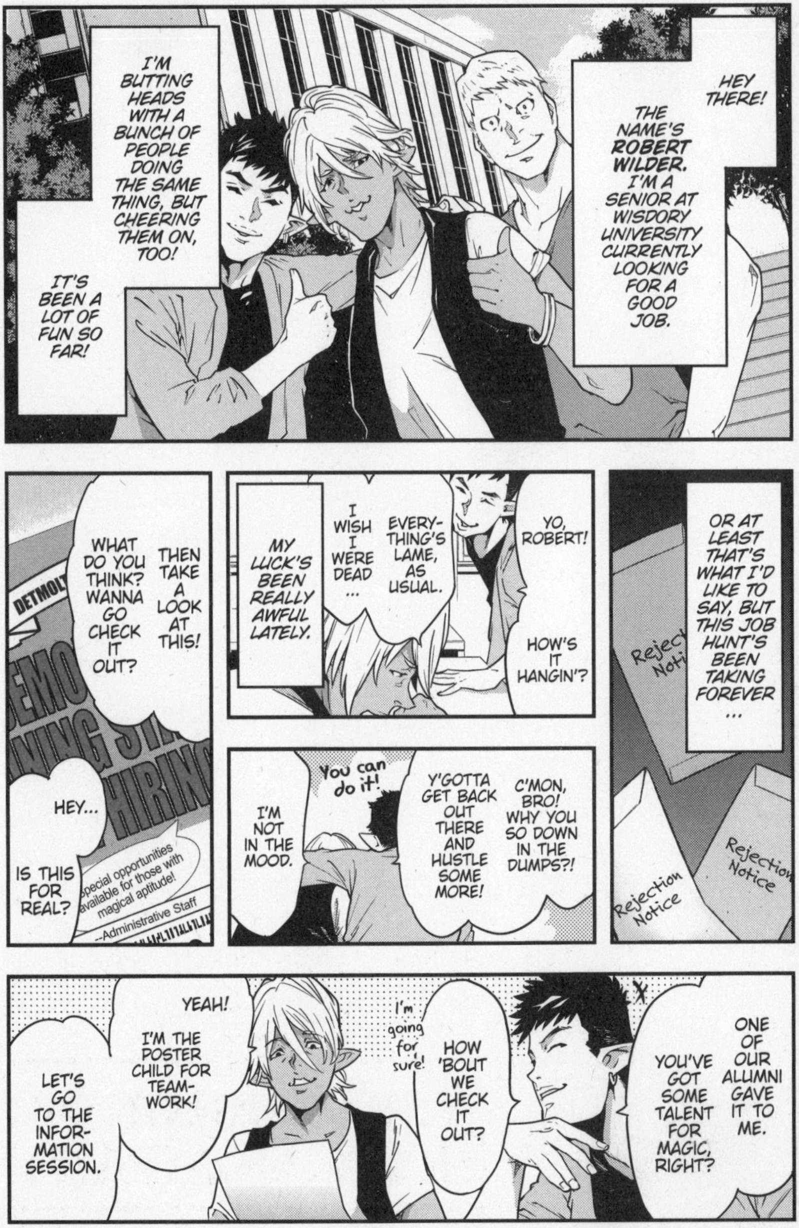
HEY THERE!
THE NAME'S ROBERT WILDER. I'M A SENIOR AT WISDORY UNIVERSITY CURRENTLY LOOKING FOR A GOOD JOB.
I'M BUTTING HEADS WITH A BUNCH OF PEOPLE DOING THE SAME THING, BUT CHEERING THEM ON, TOO!
IT'S BEEN A LOT OF FUN SO FAR!
OR AT LEAST THAT'S WHAT I'D LIKE TO SAY, BUT THIS JOB HUNT'S BEEN TAKING FOREVER ...
Rejection Notice
Rejection Notice
Rejection Notice
YO, ROBERT!
HOW'S IT HANGIN'?
EVERYTHING'S LAME, AS USUAL.
I WISH I WERE DEAD ...
MY LUCK'S BEEN REALLY AWFUL LATELY.
C'MON, BRO! WHY YOU SO DOWN IN THE DUMPS?!
Y'GOTTA GET BACK OUT THERE AND HUSTLE SOME MORE!
You can do it!
I'M NOT IN THE MOOD.
THEN TAKE A LOOK AT THIS!
WHAT DO YOU THINK? WANNA GO CHECK IT OUT?
DETMOLT
HIRING
special opportunities available for those with magical aptitude!
--Administrative Staff
HEY...
IS THIS FOR REAL?
ONE OF OUR ALUMNI GAVE IT TO ME.
YOU'VE GOT SOME TALENT FOR MAGIC, RIGHT?
HOW 'BOUT WE CHECK IT OUT?
I'm going for sure!
YEAH!
I'M THE POSTER CHILD FOR TEAMWORK!
LET'S GO TO THE INFORMATION SESSION.

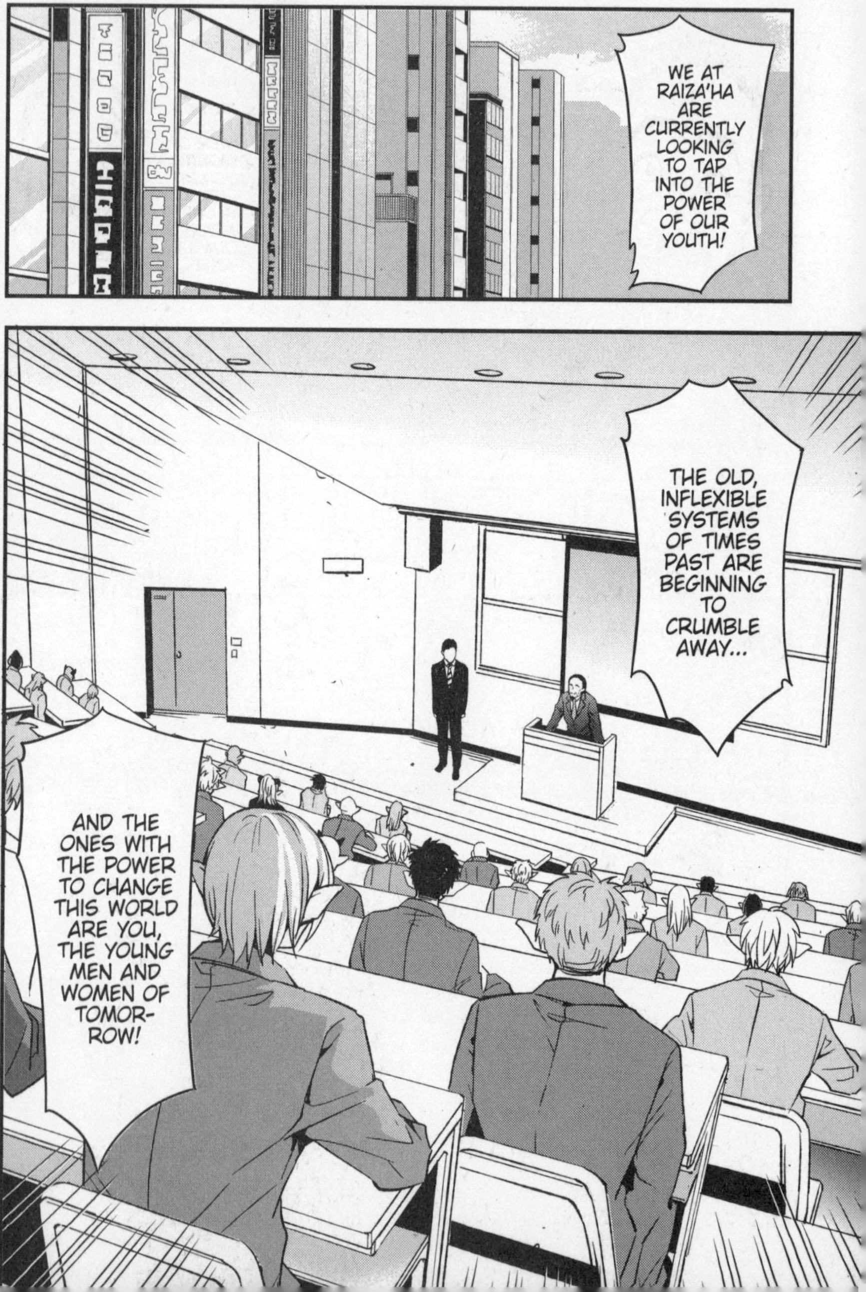
WE AT RAIZA'HA ARE CURRENTLY LOOKING TO TAP INTO THE POWER OF OUR YOUTH!
THE OLD, INFLEXIBLE SYSTEMS OF TIMES PAST ARE BEGINNING TO CRUMBLE AWAY...
AND THE ONES WITH THE POWER TO CHANGE THIS WORLD ARE YOU, THE YOUNG MEN AND WOMEN OF TOMOR-ROW!

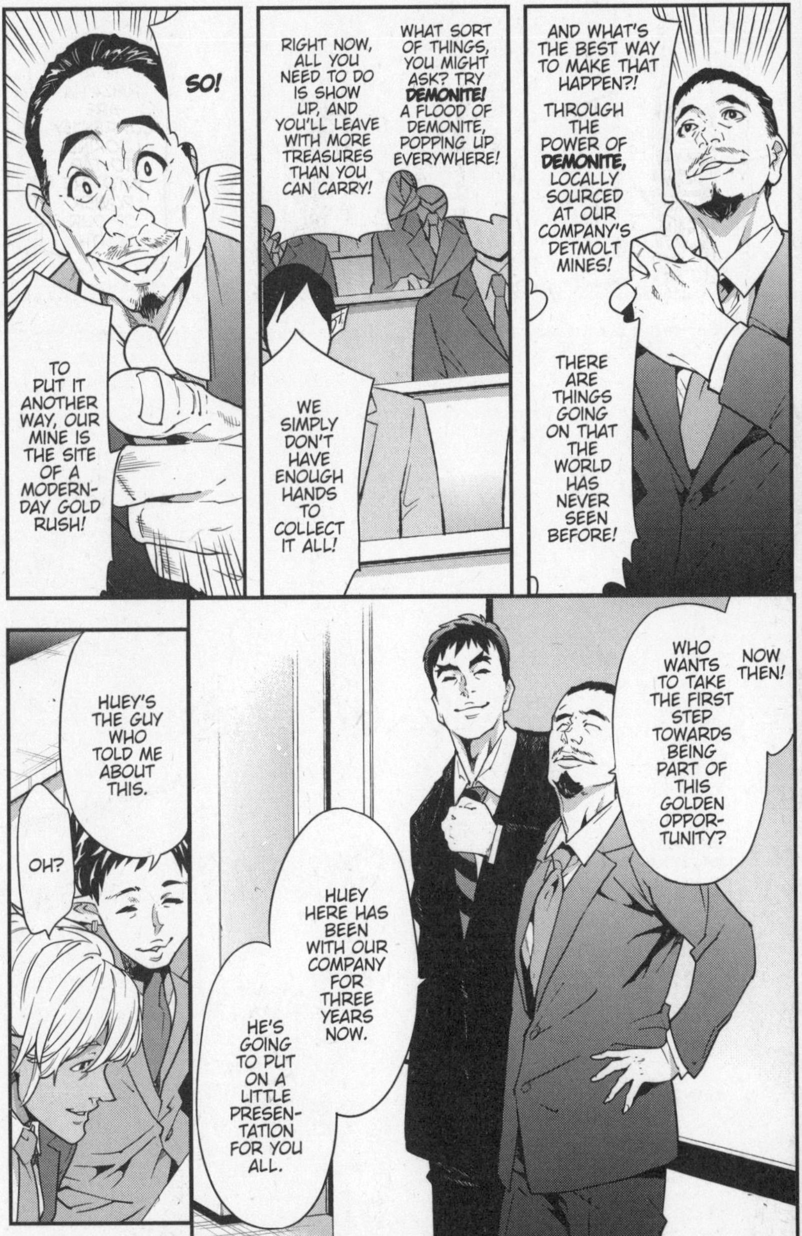
AND WHAT'S THE BEST WAY TO MAKE THAT HAPPEN?!
THROUGH THE POWER OF DEMONITE, LOCALLY SOURCED AT OUR COMPANY'S DETMOLT MINES!
THERE ARE THINGS GOING ON THAT THE WORLD HAS NEVER SEEN BEFORE!
WHAT SORT OF THINGS, YOU MIGHT ASK? TRY DEMONITE! A FLOOD OF DEMONITE, POPPING UP EVERYWHERE!
RIGHT NOW, ALL YOU NEED TO DO IS SHOW UP, AND YOU'LL LEAVE WITH MORE TREASURES THAN YOU CAN CARRY!
WE SIMPLY DON'T HAVE ENOUGH HANDS TO COLLECT IT ALL!
SO!
TO PUT IT ANOTHER WAY, OUR MINE IS THE SITE OF A MODERN-DAY GOLD RUSH!
NOW THEN!
WHO WANTS TO TAKE THE FIRST STEP TOWARDS BEING PART OF THIS GOLDEN OPPORTUNITY?
HUEY HERE HAS BEEN WITH OUR COMPANY FOR THREE YEARS NOW.
HE'S GOING TO PUT ON A LITTLE PRESENTATION FOR YOU ALL.
HUEY'S THE GUY WHO TOLD ME ABOUT THIS.
OH?

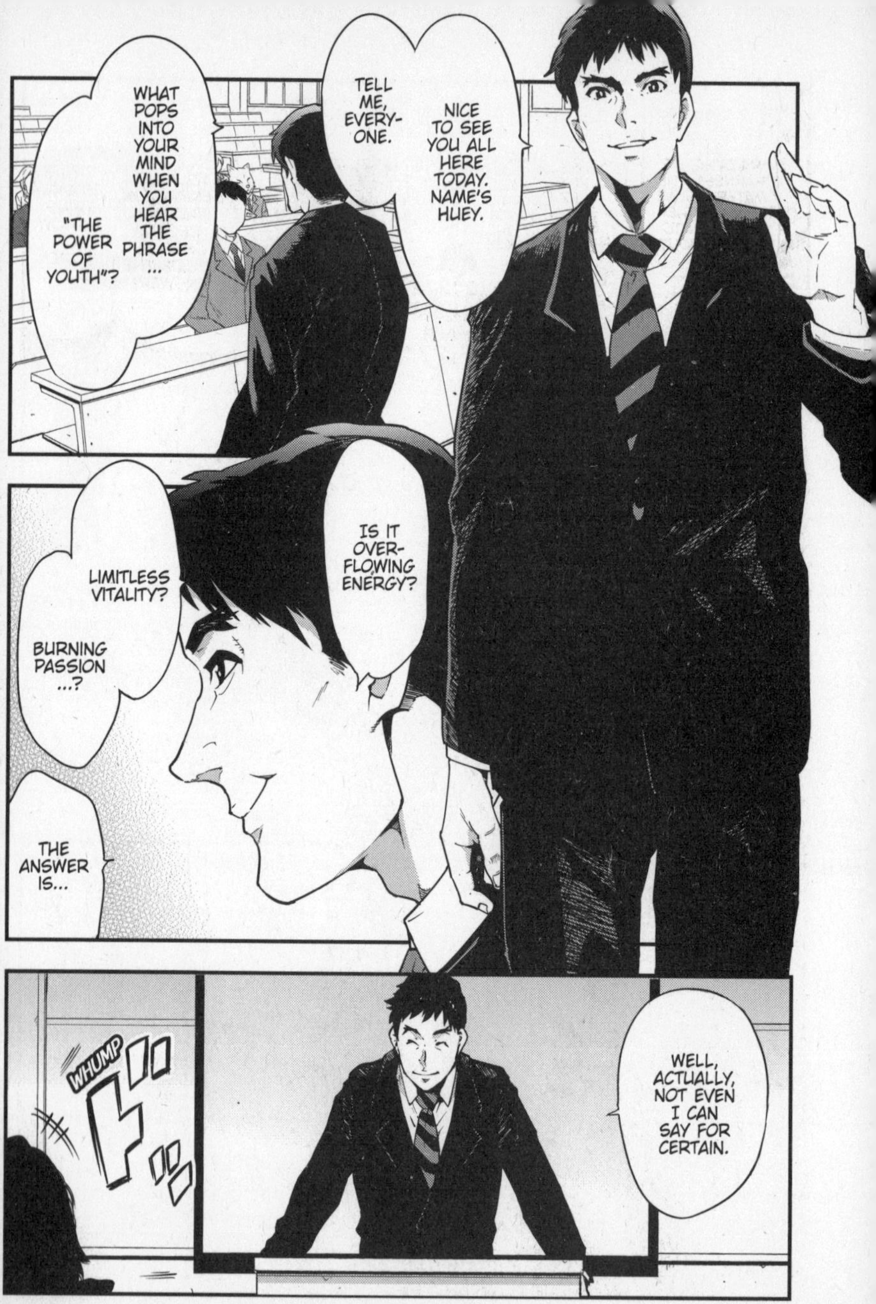
NICE TO SEE YOU ALL HERE TODAY. NAME'S HUEY.
TELL ME, EVERYONE.
WHAT POPS INTO YOUR MIND WHEN YOU HEAR THE PHRASE ...
"THE POWER OF YOUTH"?
IS IT OVER-FLOWING ENERGY?
LIMITLESS VITALITY?
BURNING PASSION ...?
THE ANSWER IS...
WELL, ACTUALLY, NOT EVEN I CAN SAY FOR CERTAIN.
WHUMP

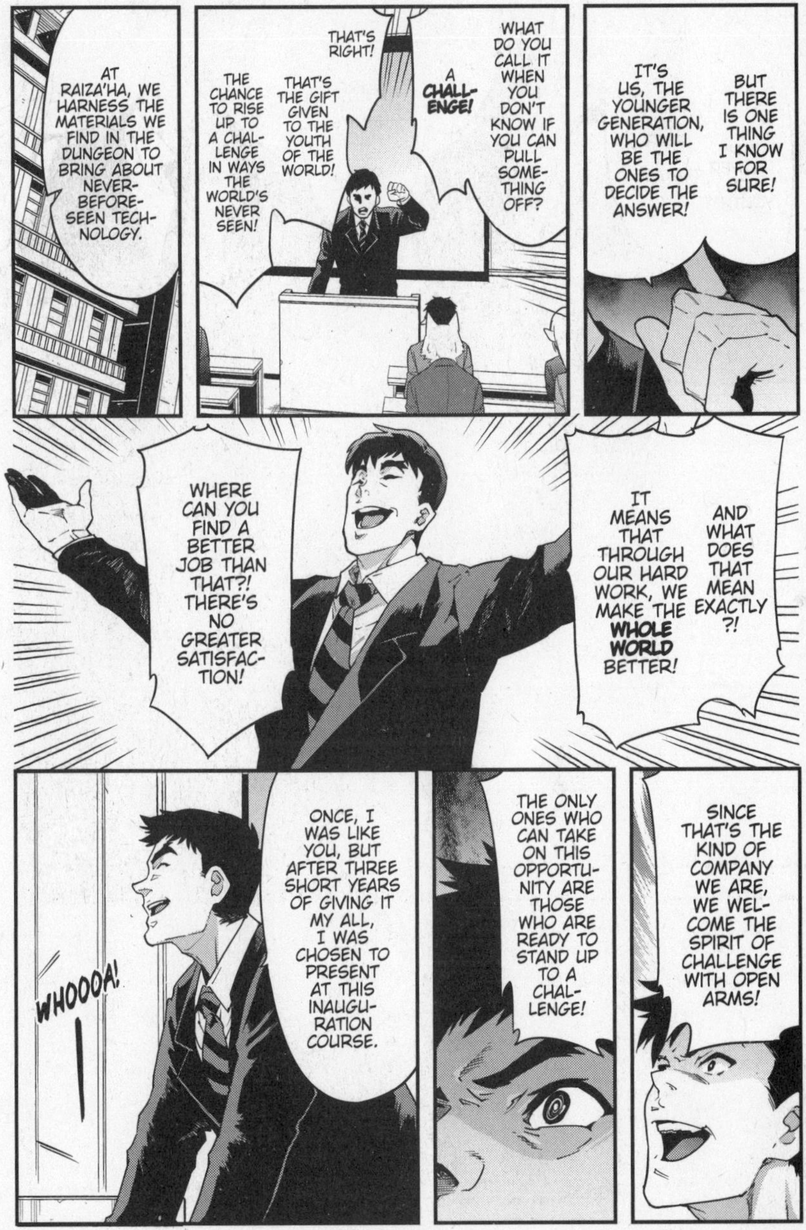
BUT THERE IS ONE THING I KNOW FOR SURE!
IT'S US, THE YOUNGER GENERATION, WHO WILL BE THE ONES TO DECIDE THE ANSWER!
WHAT DO YOU CALL IT WHEN YOU DON'T KNOW IF YOU CAN PULL SOMETHING OFF?
A **CHALLENGE!**
THAT'S RIGHT!
THAT'S THE GIFT GIVEN TO THE YOUTH OF THE WORLD!
THE CHANCE TO RISE UP TO A CHALLENGE IN WAYS THE WORLD'S NEVER SEEN!
AT RAIZA'HA, WE HARNESS THE MATERIALS WE FIND IN THE DUNGEON TO BRING ABOUT NEVER-BEFORE-SEEN TECHNOLOGY.
AND WHAT DOES THAT MEAN EXACTLY?!
IT MEANS THAT THROUGH OUR HARD WORK, WE MAKE THE **WHOLE WORLD** BETTER!
WHERE CAN YOU FIND A BETTER JOB THAN THAT?! THERE'S NO GREATER SATISFACTION!
SINCE THAT'S THE KIND OF COMPANY WE ARE, WE WELCOME THE SPIRIT OF CHALLENGE WITH OPEN ARMS!
THE ONLY ONES WHO CAN TAKE ON THIS OPPORTUNITY ARE THOSE WHO ARE READY TO STAND UP TO A CHALLENGE!
ONCE, I WAS LIKE YOU, BUT AFTER THREE SHORT YEARS OF GIVING IT MY ALL, I WAS CHOSEN TO PRESENT AT THIS INAUGURATION COURSE.
WHOOOA!

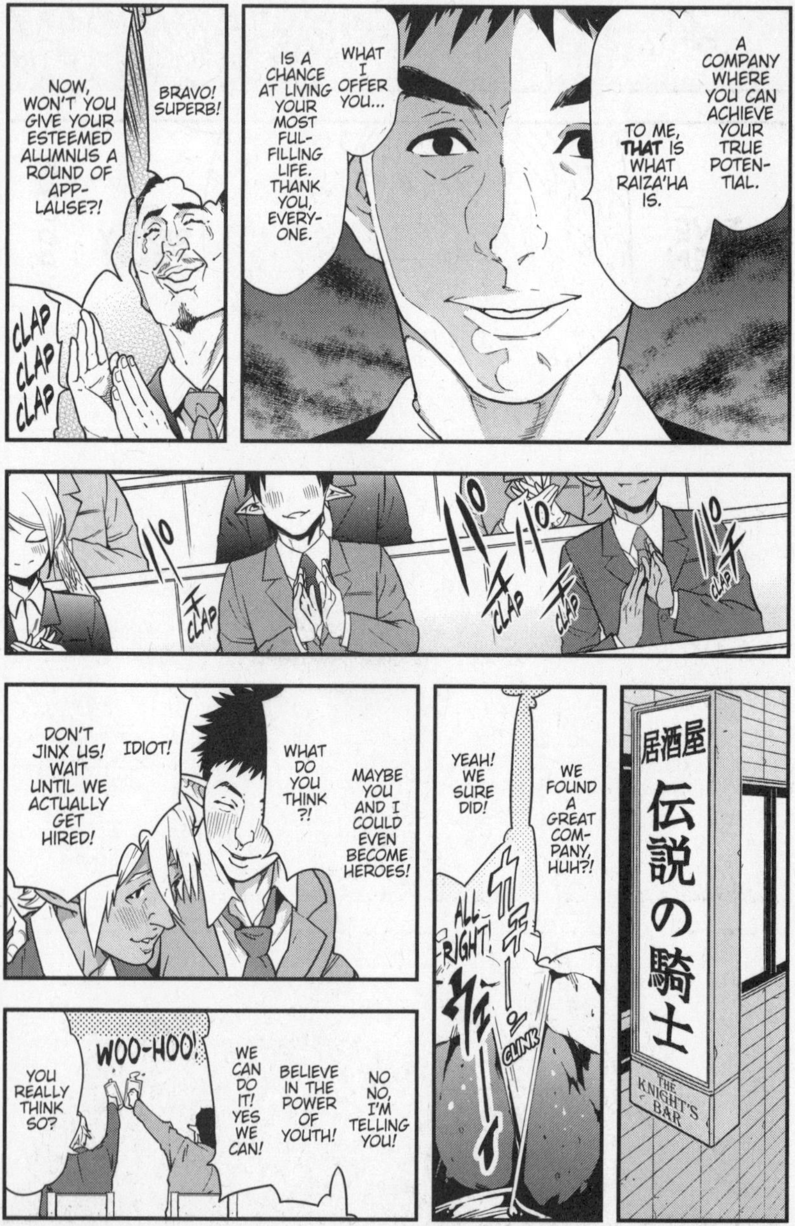
A COMPANY WHERE YOU CAN ACHIEVE YOUR TRUE POTENTIAL.
TO ME, **THAT** IS WHAT RAIZA'HA IS.
WHAT I OFFER YOU...
IS A CHANCE AT LIVING YOUR MOST FULFILLING LIFE. THANK YOU, EVERYONE.
BRAVO! SUPERB!
NOW, WON'T YOU GIVE YOUR ESTEEMED ALUMNUS A ROUND OF APPLAUSE?!
CLAP CLAP CLAP
パチ CLAP
パチ CLAP
パチ CLAP
パチ CLAP
居酒屋 伝説の騎士
THE KNIGHT'S BAR
WE FOUND A GREAT COMPANY, HUH?!
YEAH! WE SURE DID!
ALL RIGHT!
カチーン CLINK
MAYBE YOU AND I COULD EVEN BECOME HEROES!
WHAT DO YOU THINK?!
IDIOT!
DON'T JINX US! WAIT UNTIL WE ACTUALLY GET HIRED!
NO NO, I'M TELLING YOU!
BELIEVE IN THE POWER OF YOUTH!
WE CAN DO IT! YES WE CAN!
WOO-HOO!
YOU REALLY THINK SO?

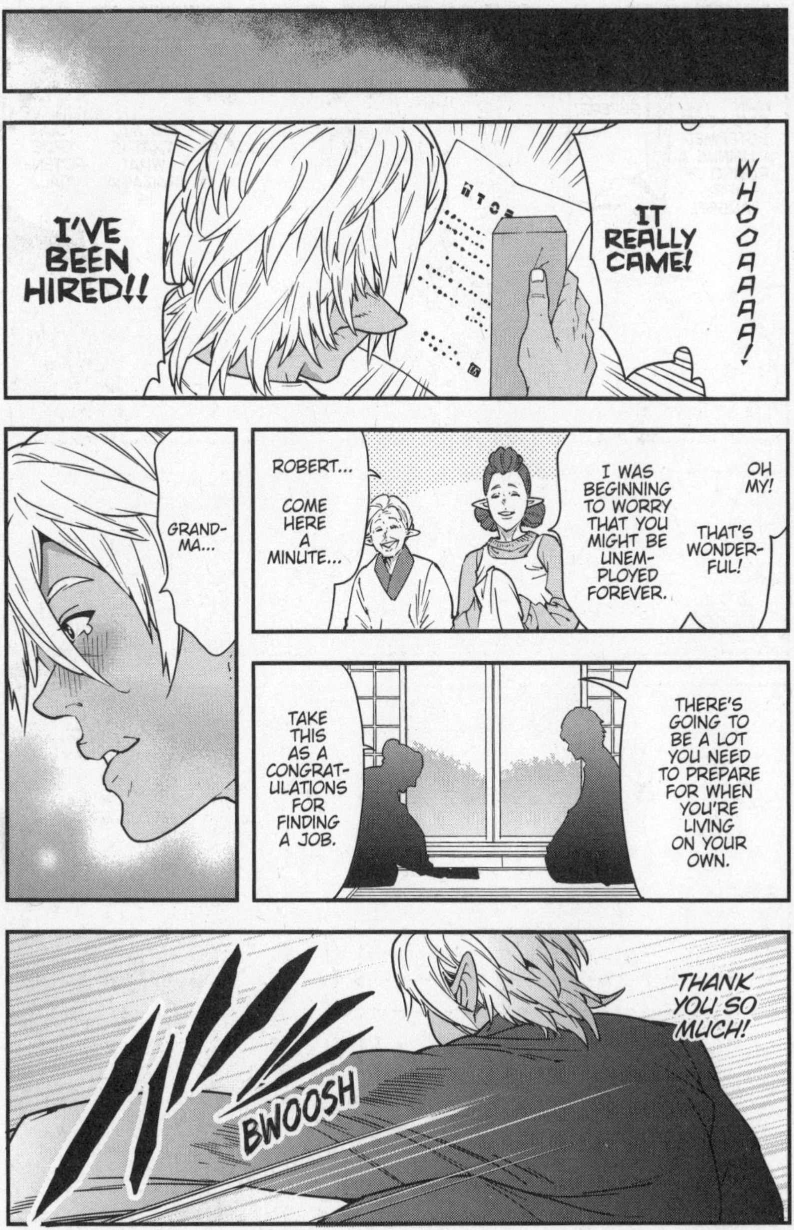
WHOOAAAAA!
IT REALLY CAME!
I'VE BEEN HIRED!!
OH MY! THAT'S WONDERFUL!
I WAS BEGINNING TO WORRY THAT YOU MIGHT BE UNEMPLOYED FOREVER.
ROBERT... COME HERE A MINUTE...
THERE'S GOING TO BE A LOT YOU NEED TO PREPARE FOR WHEN YOU'RE LIVING ON YOUR OWN.
TAKE THIS AS A CONGRATULATIONS FOR FINDING A JOB.
GRANDMA...
THANK YOU SO MUCH!
BWOOSH

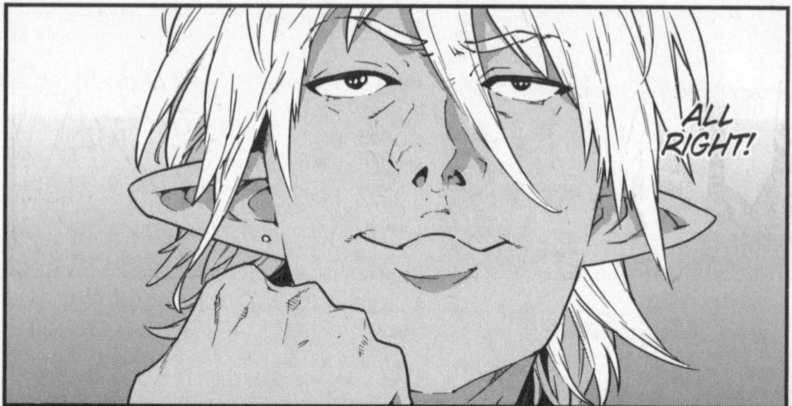
ALL RIGHT!
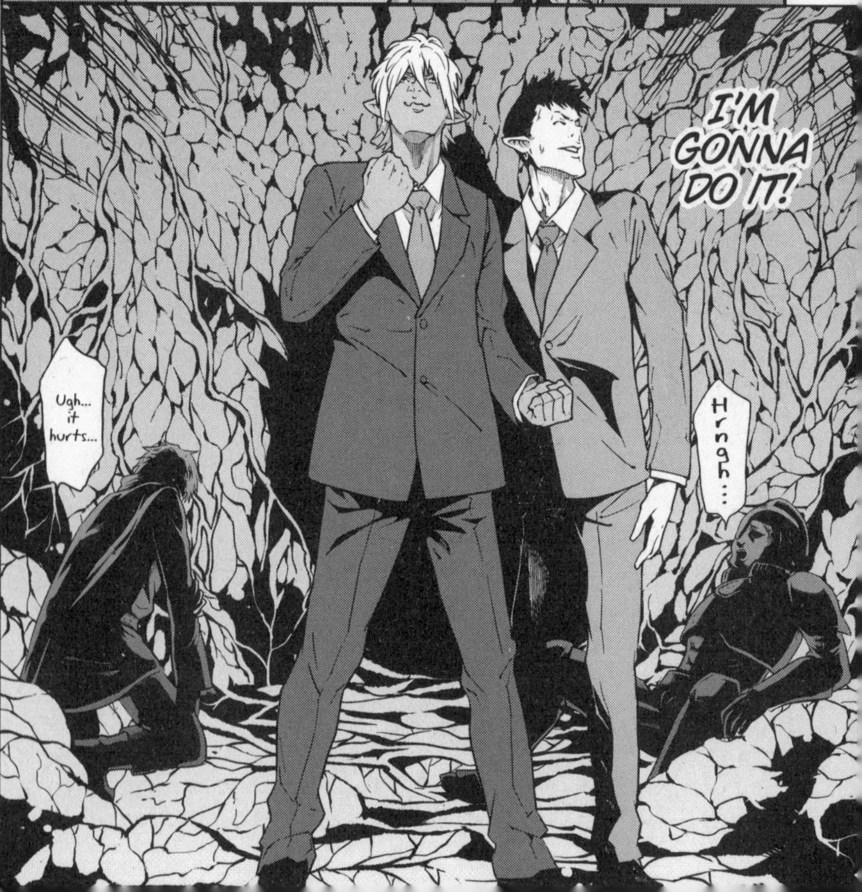
I'M GONNA DO IT!
Hrngh...
Ugh... it hurts...

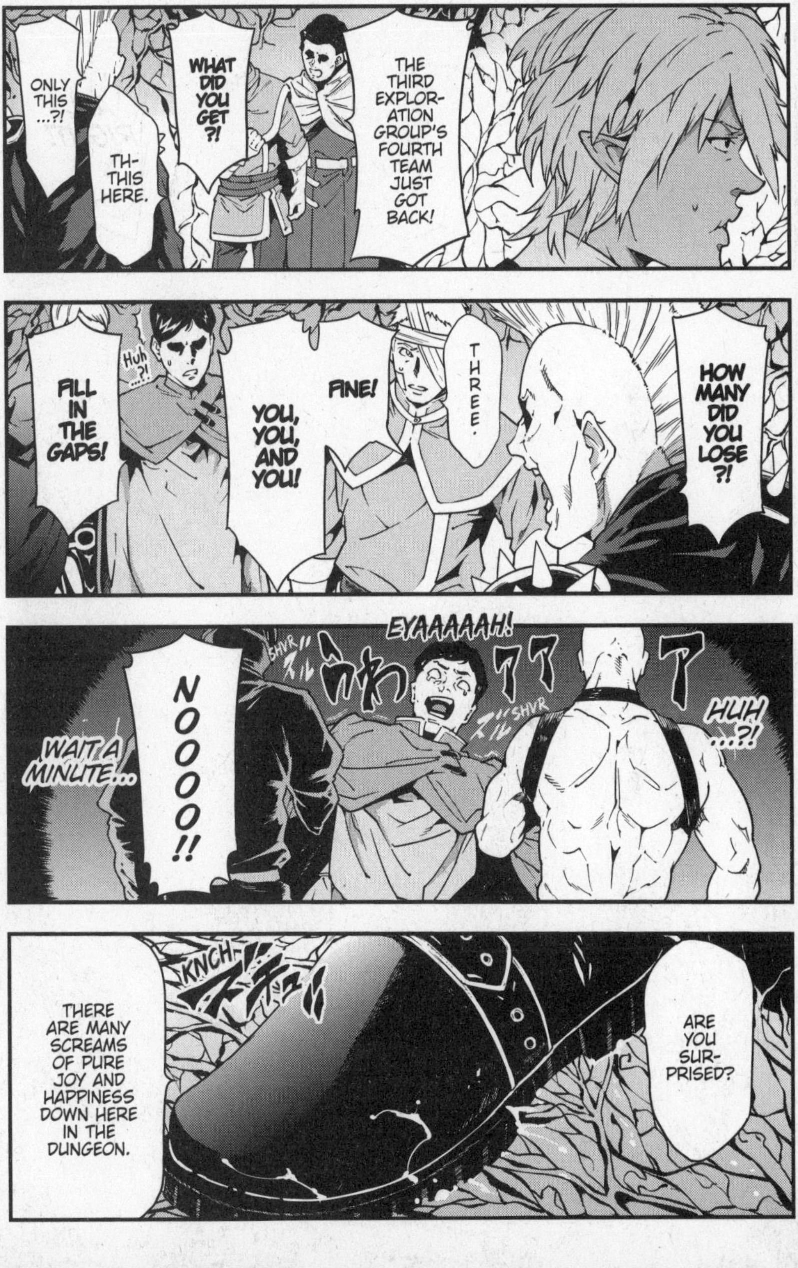
THE THIRD EXPLORATION GROUP'S FOURTH TEAM JUST GOT BACK!
WHAT DID YOU GET?!
TH-THIS HERE.
ONLY THIS...?!
HOW MANY DID YOU LOSE?!
THREE.
FINE!
YOU, YOU, AND YOU!
Huh...?!
FILL IN THE GAPS!
HUH...?!
EYAAAAAH!
うわアアア
SHVR ズル
SHVR ズル
NOOOOO!!
WAIT A MINUTE...
ARE YOU SURPRISED?
KNCH
THERE ARE MANY SCREAMS OF PURE JOY AND HAPPINESS DOWN HERE IN THE DUNGEON.

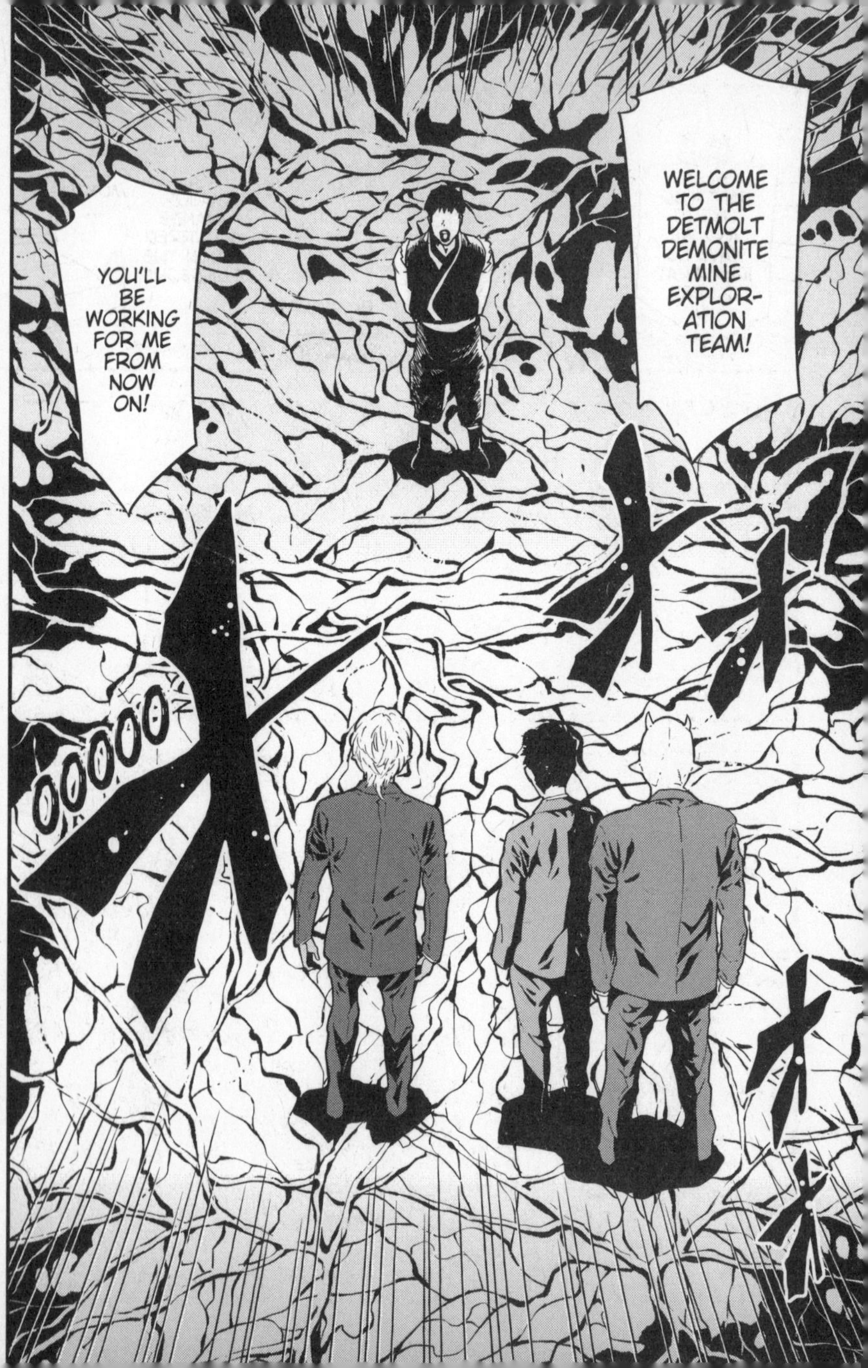
WELCOME TO THE DETMOLT DEMONITE MINE EXPLOR-ATION TEAM!
YOU'LL BE WORKING FOR ME FROM NOW ON!

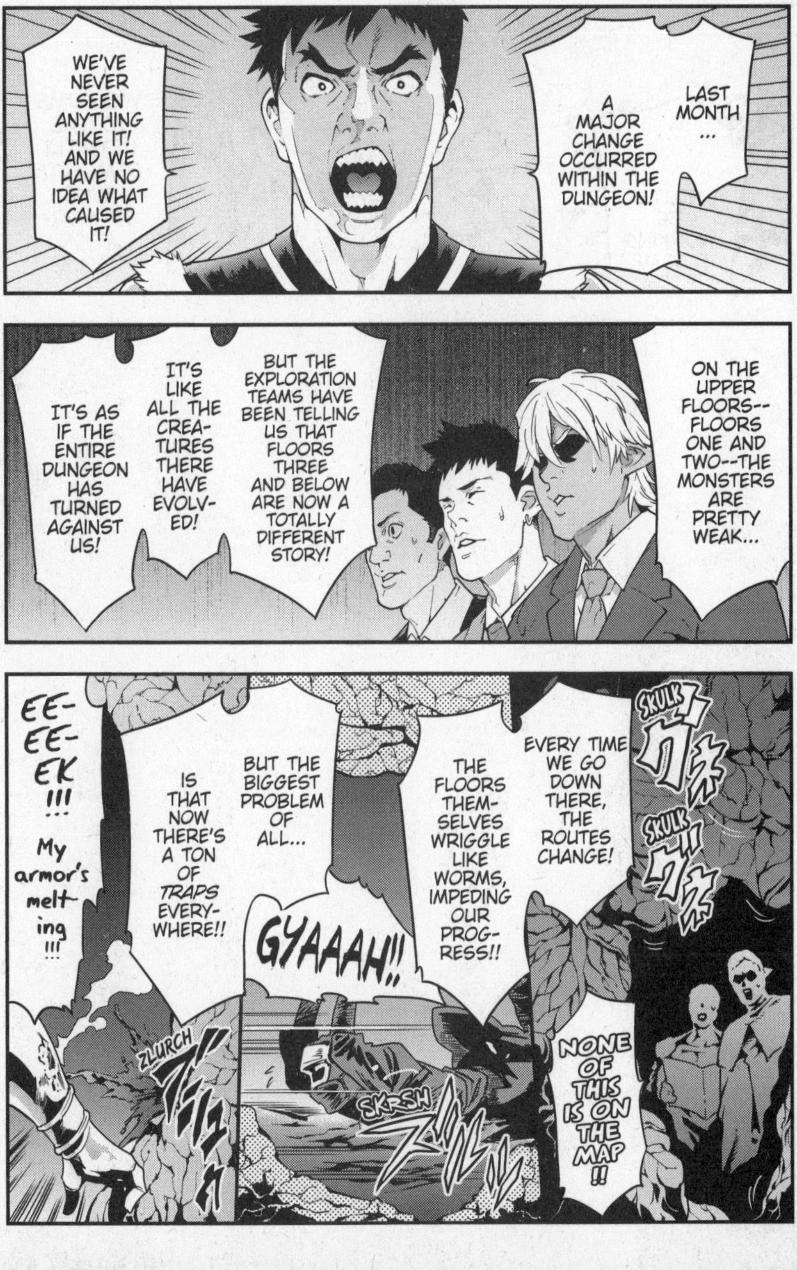
LAST MONTH ...
A MAJOR CHANGE OCCURRED WITHIN THE DUNGEON!
WE'VE NEVER SEEN ANYTHING LIKE IT! AND WE HAVE NO IDEA WHAT CAUSED IT!
ON THE UPPER FLOORS--FLOORS ONE AND TWO--THE MONSTERS ARE PRETTY WEAK...
BUT THE EXPLORATION TEAMS HAVE BEEN TELLING US THAT FLOORS THREE AND BELOW ARE NOW A TOTALLY DIFFERENT STORY!
IT'S LIKE ALL THE CREATURES THERE HAVE EVOLVED!
IT'S AS IF THE ENTIRE DUNGEON HAS TURNED AGAINST US!
SKULK
SKULK
EVERY TIME WE GO DOWN THERE, THE ROUTES CHANGE!
THE FLOORS THEMSELVES WRIGGLE LIKE WORMS, IMPEDING OUR PROGRESS!!
BUT THE BIGGEST PROBLEM OF ALL...
IS THAT NOW THERE'S A TON OF *TRAPS* EVERYWHERE!!
EEEEEK!!!...
My armor's melting!!!
NONE OF THIS IS ON THE MAP!!
SKRSH
GYAAAH!!
ZLURCH

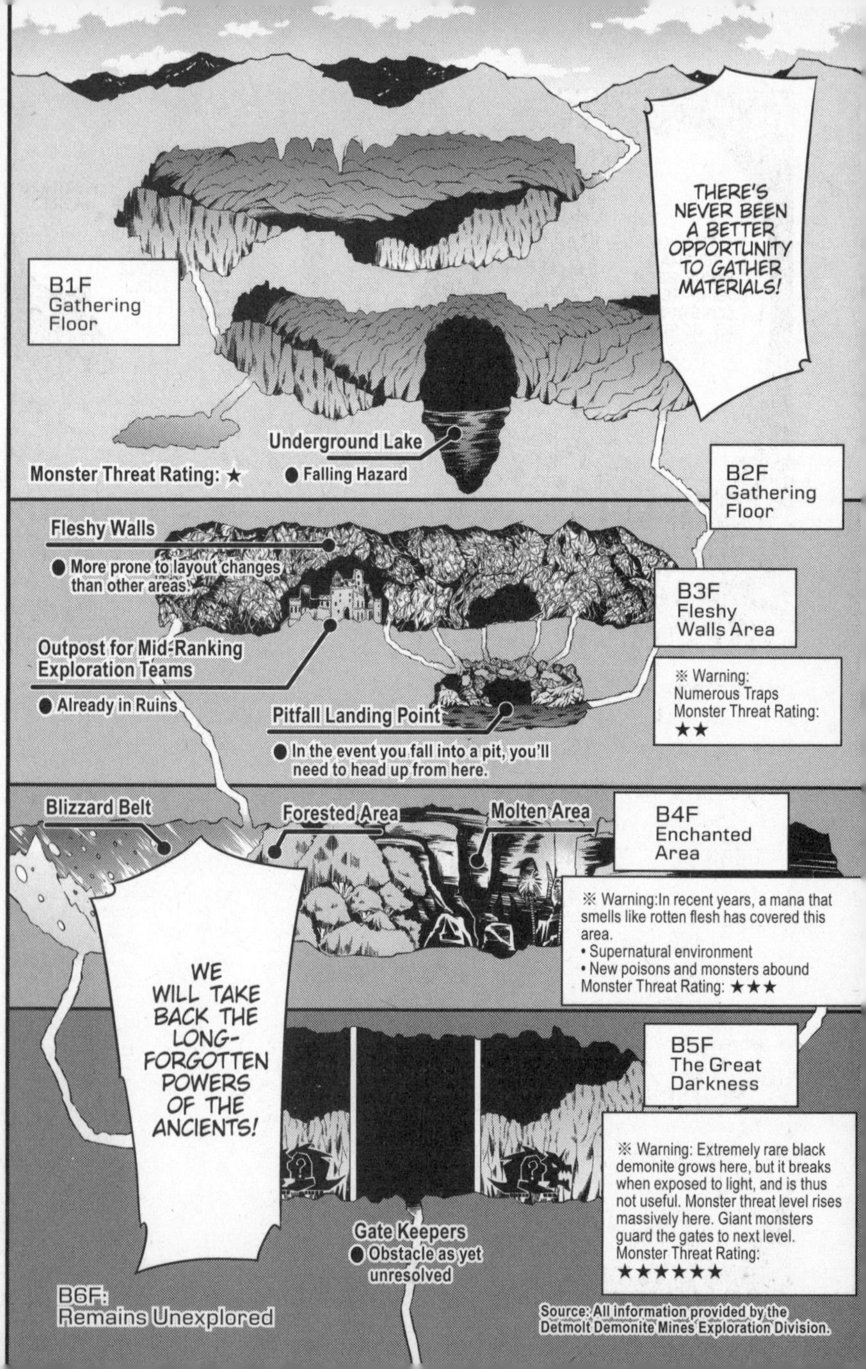

THERE'S NEVER BEEN A BETTER OPPORTUNITY TO GATHER MATERIALS!
B1F Gathering Floor
Underground Lake
Monster Threat Rating: ★
● Falling Hazard
B2F Gathering Floor
Fleshy Walls
● More prone to layout changes than other areas.
B3F Fleshy Walls Area
※ Warning: Numerous Traps Monster Threat Rating: ★★
Outpost for Mid-Ranking Exploration Teams
● Already in Ruins
Pitfall Landing Point
● In the event you fall into a pit, you'll need to head up from here.
B4F Enchanted Area
Molten Area
Forested Area
Blizzard Belt
※ Warning:In recent years, a mana that smells like rotten flesh has covered this area.
• Supernatural environment
• New poisons and monsters abound
Monster Threat Rating: ★★★
B5F The Great Darkness
WE WILL TAKE BACK THE LONG-FORGOTTEN POWERS OF THE ANCIENTS!
※ Warning: Extremely rare black demonite grows here, but it breaks when exposed to light, and is thus not useful. Monster threat level rises massively here. Giant monsters guard the gates to next level. Monster Threat Rating: ★★★★★★
Gate Keepers
● Obstacle as yet unresolved
B6F: Remains Unexplored
Source: All information provided by the Detmolt Demonite Mines Exploration Division.

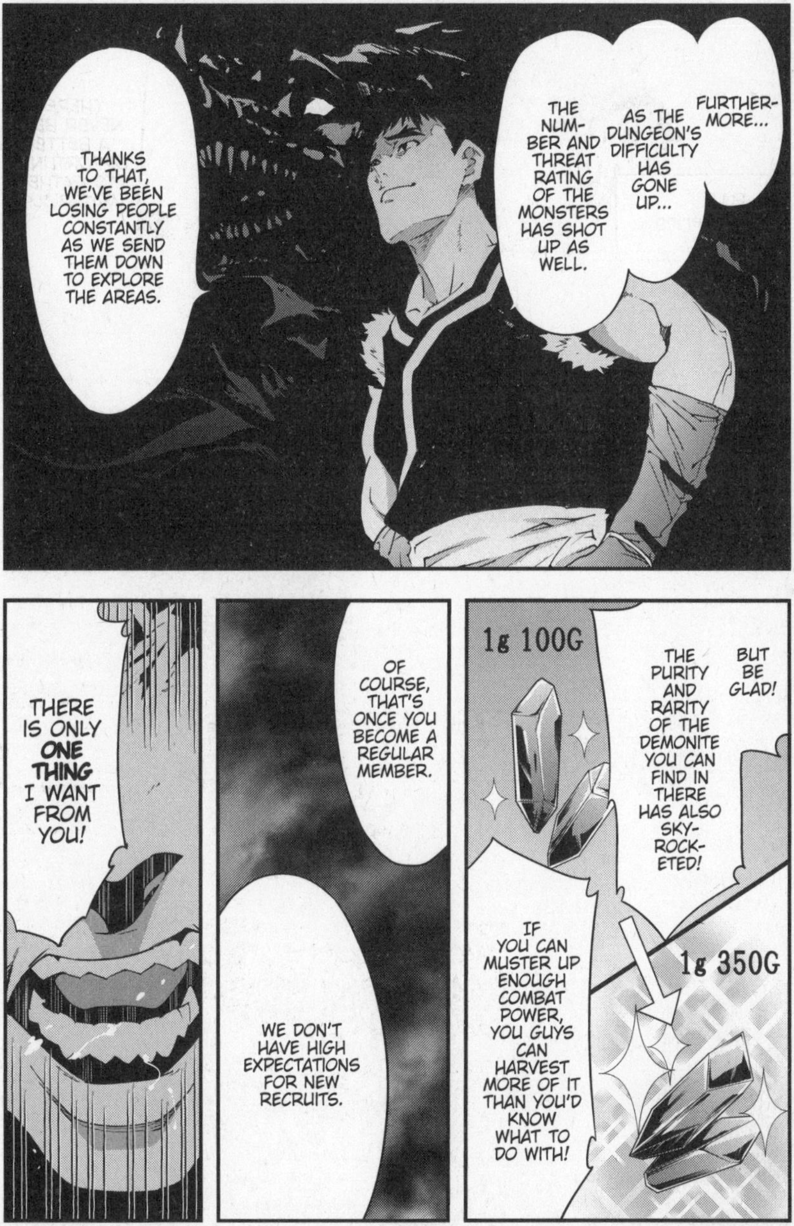
FURTHER-MORE...
AS THE DUNGEON'S DIFFICULTY HAS GONE UP...
THE NUMBER AND THREAT RATING OF THE MONSTERS HAS SHOT UP AS WELL.
THANKS TO THAT, WE'VE BEEN LOSING PEOPLE CONSTANTLY AS WE SEND THEM DOWN TO EXPLORE THE AREAS.
BUT BE GLAD!
THE PURITY AND RARITY OF THE DEMONITE YOU CAN FIND IN THERE HAS ALSO SKYROCKETED!
1g 100G
1g 350G
IF YOU CAN MUSTER UP ENOUGH COMBAT POWER, YOU GUYS CAN HARVEST MORE OF IT THAN YOU'D KNOW WHAT TO DO WITH!
OF COURSE, THAT'S ONCE YOU BECOME A REGULAR MEMBER.
WE DON'T HAVE HIGH EXPECTATIONS FOR NEW RECRUITS.
THERE IS ONLY **ONE THING** I WANT FROM YOU!

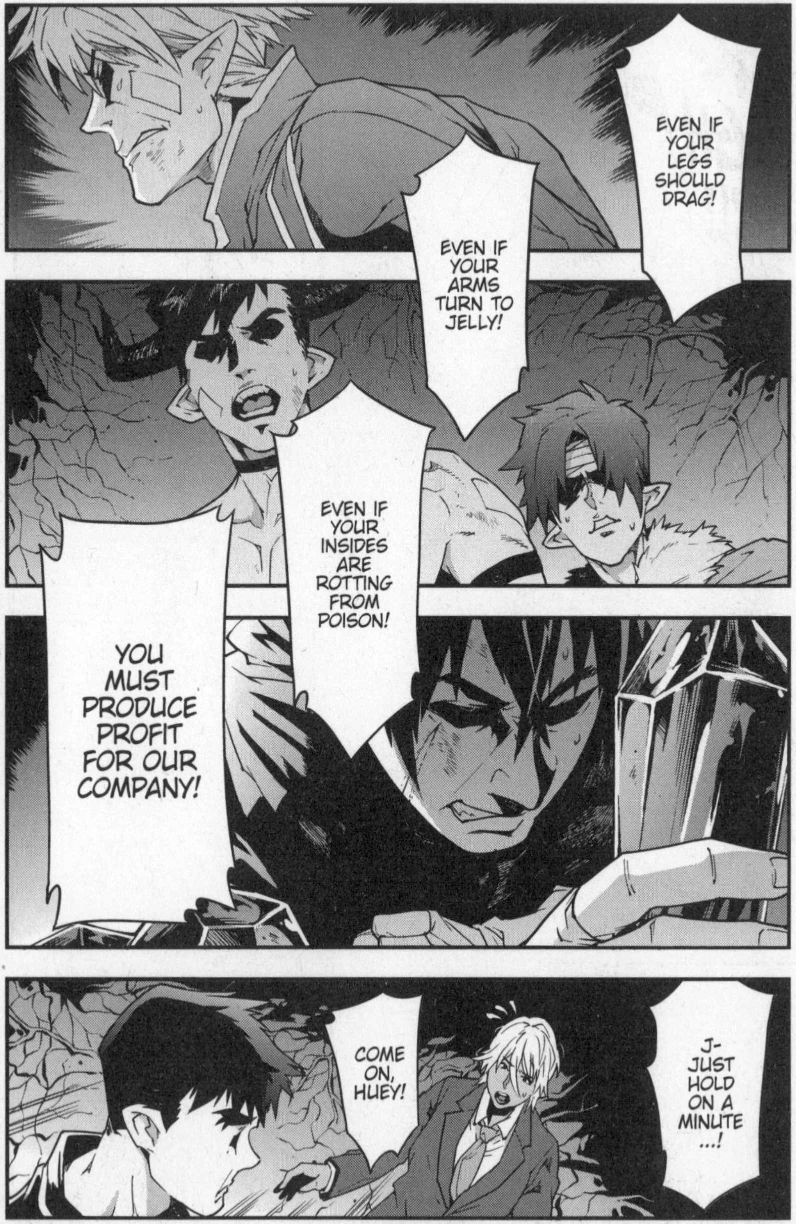
EVEN IF YOUR LEGS SHOULD DRAG!
EVEN IF YOUR ARMS TURN TO JELLY!
EVEN IF YOUR INSIDES ARE ROTTING FROM POISON!
YOU MUST PRODUCE PROFIT FOR OUR COMPANY!
J-JUST HOLD ON A MINUTE...!
COME ON, HUEY!

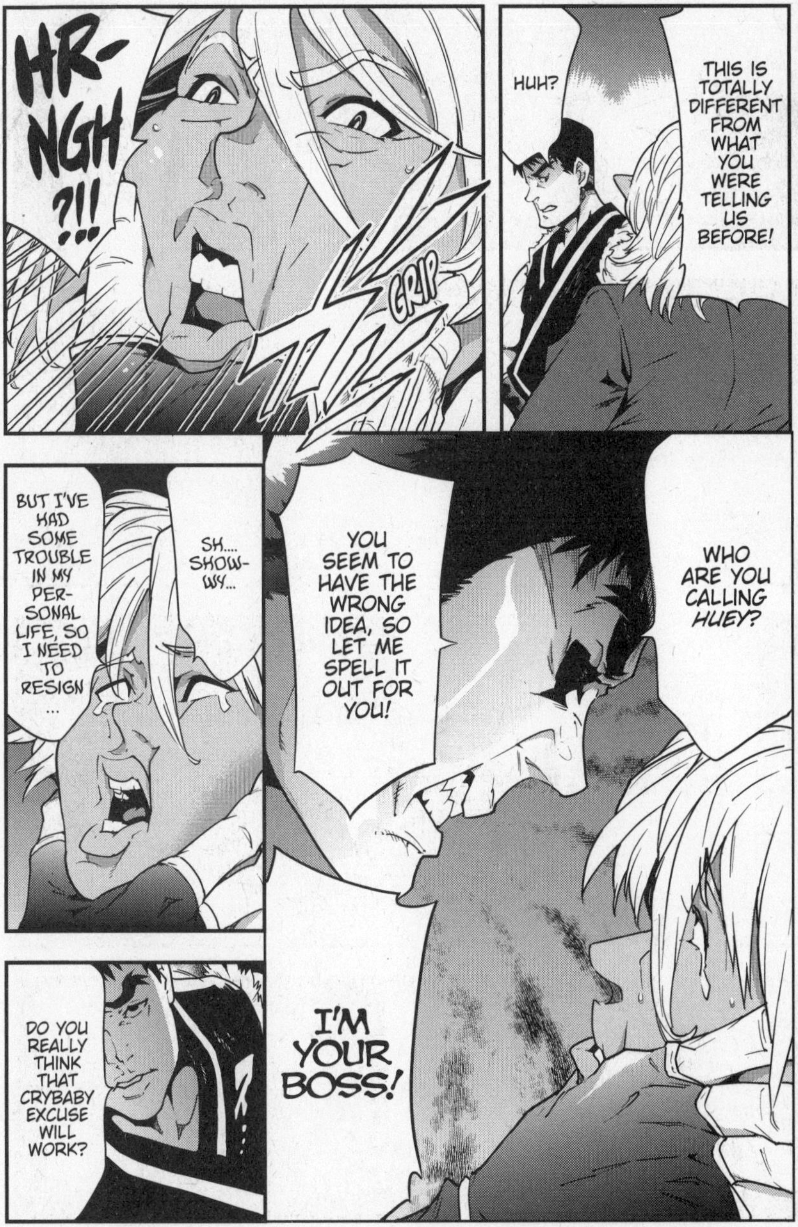
THIS IS TOTALLY DIFFERENT FROM WHAT YOU WERE TELLING US BEFORE!
HUH?
HR-NGH ?!!...
GRIP
WHO ARE YOU CALLING HUEY?
YOU SEEM TO HAVE THE WRONG IDEA, SO LET ME SPELL IT OUT FOR YOU!
I'M YOUR BOSS!
SH.... SHOW-WY...
BUT I'VE HAD SOME TROUBLE IN MY PER-SONAL LIFE, SO I NEED TO RESIGN ...
DO YOU REALLY THINK THAT CRYBABY EXCUSE WILL WORK?

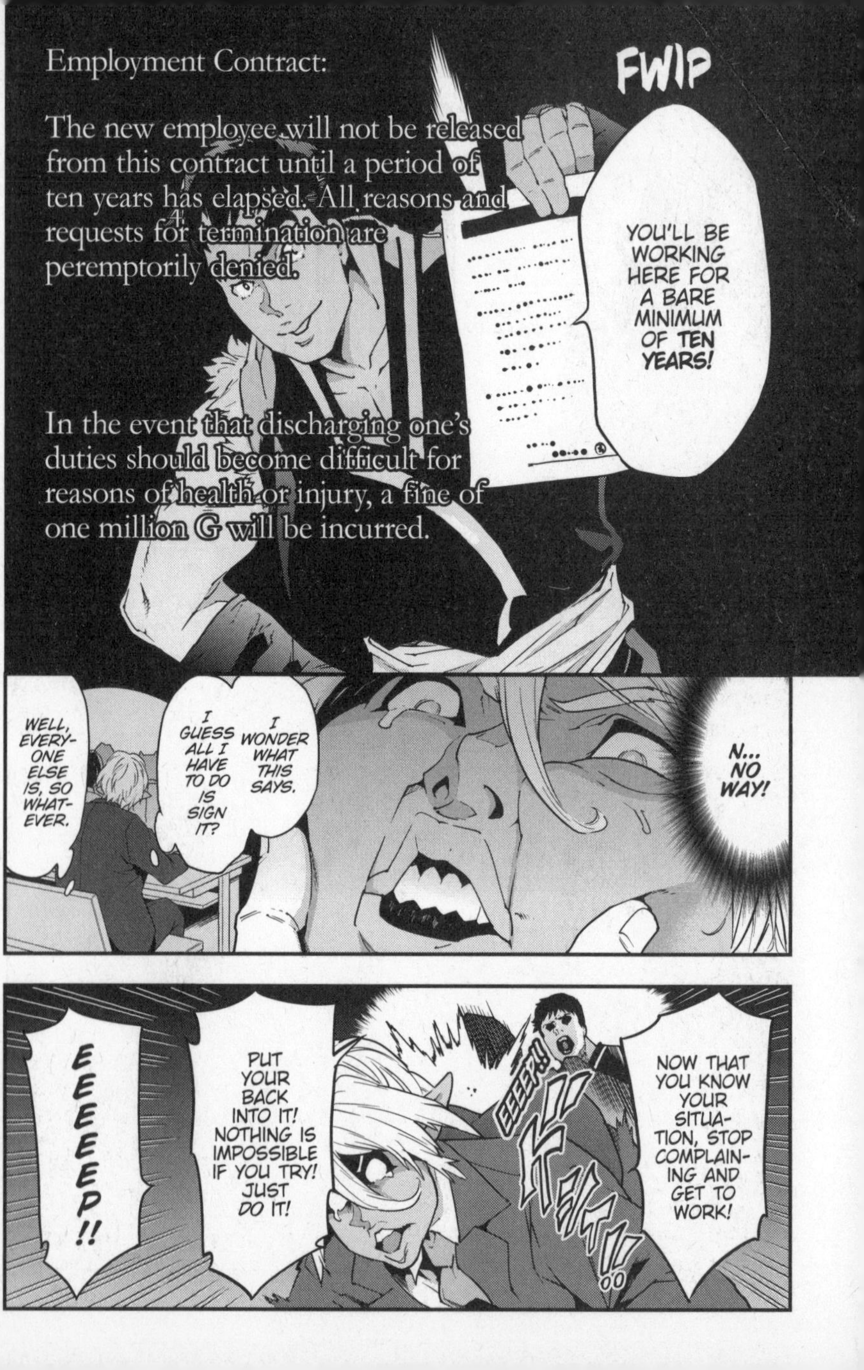
FWIP
YOU'LL BE WORKING HERE FOR A BARE MINIMUM OF TEN YEARS!
Employment Contract:
The new employee will not be released from this contract until a period of ten years has elapsed. All reasons and requests for termination are peremptorily denied.
In the event that discharging one's duties should become difficult for reasons of health or injury, a fine of one million G will be incurred.
N... NO WAY!
I WONDER WHAT THIS SAYS.
I GUESS ALL I HAVE TO DO IS SIGN IT?
WELL, EVERYONE ELSE IS, SO WHATEVER.
NOW THAT YOU KNOW YOUR SITUATION, STOP COMPLAINING AND GET TO WORK!
EEEEEP!!
PUT YOUR BACK INTO IT! NOTHING IS IMPOSSIBLE IF YOU TRY! JUST DO IT!
EEEEEEP!!

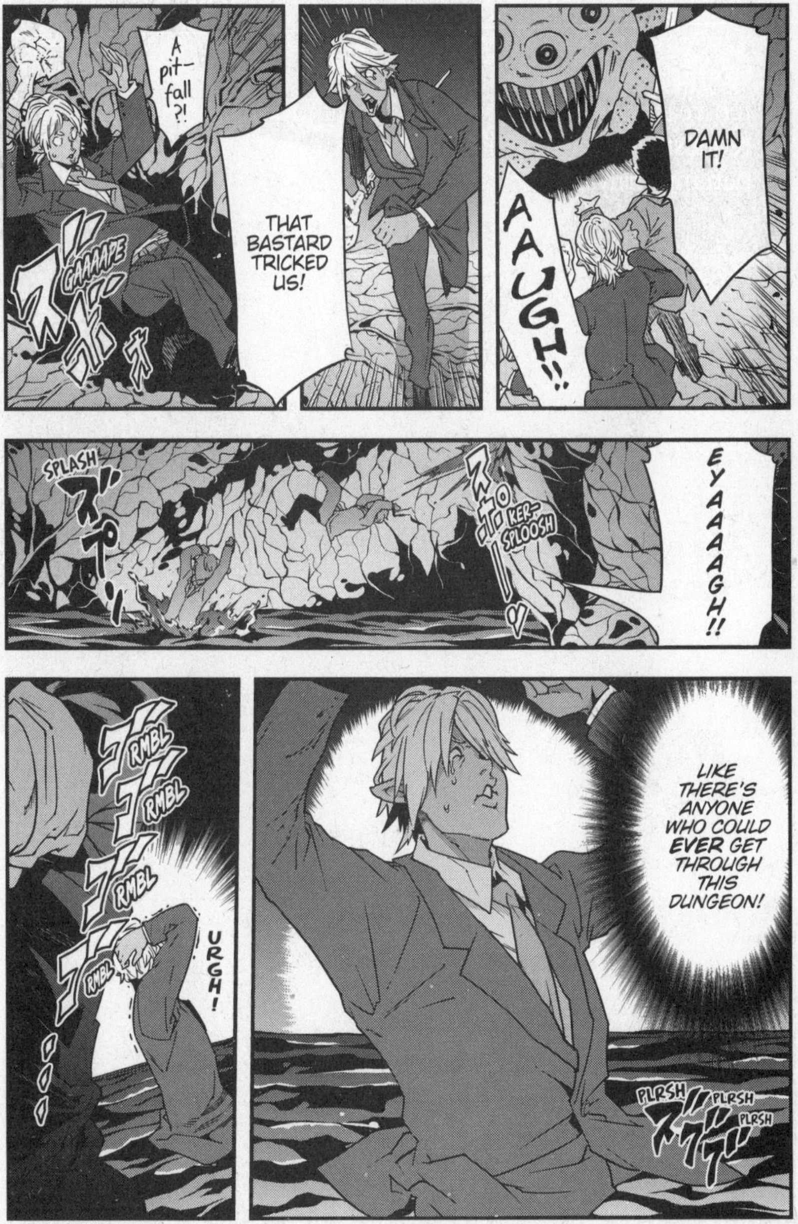
DAMN IT!
AAUGH!!
THAT BASTARD TRICKED US!
A pit-fall?!
GAAAAPE
EYAAAAAGH!!
KER-SPLOOSH
SPLASH
LIKE THERE'S ANYONE WHO COULD EVER GET THROUGH THIS DUNGEON!
PLRSH
PLRSH
PLRSH
RMBL
RMBL
RMBL
RMBL
URGH!

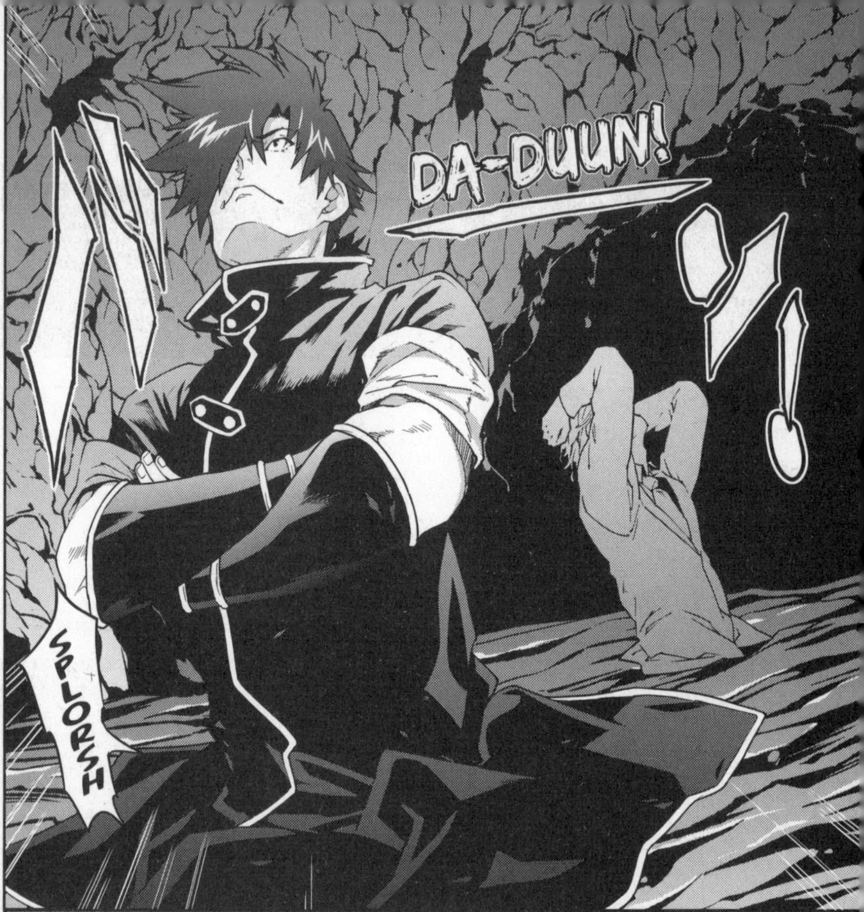
DA-DUUN!
SPLORSH

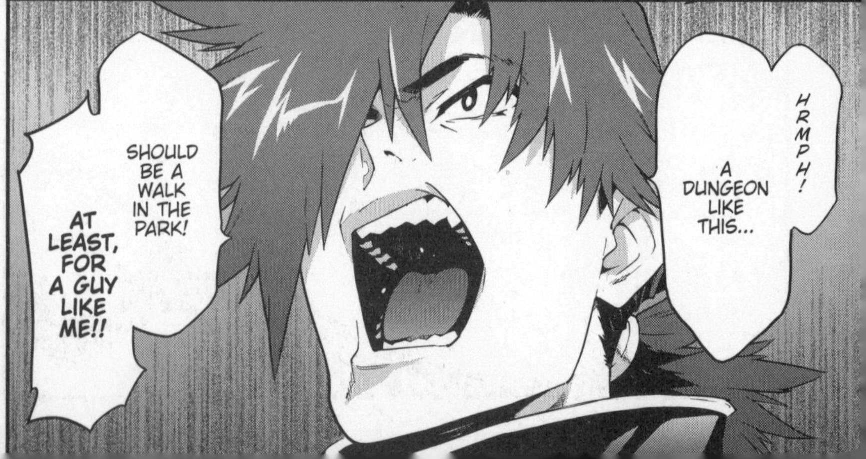
HRMPH!
A DUNGEON LIKE THIS...
SHOULD BE A WALK IN THE PARK!
AT LEAST, FOR A GUY LIKE ME!!

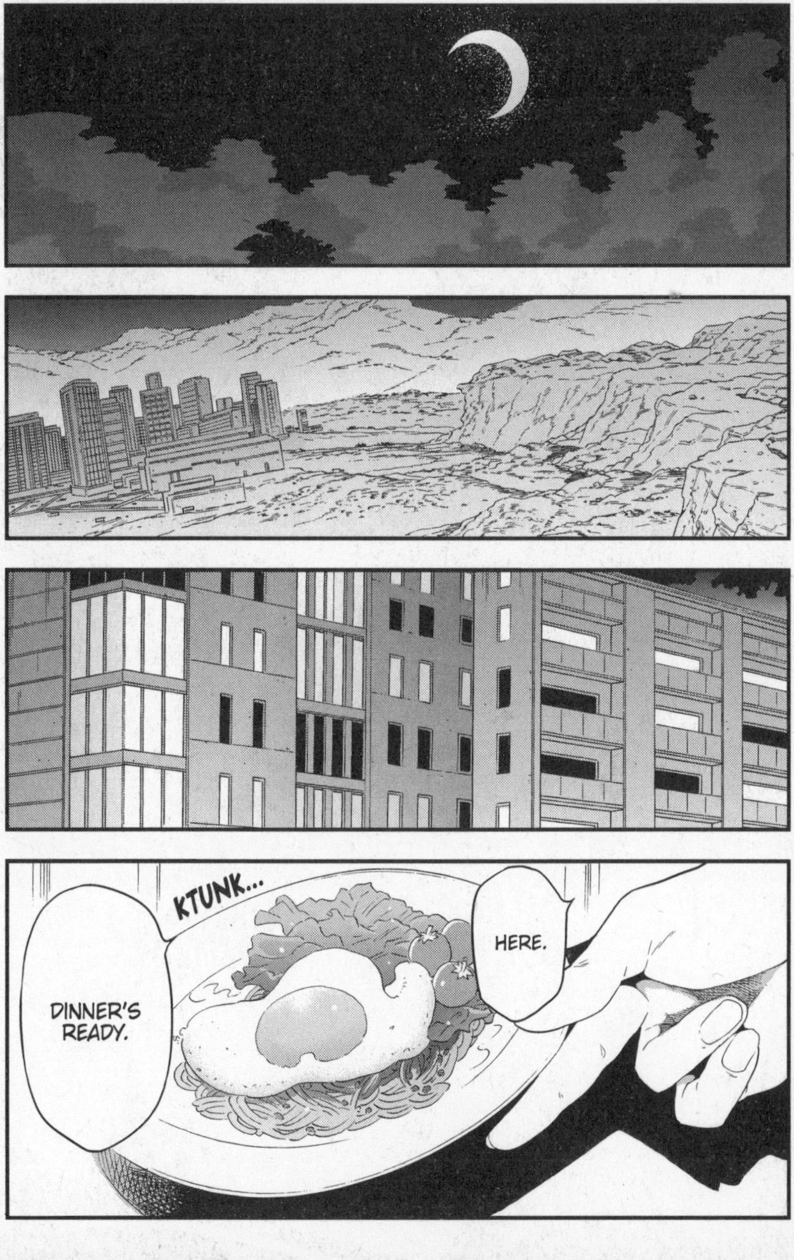
HERE.
KTUNK...
DINNER'S READY.

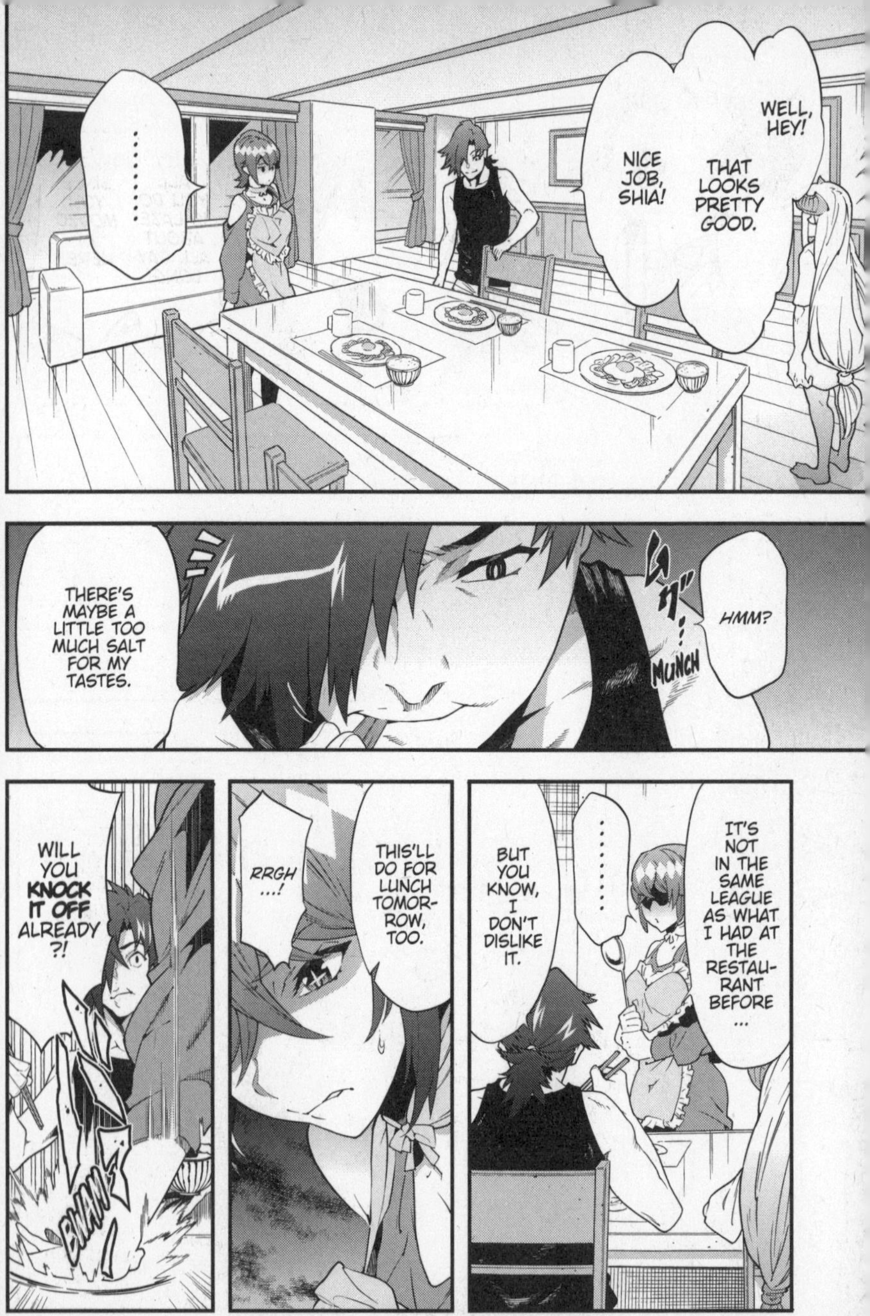
WELL, HEY! THAT LOOKS PRETTY GOOD.
NICE JOB, SHIA!
......
HMM?
MUNCH
THERE'S MAYBE A LITTLE TOO MUCH SALT FOR MY TASTES.
IT'S NOT IN THE SAME LEAGUE AS WHAT I HAD AT THE RESTAURANT BEFORE...
......
BUT YOU KNOW, I DON'T DISLIKE IT.
THIS'LL DO FOR LUNCH TOMORROW, TOO.
RRGH...!
WILL YOU **KNOCK IT OFF** ALREADY?!
BWAM

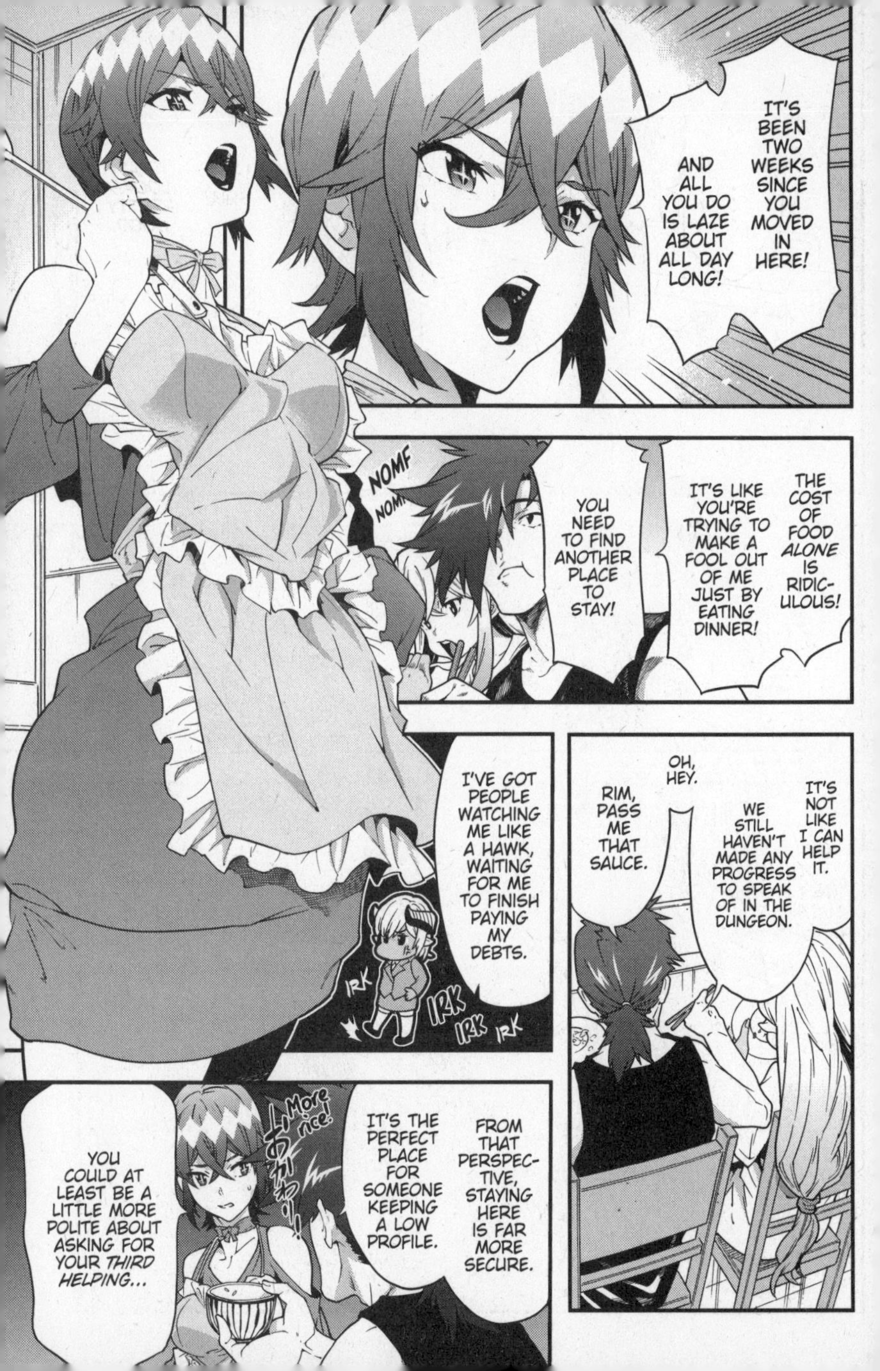
IT'S BEEN TWO WEEKS SINCE YOU MOVED IN HERE!
AND ALL YOU DO IS LAZE ABOUT ALL DAY LONG!
THE COST OF FOOD *ALONE* IS RIDICULOUS!
IT'S LIKE YOU'RE TRYING TO MAKE A FOOL OUT OF ME JUST BY EATING DINNER!
YOU NEED TO FIND ANOTHER PLACE TO STAY!
NOMF
IT'S NOT LIKE I CAN HELP IT.
WE STILL HAVEN'T MADE ANY PROGRESS TO SPEAK OF IN THE DUNGEON.
OH, HEY.
RIM, PASS ME THAT SAUCE.
I'VE GOT PEOPLE WATCHING ME LIKE A HAWK, WAITING FOR ME TO FINISH PAYING MY DEBTS.
IRK
IRK
IRK
IRK
FROM THAT PERSPECTIVE, STAYING HERE IS FAR MORE SECURE.
IT'S THE PERFECT PLACE FOR SOMEONE KEEPING A LOW PROFILE.
More rice!
YOU COULD AT LEAST BE A LITTLE MORE POLITE ABOUT ASKING FOR YOUR *THIRD HELPING*...

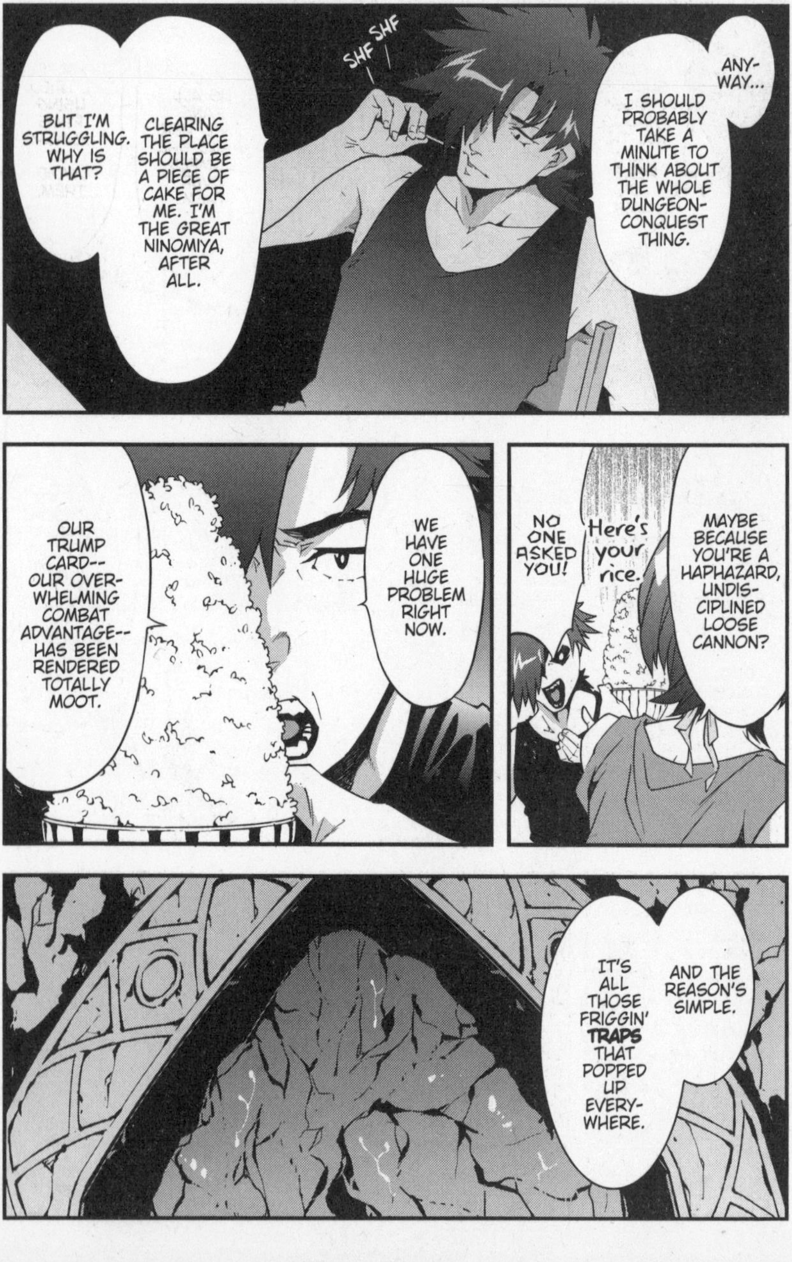
ANY-WAY... I SHOULD PROBABLY TAKE A MINUTE TO THINK ABOUT THE WHOLE DUNGEON-CONQUEST THING.
SHF SHF
CLEARING THE PLACE SHOULD BE A PIECE OF CAKE FOR ME. I'M THE GREAT NINOMIYA, AFTER ALL.
BUT I'M STRUGGLING. WHY IS THAT?
MAYBE BECAUSE YOU'RE A HAPHAZARD, UNDIS-CIPLINED LOOSE CANNON?
Here's your rice.
NO ONE ASKED YOU!
WE HAVE ONE HUGE PROBLEM RIGHT NOW.
OUR TRUMP CARD--OUR OVER-WHELMING COMBAT ADVANTAGE--HAS BEEN RENDERED TOTALLY MOOT.
AND THE REASON'S SIMPLE.
IT'S ALL THOSE FRIGGIN' **TRAPS** THAT POPPED UP EVERY-WHERE.

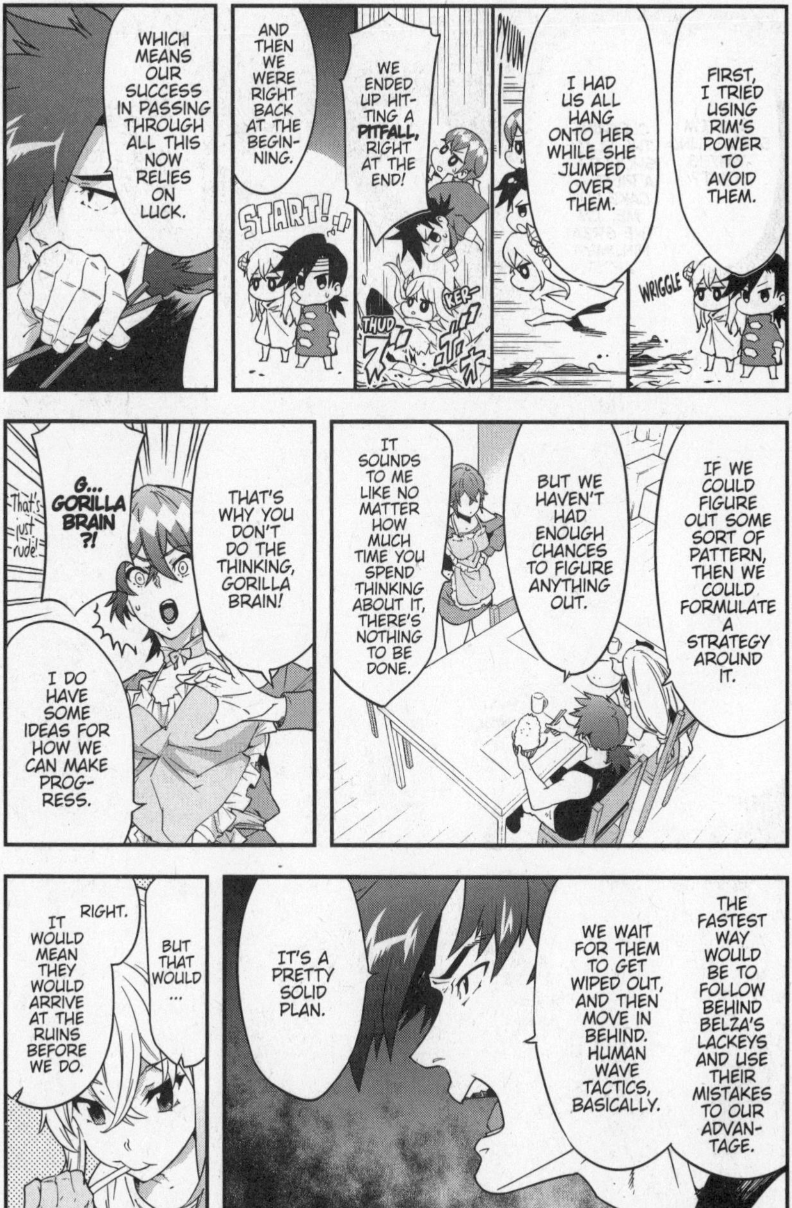
FIRST, I TRIED USING RIM'S POWER TO AVOID THEM.
WRIGGLE
I HAD US ALL HANG ONTO HER WHILE SHE JUMPED OVER THEM.
PYUUN
WE ENDED UP HITTING A **PITFALL,** RIGHT AT THE END!
KER-
THUD
AND THEN WE WERE RIGHT BACK AT THE BEGINNING.
START!
WHICH MEANS OUR SUCCESS IN PASSING THROUGH ALL THIS NOW RELIES ON LUCK.
IF WE COULD FIGURE OUT SOME SORT OF PATTERN, THEN WE COULD FORMULATE A STRATEGY AROUND IT.
BUT WE HAVEN'T HAD ENOUGH CHANCES TO FIGURE ANYTHING OUT.
IT SOUNDS TO ME LIKE NO MATTER HOW MUCH TIME YOU SPEND THINKING ABOUT IT, THERE'S NOTHING TO BE DONE.
THAT'S WHY YOU DON'T DO THE THINKING, GORILLA BRAIN!
G... GORILLA BRAIN?!
That's just rude!
I DO HAVE SOME IDEAS FOR HOW WE CAN MAKE PROGRESS.
THE FASTEST WAY WOULD BE TO FOLLOW BEHIND BELZA'S LACKEYS AND USE THEIR MISTAKES TO OUR ADVANTAGE.
WE WAIT FOR THEM TO GET WIPED OUT, AND THEN MOVE IN BEHIND. HUMAN WAVE TACTICS, BASICALLY.
IT'S A PRETTY SOLID PLAN.
BUT THAT WOULD...
RIGHT.
IT WOULD MEAN THEY WOULD ARRIVE AT THE RUINS BEFORE WE DO.

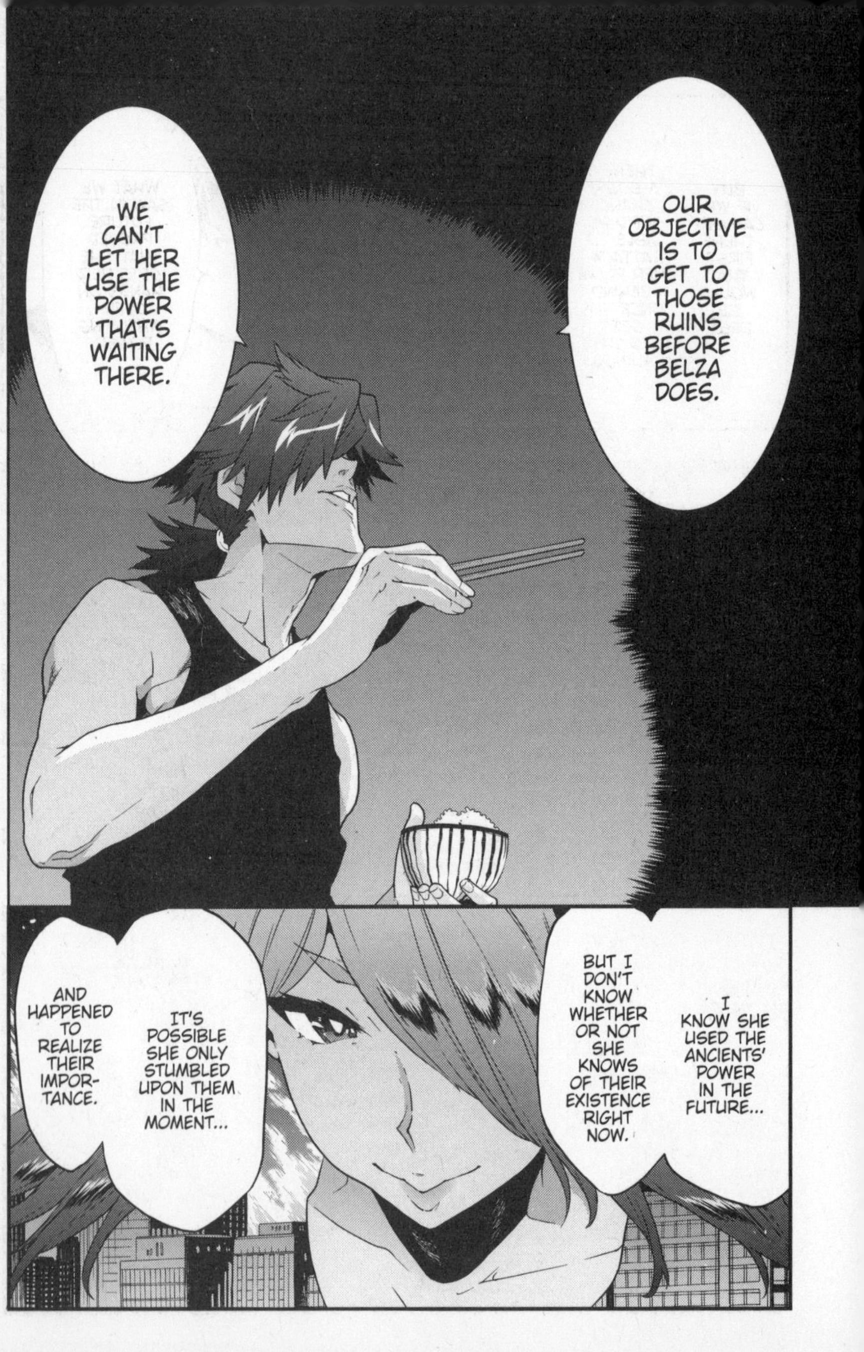
OUR OBJECTIVE IS TO GET TO THOSE RUINS BEFORE BELZA DOES.
WE CAN'T LET HER USE THE POWER THAT'S WAITING THERE.
I KNOW SHE USED THE ANCIENTS' POWER IN THE FUTURE...
BUT I DON'T KNOW WHETHER OR NOT SHE KNOWS OF THEIR EXISTENCE RIGHT NOW.
IT'S POSSIBLE SHE ONLY STUMBLED UPON THEM IN THE MOMENT...
AND HAPPENED TO REALIZE THEIR IMPOR-TANCE.

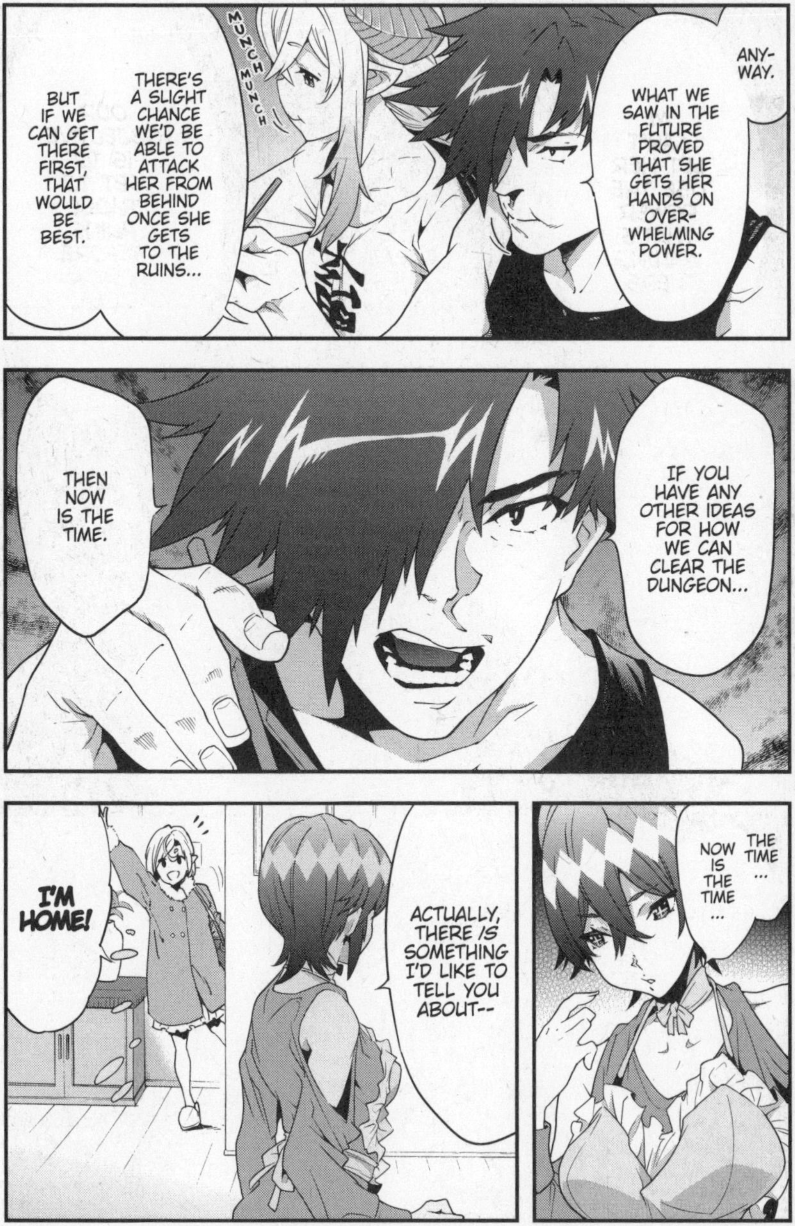
ANY-WAY.
WHAT WE SAW IN THE FUTURE PROVED THAT SHE GETS HER HANDS ON OVER-WHELMING POWER.
MUNCH MUNCH
THERE'S A SLIGHT CHANCE WE'D BE ABLE TO ATTACK HER FROM BEHIND ONCE SHE GETS TO THE RUINS...
BUT IF WE CAN GET THERE FIRST, THAT WOULD BE BEST.
IF YOU HAVE ANY OTHER IDEAS FOR HOW WE CAN CLEAR THE DUNGEON...
THEN NOW IS THE TIME.
THE TIME...
NOW IS THE TIME...
ACTUALLY, THERE *IS* SOMETHING I'D LIKE TO TELL YOU ABOUT--
I'M HOME!

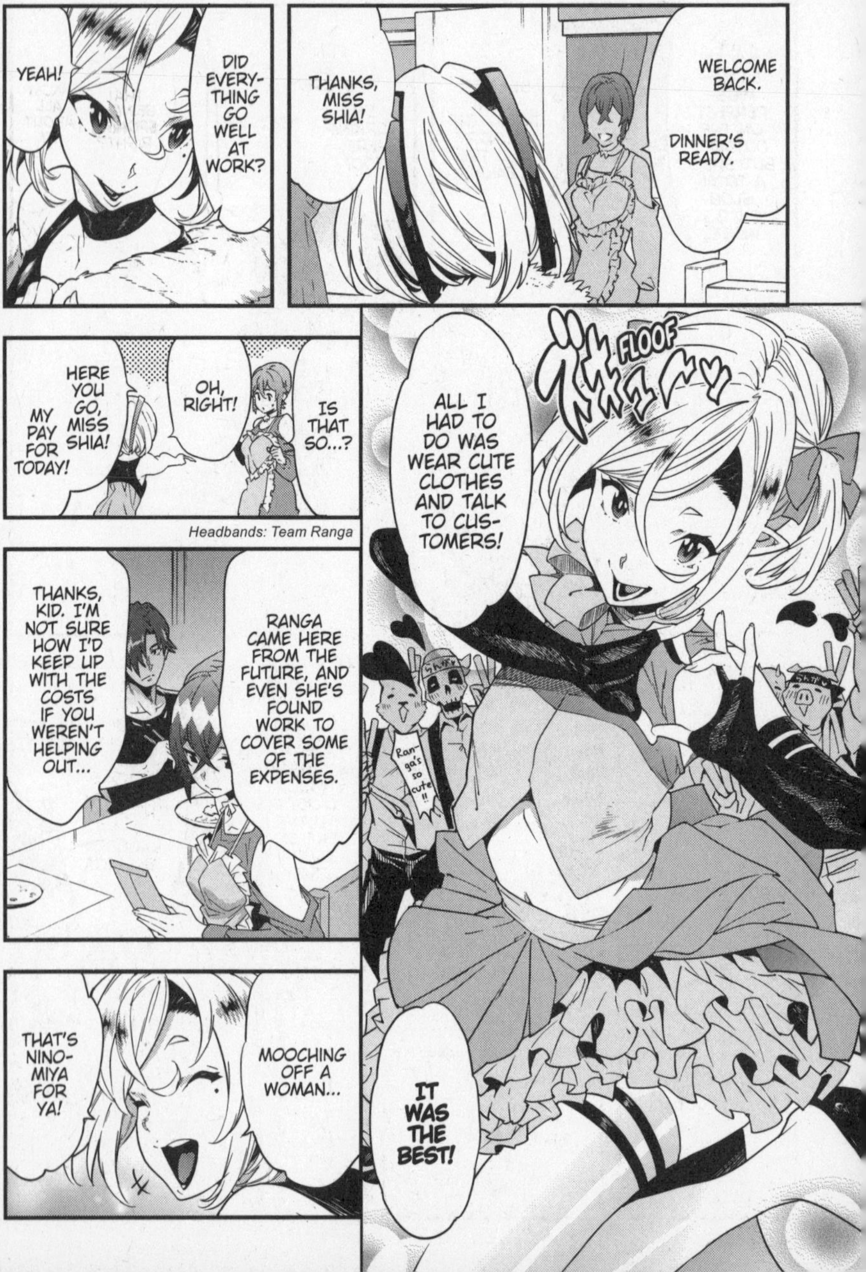
WELCOME BACK.
DINNER'S READY.
THANKS, MISS SHIA!
DID EVERYTHING GO WELL AT WORK?
YEAH!
FLOOF
ALL I HAD TO DO WAS WEAR CUTE CLOTHES AND TALK TO CUSTOMERS!
Ranga's so cute!!
IT WAS THE BEST!
IS THAT SO...?
OH, RIGHT!
HERE YOU GO, MISS SHIA!
MY PAY FOR TODAY!
Headbands: Team Ranga
RANGA CAME HERE FROM THE FUTURE, AND EVEN SHE'S FOUND WORK TO COVER SOME OF THE EXPENSES.
THANKS, KID. I'M NOT SURE HOW I'D KEEP UP WITH THE COSTS IF YOU WEREN'T HELPING OUT...
MOOCHING OFF A WOMAN...
THAT'S NINOMIYA FOR YA!

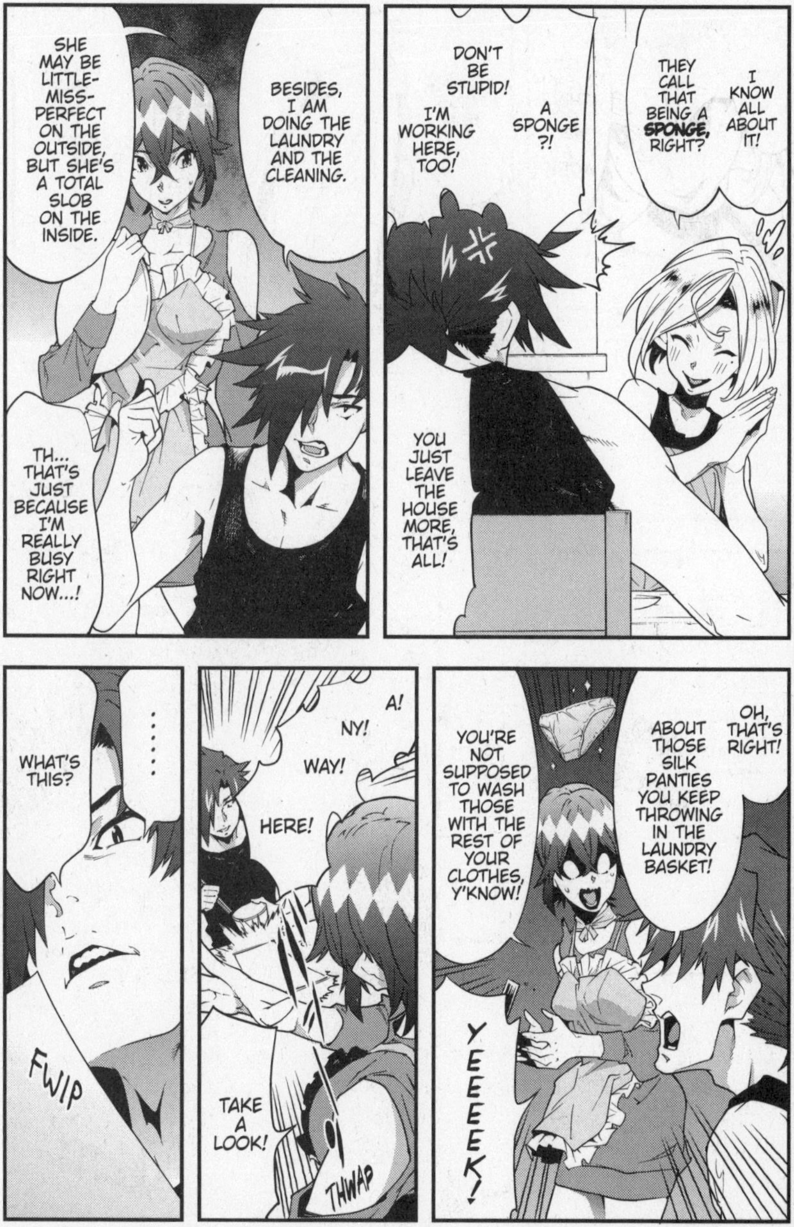
I KNOW ALL ABOUT IT!
THEY CALL THAT BEING A **SPONGE,** RIGHT?
A SPONGE ?!
DON'T BE STUPID!
I'M WORKING HERE, TOO!
YOU JUST LEAVE THE HOUSE MORE, THAT'S ALL!
BESIDES, I AM DOING THE LAUNDRY AND THE CLEANING.
SHE MAY BE LITTLE-MISS-PERFECT ON THE OUTSIDE, BUT SHE'S A TOTAL SLOB ON THE INSIDE.
TH... THAT'S JUST BECAUSE I'M REALLY BUSY RIGHT NOW...!
OH, THAT'S RIGHT!
ABOUT THOSE SILK PANTIES YOU KEEP THROWING IN THE LAUNDRY BASKET!
YOU'RE NOT SUPPOSED TO WASH THOSE WITH THE REST OF YOUR CLOTHES, Y'KNOW!
YEEEEK!
A!
NY!
WAY!
HERE!
TAKE A LOOK!
THWAP
......
WHAT'S THIS?
FWIP

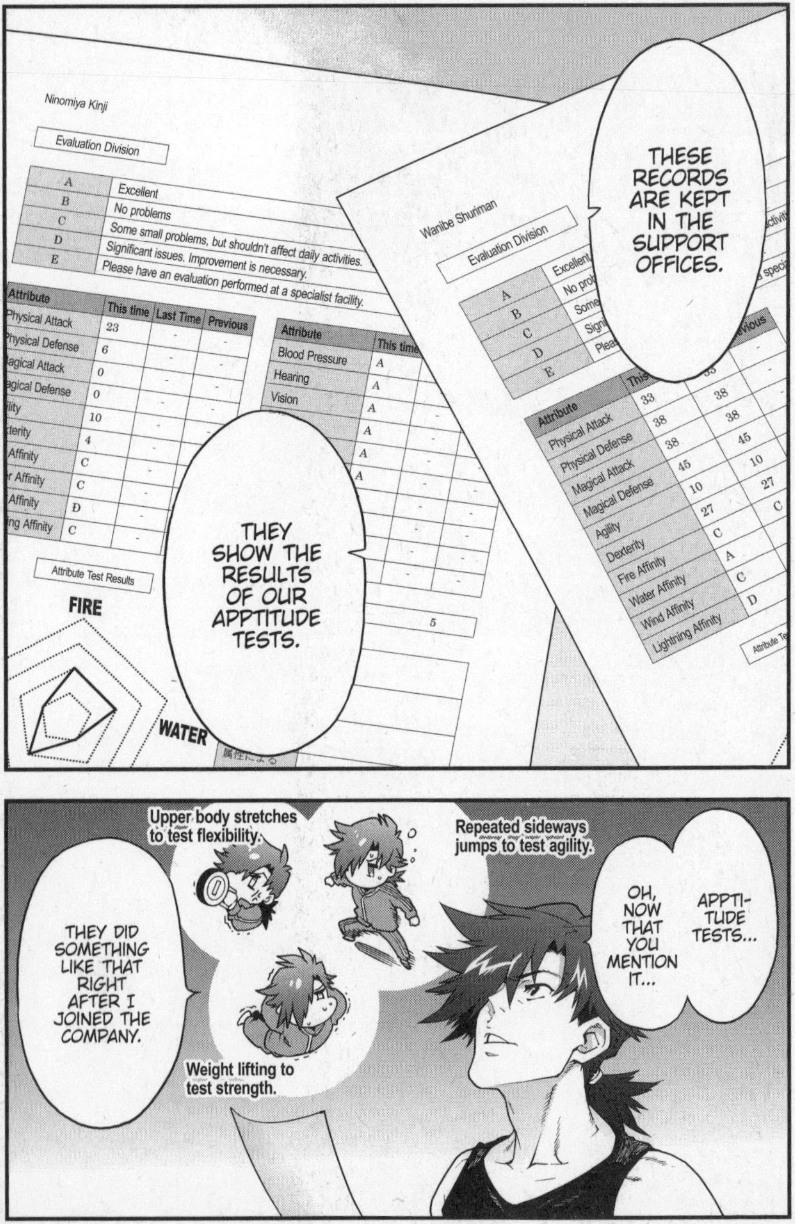
Ninomiya Kinji
Evaluation Division
A Excellent
B No problems
C Some small problems, but shouldn't affect daily activities.
D Significant issues. Improvement is necessary.
E Please have an evaluation performed at a specialist facility.
Attribute | This time | Last Time | Previous
Physical Attack 23
Physical Defense 6
Magical Attack 0
Magical Defense 0
10
4
C
C
D
C
Attribute | This time
Blood Pressure A
Hearing A
Vision A
Attribute Test Results
FIRE
WATER
Wanibe Shuriman
Evaluation Division
Attribute
Physical Attack
Physical Defense
Magical Attack
Magical Defense
Agility
Dexterity
Fire Affinity
Water Affinity
Wind Affinity
Lightning Affinity
THESE RECORDS ARE KEPT IN THE SUPPORT OFFICES.
THEY SHOW THE RESULTS OF OUR APPTITUDE TESTS.
APPTI-TUDE TESTS...
OH, NOW THAT YOU MENTION IT...
Repeated sideways jumps to test agility.
Upper body stretches to test flexibility.
THEY DID SOMETHING LIKE THAT RIGHT AFTER I JOINED THE COMPANY.
Weight lifting to test strength.

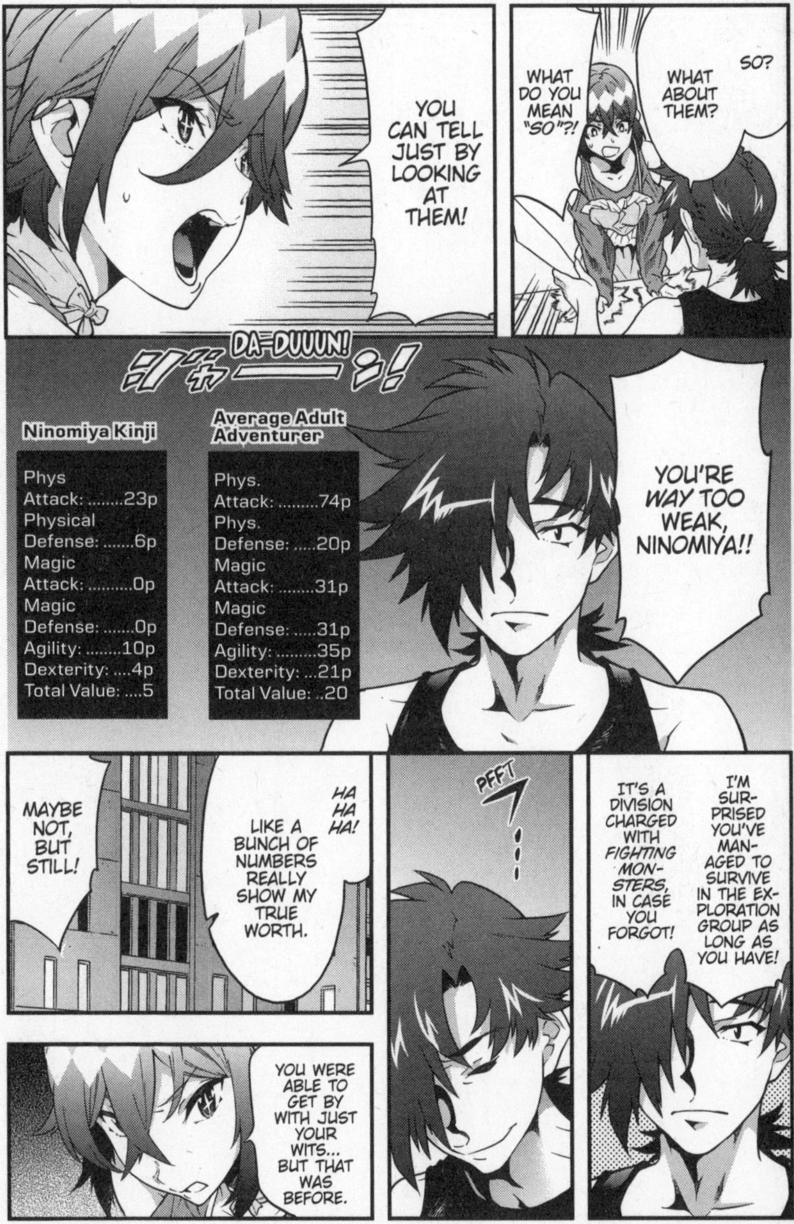
SO?
WHAT ABOUT THEM?
WHAT DO YOU MEAN "SO"?!
YOU CAN TELL JUST BY LOOKING AT THEM!
YOU'RE WAY TOO WEAK, NINOMIYA!!
DA-DUUUN!
Average Adult Adventurer
Phys. Attack: 74p
Phys. Defense: 20p
Magic Attack: 31p
Magic Defense: 31p
Agility: 35p
Dexterity: ...21p
Total Value: ..20
Ninomiya Kinji
Phys Attack: 23p
Physical Defense: 6p
Magic Attack: 0p
Magic Defense: 0p
Agility: 10p
Dexterity: 4p
Total Value: 5
I'M SURPRISED YOU'VE MANAGED TO SURVIVE IN THE EXPLORATION GROUP AS LONG AS YOU HAVE!
IT'S A DIVISION CHARGED WITH FIGHTING MONSTERS, IN CASE YOU FORGOT!
PFFT
...
HA HA HA!
LIKE A BUNCH OF NUMBERS REALLY SHOW MY TRUE WORTH.
MAYBE NOT, BUT STILL!
YOU WERE ABLE TO GET BY WITH JUST YOUR WITS... BUT THAT WAS BEFORE.

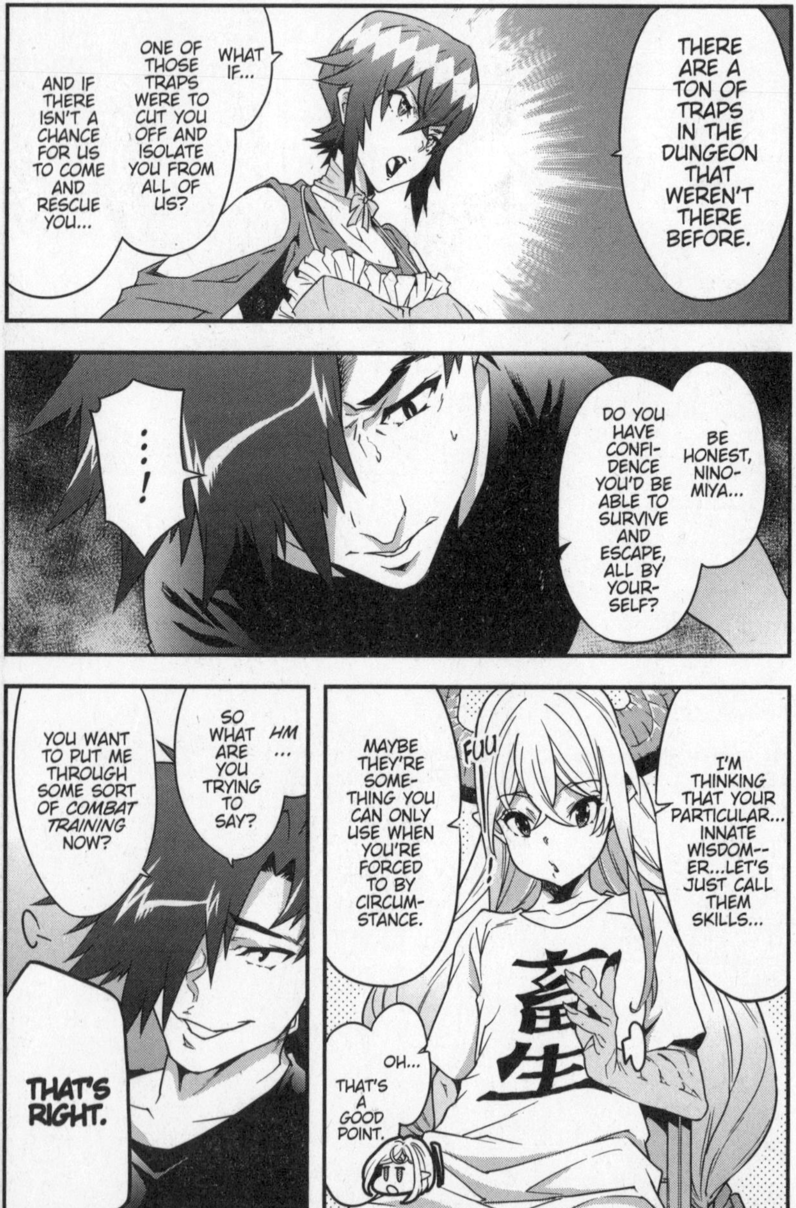
THERE ARE A TON OF TRAPS IN THE DUNGEON THAT WEREN'T THERE BEFORE.
WHAT IF...
ONE OF THOSE TRAPS WERE TO CUT YOU OFF AND ISOLATE YOU FROM ALL OF US?
AND IF THERE ISN'T A CHANCE FOR US TO COME AND RESCUE YOU...
BE HONEST, NINOMIYA...
DO YOU HAVE CONFIDENCE YOU'D BE ABLE TO SURVIVE AND ESCAPE, ALL BY YOURSELF?
...!
I'M THINKING THAT YOUR PARTICULAR... INNATE WISDOM-- ER...LET'S JUST CALL THEM SKILLS...
FUU
MAYBE THEY'RE SOMETHING YOU CAN ONLY USE WHEN YOU'RE FORCED TO BY CIRCUMSTANCE.
畜生
OH... THAT'S A GOOD POINT.
HM...
SO WHAT ARE YOU TRYING TO SAY?
YOU WANT TO PUT ME THROUGH SOME SORT OF *COMBAT TRAINING* NOW?
THAT'S RIGHT.

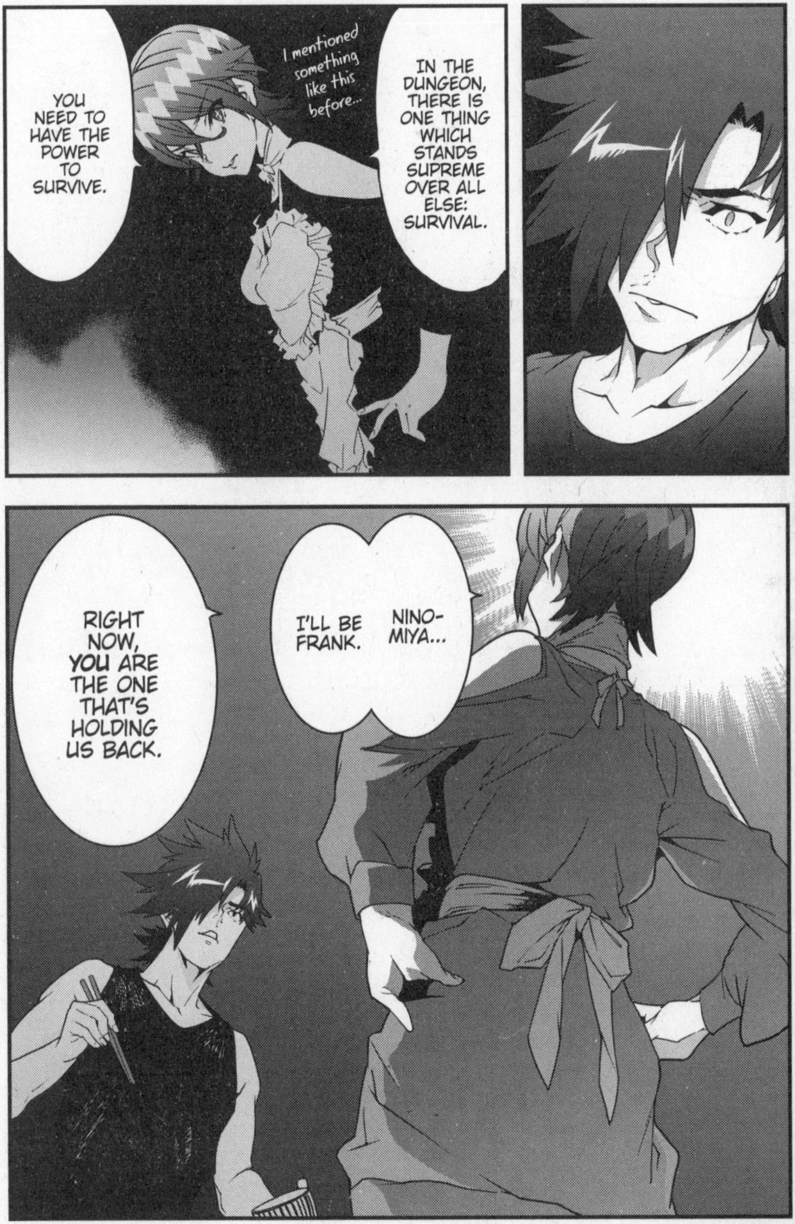
IN THE DUNGEON, THERE IS ONE THING WHICH STANDS SUPREME OVER ALL ELSE: SURVIVAL.
I mentioned something like this before...
YOU NEED TO HAVE THE POWER TO SURVIVE.
NINO-MIYA...
I'LL BE FRANK.
RIGHT NOW, **YOU** ARE THE ONE THAT'S HOLDING US BACK.

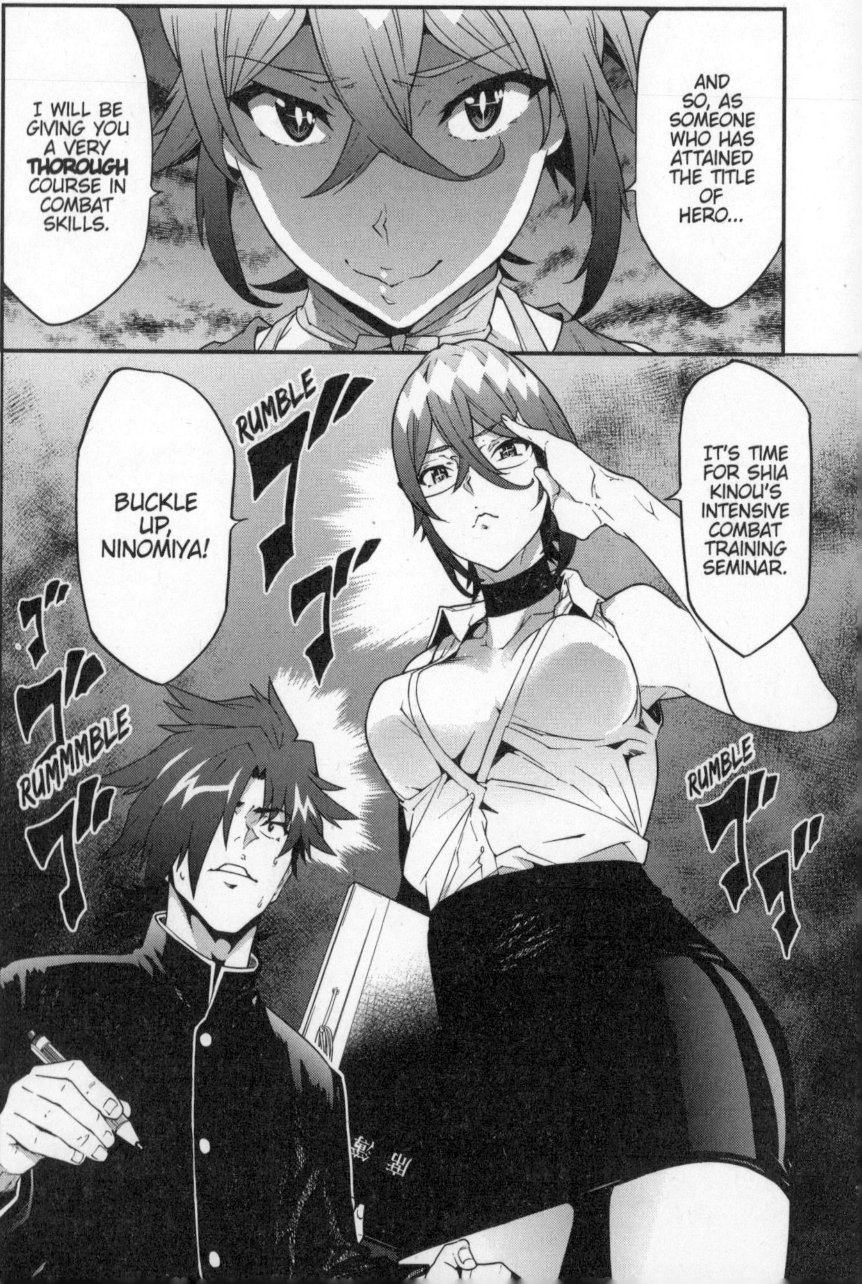
AND SO, AS SOMEONE WHO HAS ATTAINED THE TITLE OF HERO...
I WILL BE GIVING YOU A VERY **THOROUGH** COURSE IN COMBAT SKILLS.
IT'S TIME FOR SHIA KINOU'S INTENSIVE COMBAT TRAINING SEMINAR.
RUMBLE
BUCKLE UP, NINOMIYA!
RUMBLE
RUMMMBLE

Shia,
casual style.

THE DUNGEON OF
BLACK COMPANY

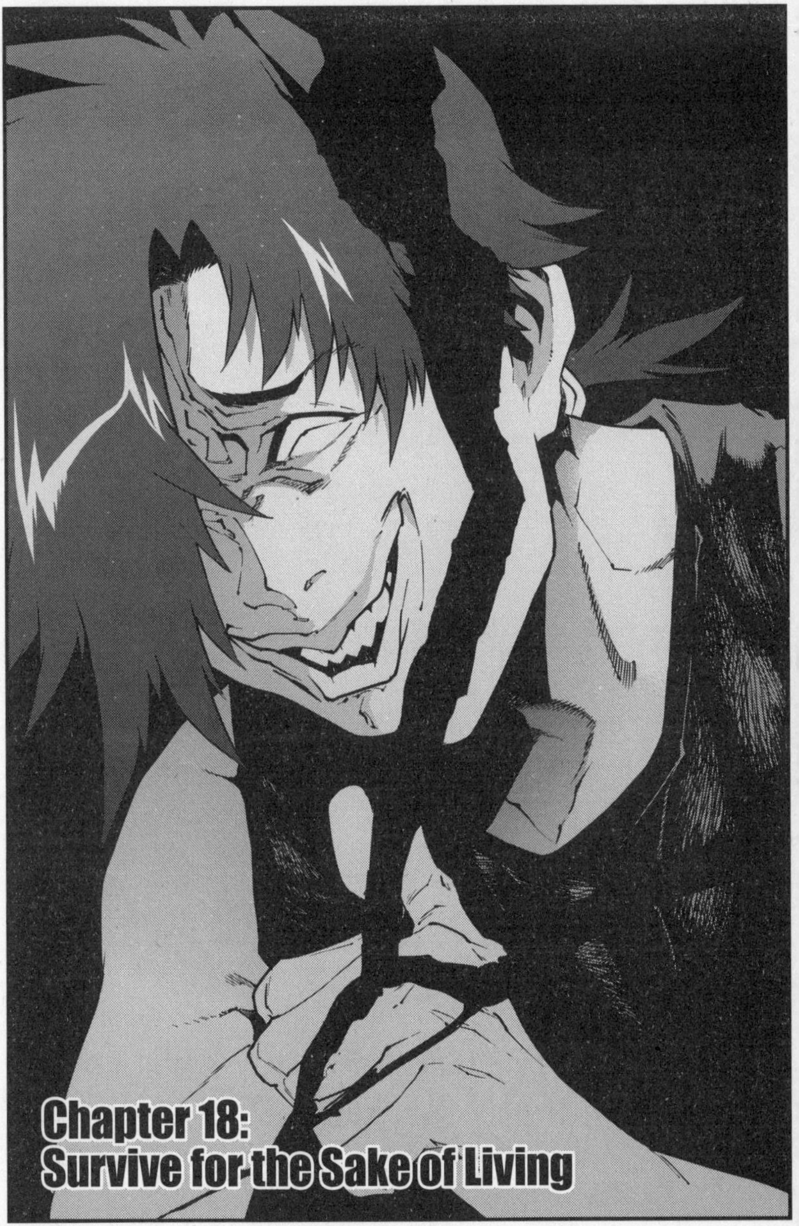
Chapter 18:
Survive for the Sake of Living

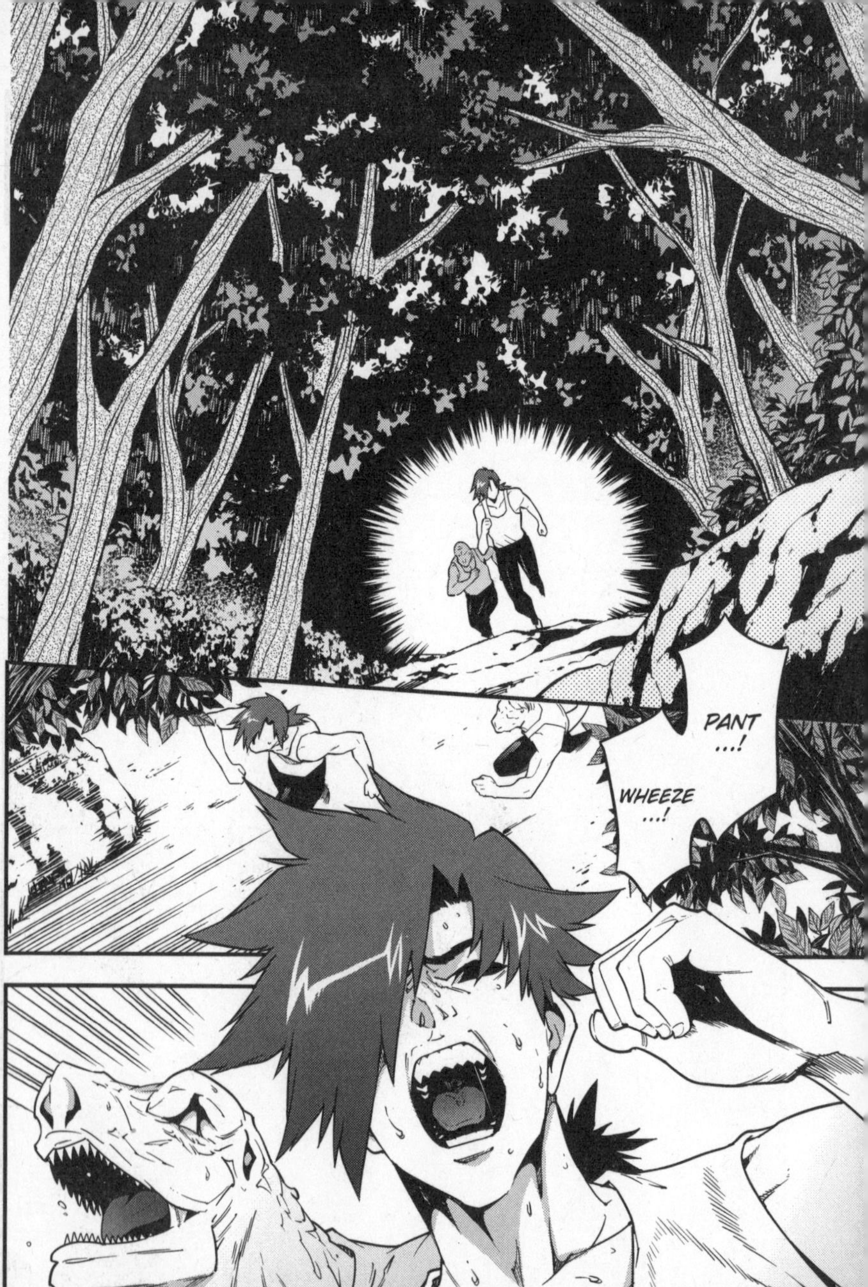
PANT ...!
WHEEZE ...!

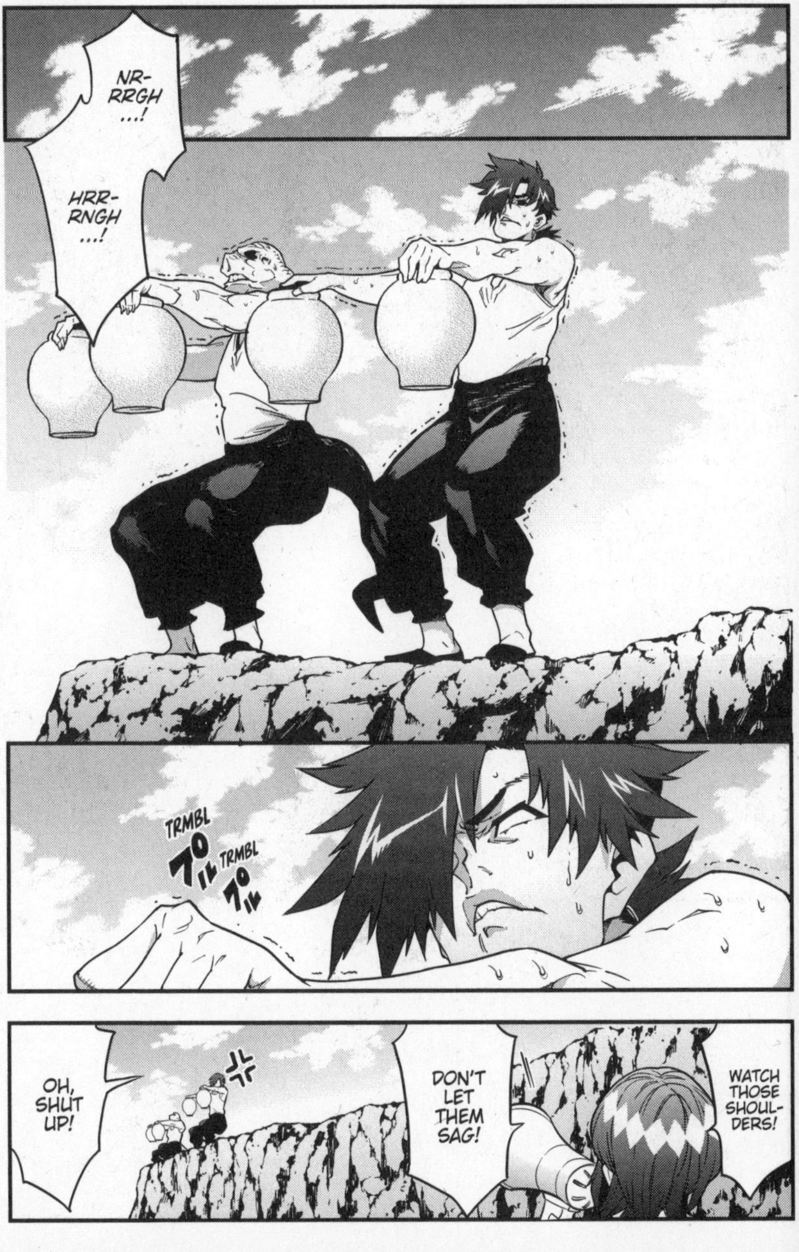
NR-RRGH ...!
HRR-RNGH ...!
TRMBL
TRMBL
WATCH THOSE SHOUL-DERS!
DON'T LET THEM SAG!
OH, SHUT UP!

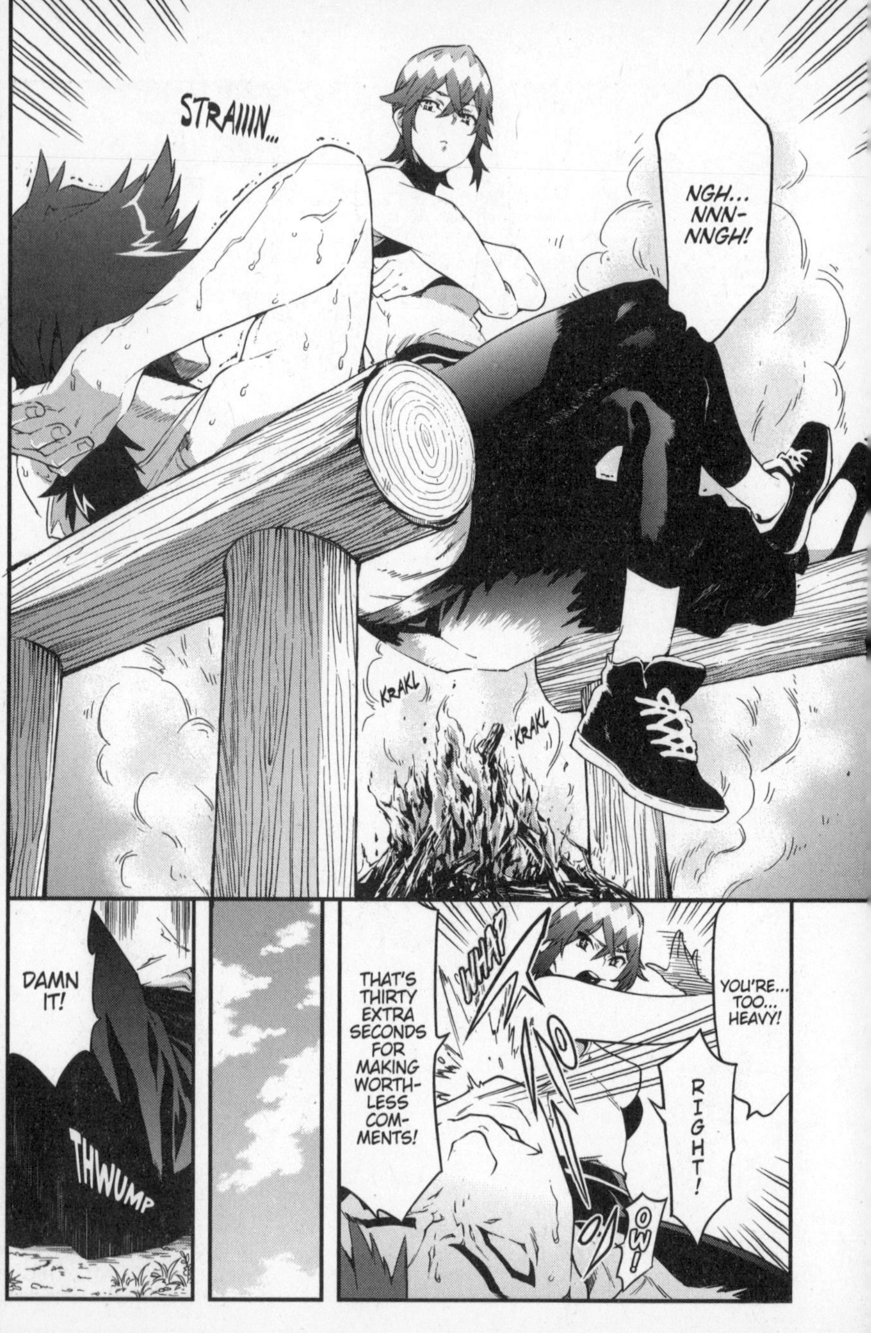
NGH... NNN-NNGH!
STRAIIIN...
KRAKL
KRAKL
YOU'RE... TOO... HEAVY!
WHAP
THAT'S THIRTY EXTRA SECONDS FOR MAKING WORTH-LESS COM-MENTS!
RIGHT!
OW!
DAMN IT!
THWUMP

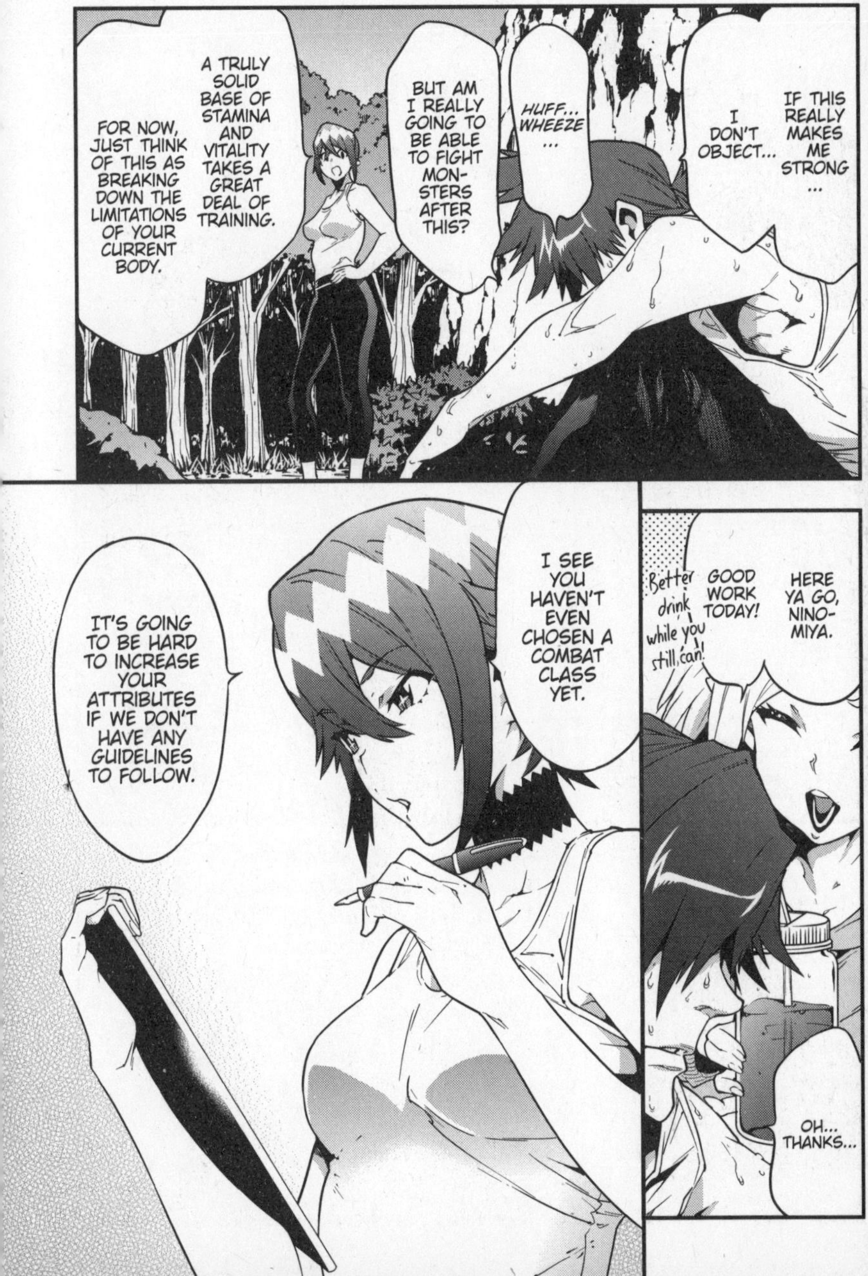
IF THIS REALLY MAKES ME STRONG ...
I DON'T OBJECT...
HUFF... WHEEZE ...
BUT AM I REALLY GOING TO BE ABLE TO FIGHT MON-STERS AFTER THIS?
A TRULY SOLID BASE OF STAMINA AND VITALITY TAKES A GREAT DEAL OF TRAINING.
FOR NOW, JUST THINK OF THIS AS BREAKING DOWN THE LIMITATIONS OF YOUR CURRENT BODY.
HERE YA GO, NINO-MIYA.
GOOD WORK TODAY!
Better drink while you still can!
OH... THANKS...
I SEE YOU HAVEN'T EVEN CHOSEN A COMBAT CLASS YET.
IT'S GOING TO BE HARD TO INCREASE YOUR ATTRIBUTES IF WE DON'T HAVE ANY GUIDELINES TO FOLLOW.

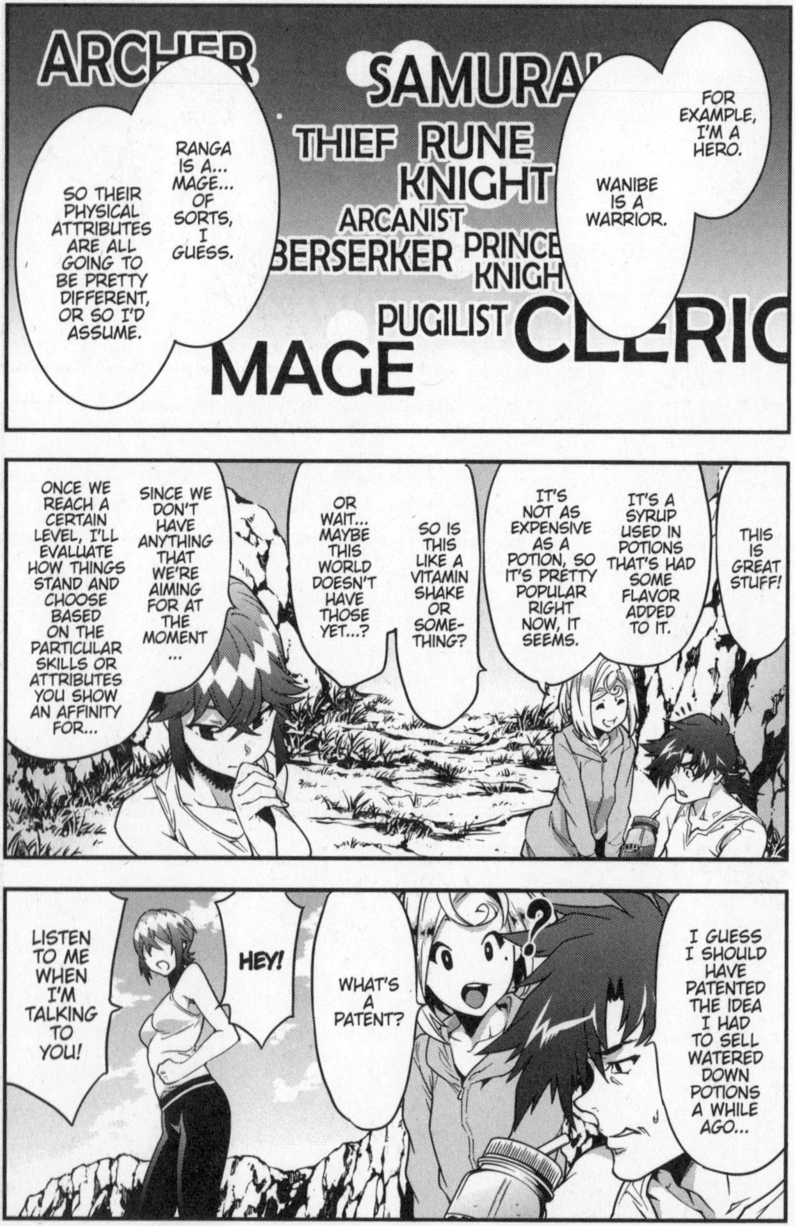
ARCHER
SAMURA
THIEF
RUNE KNIGHT
ARCANIST
BERSERKER
PRINCE KNIGH
PUGILIST
CLERIC
MAGE
FOR EXAMPLE, I'M A HERO.
WANIBE IS A WARRIOR.
RANGA IS A... MAGE... OF SORTS, I GUESS.
SO THEIR PHYSICAL ATTRIBUTES ARE ALL GOING TO BE PRETTY DIFFERENT, OR SO I'D ASSUME.
THIS IS GREAT STUFF!
IT'S A SYRUP USED IN POTIONS THAT'S HAD SOME FLAVOR ADDED TO IT.
IT'S NOT AS EXPENSIVE AS A POTION, SO IT'S PRETTY POPULAR RIGHT NOW, IT SEEMS.
SO IS THIS LIKE A VITAMIN SHAKE OR SOME-THING?
OR WAIT... MAYBE THIS WORLD DOESN'T HAVE THOSE YET...?
SINCE WE DON'T HAVE ANYTHING THAT WE'RE AIMING FOR AT THE MOMENT...
ONCE WE REACH A CERTAIN LEVEL, I'LL EVALUATE HOW THINGS STAND AND CHOOSE BASED ON THE PARTICULAR SKILLS OR ATTRIBUTES YOU SHOW AN AFFINITY FOR...
I GUESS I SHOULD HAVE PATENTED THE IDEA I HAD TO SELL WATERED DOWN POTIONS A WHILE AGO...
?
WHAT'S A PATENT?
HEY!
LISTEN TO ME WHEN I'M TALKING TO YOU!

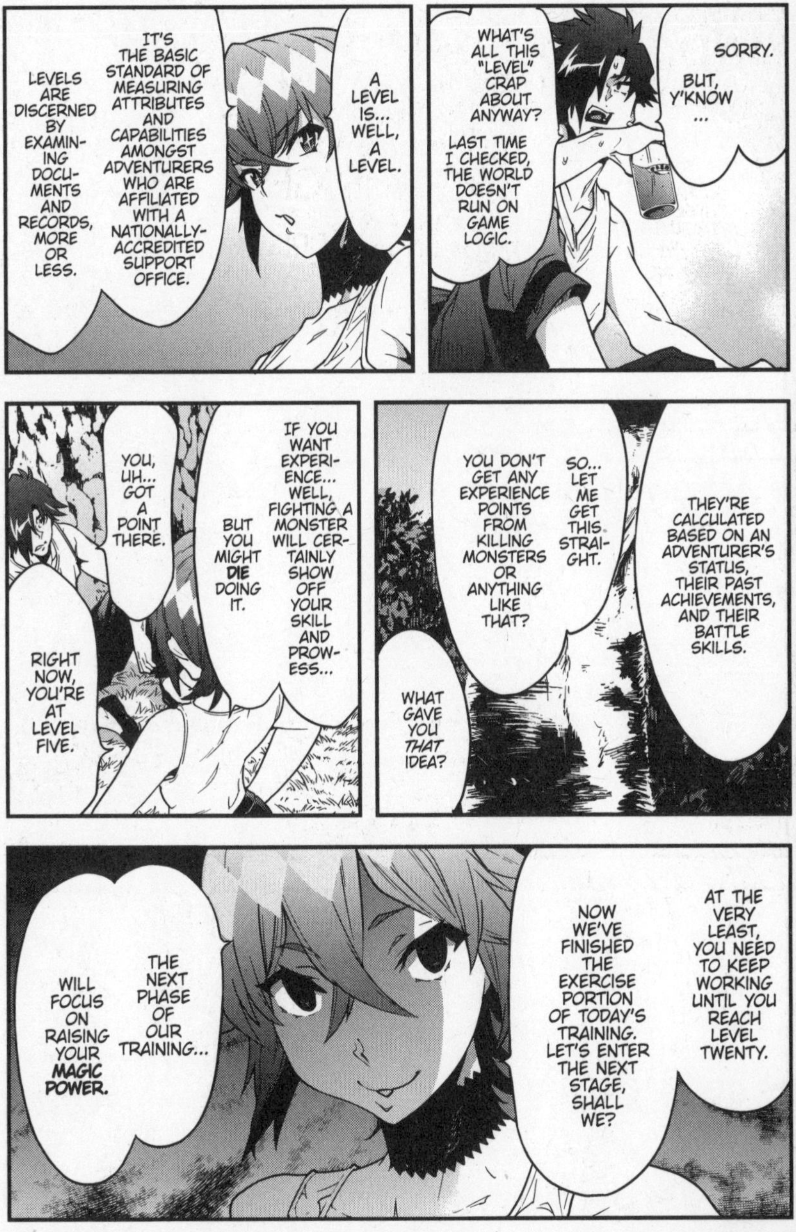
SORRY.
BUT, Y'KNOW ...
WHAT'S ALL THIS "LEVEL" CRAP ABOUT ANYWAY?
LAST TIME I CHECKED, THE WORLD DOESN'T RUN ON GAME LOGIC.
A LEVEL IS... WELL, A LEVEL.
IT'S THE BASIC STANDARD OF MEASURING ATTRIBUTES AND CAPABILITIES AMONGST ADVENTURERS WHO ARE AFFILIATED WITH A NATIONALLY-ACCREDITED SUPPORT OFFICE.
LEVELS ARE DISCERNED BY EXAMINING DOCUMENTS AND RECORDS, MORE OR LESS.
THEY'RE CALCULATED BASED ON AN ADVENTURER'S STATUS, THEIR PAST ACHIEVEMENTS, AND THEIR BATTLE SKILLS.
SO... LET ME GET THIS STRAIGHT.
YOU DON'T GET ANY EXPERIENCE POINTS FROM KILLING MONSTERS OR ANYTHING LIKE THAT?
WHAT GAVE YOU *THAT* IDEA?
IF YOU WANT EXPERIENCE... WELL, FIGHTING A MONSTER WILL CERTAINLY SHOW OFF YOUR SKILL AND PROWESS...
BUT YOU MIGHT **DIE** DOING IT.
YOU, UH... GOT A POINT THERE.
RIGHT NOW, YOU'RE AT LEVEL FIVE.
AT THE VERY LEAST, YOU NEED TO KEEP WORKING UNTIL YOU REACH LEVEL TWENTY.
NOW WE'VE FINISHED THE EXERCISE PORTION OF TODAY'S TRAINING. LET'S ENTER THE NEXT STAGE, SHALL WE?
THE NEXT PHASE OF OUR TRAINING...
WILL FOCUS ON RAISING YOUR **MAGIC POWER.**

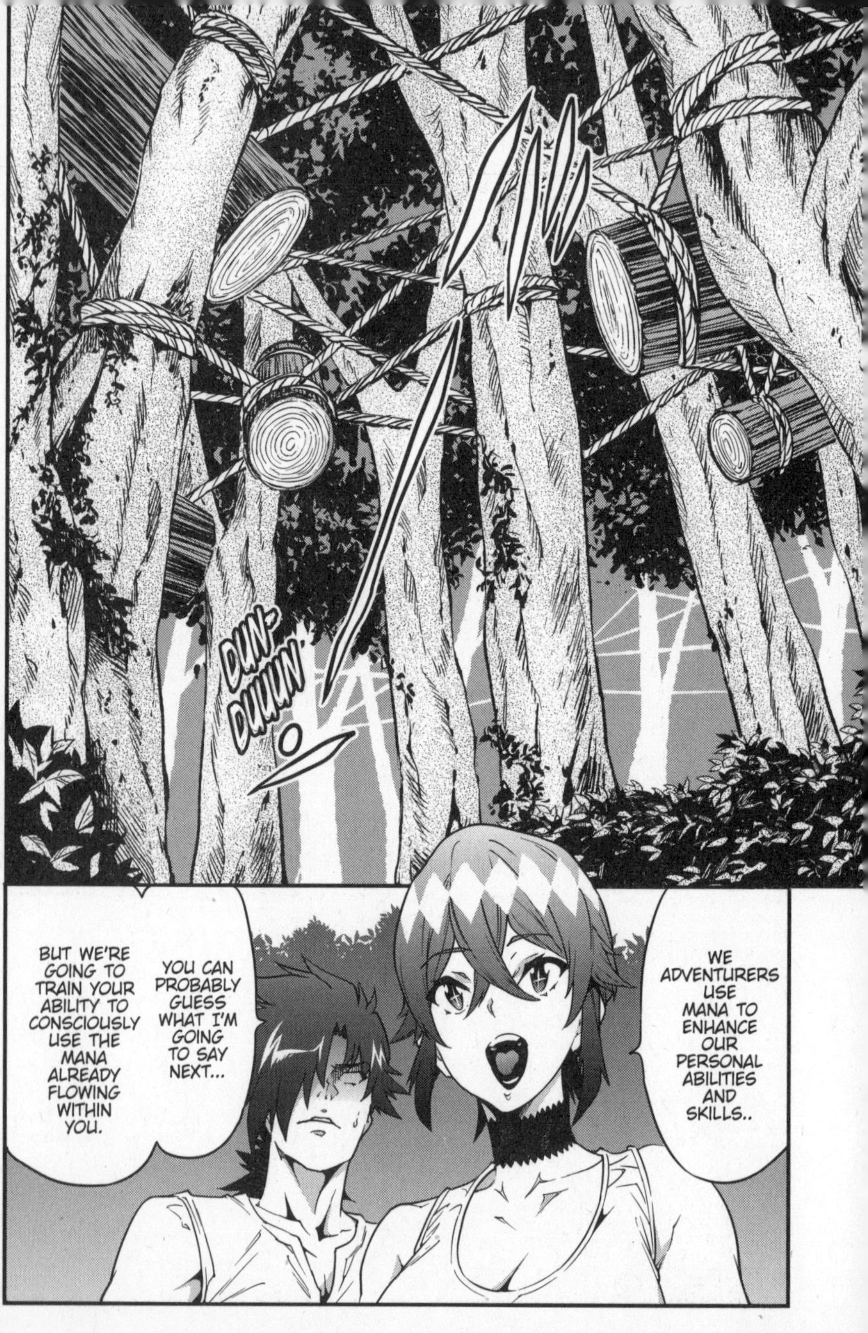
DUN-DUUUN
WE ADVENTURERS USE MANA TO ENHANCE OUR PERSONAL ABILITIES AND SKILLS..
YOU CAN PROBABLY GUESS WHAT I'M GOING TO SAY NEXT...
BUT WE'RE GOING TO TRAIN YOUR ABILITY TO CONSCIOUSLY USE THE MANA ALREADY FLOWING WITHIN YOU.

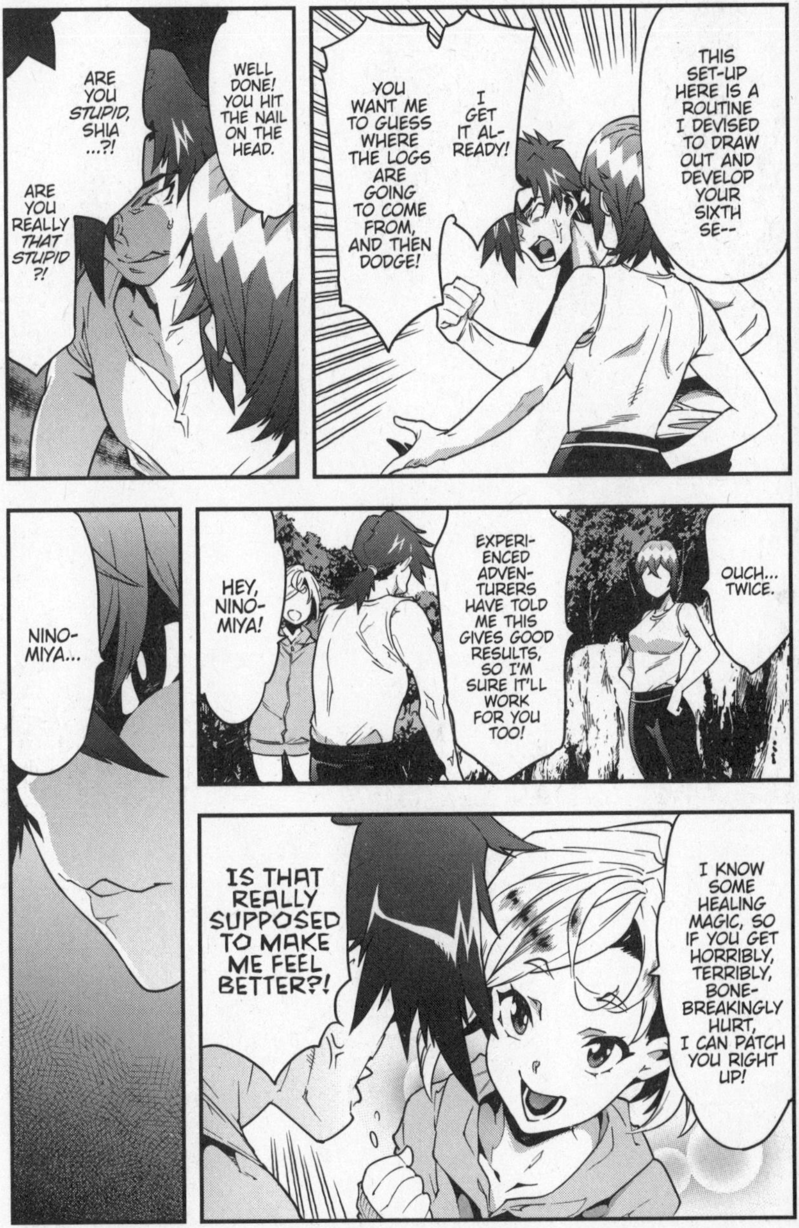
THIS SET-UP HERE IS A ROUTINE I DEVISED TO DRAW OUT AND DEVELOP YOUR SIXTH SE--
I GET IT AL-READY!
YOU WANT ME TO GUESS WHERE THE LOGS ARE GOING TO COME FROM, AND THEN DODGE!
WELL DONE! YOU HIT THE NAIL ON THE HEAD.
ARE YOU *STUPID*, SHIA ...?!
ARE YOU REALLY *THAT STUPID* ?!
OUCH... TWICE.
EXPERIENCED ADVENTURERS HAVE TOLD ME THIS GIVES GOOD RESULTS, SO I'M SURE IT'LL WORK FOR YOU TOO!
HEY, NINO-MIYA!
I KNOW SOME HEALING MAGIC, SO IF YOU GET HORRIBLY, TERRIBLY, BONE-BREAKINGLY HURT, I CAN PATCH YOU RIGHT UP!
IS THAT REALLY SUPPOSED TO MAKE ME FEEL BETTER?!
NINO-MIYA...

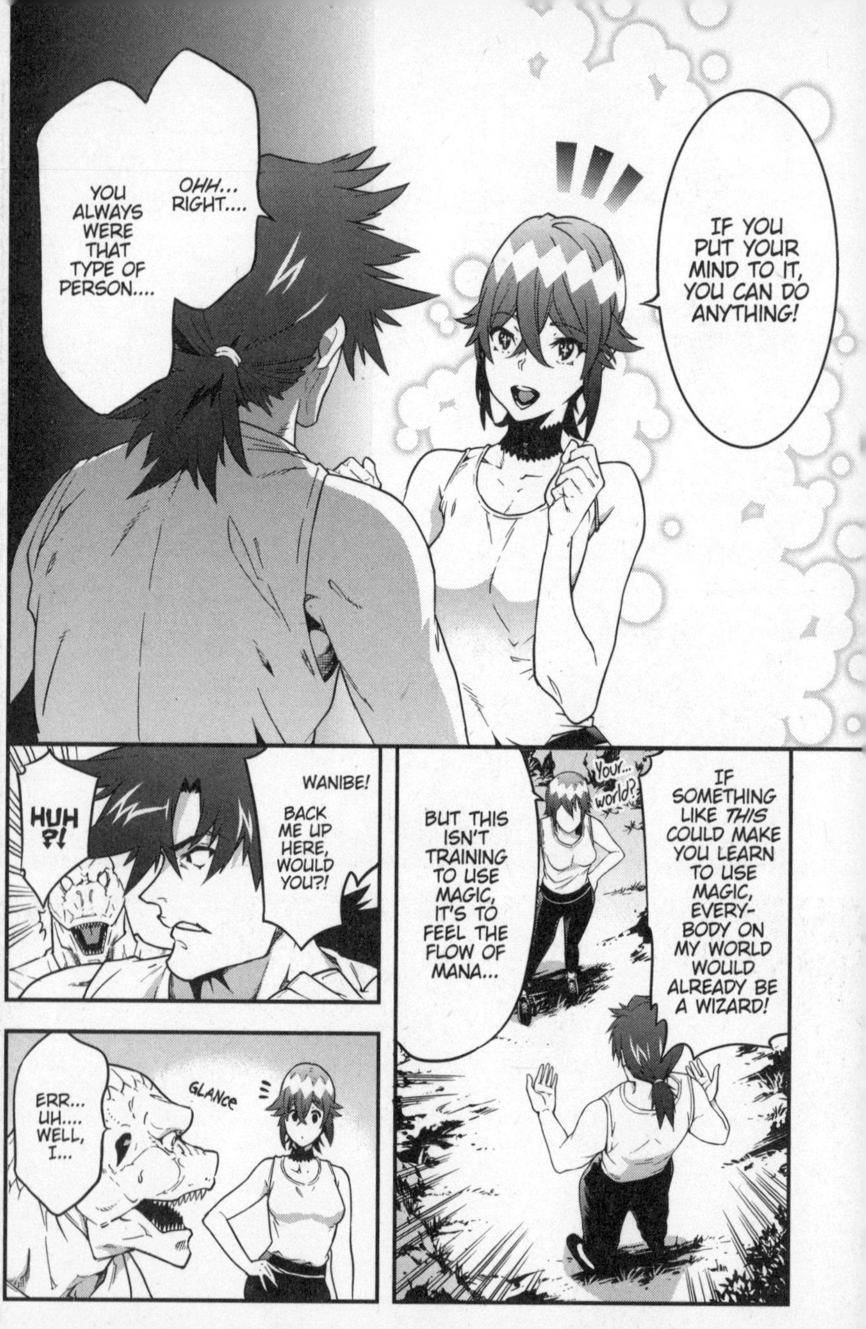
IF YOU PUT YOUR MIND TO IT, YOU CAN DO ANYTHING!
OHH... RIGHT....
YOU ALWAYS WERE THAT TYPE OF PERSON....
IF SOMETHING LIKE *THIS* COULD MAKE YOU LEARN TO USE MAGIC, EVERY-BODY ON MY WORLD WOULD ALREADY BE A WIZARD!
Your... world?
BUT THIS ISN'T TRAINING TO USE MAGIC, IT'S TO FEEL THE FLOW OF MANA...
WANIBE!
BACK ME UP HERE, WOULD YOU?!
HUH ?!
GLANCE
ERR... UH.... WELL, I...

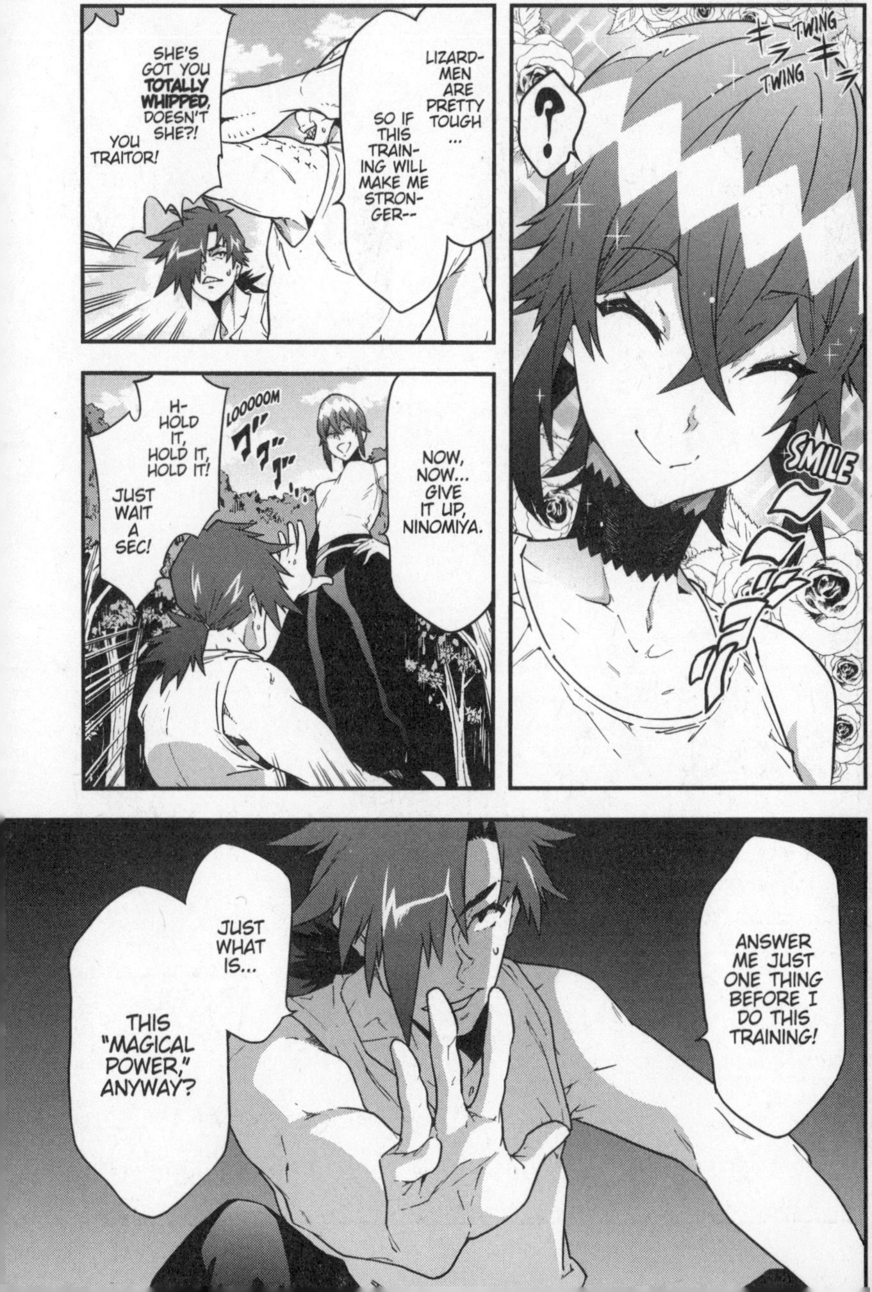
TWING
TWING
?
SMILE
LIZARD-MEN ARE PRETTY TOUGH...
SO IF THIS TRAINING WILL MAKE ME STRONGER--
SHE'S GOT YOU **TOTALLY WHIPPED**, DOESN'T SHE?!
YOU TRAITOR!
NOW, NOW... GIVE IT UP, NINOMIYA.
LOOOOOM
H-HOLD IT, HOLD IT, HOLD IT!
JUST WAIT A SEC!
ANSWER ME JUST ONE THING BEFORE I DO THIS TRAINING!
JUST WHAT IS...
THIS "MAGICAL POWER," ANYWAY?

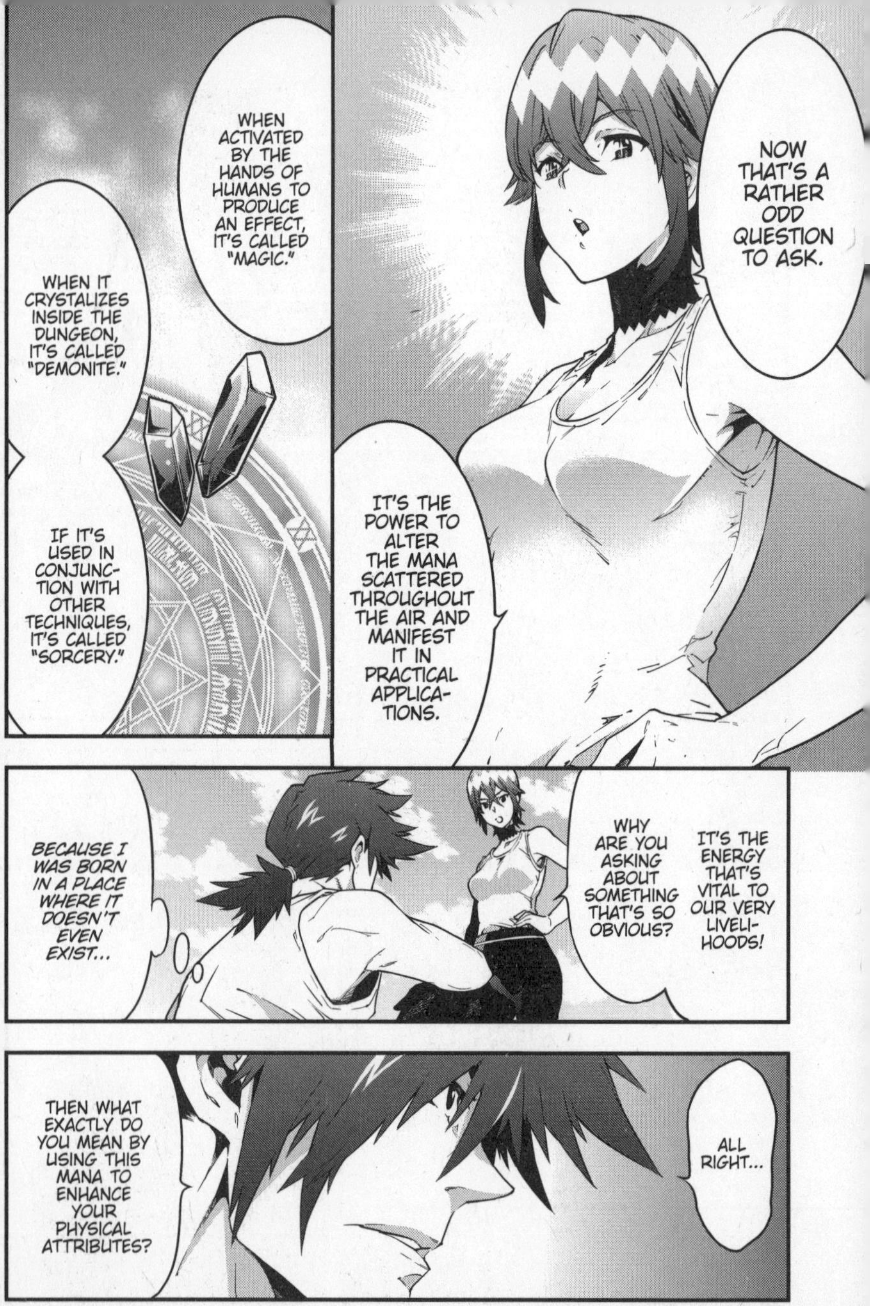
NOW THAT'S A RATHER ODD QUESTION TO ASK.
IT'S THE POWER TO ALTER THE MANA SCATTERED THROUGHOUT THE AIR AND MANIFEST IT IN PRACTICAL APPLICATIONS.
WHEN ACTIVATED BY THE HANDS OF HUMANS TO PRODUCE AN EFFECT, IT'S CALLED "MAGIC."
WHEN IT CRYSTALIZES INSIDE THE DUNGEON, IT'S CALLED "DEMONITE."
IF IT'S USED IN CONJUNCTION WITH OTHER TECHNIQUES, IT'S CALLED "SORCERY."
IT'S THE ENERGY THAT'S VITAL TO OUR VERY LIVELIHOODS!
WHY ARE YOU ASKING ABOUT SOMETHING THAT'S SO OBVIOUS?
BECAUSE I WAS BORN IN A PLACE WHERE IT DOESN'T EVEN EXIST...
ALL RIGHT...
THEN WHAT EXACTLY DO YOU MEAN BY USING THIS MANA TO ENHANCE YOUR PHYSICAL ATTRIBUTES?

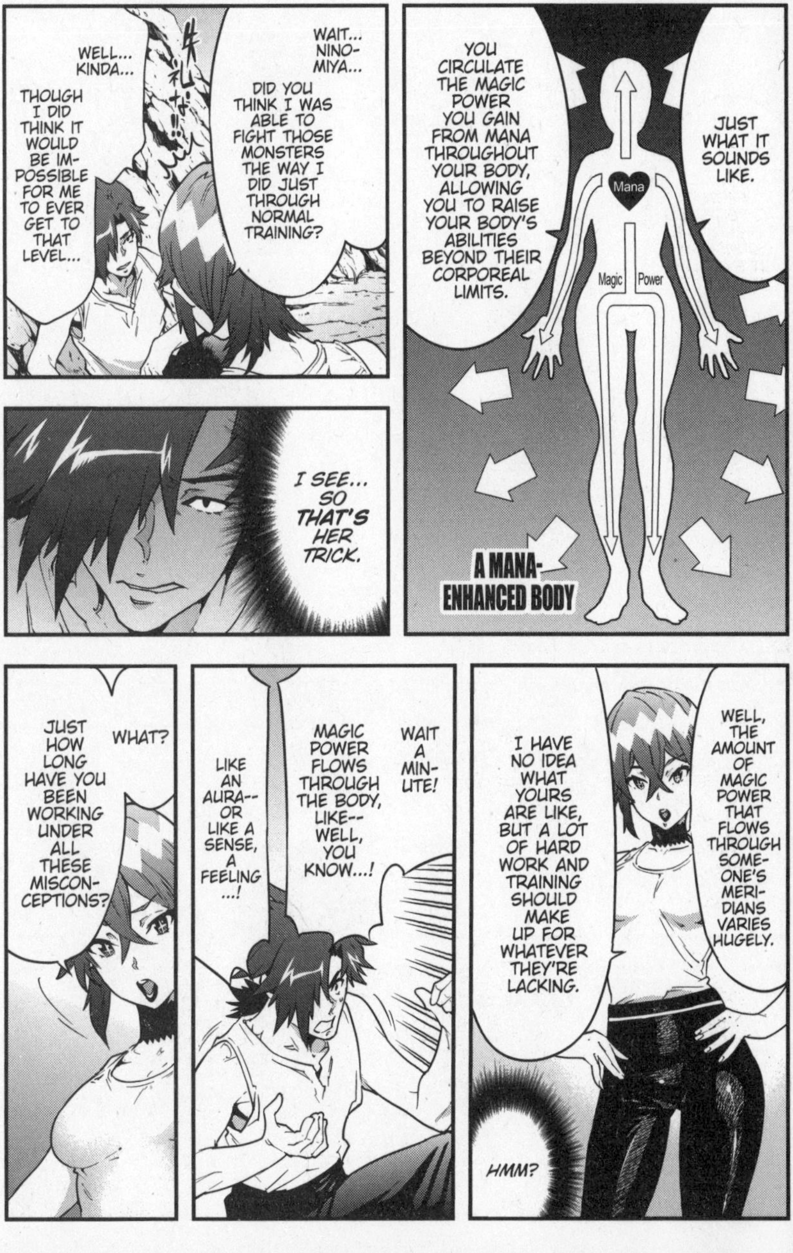
JUST WHAT IT SOUNDS LIKE.
YOU CIRCULATE THE MAGIC POWER YOU GAIN FROM MANA THROUGHOUT YOUR BODY, ALLOWING YOU TO RAISE YOUR BODY'S ABILITIES BEYOND THEIR CORPOREAL LIMITS.
Mana
Magic Power
A MANA-ENHANCED BODY
WAIT... NINO-MIYA...
DID YOU THINK I WAS ABLE TO FIGHT THOSE MONSTERS THE WAY I DID JUST THROUGH NORMAL TRAINING?
失礼な!!
WELL... KINDA...
THOUGH I DID THINK IT WOULD BE IM-POSSIBLE FOR ME TO EVER GET TO THAT LEVEL...
I SEE... SO ***THAT'S*** HER TRICK.
WELL, THE AMOUNT OF MAGIC POWER THAT FLOWS THROUGH SOME-ONE'S MERI-DIANS VARIES HUGELY.
I HAVE NO IDEA WHAT YOURS ARE LIKE, BUT A LOT OF HARD WORK AND TRAINING SHOULD MAKE UP FOR WHATEVER THEY'RE LACKING.
HMM?
WAIT A MIN-UTE!
MAGIC POWER FLOWS THROUGH THE BODY, LIKE-- WELL, YOU KNOW...!
LIKE AN AURA-- OR LIKE A SENSE, A FEELING ...!
WHAT?
JUST HOW LONG HAVE YOU BEEN WORKING UNDER ALL THESE MISCON-CEPTIONS?

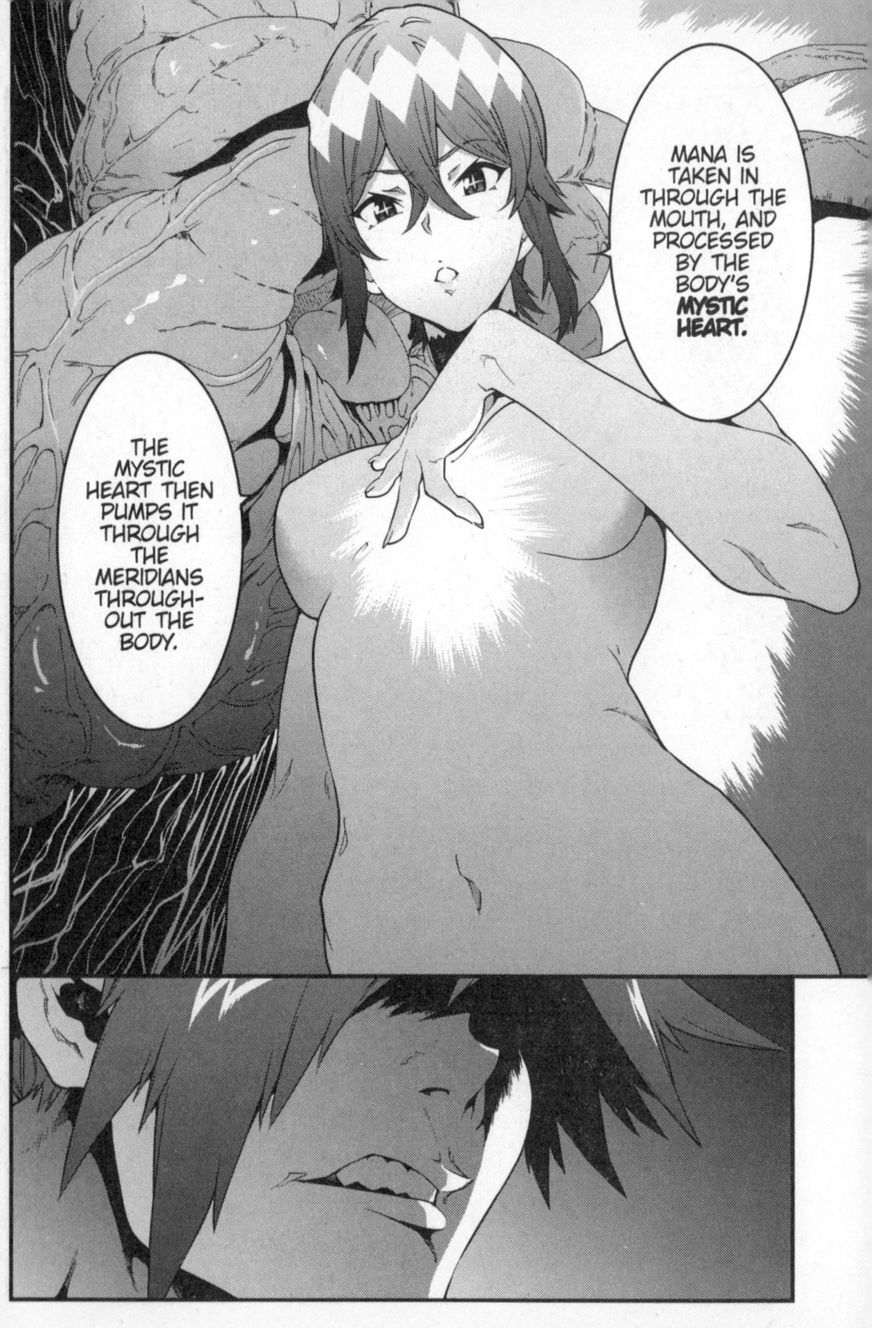
MANA IS TAKEN IN THROUGH THE MOUTH, AND PROCESSED BY THE BODY'S **MYSTIC HEART.**
THE MYSTIC HEART THEN PUMPS IT THROUGH THE MERIDIANS THROUGH-OUT THE BODY.

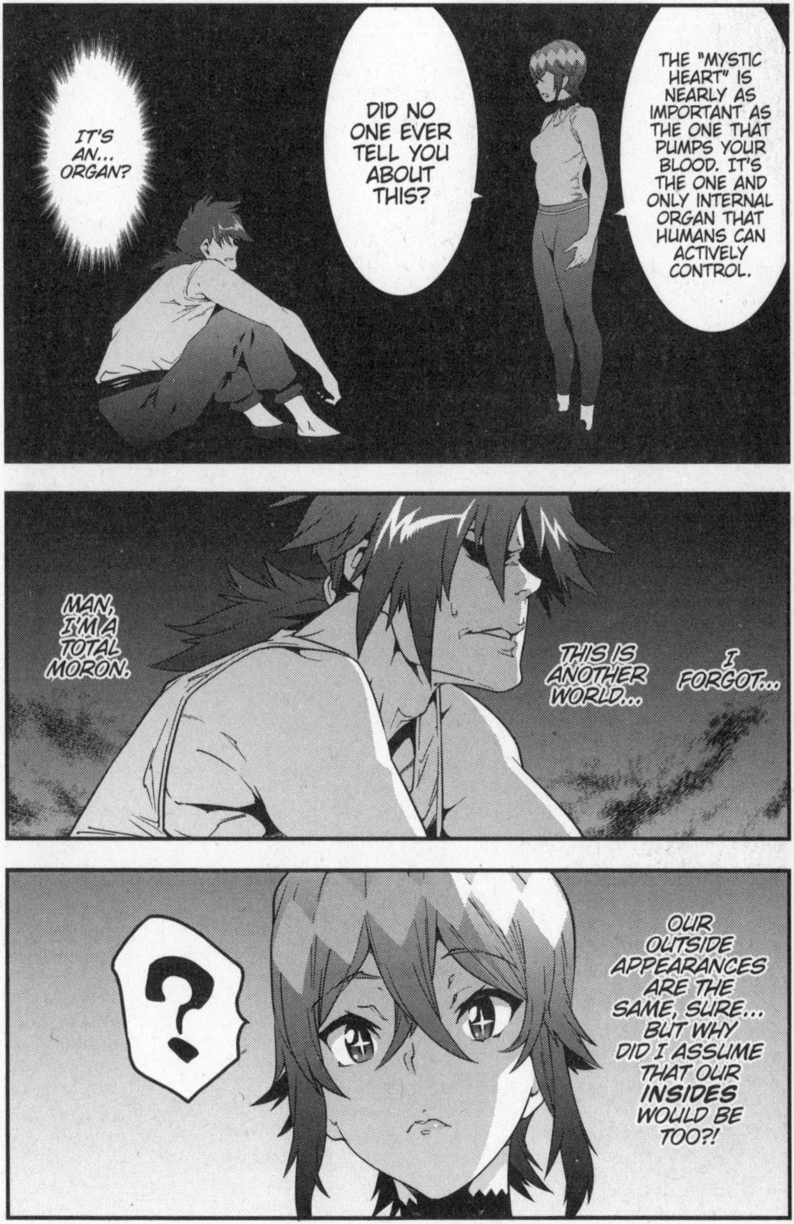
THE "MYSTIC HEART" IS NEARLY AS IMPORTANT AS THE ONE THAT PUMPS YOUR BLOOD. IT'S THE ONE AND ONLY INTERNAL ORGAN THAT HUMANS CAN ACTIVELY CONTROL.
DID NO ONE EVER TELL YOU ABOUT THIS?
IT'S AN... ORGAN?
I FORGOT...
THIS IS ANOTHER WORLD...
MAN, I'M A TOTAL MORON.
OUR OUTSIDE APPEARANCES ARE THE SAME, SURE... BUT WHY DID I ASSUME THAT OUR **INSIDES** WOULD BE TOO?!
?

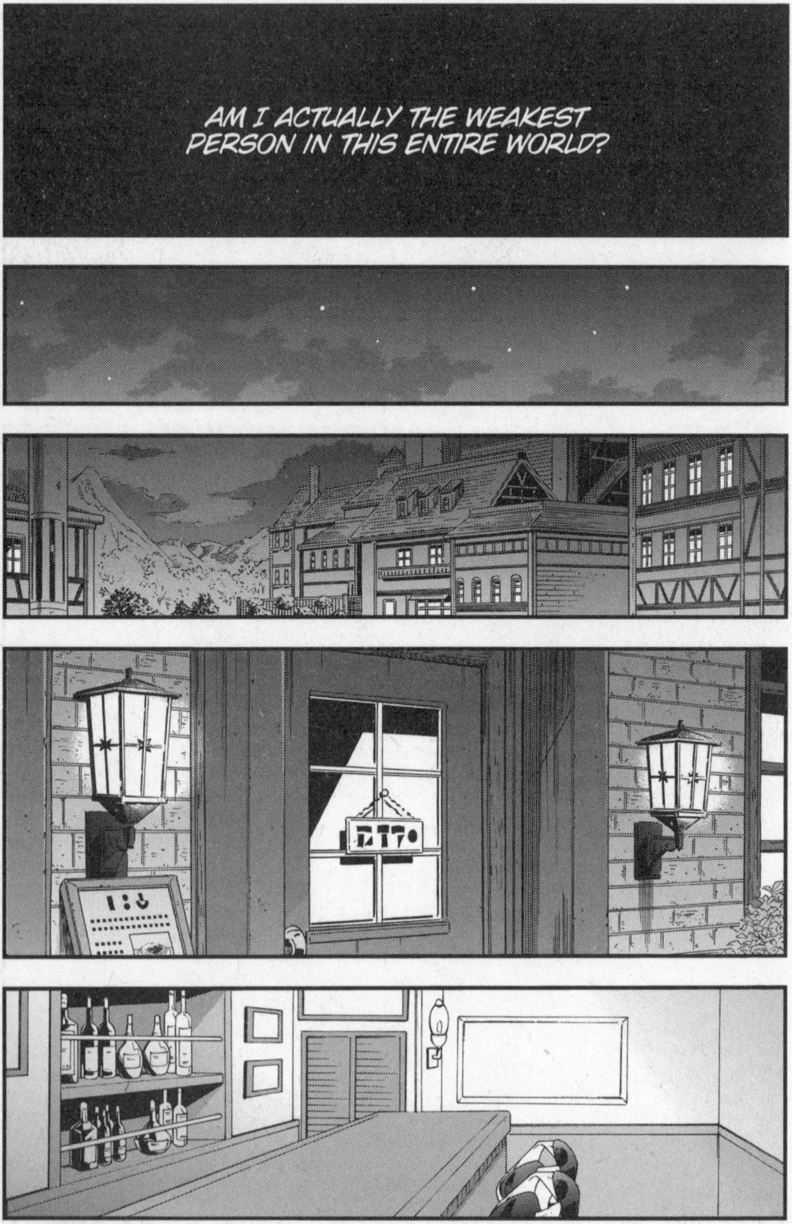
AM I ACTUALLY THE WEAKEST PERSON IN THIS ENTIRE WORLD?

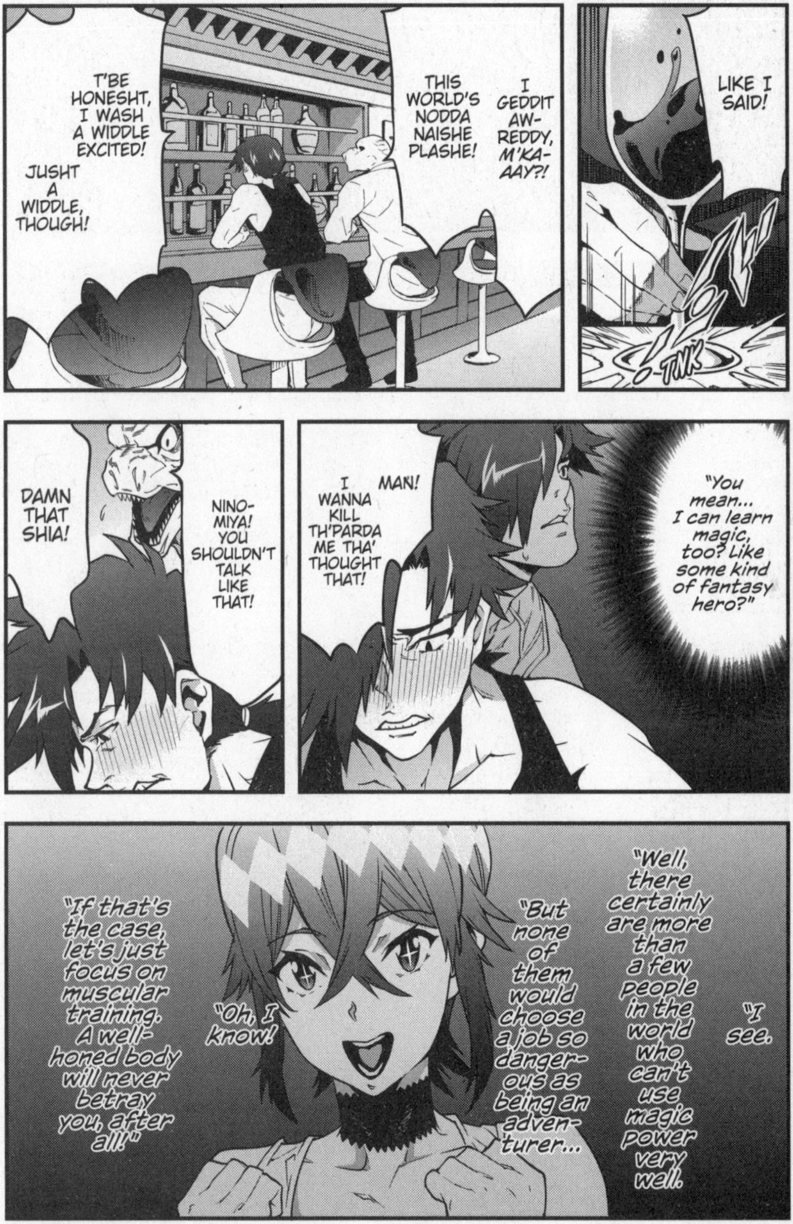
LIKE I SAID!
TNK
I GEDDIT AW-REDDY, M'KA-AAY?!
THIS WORLD'S NODDA NAISHE PLASHE!
T'BE HONESHT, I WASH A WIDDLE EXCITED!
JUSHT A WIDDLE, THOUGH!
"You mean... I can learn magic, too? Like some kind of fantasy hero?"
MAN!
I WANNA KILL TH'PARDA ME THA' THOUGHT THAT!
NINO-MIYA! YOU SHOULDN'T TALK LIKE THAT!
DAMN THAT SHIA!
"I see.
"Well, there certainly are more than a few people in the world who can't use magic power very well.
"But none of them would choose a job so danger-ous as being an adven-turer...
"Oh, I know!
"If that's the case, let's just focus on muscular training. A well-honed body will never betray you, after all!"

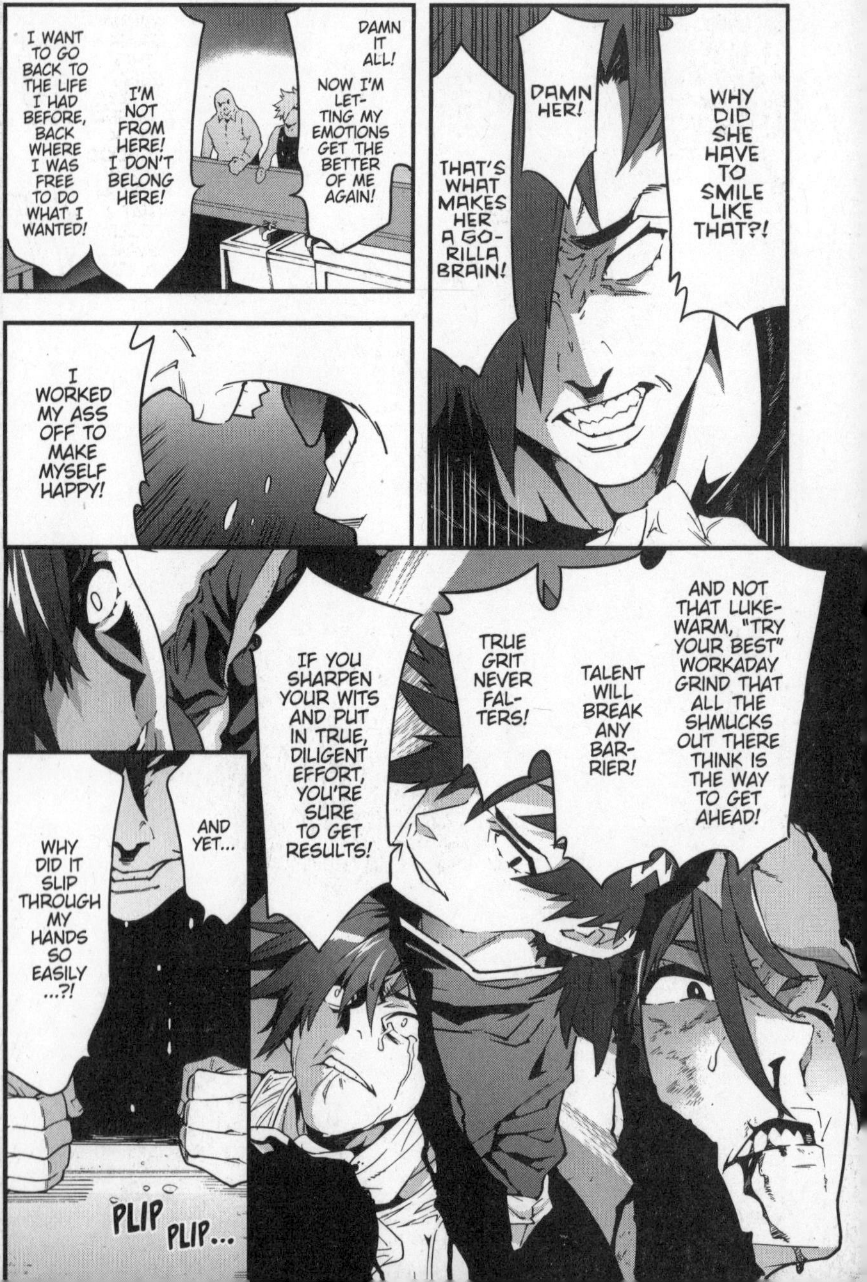
WHY DID SHE HAVE TO SMILE LIKE THAT?!
DAMN HER!
THAT'S WHAT MAKES HER A GO-RILLA BRAIN!
DAMN IT ALL!
NOW I'M LET-TING MY EMOTIONS GET THE BETTER OF ME AGAIN!
I'M NOT FROM HERE! I DON'T BELONG HERE!
I WANT TO GO BACK TO THE LIFE I HAD BEFORE, BACK WHERE I WAS FREE TO DO WHAT I WANTED!
I WORKED MY ASS OFF TO MAKE MYSELF HAPPY!
AND NOT THAT LUKE-WARM, "TRY YOUR BEST" WORKADAY GRIND THAT ALL THE SHMUCKS OUT THERE THINK IS THE WAY TO GET AHEAD!
TALENT WILL BREAK ANY BAR-RIER!
TRUE GRIT NEVER FAL-TERS!
IF YOU SHARPEN YOUR WITS AND PUT IN TRUE, DILIGENT EFFORT, YOU'RE SURE TO GET RESULTS!
AND YET...
WHY DID IT SLIP THROUGH MY HANDS SO EASILY ...?!
PLIP PLIP...

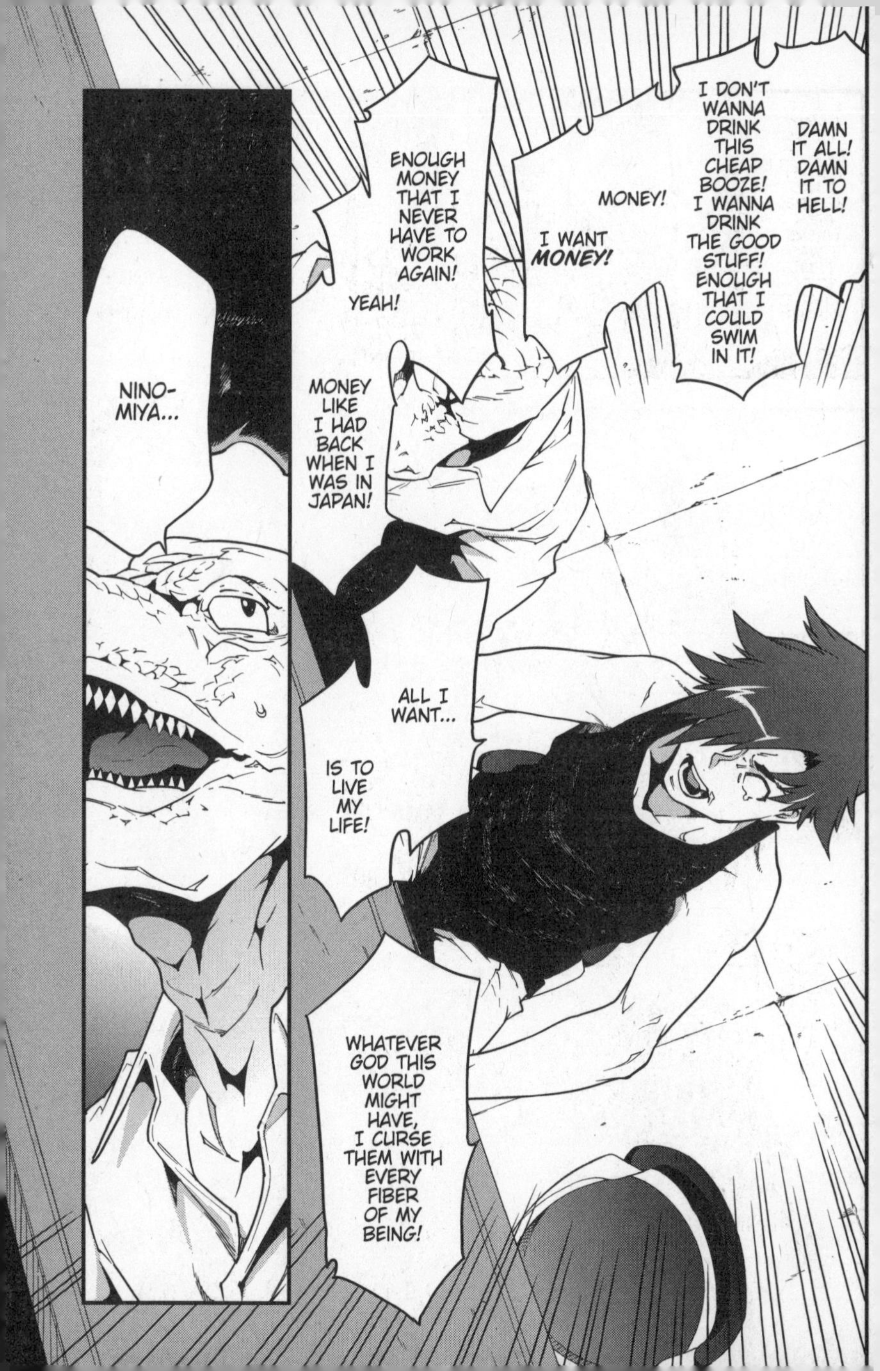

DAMN IT ALL! DAMN IT TO HELL!
I DON'T WANNA DRINK THIS CHEAP BOOZE! I WANNA DRINK THE GOOD STUFF! ENOUGH THAT I COULD SWIM IN IT!
MONEY!
I WANT MONEY!
ENOUGH MONEY THAT I NEVER HAVE TO WORK AGAIN!
YEAH!
MONEY LIKE I HAD BACK WHEN I WAS IN JAPAN!
ALL I WANT...
IS TO LIVE MY LIFE!
WHATEVER GOD THIS WORLD MIGHT HAVE, I CURSE THEM WITH EVERY FIBER OF MY BEING!
NINO-MIYA...

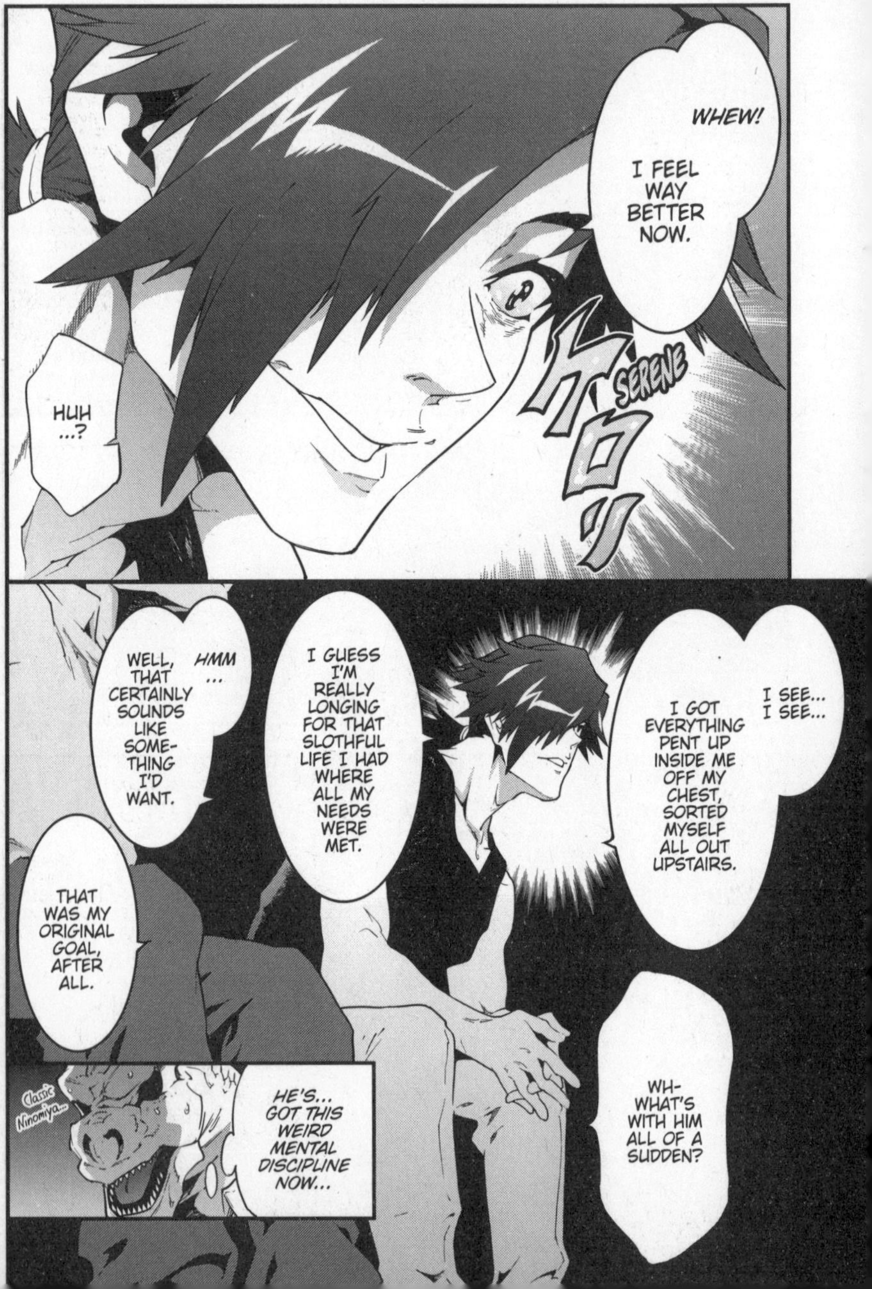
WHEW! I FEEL WAY BETTER NOW.
SERENE
HUH ...?
I SEE... I SEE...
I GOT EVERYTHING PENT UP INSIDE ME OFF MY CHEST, SORTED MYSELF ALL OUT UPSTAIRS.
I GUESS I'M REALLY LONGING FOR THAT SLOTHFUL LIFE I HAD WHERE ALL MY NEEDS WERE MET.
HMM ...
WELL, THAT CERTAINLY SOUNDS LIKE SOMETHING I'D WANT.
THAT WAS MY ORIGINAL GOAL, AFTER ALL.
WH- WHAT'S WITH HIM ALL OF A SUDDEN?
HE'S... GOT THIS WEIRD MENTAL DISCIPLINE NOW...
Classic Ninomiya...

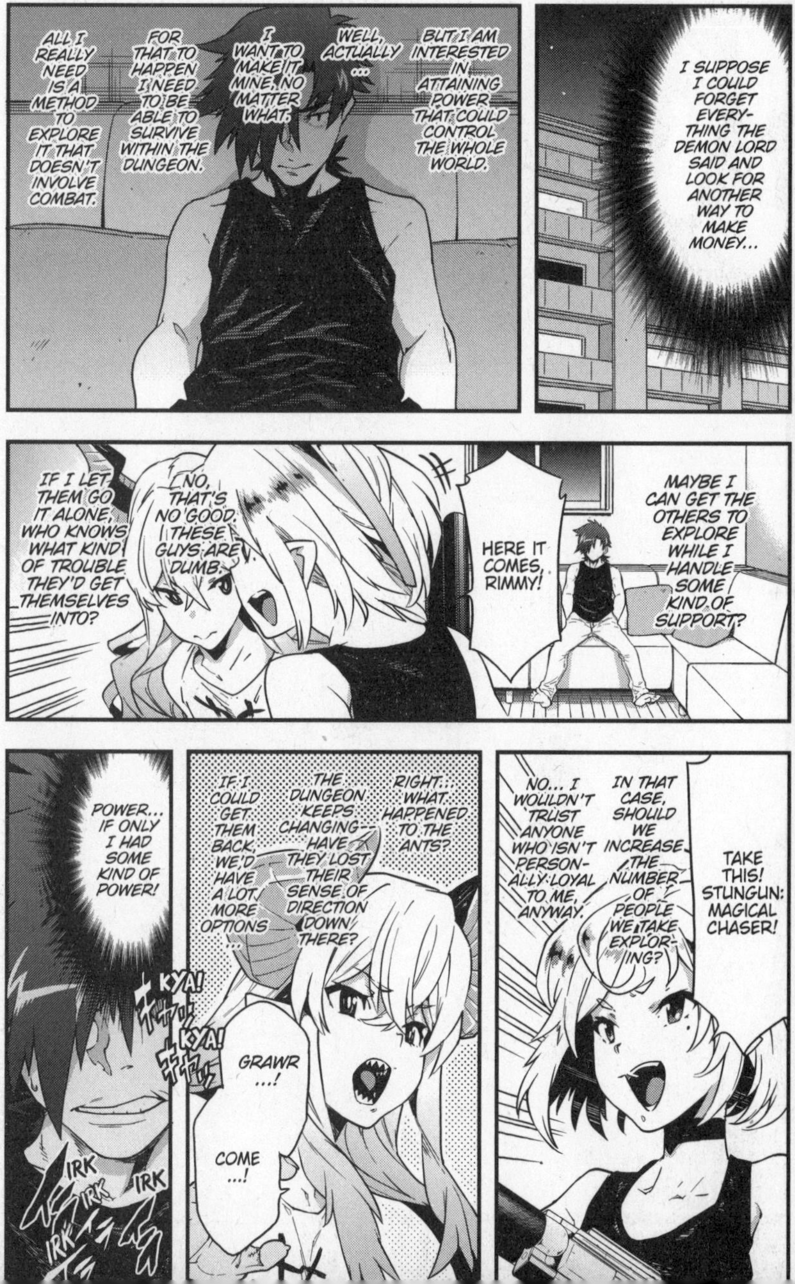
I SUPPOSE I COULD FORGET EVERY-THING THE DEMON LORD SAID AND LOOK FOR ANOTHER WAY TO MAKE MONEY...
BUT I AM INTERESTED IN ATTAINING POWER THAT COULD CONTROL THE WHOLE WORLD.
WELL, ACTUALLY...
I WANT TO MAKE IT MINE, NO MATTER WHAT.
FOR THAT TO HAPPEN I NEED TO BE ABLE TO SURVIVE WITHIN THE DUNGEON.
ALL I REALLY NEED IS A METHOD TO EXPLORE IT THAT DOESN'T INVOLVE COMBAT.
MAYBE I CAN GET THE OTHERS TO EXPLORE WHILE I HANDLE SOME KIND OF SUPPORT?
HERE IT COMES, RIMMY!
NO, THAT'S NO GOOD. THESE GUYS ARE DUMB.
IF I LET THEM GO IT ALONE, WHO KNOWS WHAT KIND OF TROUBLE THEY'D GET THEMSELVES INTO?
TAKE THIS! STUNGUN: MAGICAL CHASER!
IN THAT CASE, SHOULD WE INCREASE THE NUMBER OF PEOPLE WE TAKE EXPLOR-ING?
NO... I WOULDN'T TRUST ANYONE WHO ISN'T PERSON-ALLY LOYAL TO ME, ANYWAY.
RIGHT. WHAT HAPPENED TO THE ANTS?
THE DUNGEON KEEPS CHANGING—HAVE THEY LOST THEIR SENSE OF DIRECTION DOWN THERE?
IF I COULD GET THEM BACK, WE'D HAVE A LOT MORE OPTIONS...
GRAWR...!
COME...!
POWER... IF ONLY I HAD SOME KIND OF POWER!
KYA!
KYA!
IRK
IRK
IRK
IRK

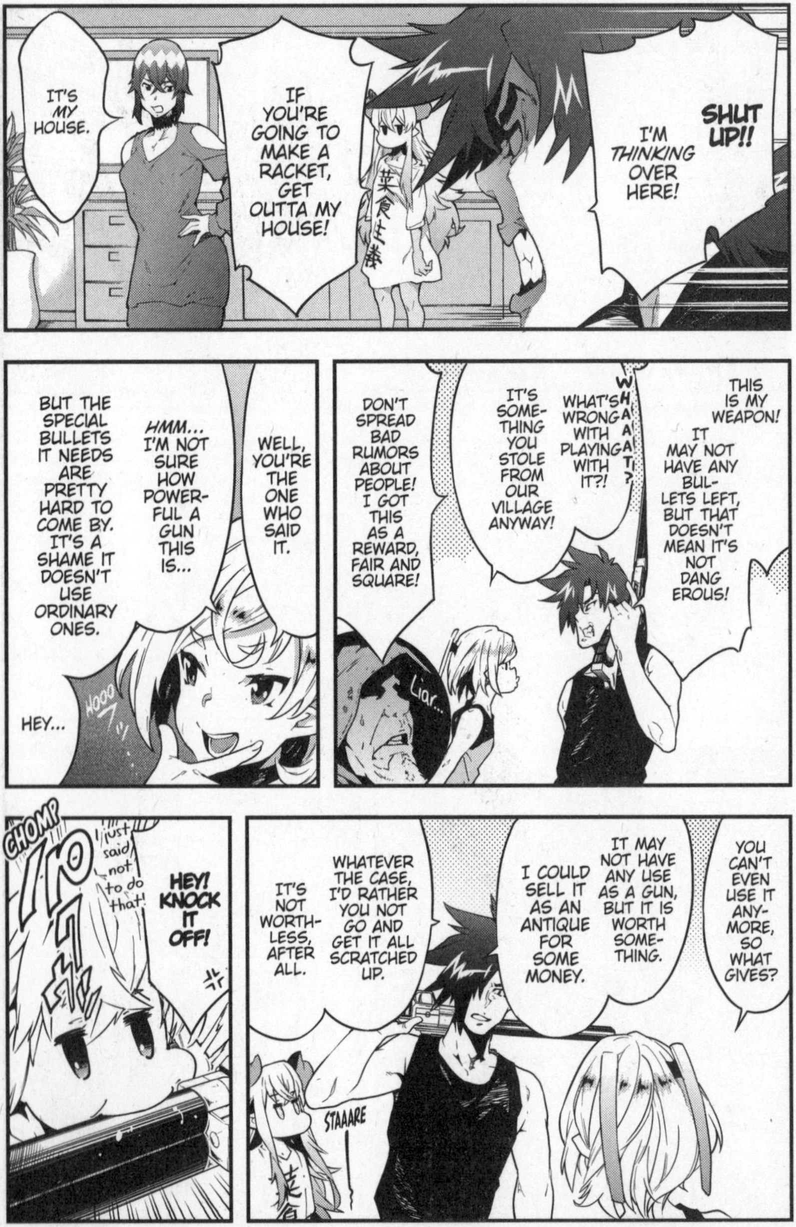
SHUT UP!!
I'M THINKING OVER HERE!
IF YOU'RE GOING TO MAKE A RACKET, GET OUTTA MY HOUSE!
IT'S MY HOUSE.
THIS IS MY WEAPON!
IT MAY NOT HAVE ANY BULLETS LEFT, BUT THAT DOESN'T MEAN IT'S NOT DANGEROUS!
WHAAAT?
WHAT'S WRONG WITH PLAYING WITH IT?!
IT'S SOMETHING YOU STOLE FROM OUR VILLAGE ANYWAY!
DON'T SPREAD BAD RUMORS ABOUT PEOPLE! I GOT THIS AS A REWARD, FAIR AND SQUARE!
Liar...
WELL, YOU'RE THE ONE WHO SAID IT.
HMM... I'M NOT SURE HOW POWERFUL A GUN THIS IS...
BUT THE SPECIAL BULLETS IT NEEDS ARE PRETTY HARD TO COME BY. IT'S A SHAME IT DOESN'T USE ORDINARY ONES.
HOOO
HEY...
YOU CAN'T EVEN USE IT ANYMORE, SO WHAT GIVES?
IT MAY NOT HAVE ANY USE AS A GUN, BUT IT IS WORTH SOMETHING.
I COULD SELL IT AS AN ANTIQUE FOR SOME MONEY.
WHATEVER THE CASE, I'D RATHER YOU NOT GO AND GET IT ALL SCRATCHED UP.
IT'S NOT WORTHLESS, AFTER ALL.
STAAARE
HEY! KNOCK IT OFF!
I just said not to do that!
CHOMP

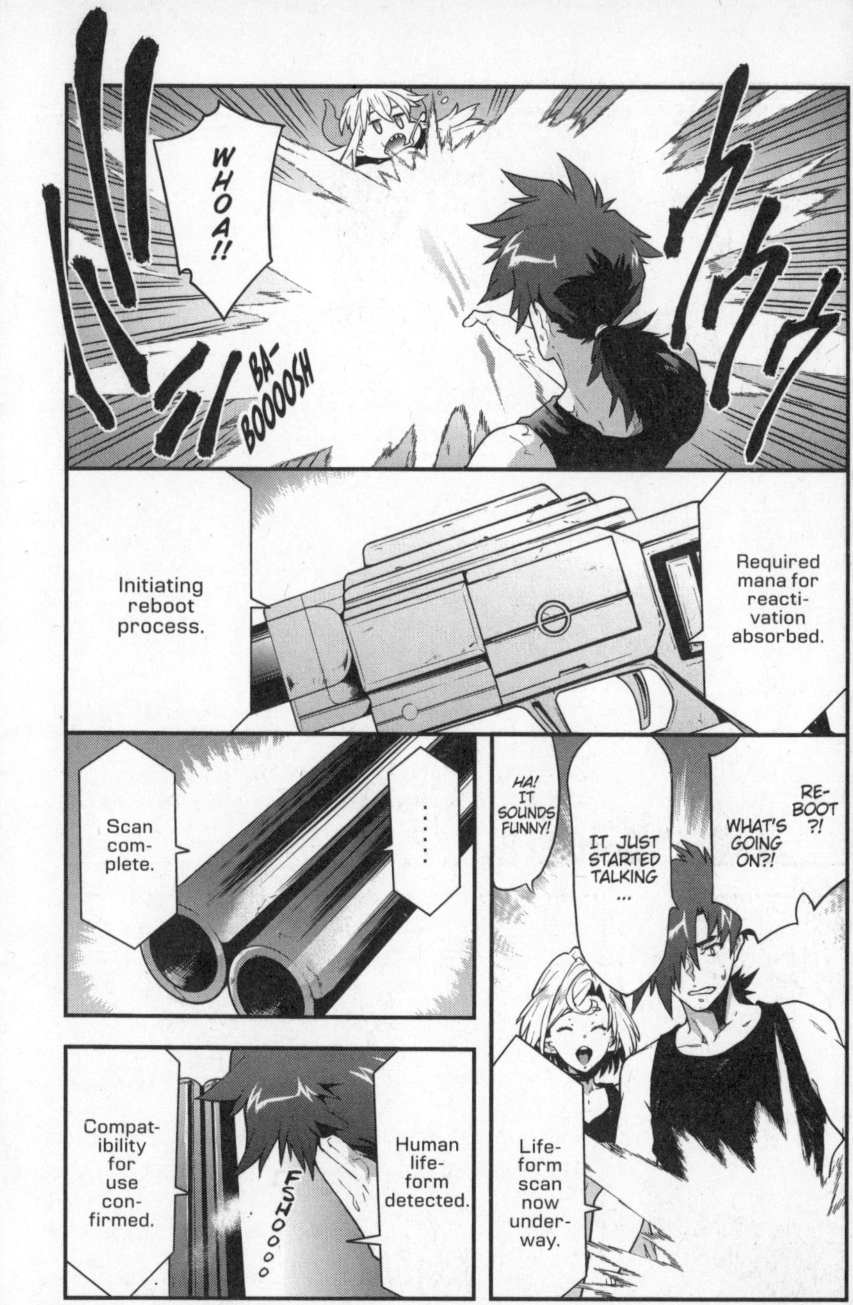
WHOA!!
BA-BOOOOSH
Required mana for reacti-vation absorbed.
Initiating reboot process.
RE-BOOT?!
WHAT'S GOING ON?!
IT JUST STARTED TALKING...
HA! IT SOUNDS FUNNY!
Life-form scan now under-way.
......
Scan com-plete.
Human life-form detected.
FSHOOOOO
Compat-ibility for use con-firmed.

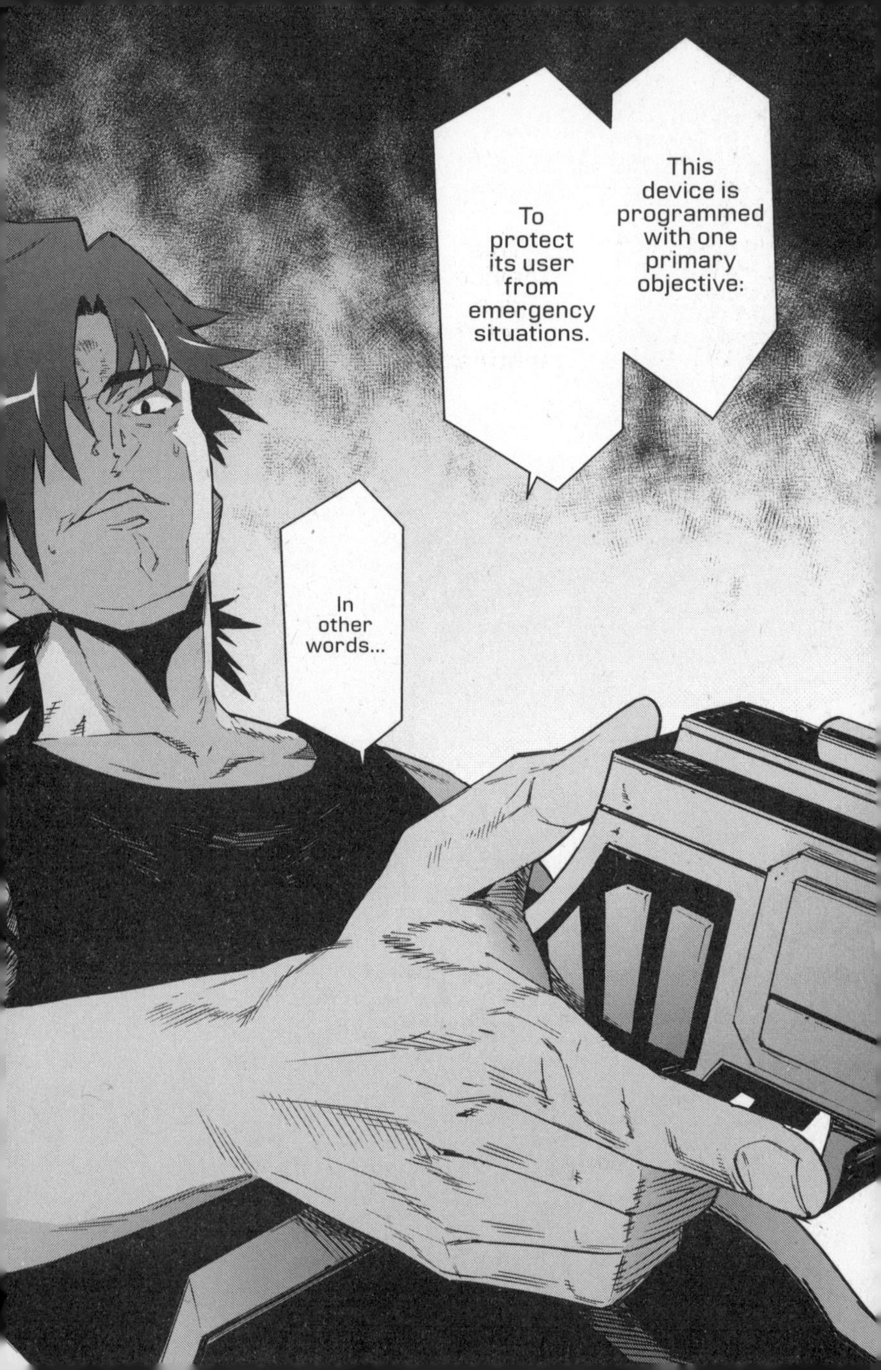
This device is programmed with one primary objective:
To protect its user from emergency situations.
In other words...

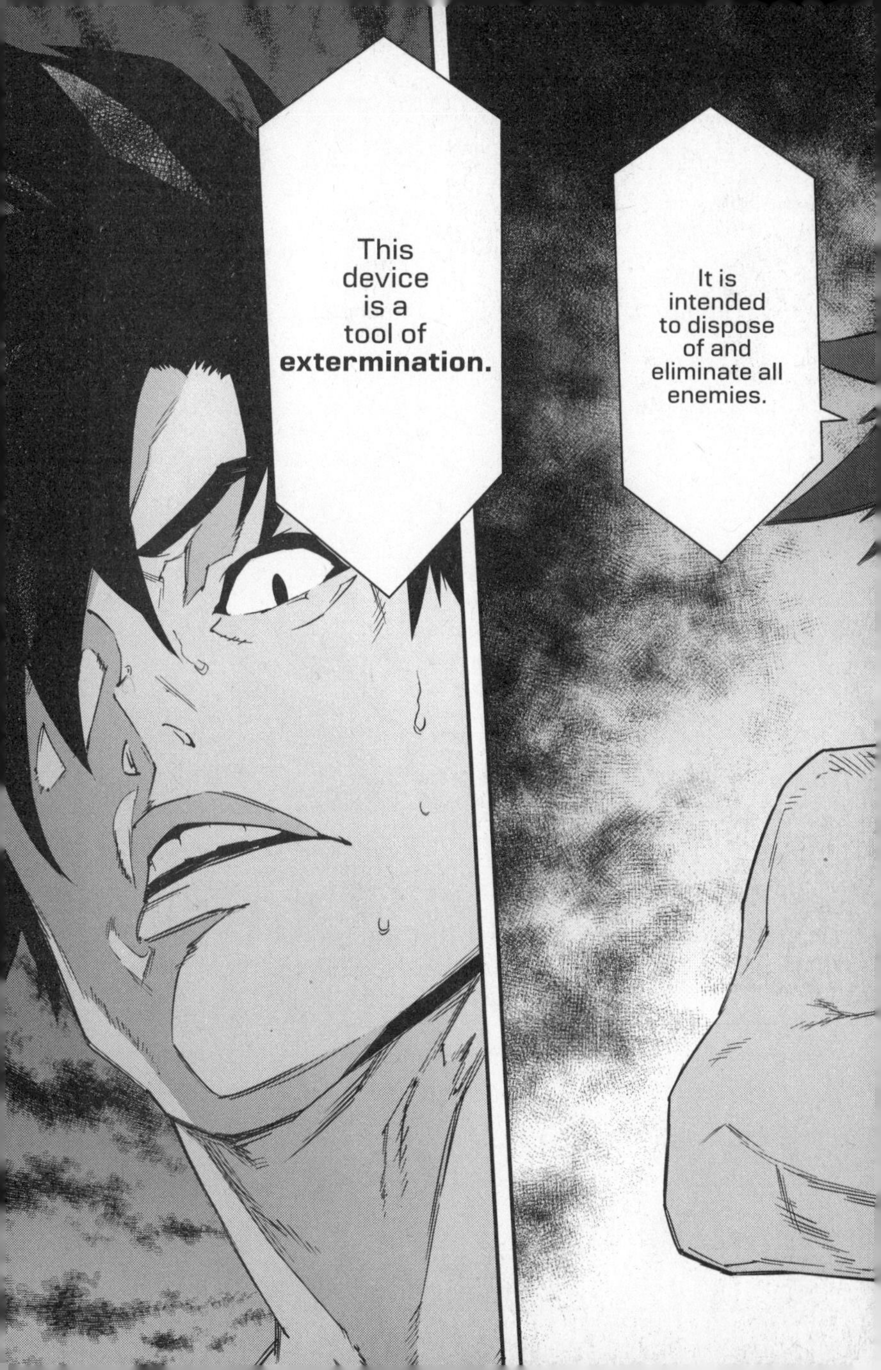
This device is a tool of **extermination.**
It is intended to dispose of and eliminate all enemies.

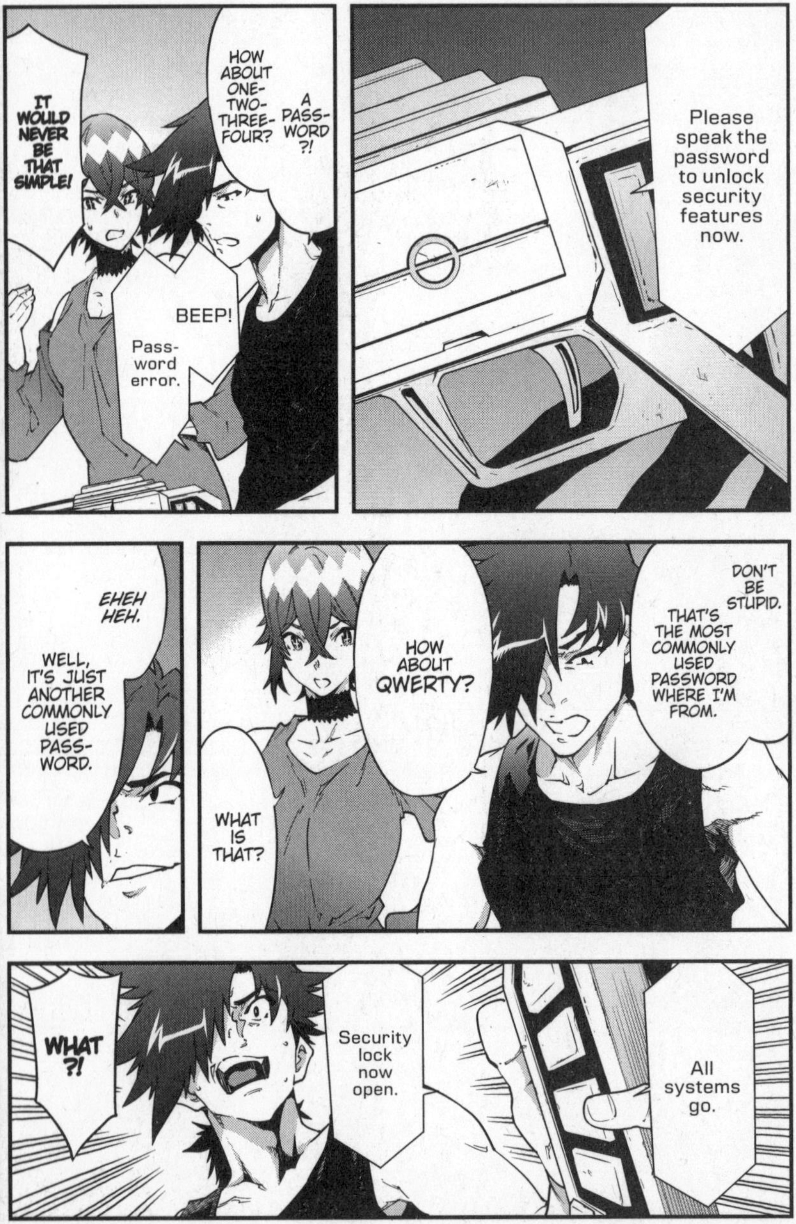
Please speak the password to unlock security features now.
A PASSWORD?!
HOW ABOUT ONE-TWO-THREE-FOUR?
IT WOULD NEVER BE THAT SIMPLE!
BEEP!
Password error.
DON'T BE STUPID.
THAT'S THE MOST COMMONLY USED PASSWORD WHERE I'M FROM.
HOW ABOUT QWERTY?
WHAT IS THAT?
EHEH HEH.
WELL, IT'S JUST ANOTHER COMMONLY USED PASSWORD.
All systems go.
Security lock now open.
WHAT?!

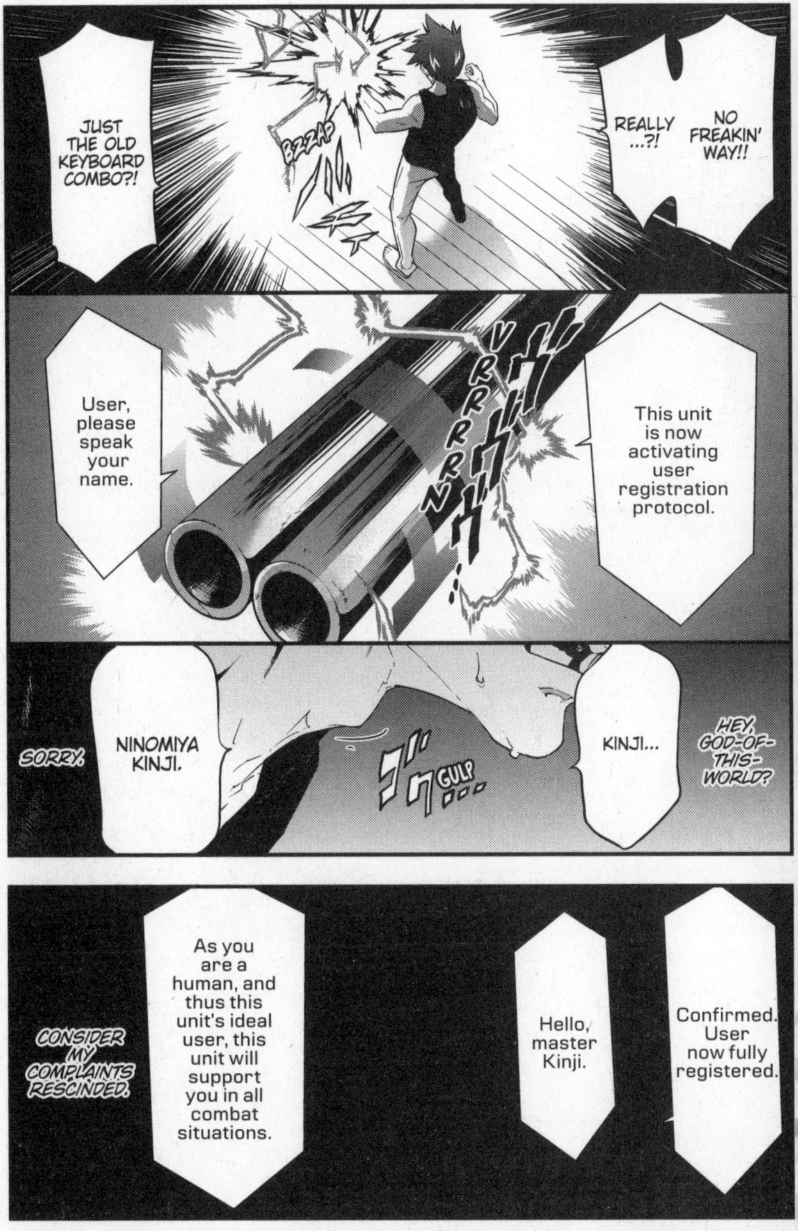
NO FREAKIN' WAY!!
REALLY ...?!
JUST THE OLD KEYBOARD COMBO?!
BZZAP
This unit is now activating user registration protocol.
VRRRRRN
User, please speak your name.
HEY, GOD-OF-THIS-WORLD?
KINJI...
GULP...
NINOMIYA KINJI.
SORRY.
Confirmed. User now fully registered.
Hello, master Kinji.
As you are a human, and thus this unit's ideal user, this unit will support you in all combat situations.
CONSIDER MY COMPLAINTS RESCINDED.

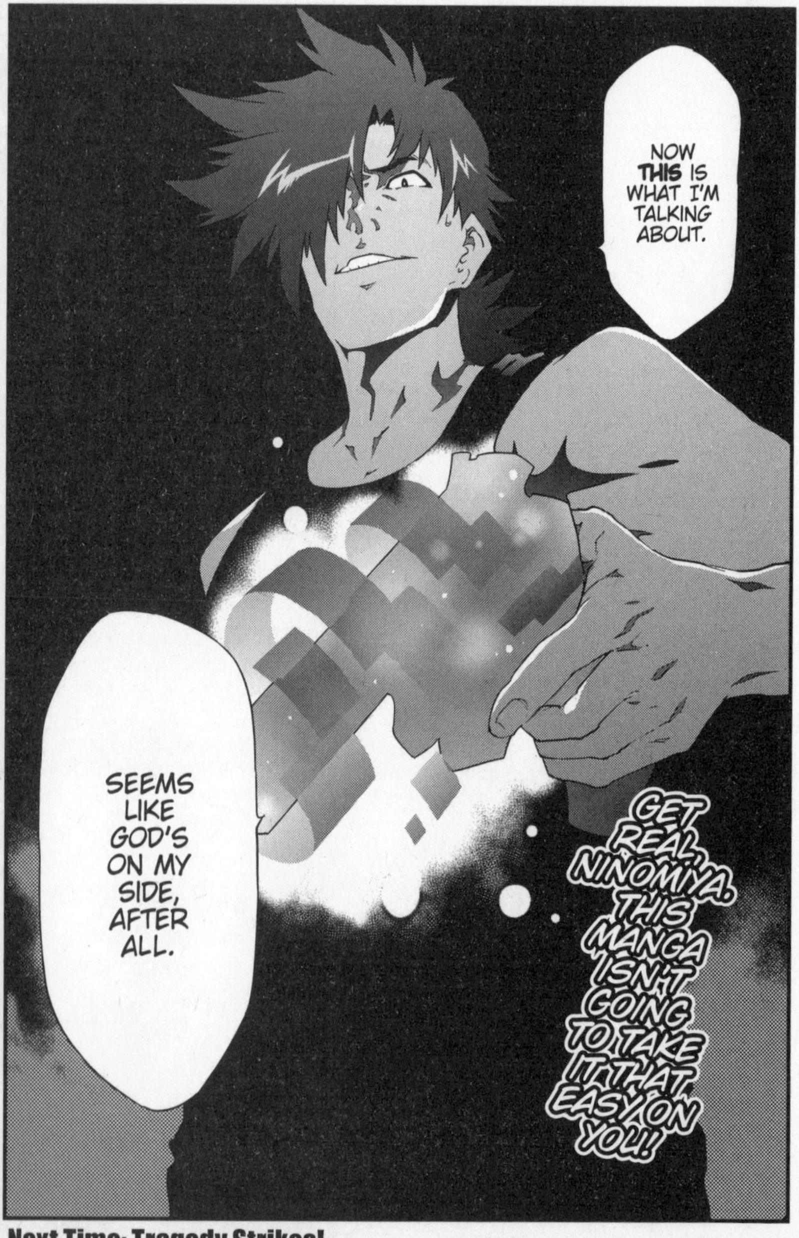
NOW THIS IS WHAT I'M TALKING ABOUT.
SEEMS LIKE GOD'S ON MY SIDE, AFTER ALL.
GET REAL, NINOMIYA. THIS MANGA ISN'T GOING TO TAKE IT THAT EASY ON YOU!!

Next Time: Tragedy Strikes!

菜食主義
vegetarian

Rim,
casual style.

THE DUNGEON OF
BLACK COMPANY

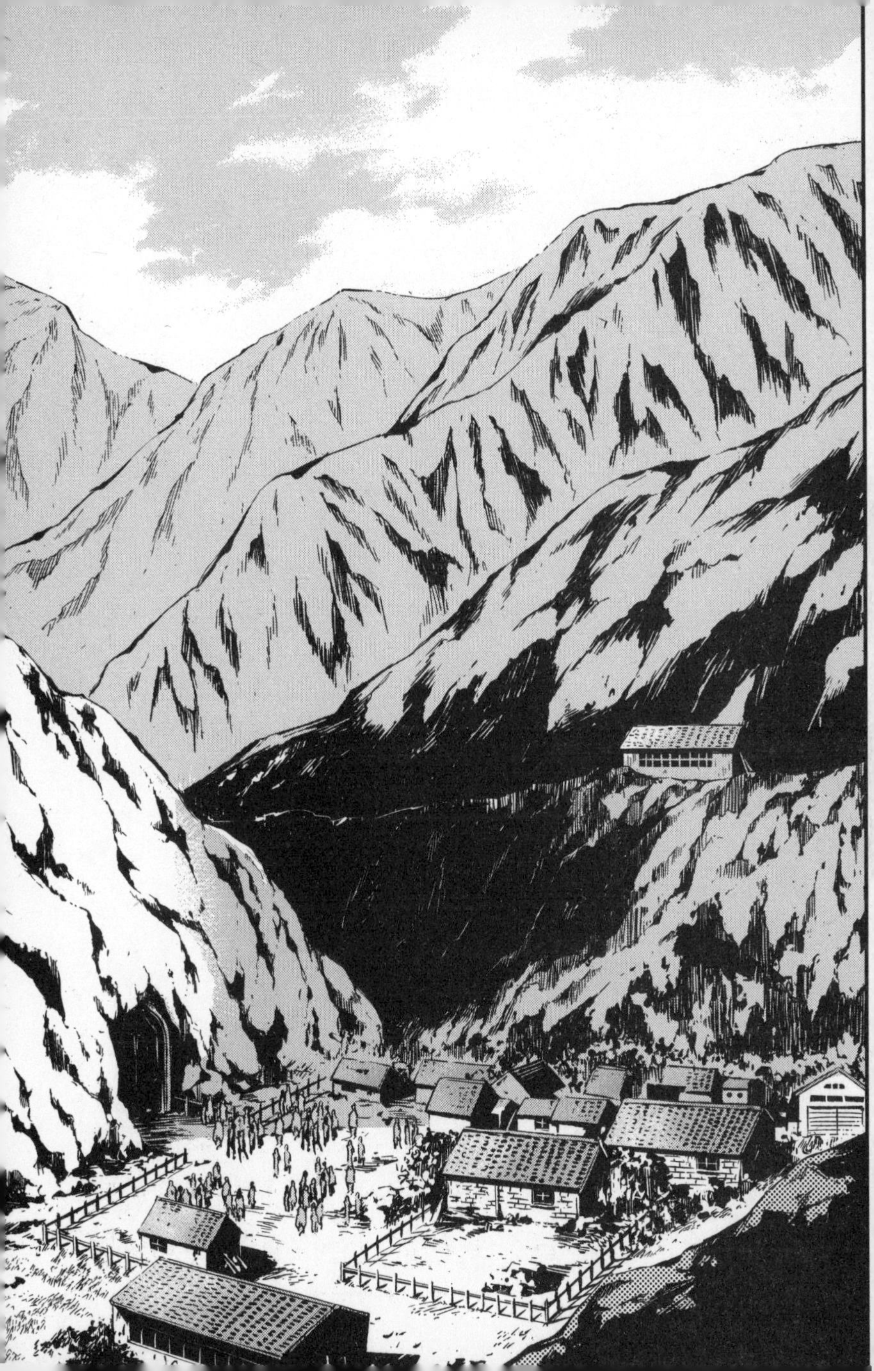

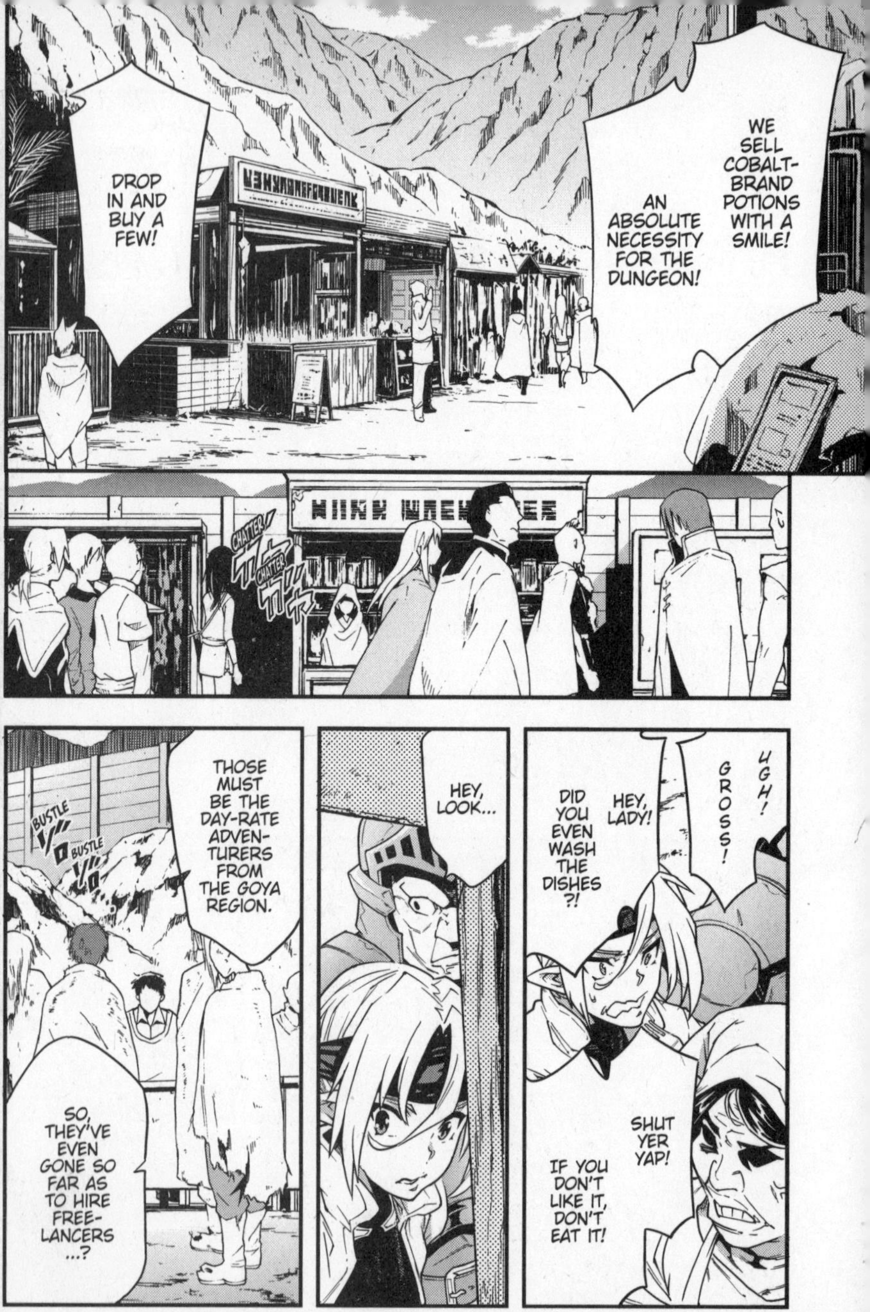
WE SELL COBALT-BRAND POTIONS WITH A SMILE!
AN ABSOLUTE NECESSITY FOR THE DUNGEON!
DROP IN AND BUY A FEW!
CHATTER CHATTER
UGH! GROSS!
HEY, LADY!
DID YOU EVEN WASH THE DISHES?!
SHUT YER YAP!
IF YOU DON'T LIKE IT, DON'T EAT IT!
HEY, LOOK...
THOSE MUST BE THE DAY-RATE ADVEN-TURERS FROM THE GOYA REGION.
BUSTLE BUSTLE
SO, THEY'VE EVEN GONE SO FAR AS TO HIRE FREE-LANCERS...?

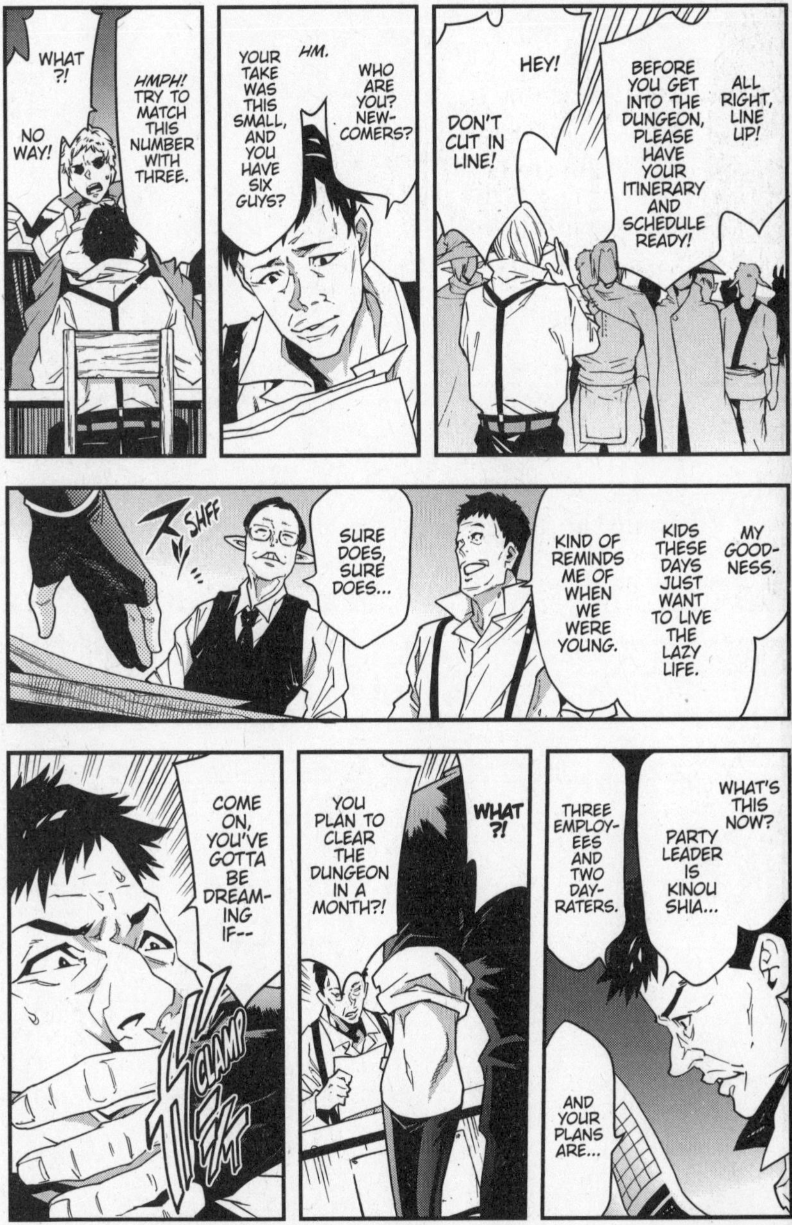
ALL RIGHT, LINE UP!
BEFORE YOU GET INTO THE DUNGEON, PLEASE HAVE YOUR ITINERARY AND SCHEDULE READY!
HEY!
DON'T CUT IN LINE!
WHO ARE YOU? NEW-COMERS?
HM.
YOUR TAKE WAS THIS SMALL, AND YOU HAVE SIX GUYS?
HMPH! TRY TO MATCH THIS NUMBER WITH THREE.
WHAT?!
NO WAY!
MY GOODNESS.
KIDS THESE DAYS JUST WANT TO LIVE THE LAZY LIFE.
KIND OF REMINDS ME OF WHEN WE WERE YOUNG.
SURE DOES, SURE DOES...
SHFF
WHAT'S THIS NOW?
PARTY LEADER IS KINOU SHIA...
THREE EMPLOY-EES AND TWO DAY-RATERS.
AND YOUR PLANS ARE...
WHAT?!
YOU PLAN TO CLEAR THE DUNGEON IN A MONTH?!
COME ON, YOU'VE GOTTA BE DREAMING IF--
CLAMP

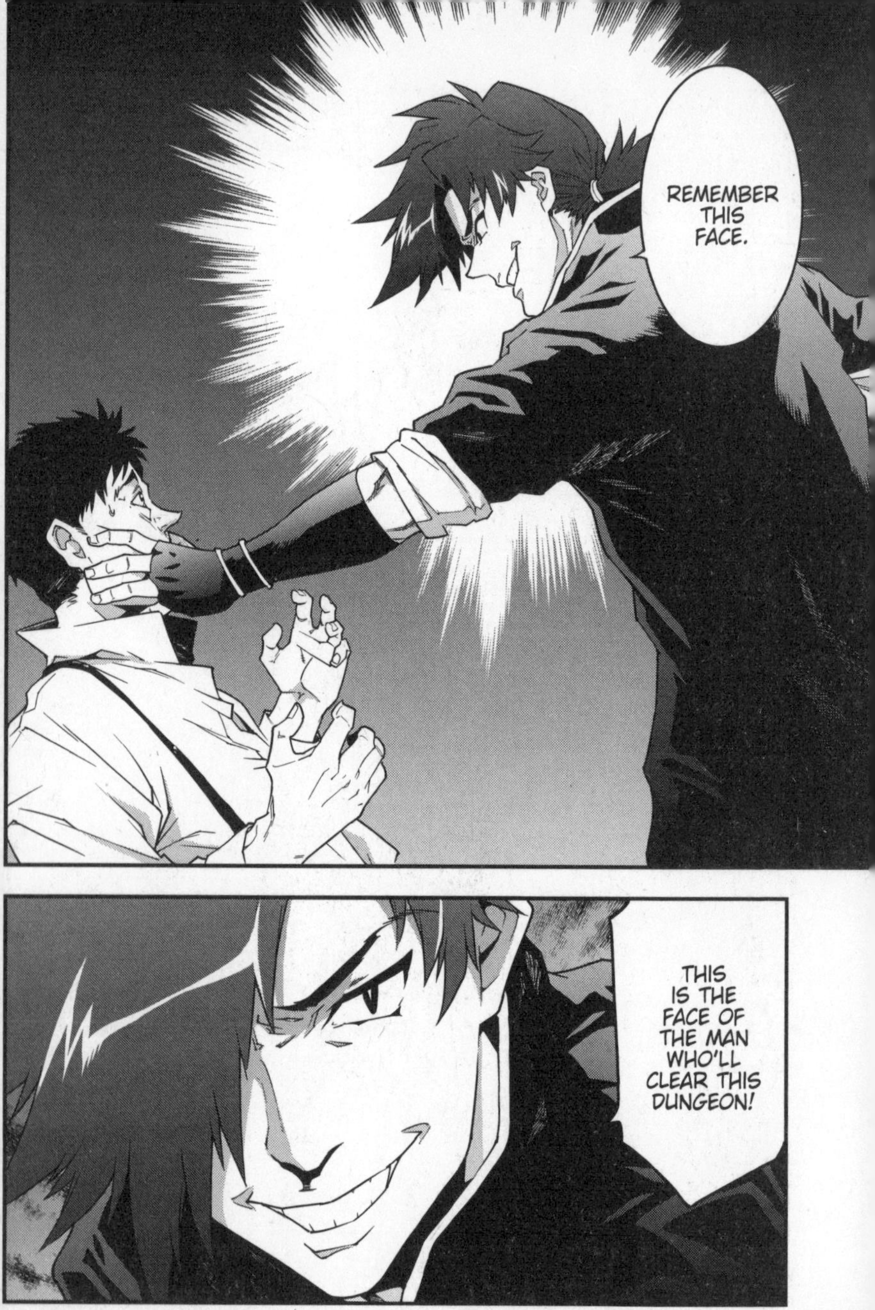
REMEMBER THIS FACE.
THIS IS THE FACE OF THE MAN WHO'LL CLEAR THIS DUNGEON!

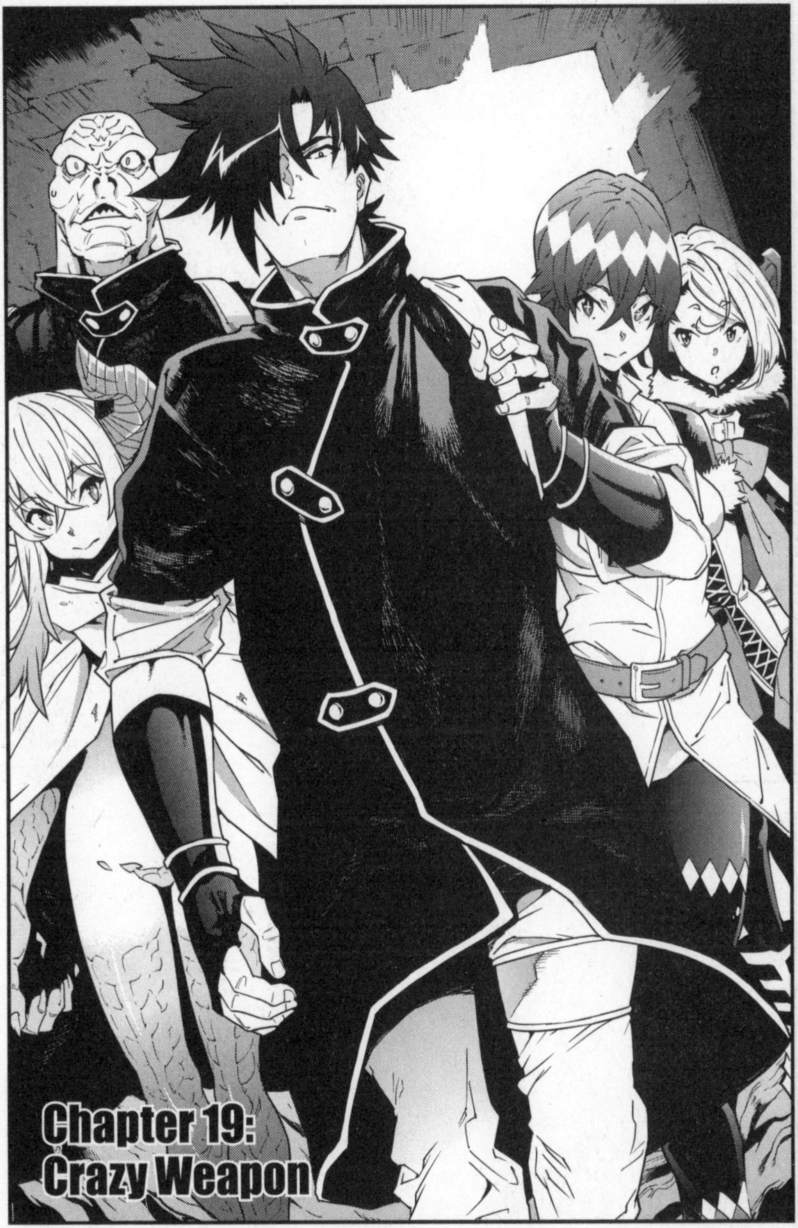
Chapter 19:
Crazy Weapon

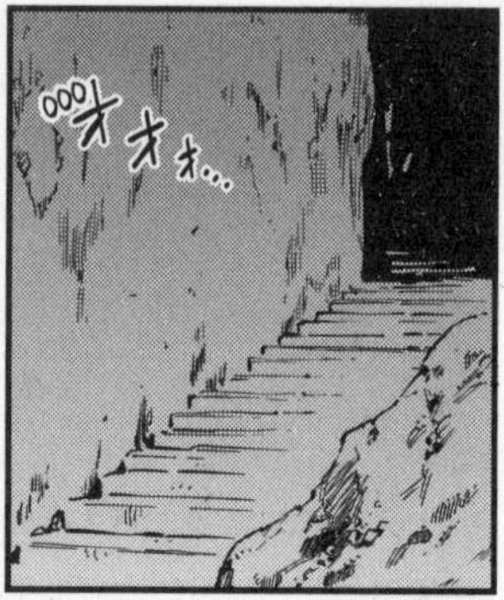
OOO オォォ...

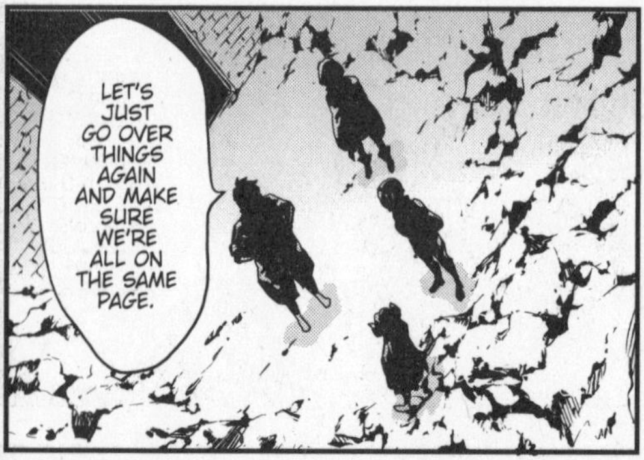
LET'S JUST GO OVER THINGS AGAIN AND MAKE SURE WE'RE ALL ON THE SAME PAGE.

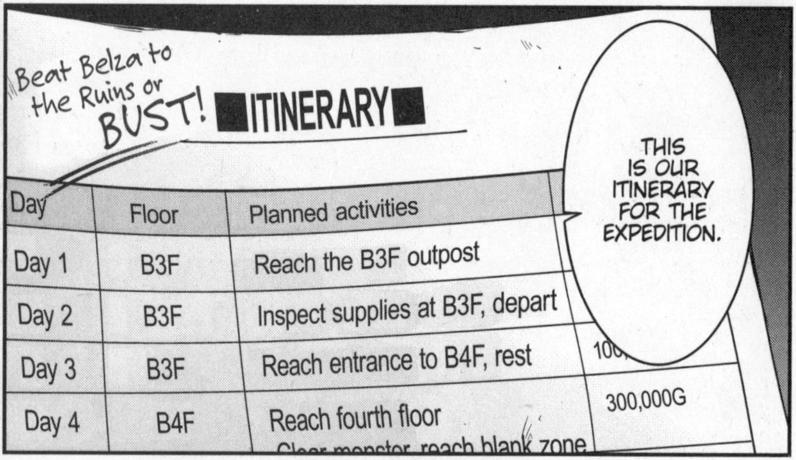
THIS IS OUR ITINERARY FOR THE EXPEDITION.
Beat Belza to the Ruins or BUST!
ITINERARY
Day
Floor
Planned activities
Day 1
B3F
Reach the B3F outpost
Day 2
B3F
Inspect supplies at B3F, depart
Day 3
B3F
Reach entrance to B4F, rest
Day 4
B4F
Reach fourth floor
300,000G

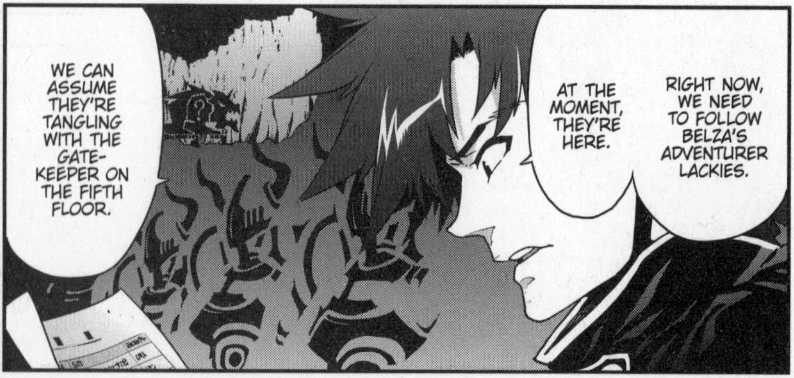
RIGHT NOW, WE NEED TO FOLLOW BELZA'S ADVENTURER LACKIES.
AT THE MOMENT, THEY'RE HERE.
WE CAN ASSUME THEY'RE TANGLING WITH THE GATE-KEEPER ON THE FIFTH FLOOR.

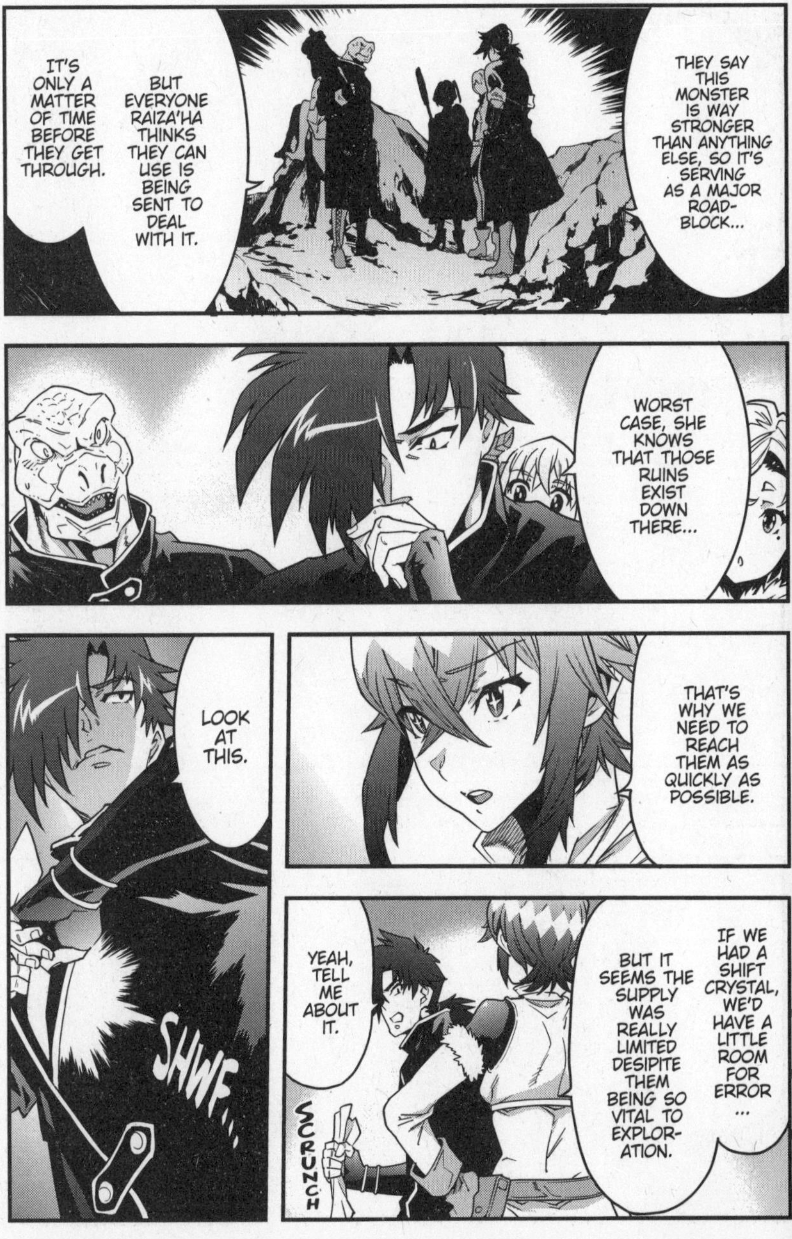
THEY SAY THIS MONSTER IS WAY STRONGER THAN ANYTHING ELSE, SO IT'S SERVING AS A MAJOR ROAD-BLOCK...
BUT EVERYONE RAIZA'HA THINKS THEY CAN USE IS BEING SENT TO DEAL WITH IT.
IT'S ONLY A MATTER OF TIME BEFORE THEY GET THROUGH.
WORST CASE, SHE KNOWS THAT THOSE RUINS EXIST DOWN THERE...
THAT'S WHY WE NEED TO REACH THEM AS QUICKLY AS POSSIBLE.
IF WE HAD A SHIFT CRYSTAL, WE'D HAVE A LITTLE ROOM FOR ERROR...
BUT IT SEEMS THE SUPPLY WAS REALLY LIMITED DESIPITE THEM BEING SO VITAL TO EXPLOR-ATION.
YEAH, TELL ME ABOUT IT.
SCRUNCH
LOOK AT THIS.
SHWF...

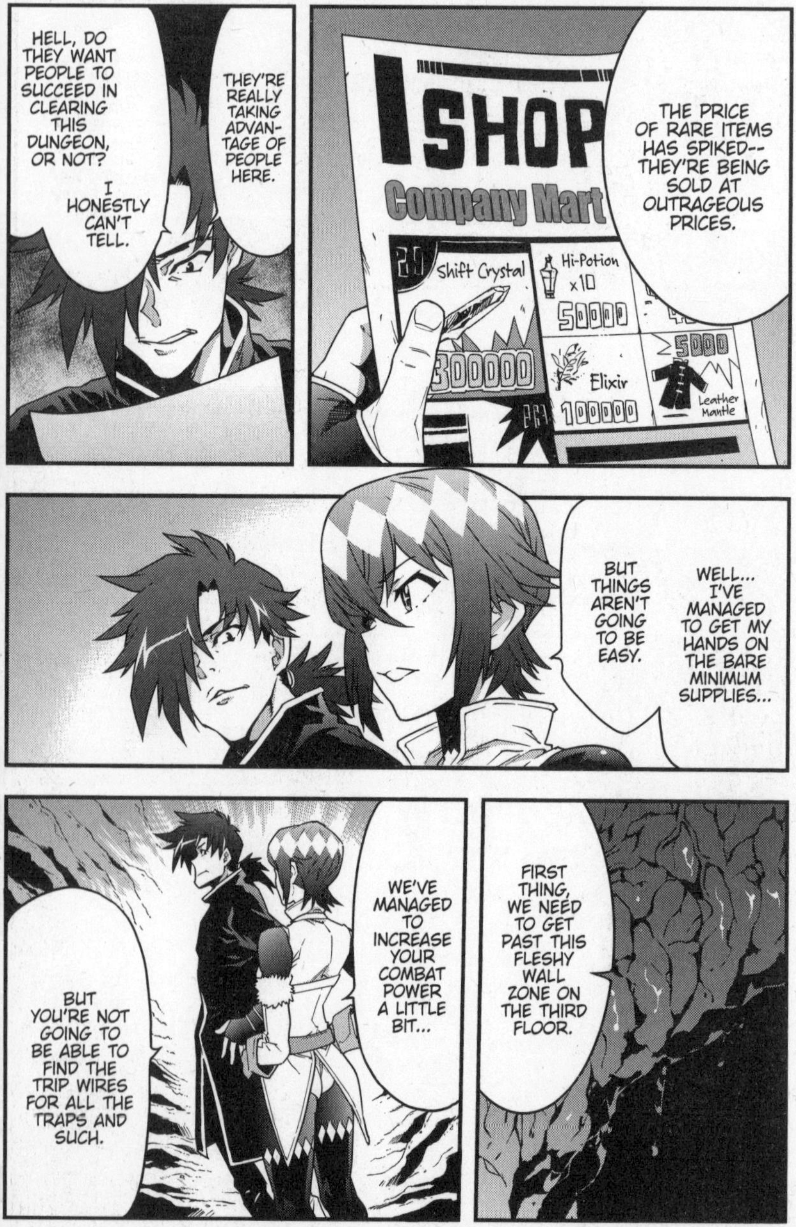
THE PRICE OF RARE ITEMS HAS SPIKED-- THEY'RE BEING SOLD AT OUTRAGEOUS PRICES.
SHOP
Company Mart
Shift Crystal
Hi-Potion
x10
Elixir
100000
Leather Mantle
THEY'RE REALLY TAKING ADVANTAGE OF PEOPLE HERE.
HELL, DO THEY WANT PEOPLE TO SUCCEED IN CLEARING THIS DUNGEON, OR NOT?
I HONESTLY CAN'T TELL.
WELL... I'VE MANAGED TO GET MY HANDS ON THE BARE MINIMUM SUPPLIES...
BUT THINGS AREN'T GOING TO BE EASY.
FIRST THING, WE NEED TO GET PAST THIS FLESHY WALL ZONE ON THE THIRD FLOOR.
WE'VE MANAGED TO INCREASE YOUR COMBAT POWER A LITTLE BIT...
BUT YOU'RE NOT GOING TO BE ABLE TO FIND THE TRIP WIRES FOR ALL THE TRAPS AND SUCH.

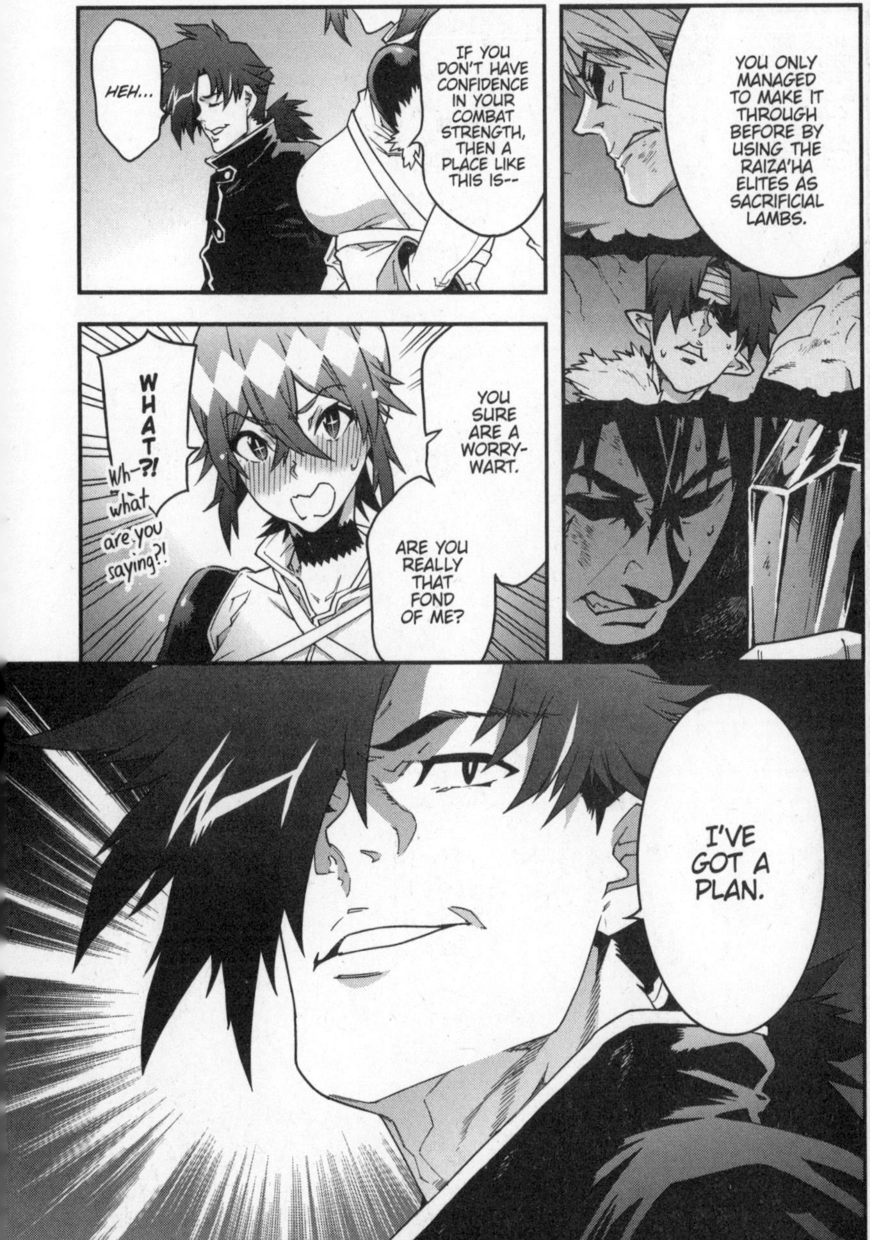
YOU ONLY MANAGED TO MAKE IT THROUGH BEFORE BY USING THE RAIZA'HA ELITES AS SACRIFICIAL LAMBS.
IF YOU DON'T HAVE CONFIDENCE IN YOUR COMBAT STRENGTH, THEN A PLACE LIKE THIS IS--
HEH...
YOU SURE ARE A WORRY-WART.
ARE YOU REALLY THAT FOND OF ME?
WHAT
Wh-?! what are you saying?!
I'VE GOT A PLAN.

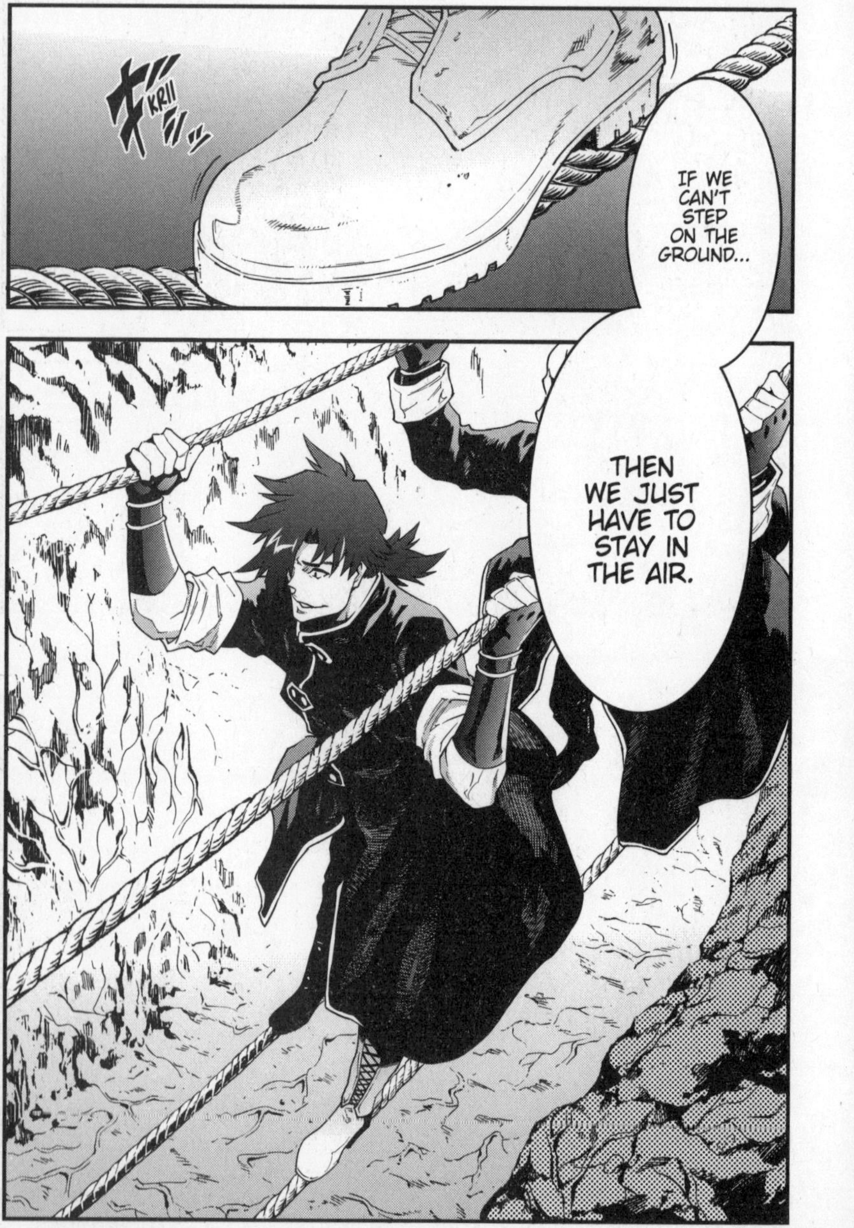
IF WE CAN'T STEP ON THE GROUND...
KRII
THEN WE JUST HAVE TO STAY IN THE AIR.

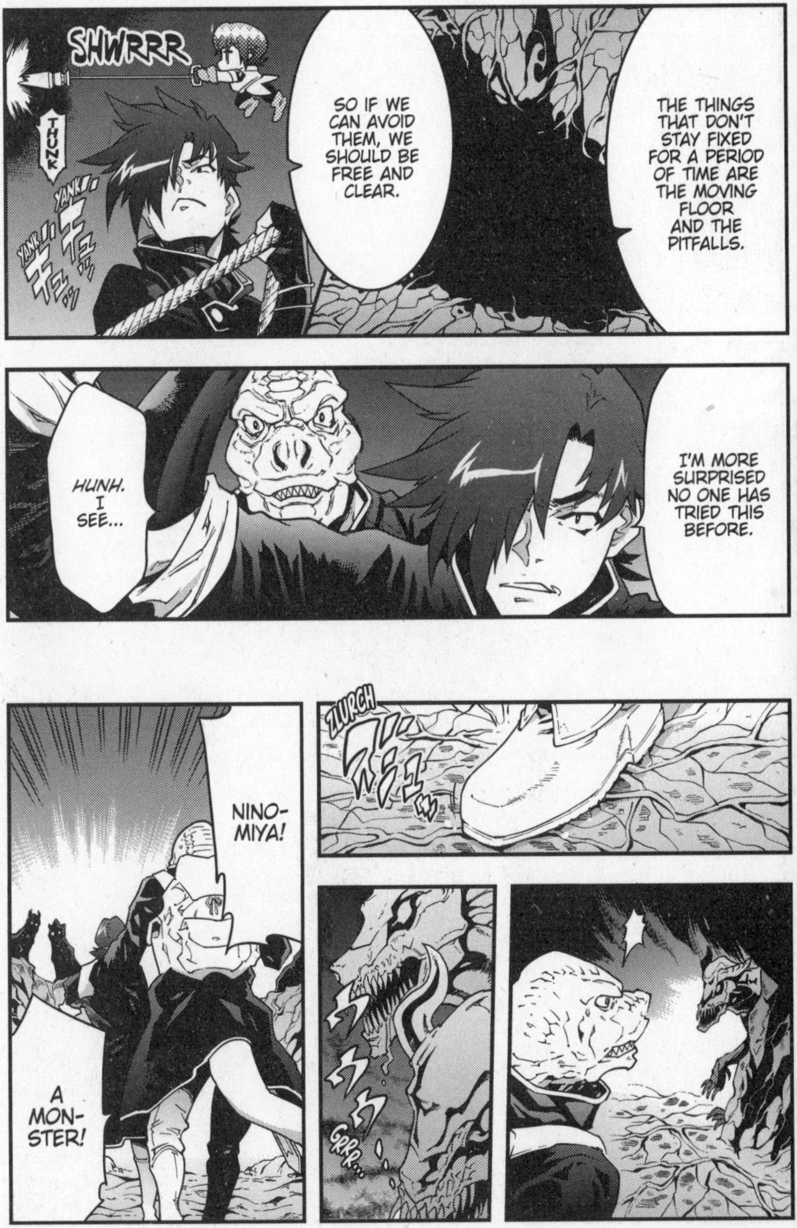
THE THINGS THAT DON'T STAY FIXED FOR A PERIOD OF TIME ARE THE MOVING FLOOR AND THE PITFALLS.
SO IF WE CAN AVOID THEM, WE SHOULD BE FREE AND CLEAR.
SHWRRR
THUNK
YANK
YANK
I'M MORE SURPRISED NO ONE HAS TRIED THIS BEFORE.
HUNH. I SEE...
ZLURCH
GRRR...
NINO-MIYA!
A MON-STER!

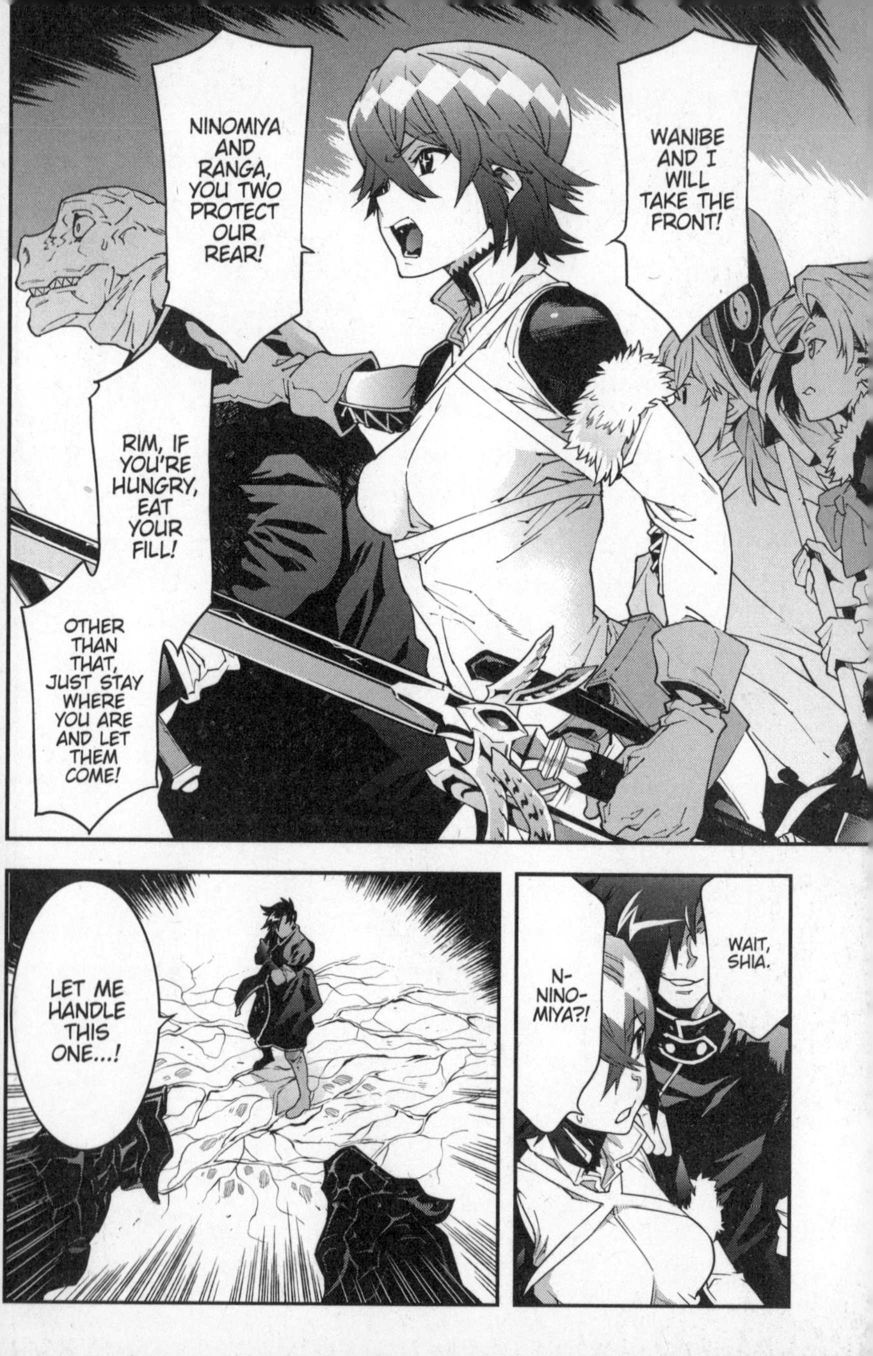
WANIBE AND I WILL TAKE THE FRONT!
NINOMIYA AND RANGA, YOU TWO PROTECT OUR REAR!
RIM, IF YOU'RE HUNGRY, EAT YOUR FILL!
OTHER THAN THAT, JUST STAY WHERE YOU ARE AND LET THEM COME!
WAIT, SHIA.
N-NINO-MIYA?!
LET ME HANDLE THIS ONE...!

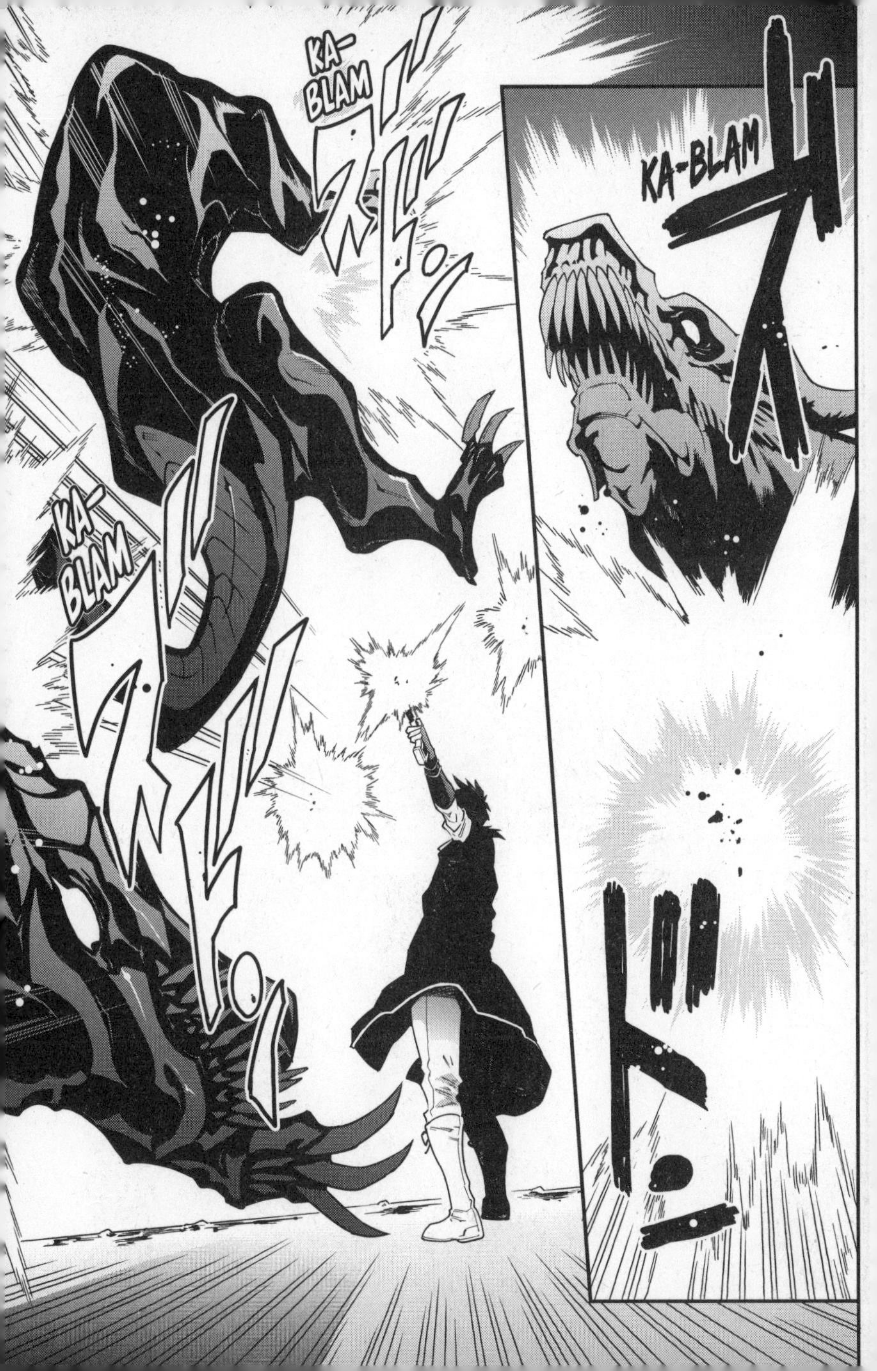
KA-BLAM
KA-
BLAM
KA-
BLAM

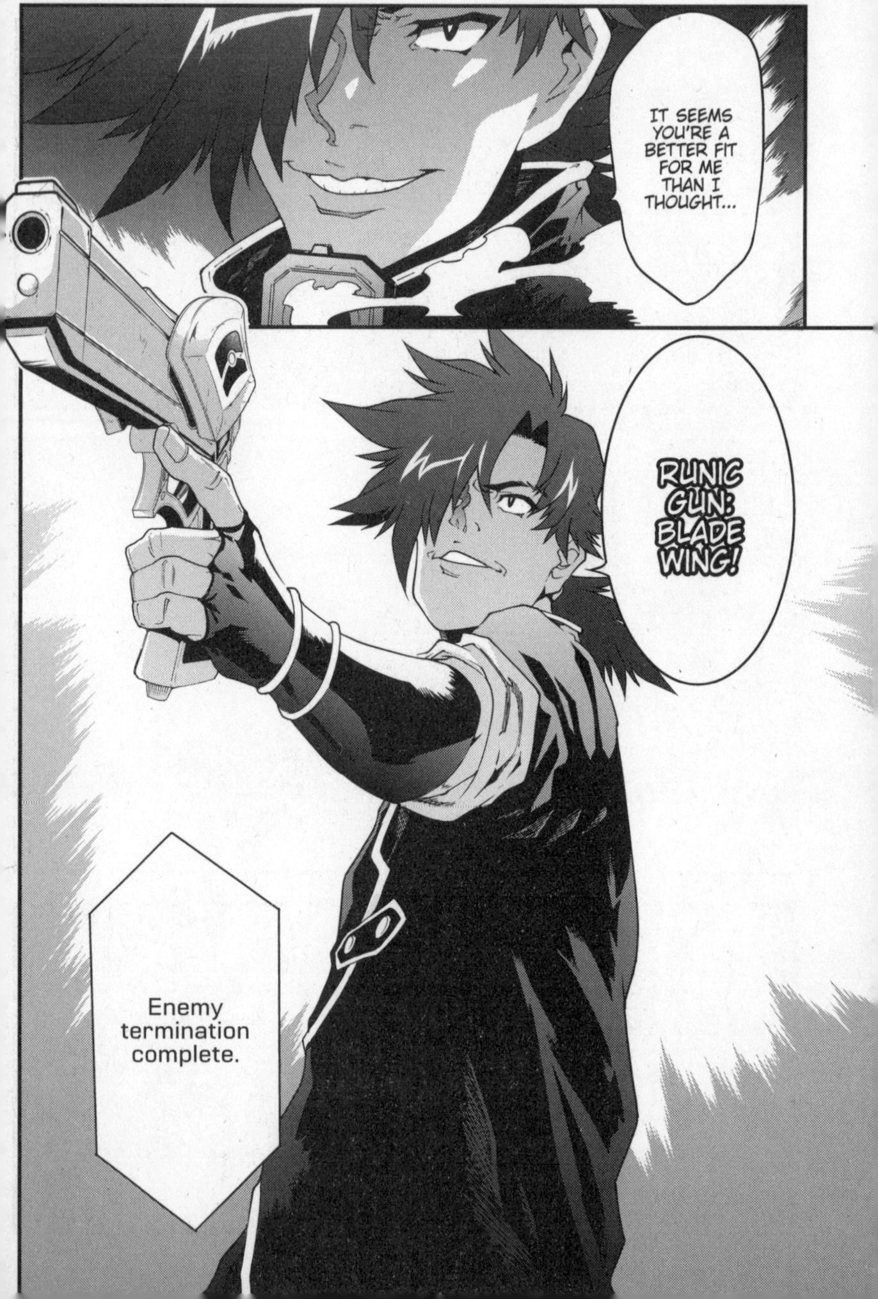
IT SEEMS YOU'RE A BETTER FIT FOR ME THAN I THOUGHT...
RUNIC GUN: BLADE WING!
Enemy termination complete.

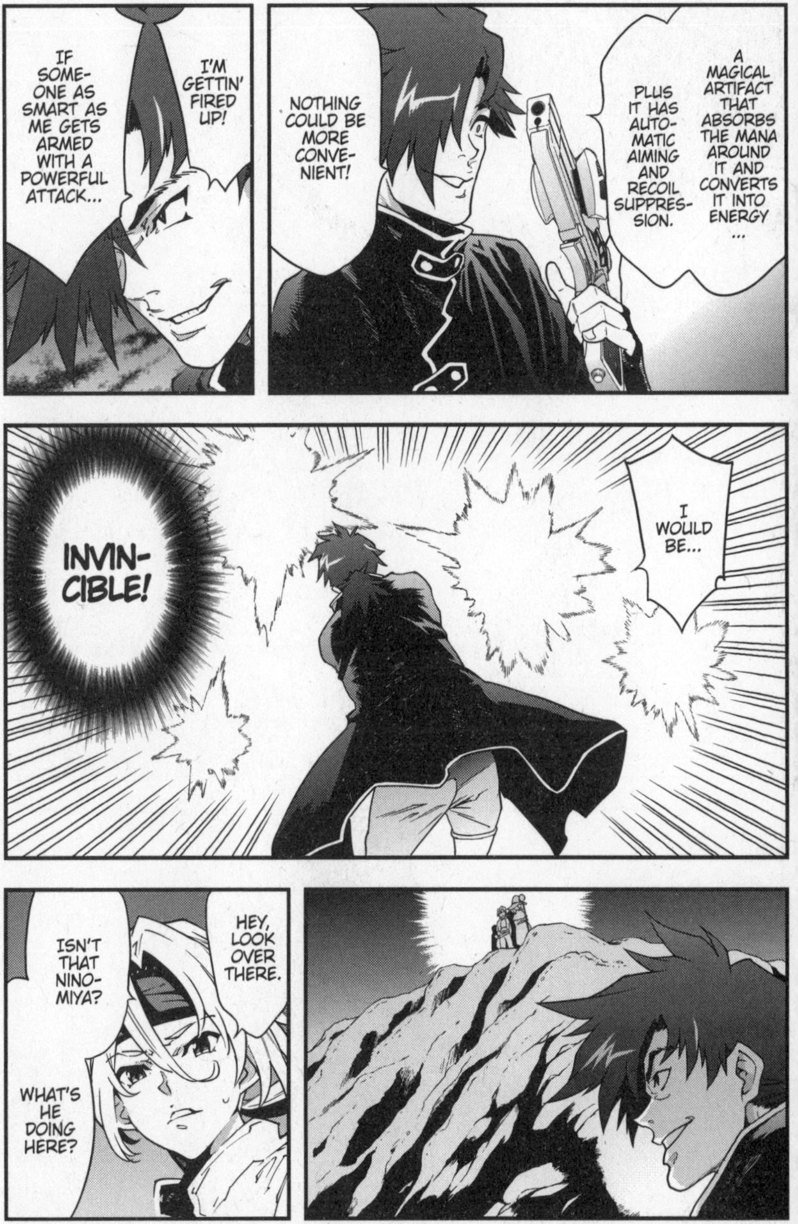
A MAGICAL ARTIFACT THAT ABSORBS THE MANA AROUND IT AND CONVERTS IT INTO ENERGY ...
PLUS IT HAS AUTOMATIC AIMING AND RECOIL SUPPRESSION.
NOTHING COULD BE MORE CONVENIENT!
I'M GETTIN' FIRED UP!
IF SOMEONE AS SMART AS ME GETS ARMED WITH A POWERFUL ATTACK...
I WOULD BE...
INVINCIBLE!
HEY, LOOK OVER THERE.
ISN'T THAT NINOMIYA?
WHAT'S HE DOING HERE?

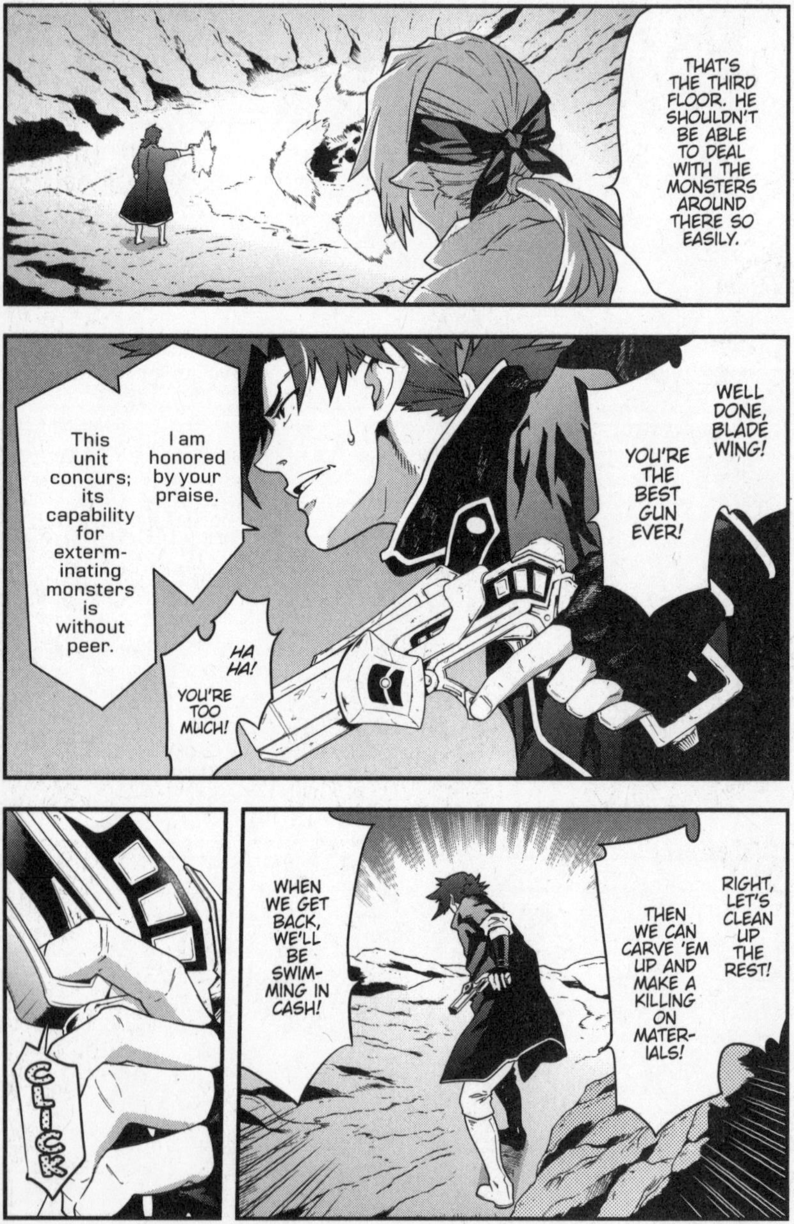
THAT'S THE THIRD FLOOR. HE SHOULDN'T BE ABLE TO DEAL WITH THE MONSTERS AROUND THERE SO EASILY.
WELL DONE, BLADE WING!
YOU'RE THE BEST GUN EVER!
I am honored by your praise.
This unit concurs; its capability for extermi-nating monsters is without peer.
HA HA!
YOU'RE TOO MUCH!
RIGHT, LET'S CLEAN UP THE REST!
THEN WE CAN CARVE 'EM UP AND MAKE A KILLING ON MATER-IALS!
WHEN WE GET BACK, WE'LL BE SWIM-MING IN CASH!
CLICK

SILENCE

NO WAY!

WHAT'S WRONG, NINO-MIYA?

DID YOU BREAK IT?

COME ON, WORK!

HUH ?!

CLICK

CLICK

CLICK

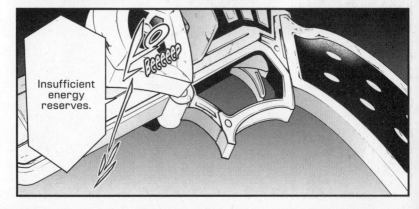

Beeeeep

Insufficient energy reserves.

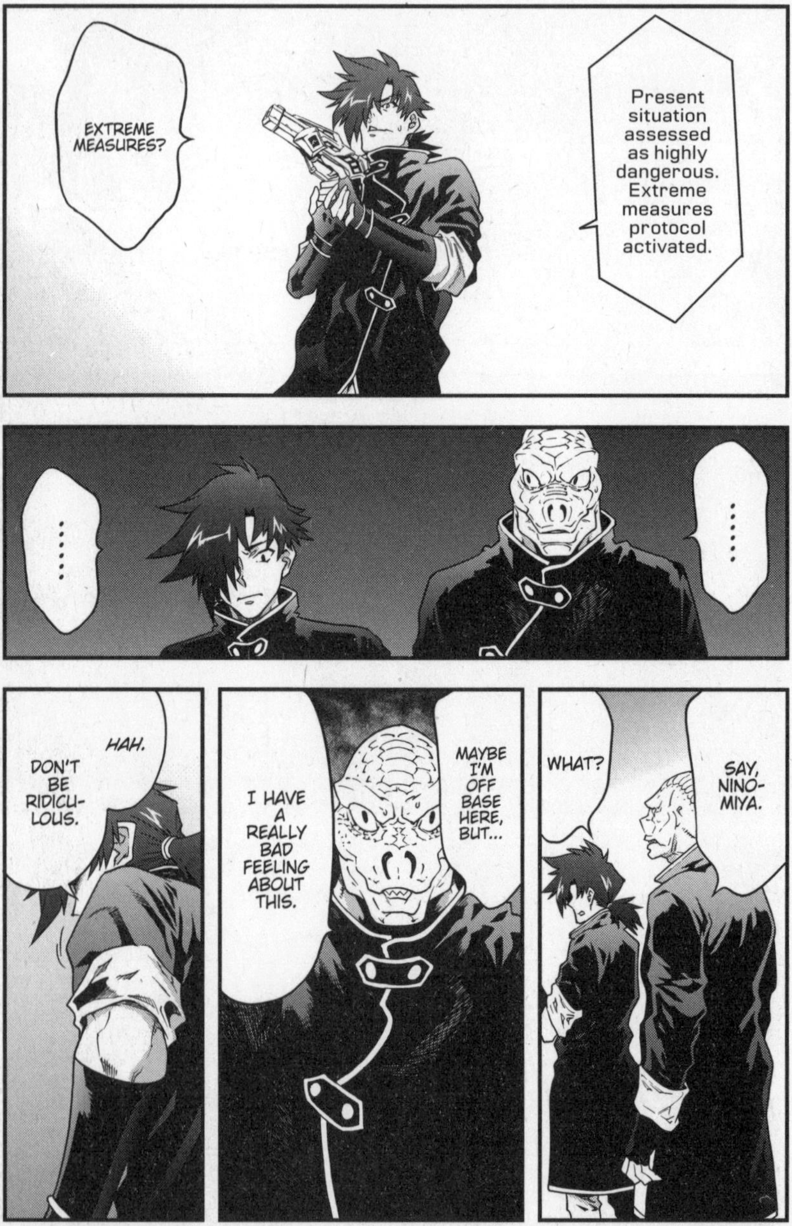
Present situation assessed as highly dangerous. Extreme measures protocol activated.
EXTREME MEASURES?
......
......
SAY, NINO-MIYA.
WHAT?
MAYBE I'M OFF BASE HERE, BUT...
I HAVE A REALLY BAD FEELING ABOUT THIS.
HAH.
DON'T BE RIDICU-LOUS.

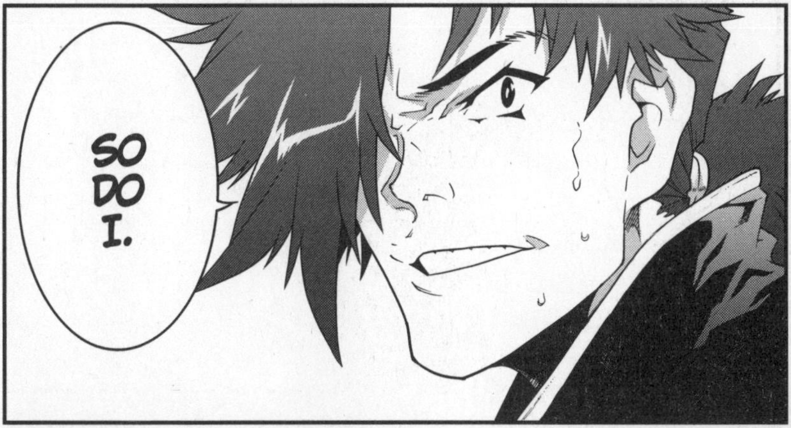
SO DO I.
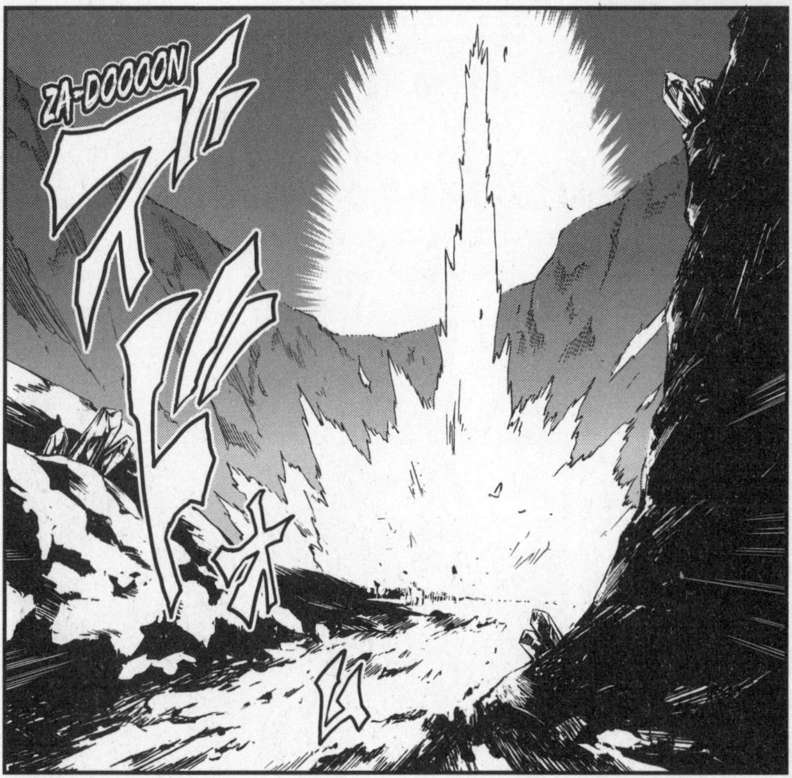
ZA-DOOOON

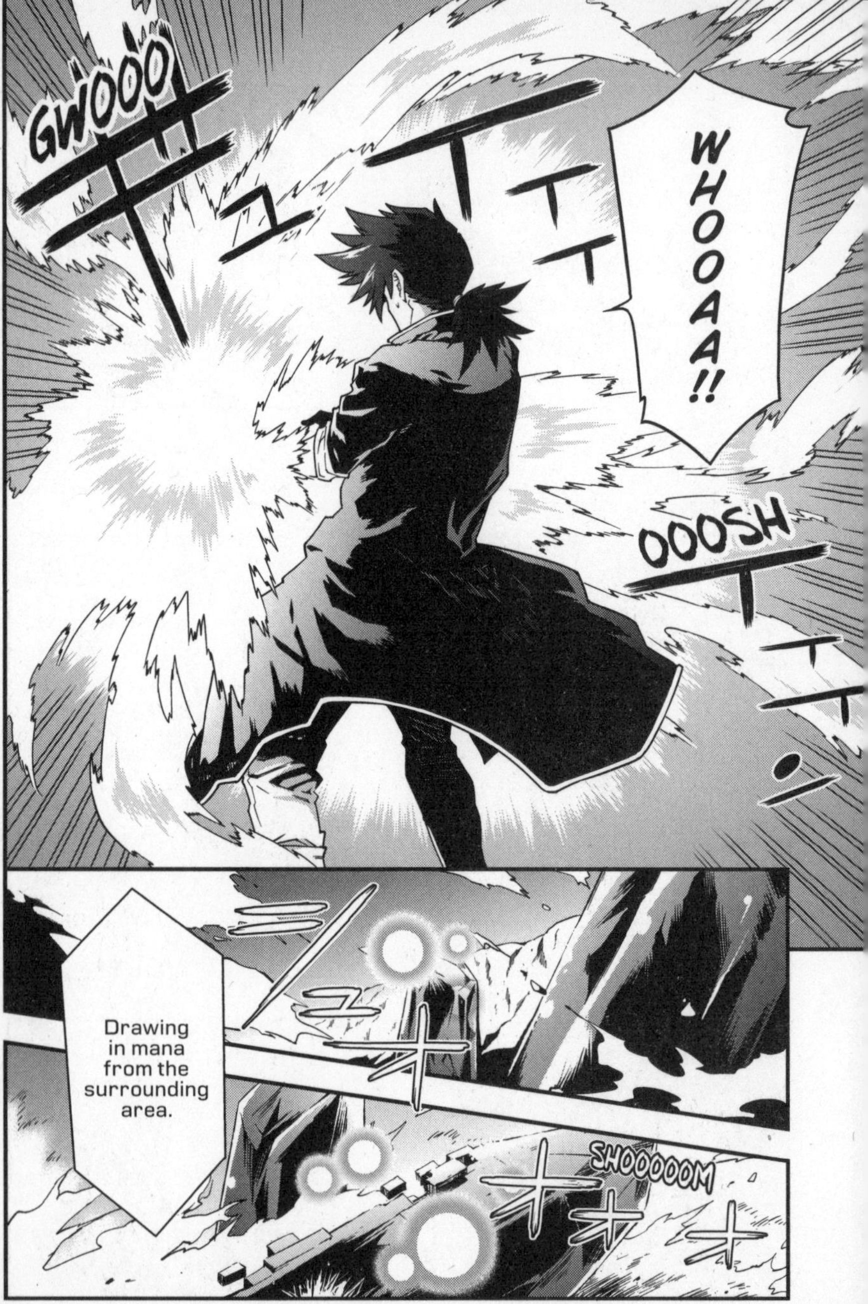
WHOOOAA!!
GWOOO
OOOSH
Drawing in mana from the surrounding area.
SHOOOOOM

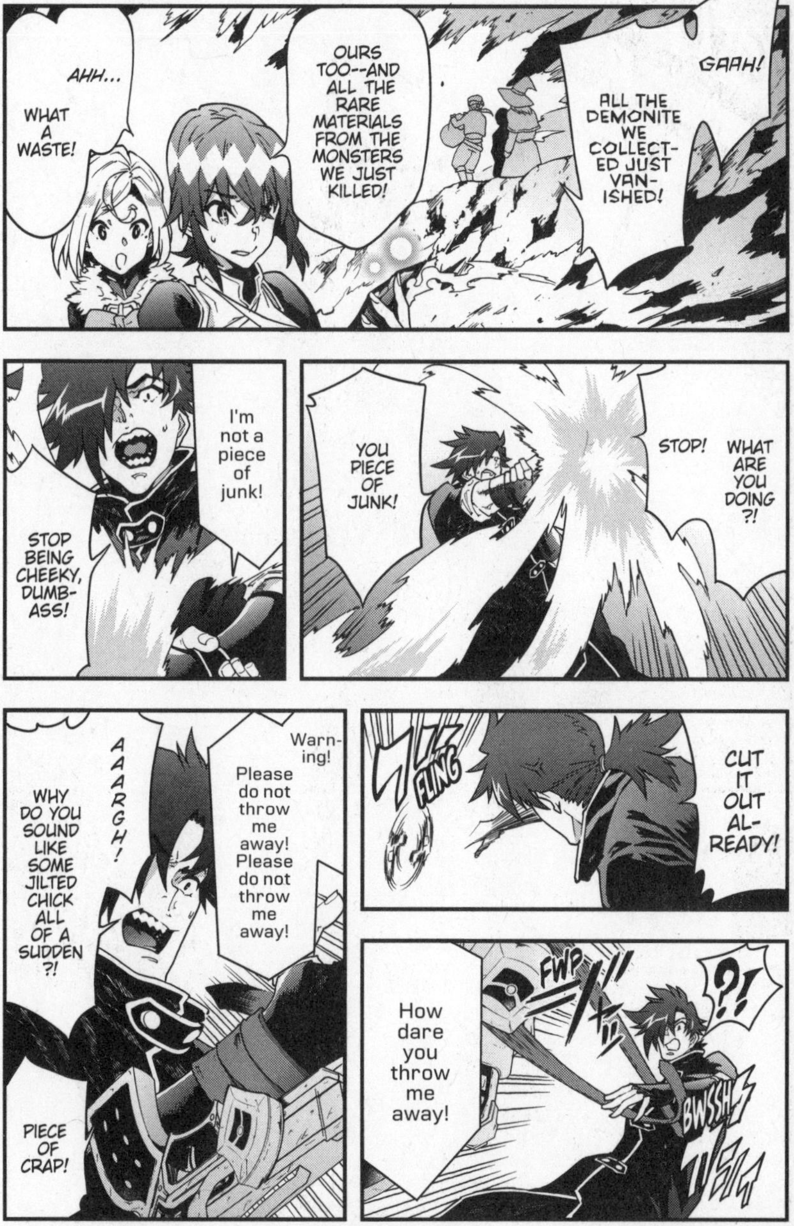
GAAH!
ALL THE DEMONITE WE COLLECTED JUST VANISHED!
OURS TOO--AND ALL THE RARE MATERIALS FROM THE MONSTERS WE JUST KILLED!
AHH... WHAT A WASTE!
WHAT ARE YOU DOING?!
STOP!
YOU PIECE OF JUNK!
I'm not a piece of junk!
STOP BEING CHEEKY, DUMBASS!
CUT IT OUT ALREADY!
FLING
?!
FWP
BWSSH
How dare you throw me away!
Warning! Please do not throw me away! Please do not throw me away!
AAARGH!
WHY DO YOU SOUND LIKE SOME JILTED CHICK ALL OF A SUDDEN?!
PIECE OF CRAP!

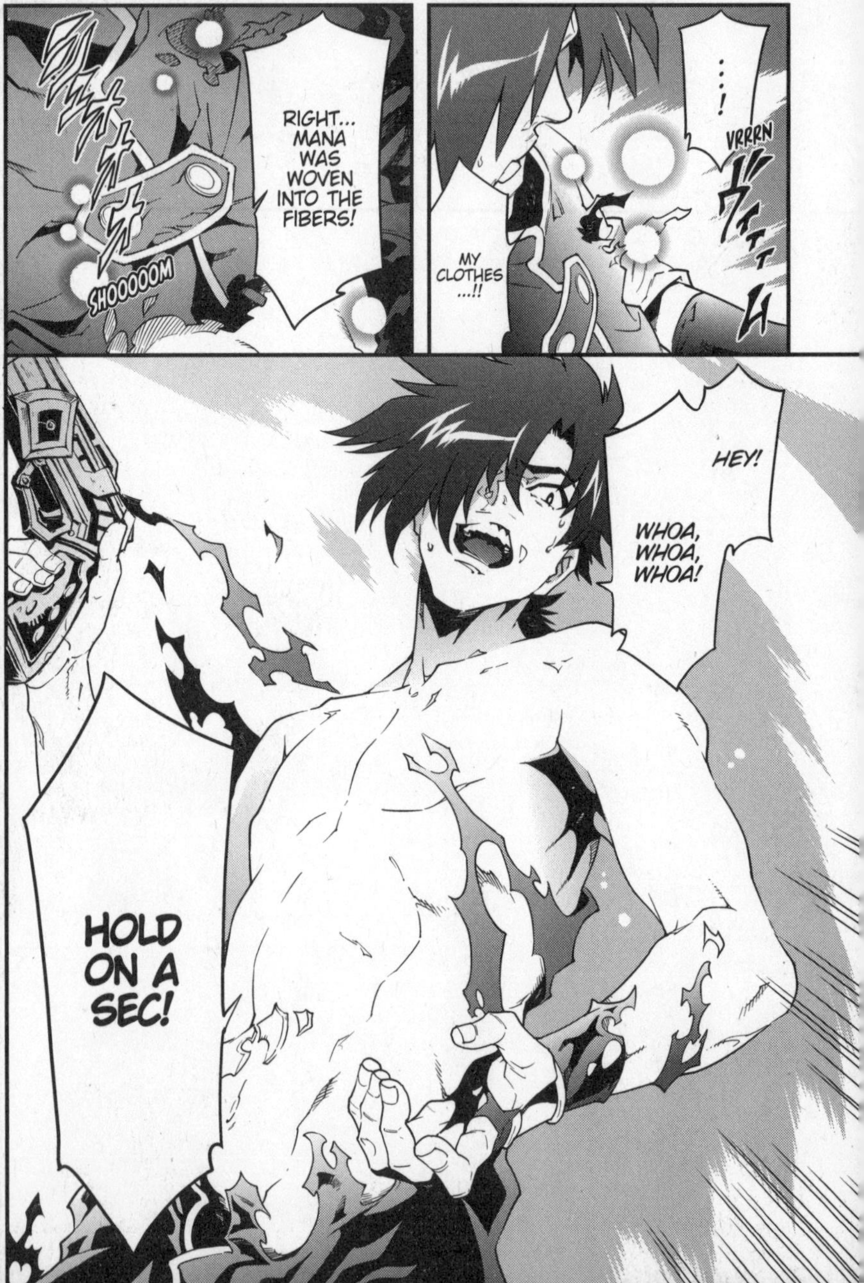
...!
VRRRN
MY CLOTHES ...!!
RIGHT... MANA WAS WOVEN INTO THE FIBERS!
SHOOOOOM
HEY!
WHOA, WHOA, WHOA!
HOLD ON A SEC!

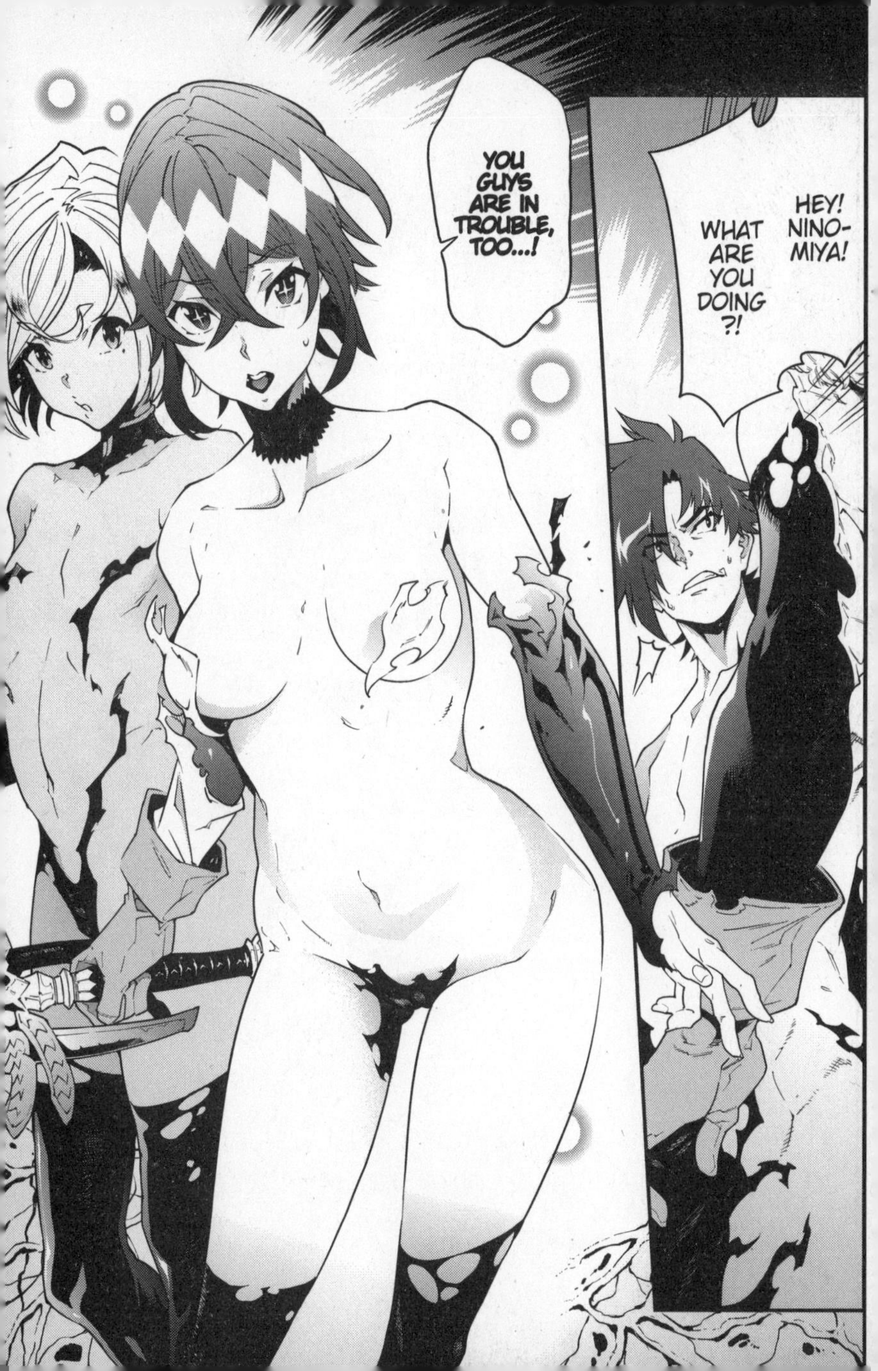
HEY! NINO-MIYA!
WHAT ARE YOU DOING ?!
YOU GUYS ARE IN TROUBLE, TOO...!

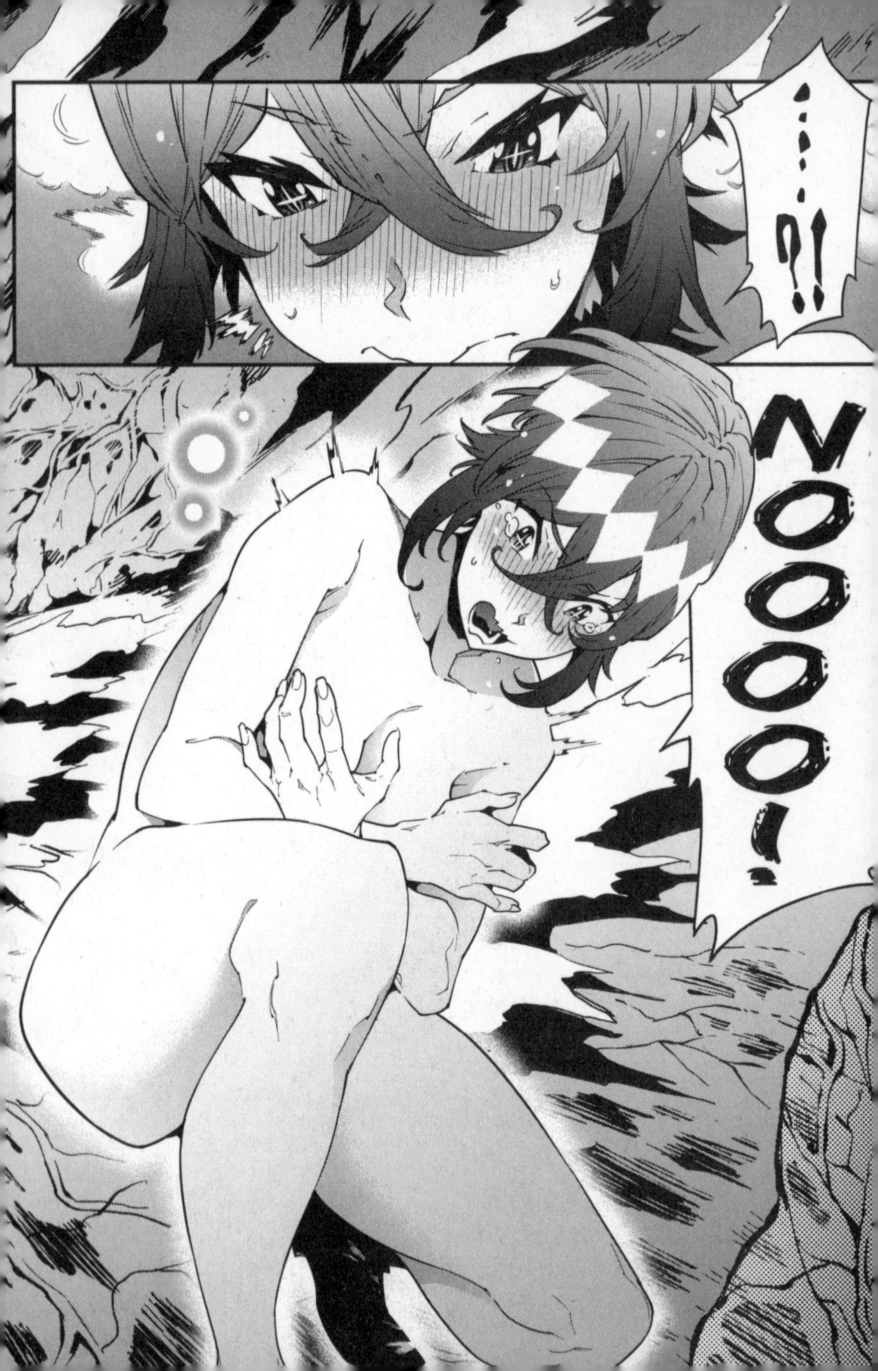
...?!!
NOOOO!

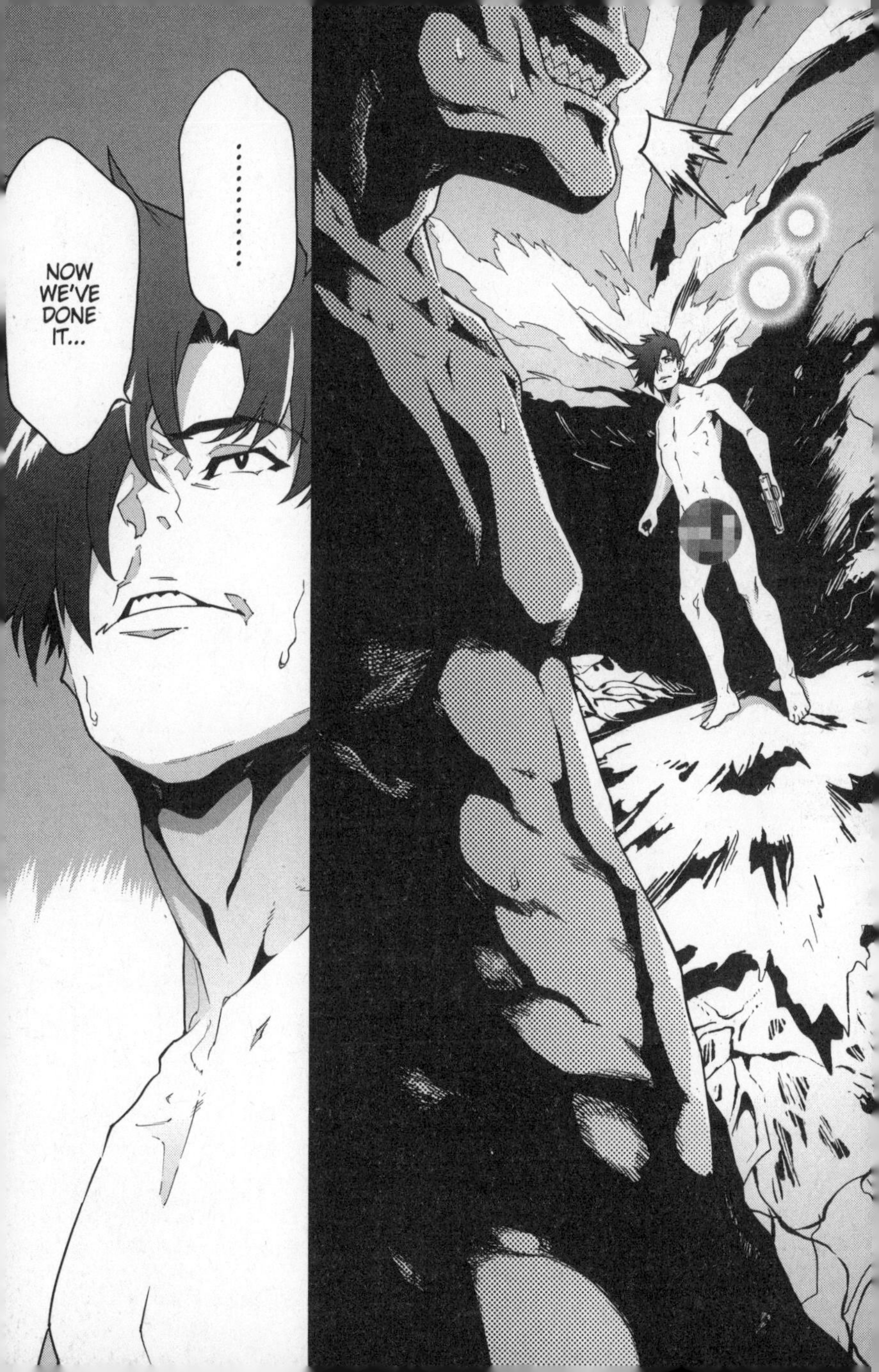
......
NOW WE'VE DONE IT...

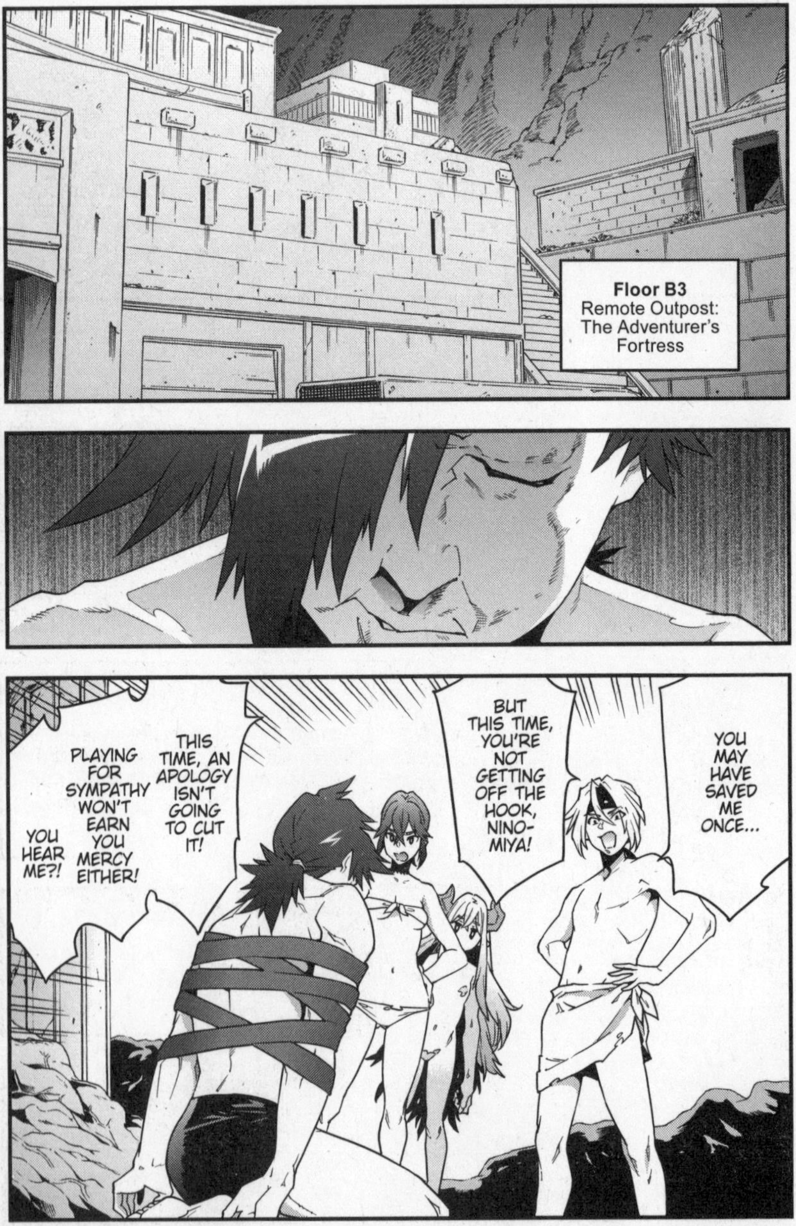
Floor B3
Remote Outpost: The Adventurer's Fortress
YOU MAY HAVE SAVED ME ONCE...
BUT THIS TIME, YOU'RE NOT GETTING OFF THE HOOK, NINO-MIYA!
THIS TIME, AN APOLOGY ISN'T GOING TO CUT IT!
PLAYING FOR SYMPATHY WON'T EARN YOU MERCY EITHER!
YOU HEAR ME?!

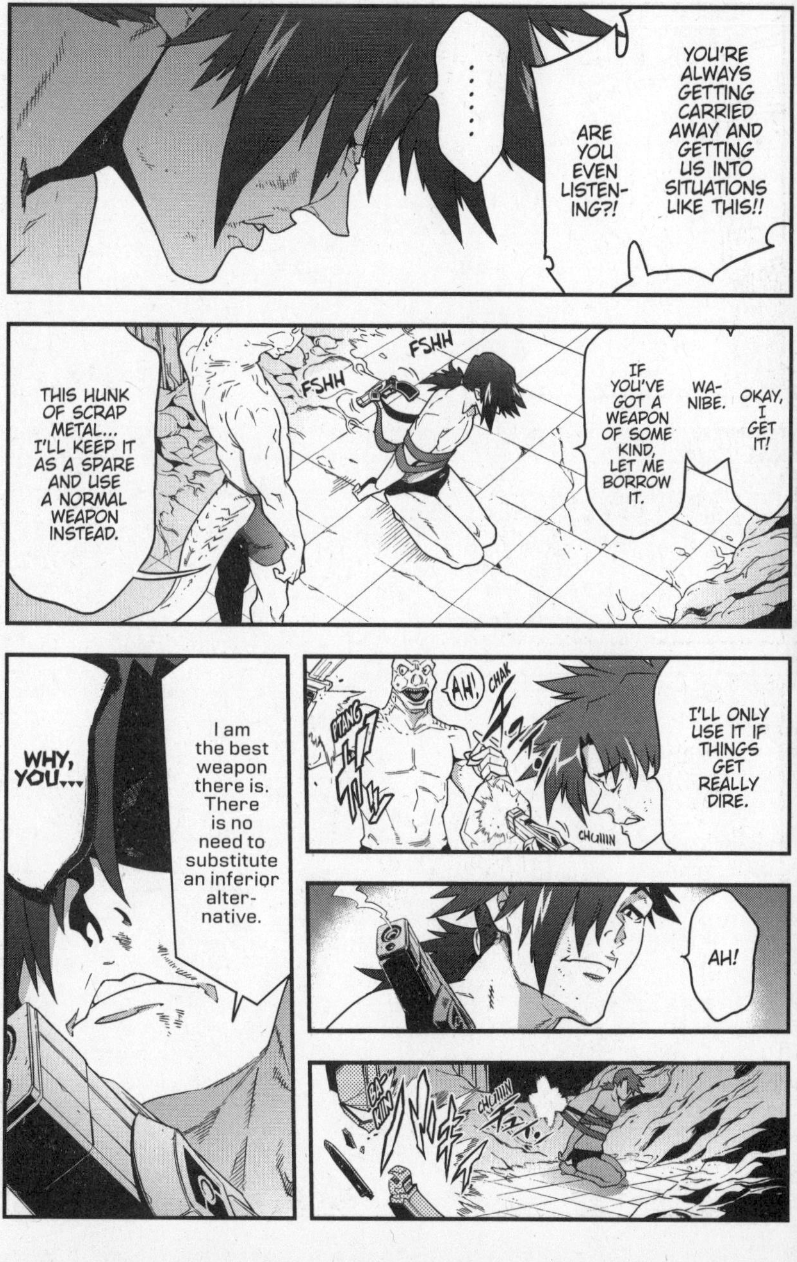
YOU'RE ALWAYS GETTING CARRIED AWAY AND GETTING US INTO SITUATIONS LIKE THIS!!
ARE YOU EVEN LISTENING?!
......
OKAY, I GET IT!
WANIBE.
IF YOU'VE GOT A WEAPON OF SOME KIND, LET ME BORROW IT.
FSHH
FSHH
THIS HUNK OF SCRAP METAL... I'LL KEEP IT AS A SPARE AND USE A NORMAL WEAPON INSTEAD.
I'LL ONLY USE IT IF THINGS GET REALLY DIRE.
CHAK
AH!
PTANG
CHUIIIN
AH!
CHUIIIN
GA-KIIN
I am the best weapon there is. There is no need to substitute an inferior alternative.
WHY, YOU...

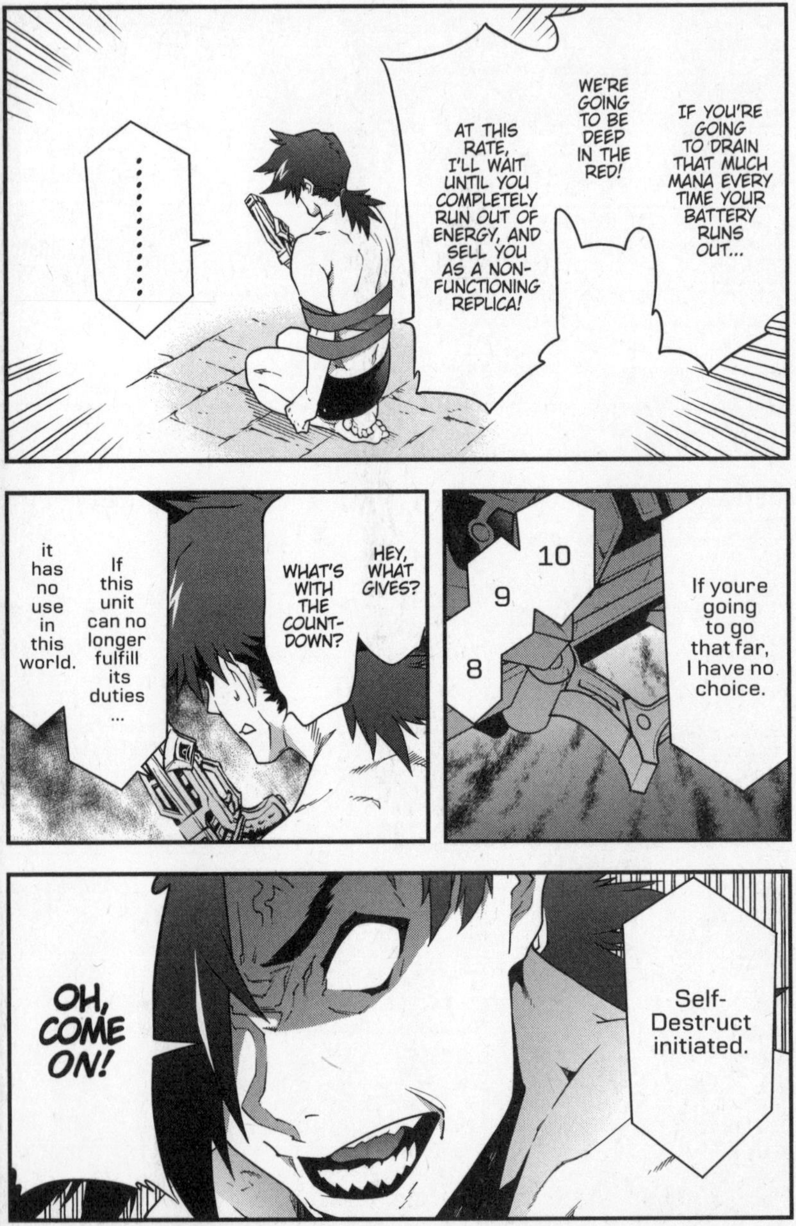
IF YOU'RE GOING TO DRAIN THAT MUCH MANA EVERY TIME YOUR BATTERY RUNS OUT...
WE'RE GOING TO BE DEEP IN THE RED!
AT THIS RATE, I'LL WAIT UNTIL YOU COMPLETELY RUN OUT OF ENERGY, AND SELL YOU AS A NON-FUNCTIONING REPLICA!
......
If youre going to go that far, I have no choice.
10
9
8
HEY, WHAT GIVES?
WHAT'S WITH THE COUNT-DOWN?
If this unit can no longer fulfill its duties ...
it has no use in this world.
Self-Destruct initiated.
OH, COME ON!

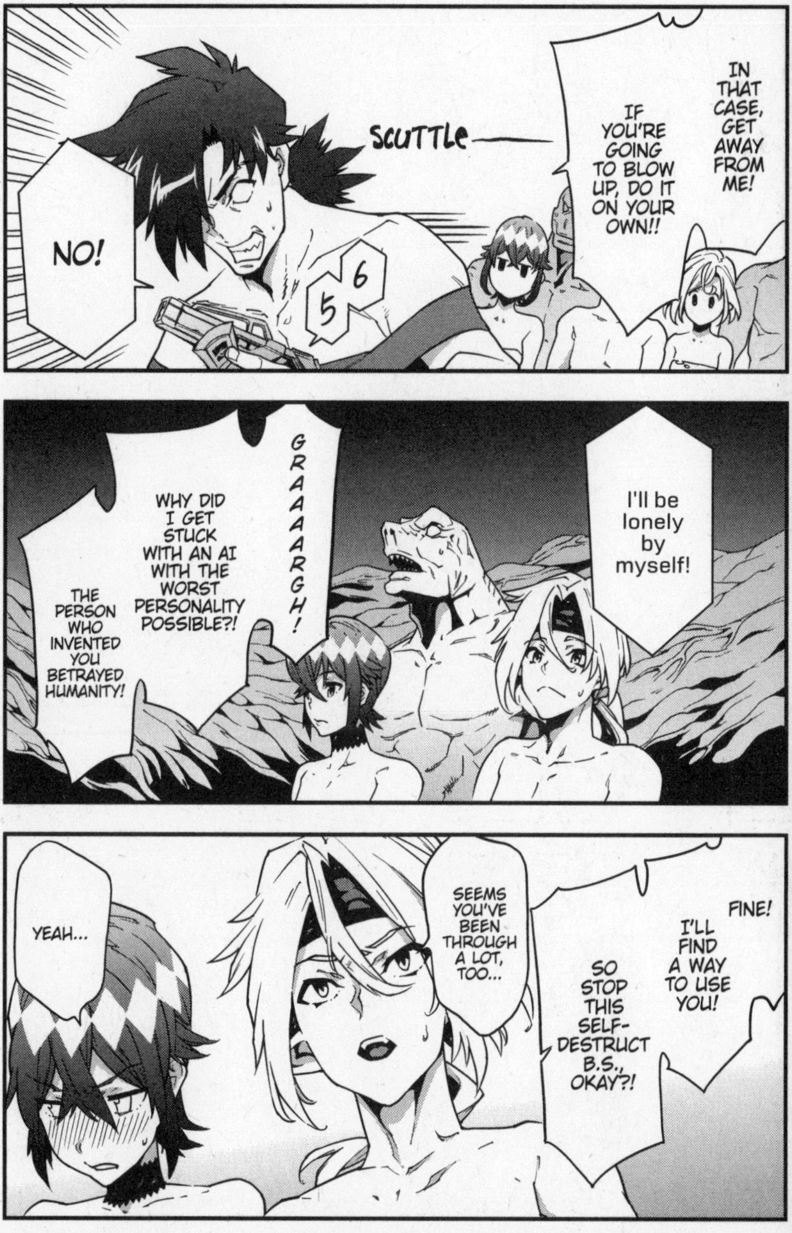
IN THAT CASE, GET AWAY FROM ME!
IF YOU'RE GOING TO BLOW UP, DO IT ON YOUR OWN!!
SCUTTLE
6
5
NO!
I'll be lonely by myself!
GRAAAAARGH!
WHY DID I GET STUCK WITH AN AI WITH THE WORST PERSONALITY POSSIBLE?!
THE PERSON WHO INVENTED YOU BETRAYED HUMANITY!
FINE!
I'LL FIND A WAY TO USE YOU!
SO STOP THIS SELF-DESTRUCT B.S., OKAY?!
SEEMS YOU'VE BEEN THROUGH A LOT, TOO...
YEAH...

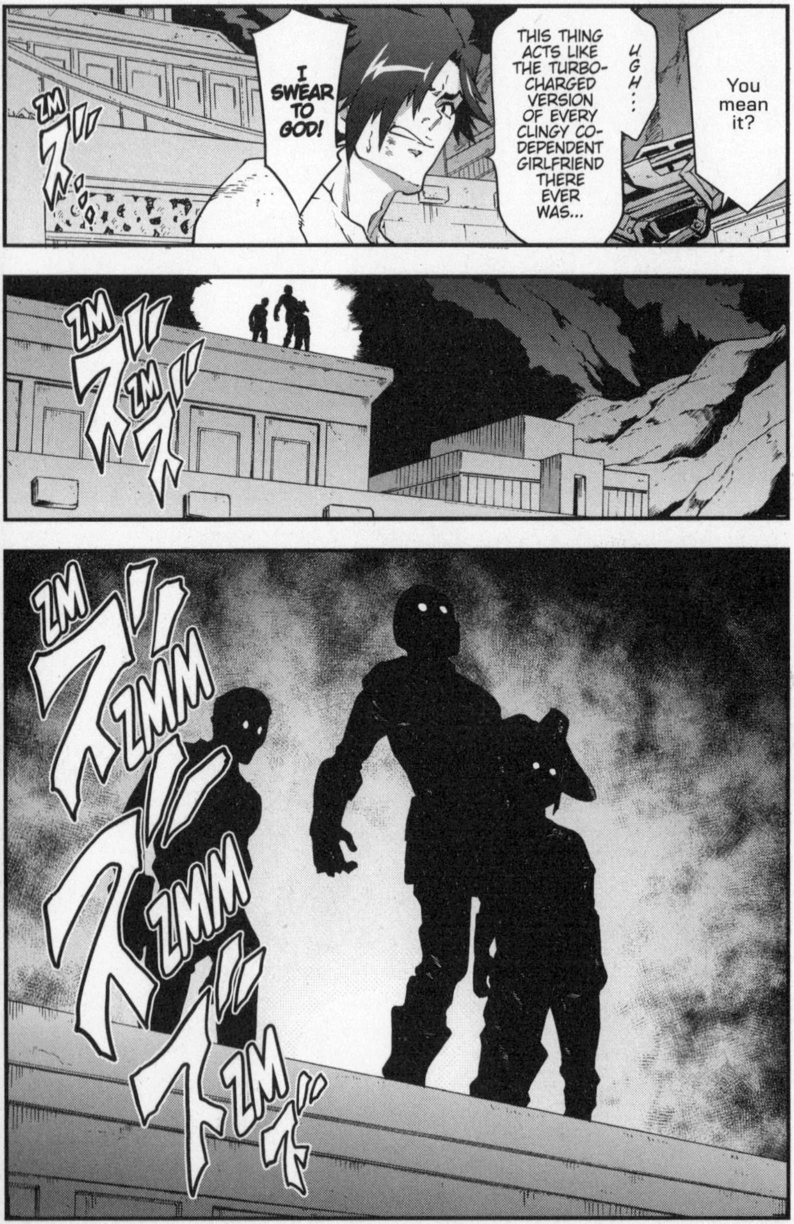
You mean it?
UGH...
THIS THING ACTS LIKE THE TURBO-CHARGED VERSION OF EVERY CLINGY CO-DEPENDENT GIRLFRIEND THERE EVER WAS...
I SWEAR TO GOD!
ZM
ZM
ZM
ZM
ZMM
ZMM
ZM

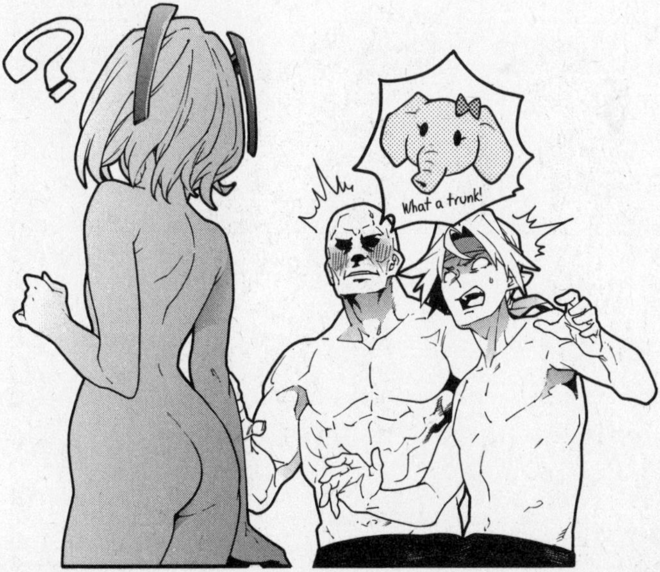
What a trunk!

THE DUNGEON OF
BLACK COMPANY

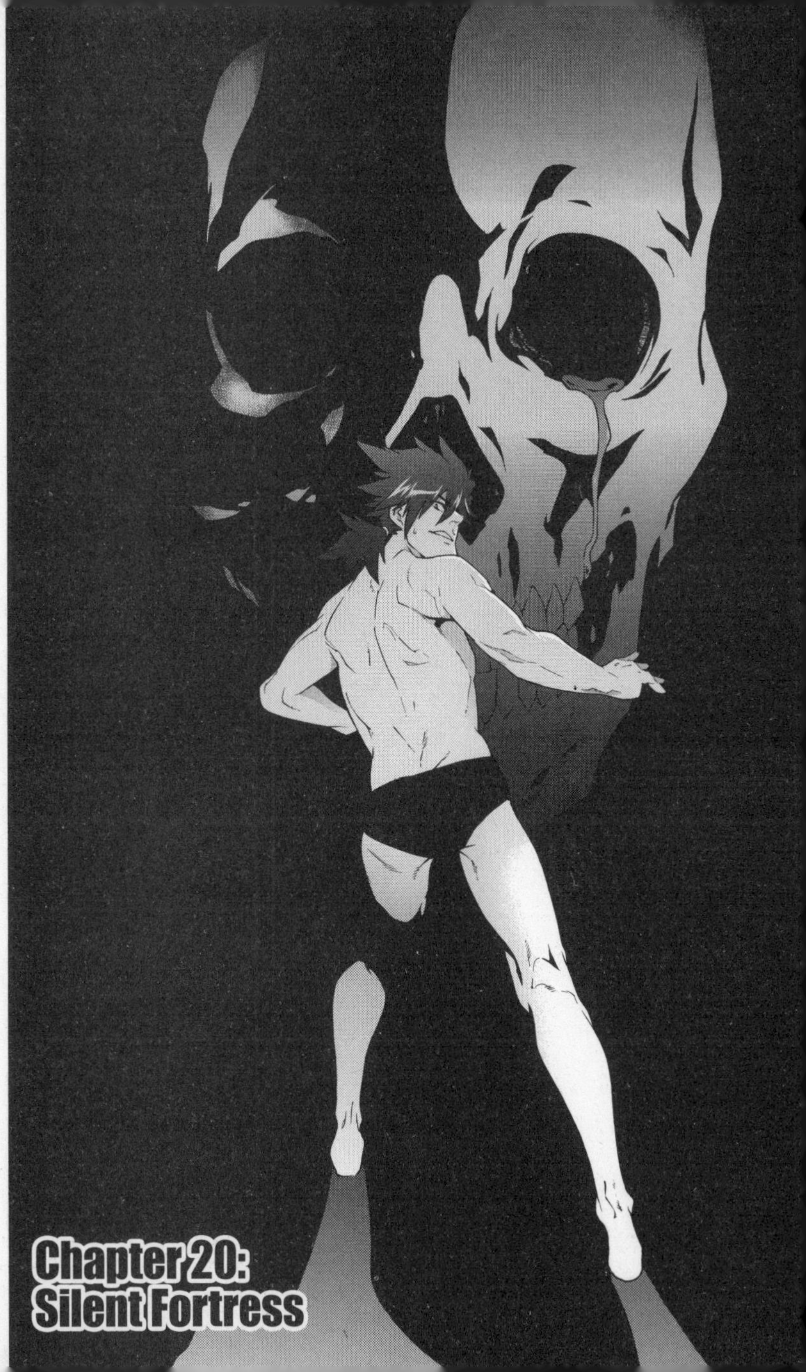
Chapter 20:
Silent Fortress

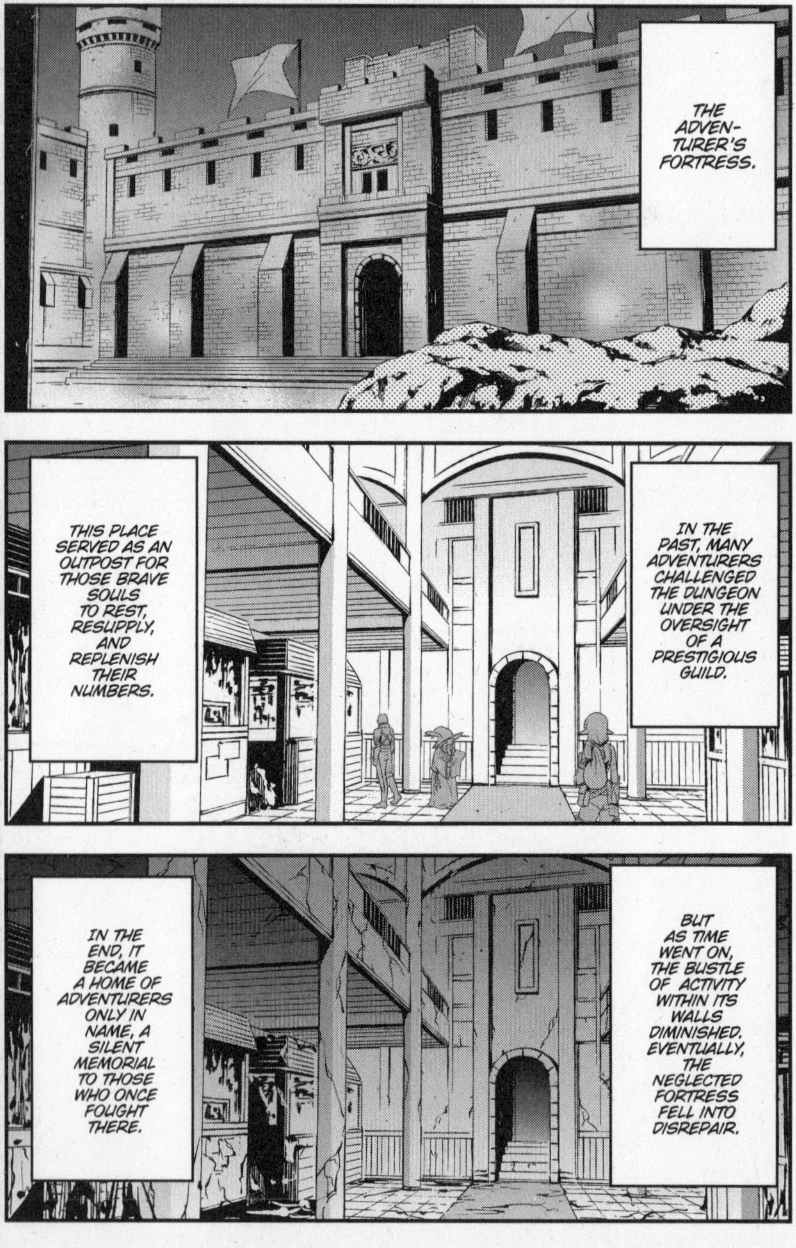
THE ADVENTURER'S FORTRESS.
IN THE PAST, MANY ADVENTURERS CHALLENGED THE DUNGEON UNDER THE OVERSIGHT OF A PRESTIGIOUS GUILD.
THIS PLACE SERVED AS AN OUTPOST FOR THOSE BRAVE SOULS TO REST, RESUPPLY, AND REPLENISH THEIR NUMBERS.
BUT AS TIME WENT ON, THE BUSTLE OF ACTIVITY WITHIN ITS WALLS DIMINISHED. EVENTUALLY, THE NEGLECTED FORTRESS FELL INTO DISREPAIR.
IN THE END, IT BECAME A HOME OF ADVENTURERS ONLY IN NAME, A SILENT MEMORIAL TO THOSE WHO ONCE FOUGHT THERE.

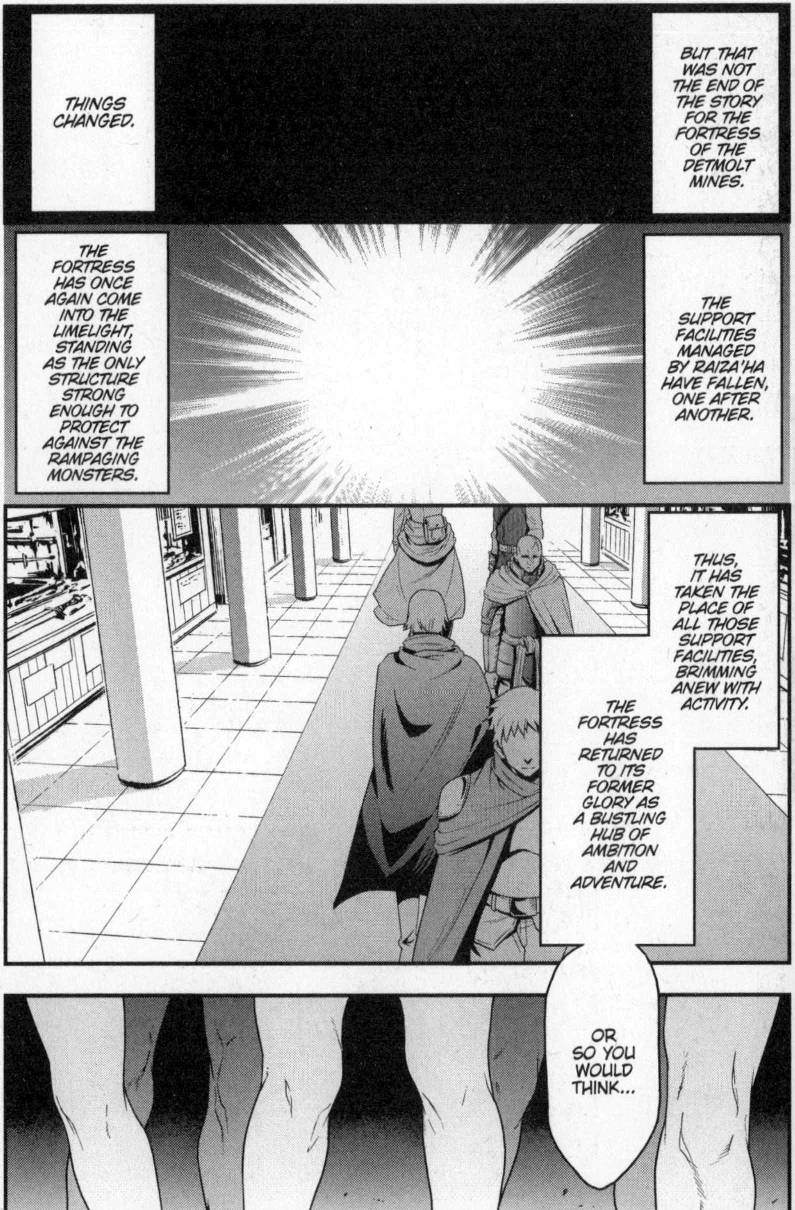
BUT THAT WAS NOT THE END OF THE STORY FOR THE FORTRESS OF THE DETMOLT MINES.
THINGS CHANGED.
THE SUPPORT FACILITIES MANAGED BY RAIZA'HA HAVE FALLEN, ONE AFTER ANOTHER.
THE FORTRESS HAS ONCE AGAIN COME INTO THE LIMELIGHT, STANDING AS THE ONLY STRUCTURE STRONG ENOUGH TO PROTECT AGAINST THE RAMPAGING MONSTERS.
THUS, IT HAS TAKEN THE PLACE OF ALL THOSE SUPPORT FACILITIES, BRIMMING ANEW WITH ACTIVITY.
THE FORTRESS HAS RETURNED TO ITS FORMER GLORY AS A BUSTLING HUB OF AMBITION AND ADVENTURE.
OR SO YOU WOULD THINK...

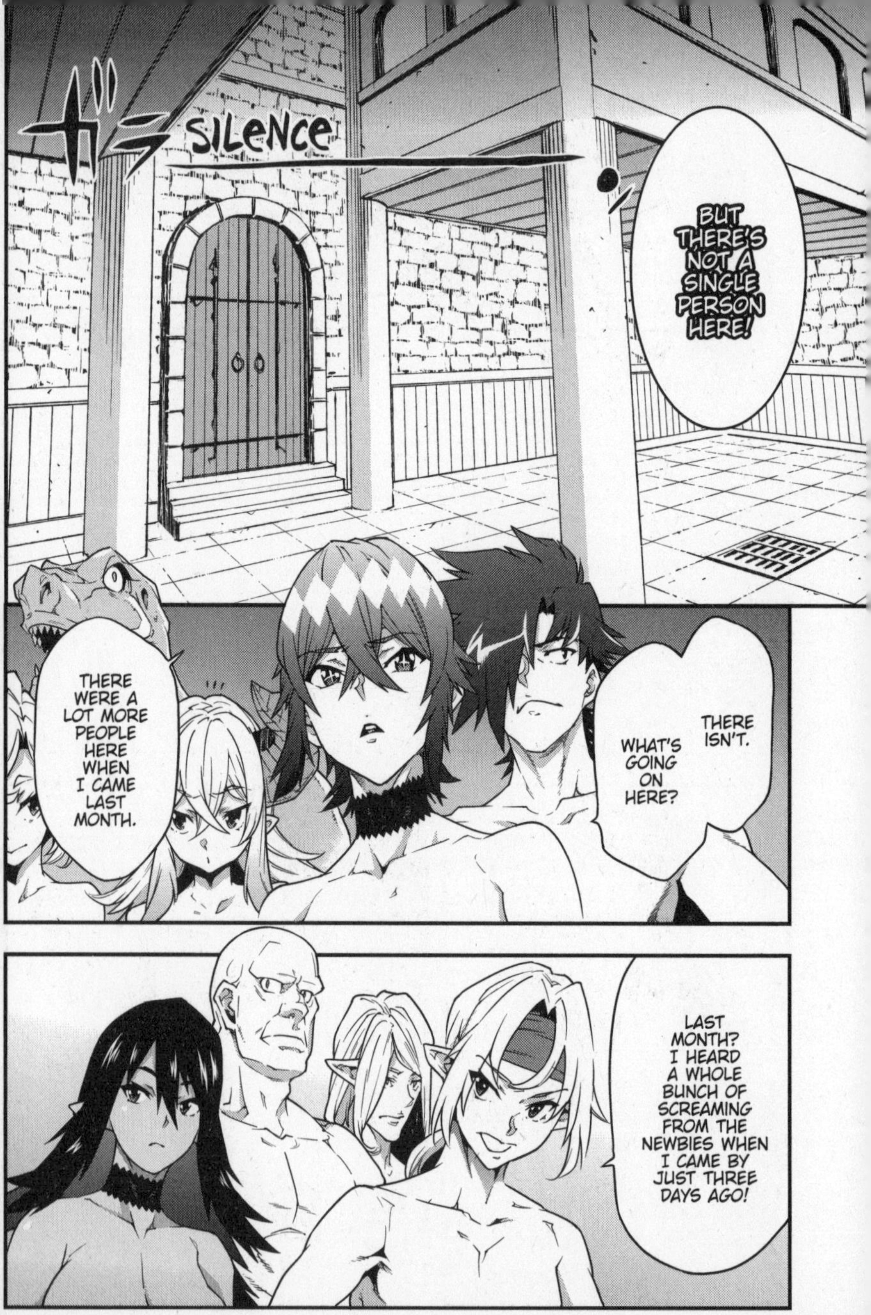
BUT THERE'S NOT A SINGLE PERSON HERE!
SILENCE
THERE ISN'T. WHAT'S GOING ON HERE?
THERE WERE A LOT MORE PEOPLE HERE WHEN I CAME LAST MONTH.
LAST MONTH? I HEARD A WHOLE BUNCH OF SCREAMING FROM THE NEWBIES WHEN I CAME BY JUST THREE DAYS AGO!

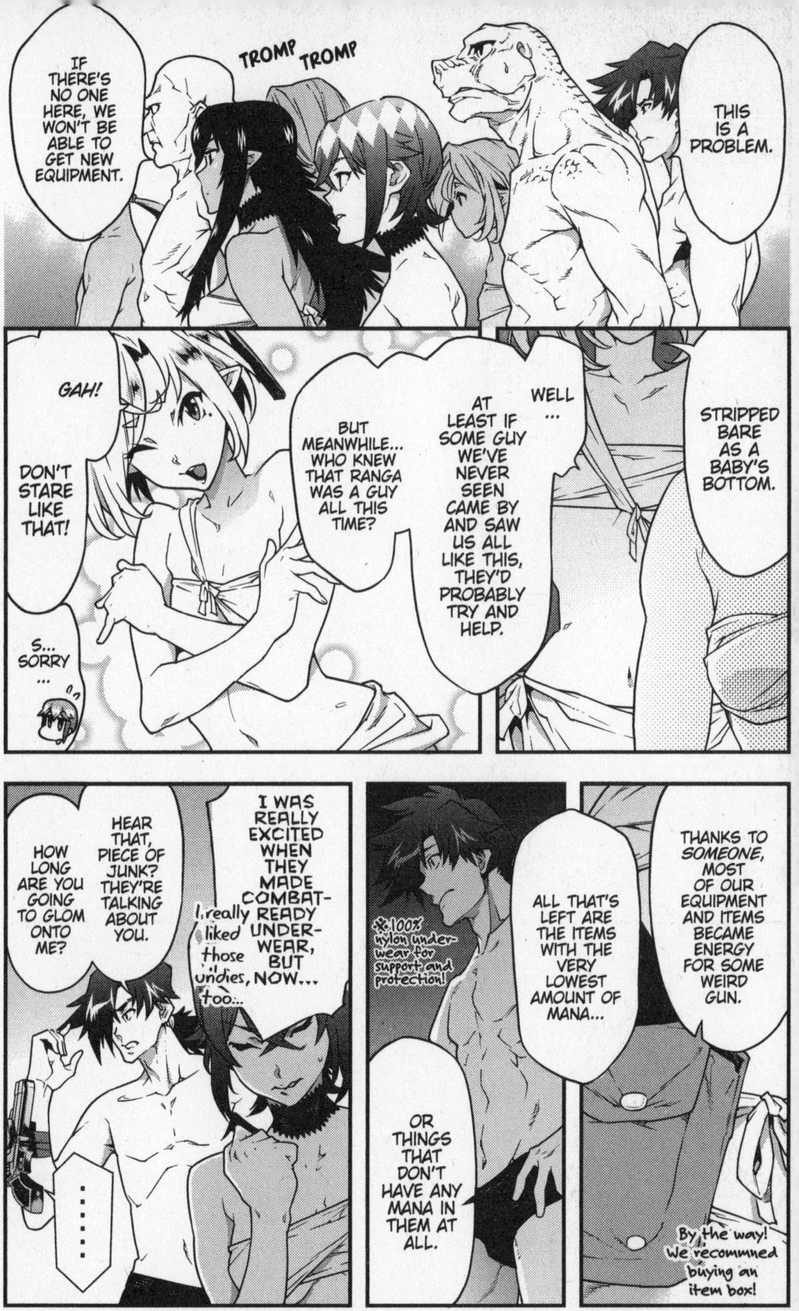
THIS IS A PROBLEM.
TROMP TROMP
IF THERE'S NO ONE HERE, WE WON'T BE ABLE TO GET NEW EQUIPMENT.
STRIPPED BARE AS A BABY'S BOTTOM.
WELL...
AT LEAST IF SOME GUY WE'VE NEVER SEEN CAME BY AND SAW US ALL LIKE THIS, THEY'D PROBABLY TRY AND HELP.
BUT MEANWHILE... WHO KNEW THAT RANGA WAS A GUY ALL THIS TIME?
GAH!
DON'T STARE LIKE THAT!
S... SORRY...
THANKS TO *SOMEONE*, MOST OF OUR EQUIPMENT AND ITEMS BECAME ENERGY FOR SOME WEIRD GUN.
By the way! We recommned buying an item box!
ALL THAT'S LEFT ARE THE ITEMS WITH THE VERY LOWEST AMOUNT OF MANA...
※100% nylon underwear for support and protection!
OR THINGS THAT DON'T HAVE ANY MANA IN THEM AT ALL.
I WAS REALLY EXCITED WHEN THEY MADE COMBAT-READY UNDERWEAR, BUT NOW...
I really liked those undies, too...
HEAR THAT, PIECE OF JUNK? THEY'RE TALKING ABOUT YOU.
HOW LONG ARE YOU GOING TO GLOM ONTO ME?
......

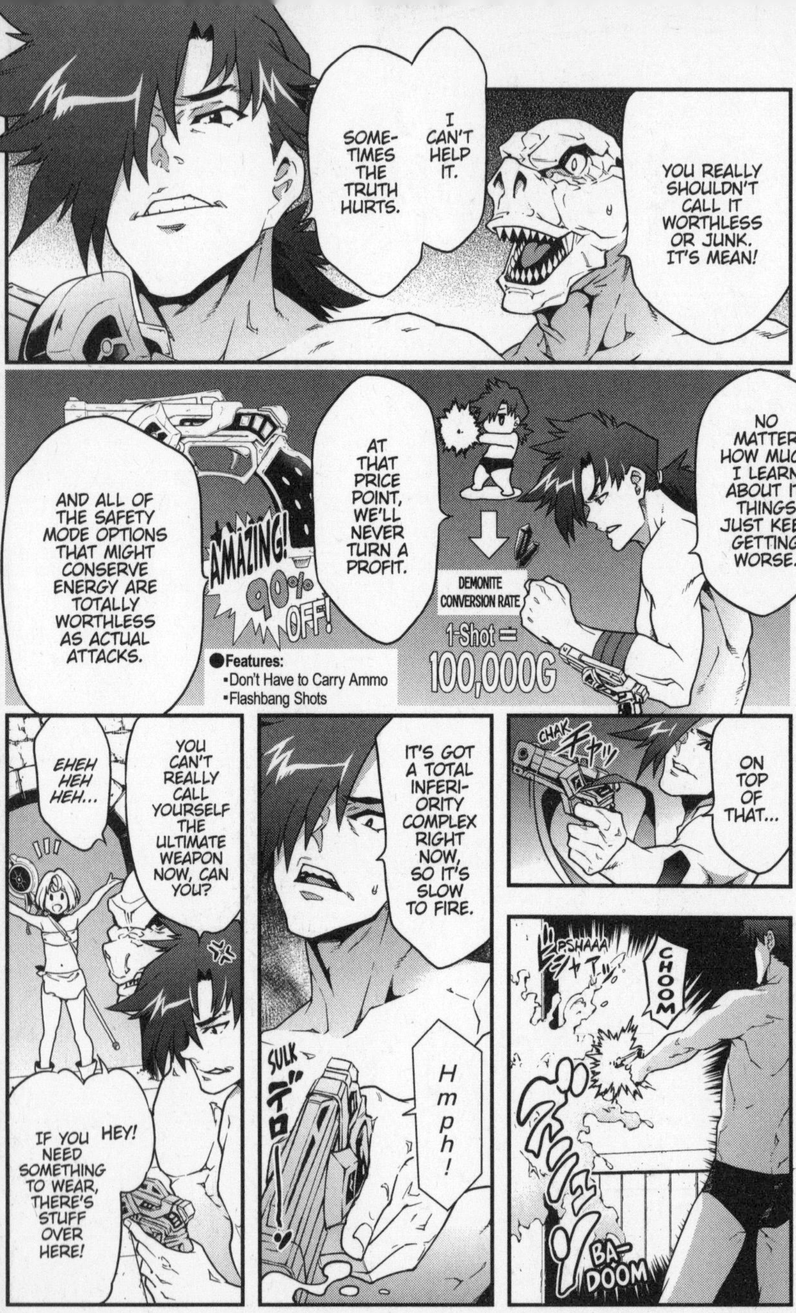
YOU REALLY SHOULDN'T CALL IT WORTHLESS OR JUNK. IT'S MEAN!
I CAN'T HELP IT.
SOME-TIMES THE TRUTH HURTS.
NO MATTER HOW MUCH I LEARN ABOUT IT, THINGS JUST KEEP GETTING WORSE.
DEMONITE CONVERSION RATE
1-Shot = 100,000G
AT THAT PRICE POINT, WE'LL NEVER TURN A PROFIT.
AMAZING! 90% OFF!
●Features:
▪Don't Have to Carry Ammo
▪Flashbang Shots
AND ALL OF THE SAFETY MODE OPTIONS THAT MIGHT CONSERVE ENERGY ARE TOTALLY WORTHLESS AS ACTUAL ATTACKS.
CHAK
ON TOP OF THAT...
PSHAAA
CHOOM
BA-DOOM
IT'S GOT A TOTAL INFERI-ORITY COMPLEX RIGHT NOW, SO IT'S SLOW TO FIRE.
Hmph!
SULK
YOU CAN'T REALLY CALL YOURSELF THE ULTIMATE WEAPON NOW, CAN YOU?
EHEH HEH HEH...
HEY!
IF YOU NEED SOMETHING TO WEAR, THERE'S STUFF OVER HERE!

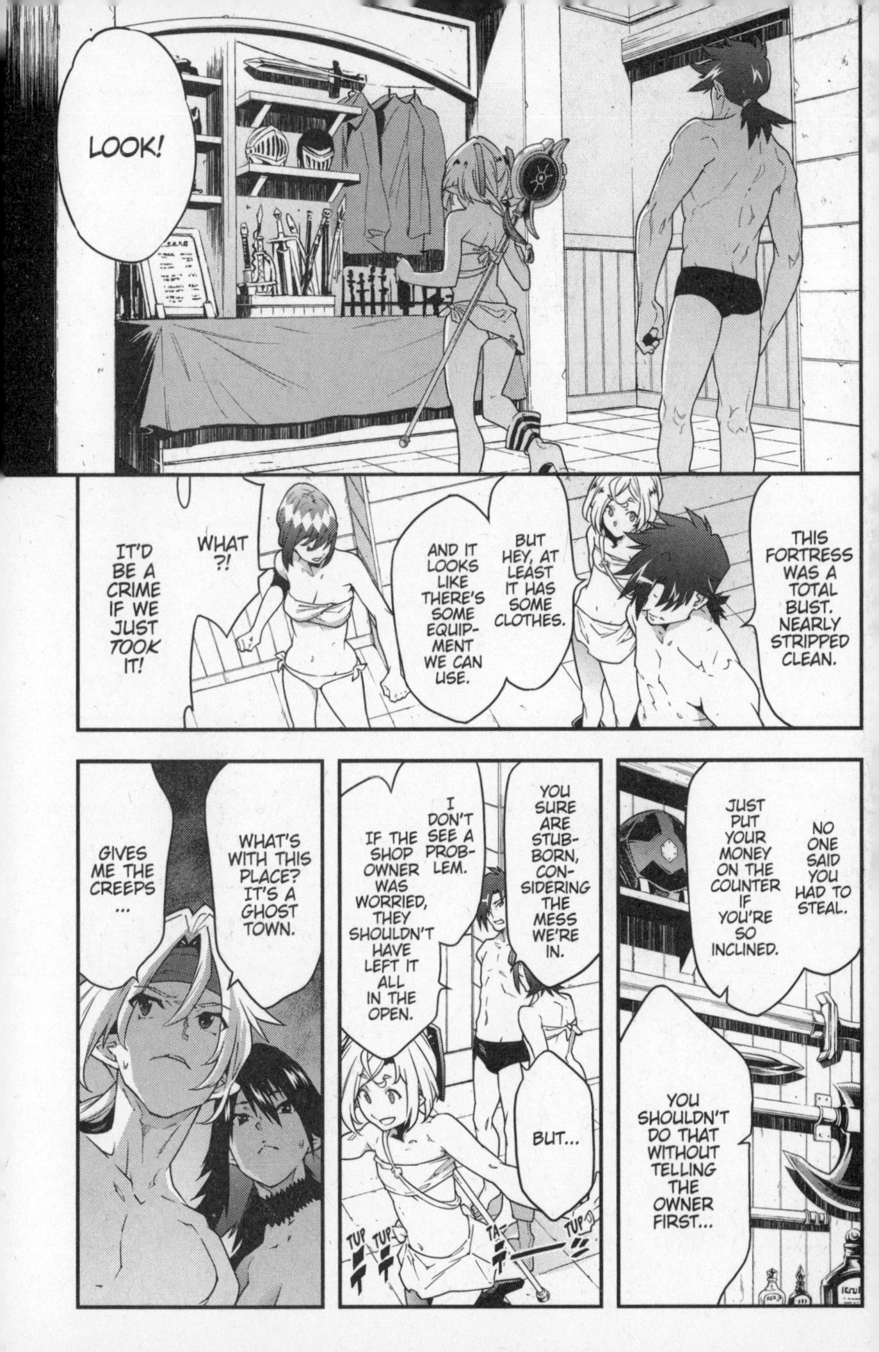
LOOK!
THIS FORTRESS WAS A TOTAL BUST. NEARLY STRIPPED CLEAN.
BUT HEY, AT LEAST IT HAS SOME CLOTHES.
AND IT LOOKS LIKE THERE'S SOME EQUIPMENT WE CAN USE.
WHAT?!
IT'D BE A CRIME IF WE JUST *TOOK* IT!
NO ONE SAID YOU HAD TO STEAL.
JUST PUT YOUR MONEY ON THE COUNTER IF YOU'RE SO INCLINED.
YOU SHOULDN'T DO THAT WITHOUT TELLING THE OWNER FIRST...
YOU SURE ARE STUBBORN, CONSIDERING THE MESS WE'RE IN.
I DON'T SEE A PROBLEM.
IF THE SHOP OWNER WAS WORRIED, THEY SHOULDN'T HAVE LEFT IT ALL IN THE OPEN.
BUT...
TUP TUP TA TUP
WHAT'S WITH THIS PLACE? IT'S A GHOST TOWN.
GIVES ME THE CREEPS...

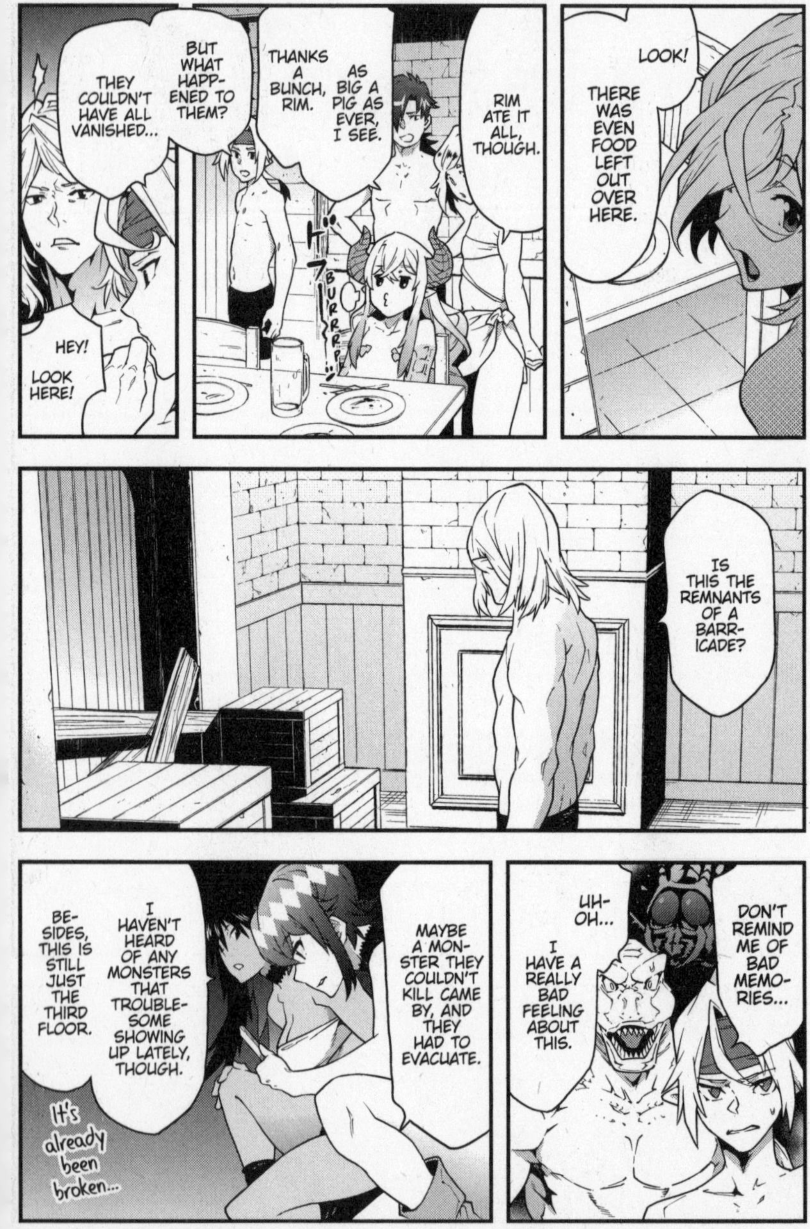
LOOK!
THERE WAS EVEN FOOD LEFT OUT OVER HERE.
RIM ATE IT ALL, THOUGH.
THANKS A BUNCH, RIM. AS BIG A PIG AS EVER, I SEE.
BURRRP
BUT WHAT HAPPENED TO THEM?
THEY COULDN'T HAVE ALL VANISHED...
HEY!
LOOK HERE!
IS THIS THE REMNANTS OF A BARRICADE?
UH-OH...
I HAVE A REALLY BAD FEELING ABOUT THIS.
DON'T REMIND ME OF BAD MEMORIES...
MAYBE A MONSTER THEY COULDN'T KILL CAME BY, AND THEY HAD TO EVACUATE.
I HAVEN'T HEARD OF ANY MONSTERS THAT TROUBLESOME SHOWING UP LATELY, THOUGH.
BESIDES, THIS IS STILL JUST THE THIRD FLOOR.
It's already been broken...

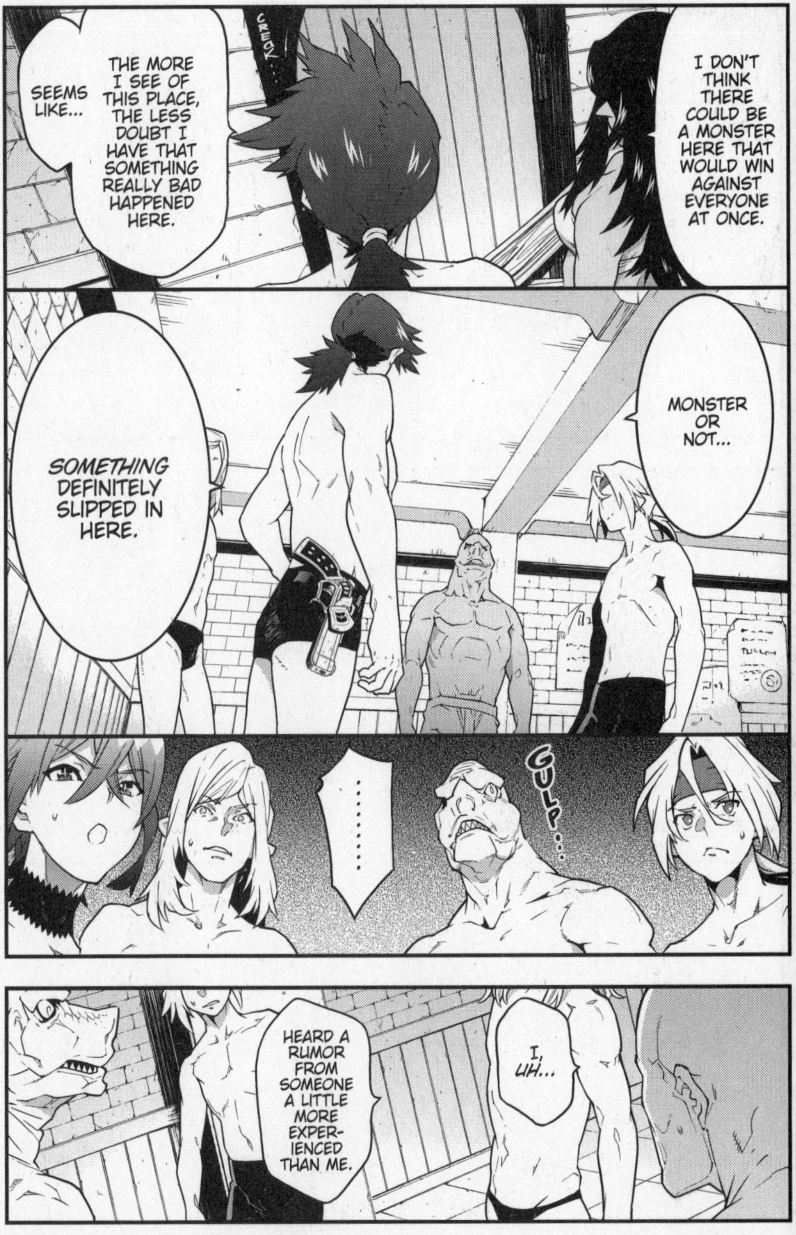
I DON'T THINK THERE COULD BE A MONSTER HERE THAT WOULD WIN AGAINST EVERYONE AT ONCE.
CREAK...
SEEMS LIKE... THE MORE I SEE OF THIS PLACE, THE LESS DOUBT I HAVE THAT SOMETHING REALLY BAD HAPPENED HERE.
MONSTER OR NOT...
SOMETHING DEFINITELY SLIPPED IN HERE.
GULP...
......
I, UH...
HEARD A RUMOR FROM SOMEONE A LITTLE MORE EXPERI-IENCED THAN ME.

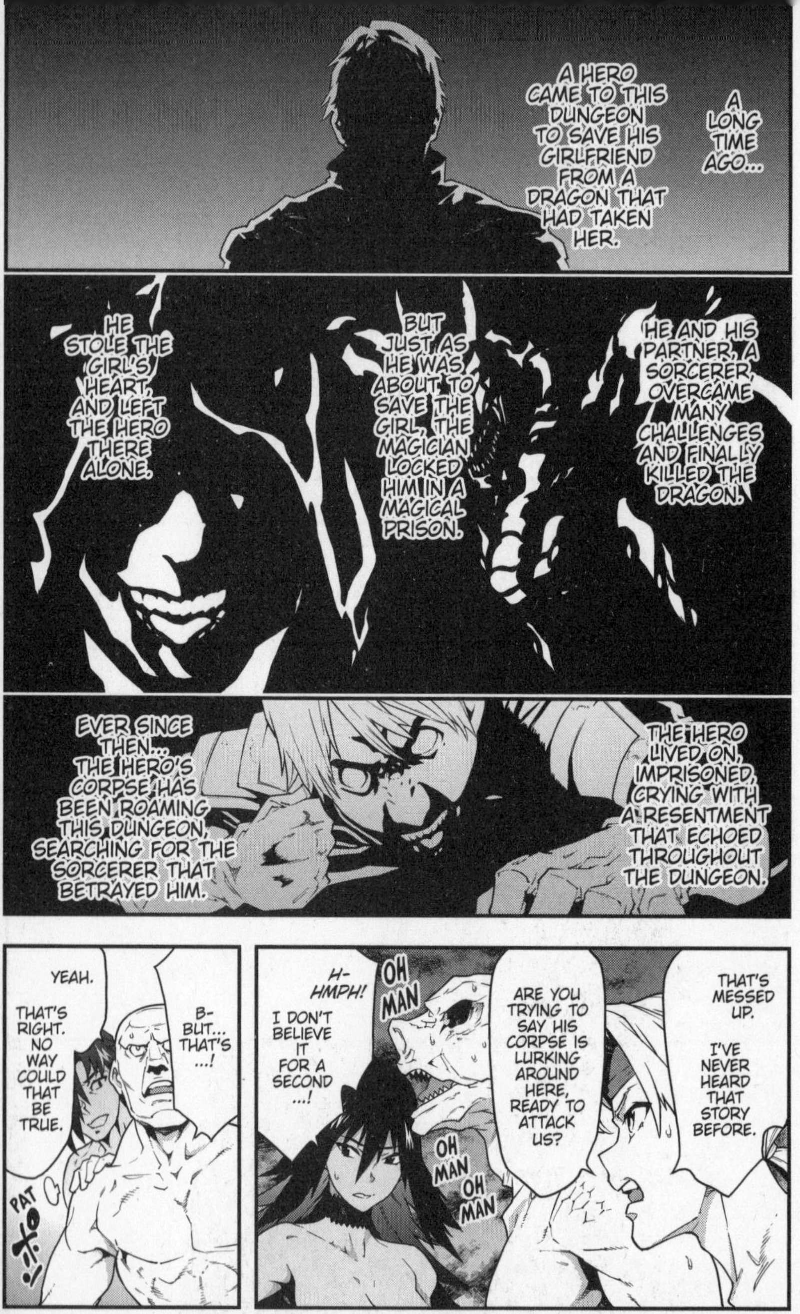
A LONG TIME AGO...
A HERO CAME TO THIS DUNGEON TO SAVE HIS GIRLFRIEND FROM A DRAGON THAT HAD TAKEN HER.
HE AND HIS PARTNER, A SORCERER, OVERCAME MANY CHALLENGES AND FINALLY KILLED THE DRAGON.
BUT JUST AS HE WAS ABOUT TO SAVE THE GIRL, THE MAGICIAN LOCKED HIM IN A MAGICAL PRISON.
HE STOLE THE GIRL'S HEART, AND LEFT THE HERO THERE ALONE.
THE HERO LIVED ON, IMPRISONED, CRYING WITH A RESENTMENT THAT ECHOED THROUGHOUT THE DUNGEON.
EVER SINCE THEN... THE HERO'S CORPSE HAS BEEN ROAMING THIS DUNGEON, SEARCHING FOR THE SORCERER THAT BETRAYED HIM.
THAT'S MESSED UP.
I'VE NEVER HEARD THAT STORY BEFORE.
ARE YOU TRYING TO SAY HIS CORPSE IS LURKING AROUND HERE, READY TO ATTACK US?
OH MAN
H-HMPH!
I DON'T BELIEVE IT FOR A SECOND ...!
OH MAN OH MAN OH MAN
B-BUT... THAT'S ...!
YEAH.
THAT'S RIGHT. NO WAY COULD THAT BE TRUE.
PAT

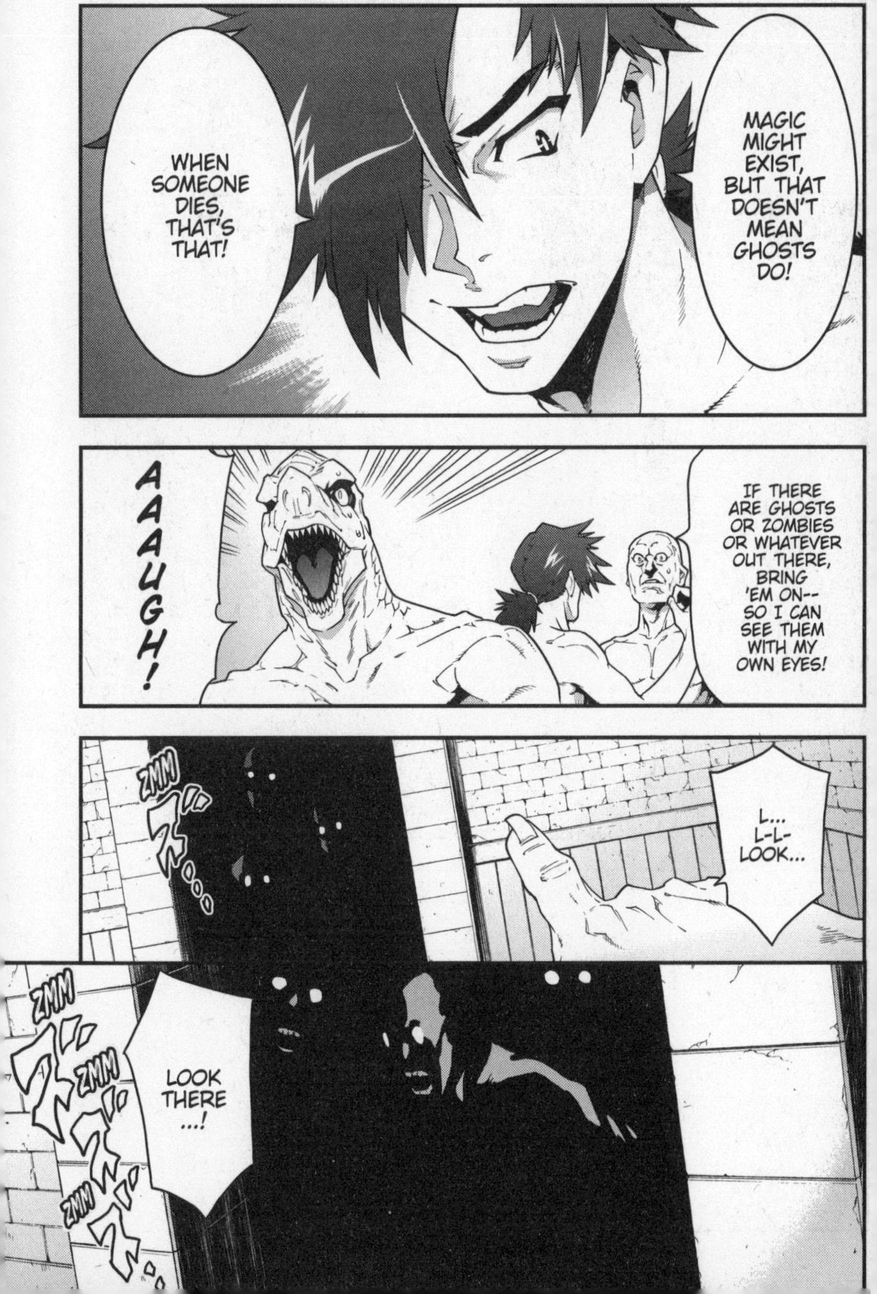
MAGIC MIGHT EXIST, BUT THAT DOESN'T MEAN GHOSTS DO!
WHEN SOMEONE DIES, THAT'S THAT!
IF THERE ARE GHOSTS OR ZOMBIES OR WHATEVER OUT THERE, BRING 'EM ON--SO I CAN SEE THEM WITH MY OWN EYES!
AAAAUGH!
L... L-L-LOOK...
ZMM
LOOK THERE ...!
ZMM
ZMM
ZMM

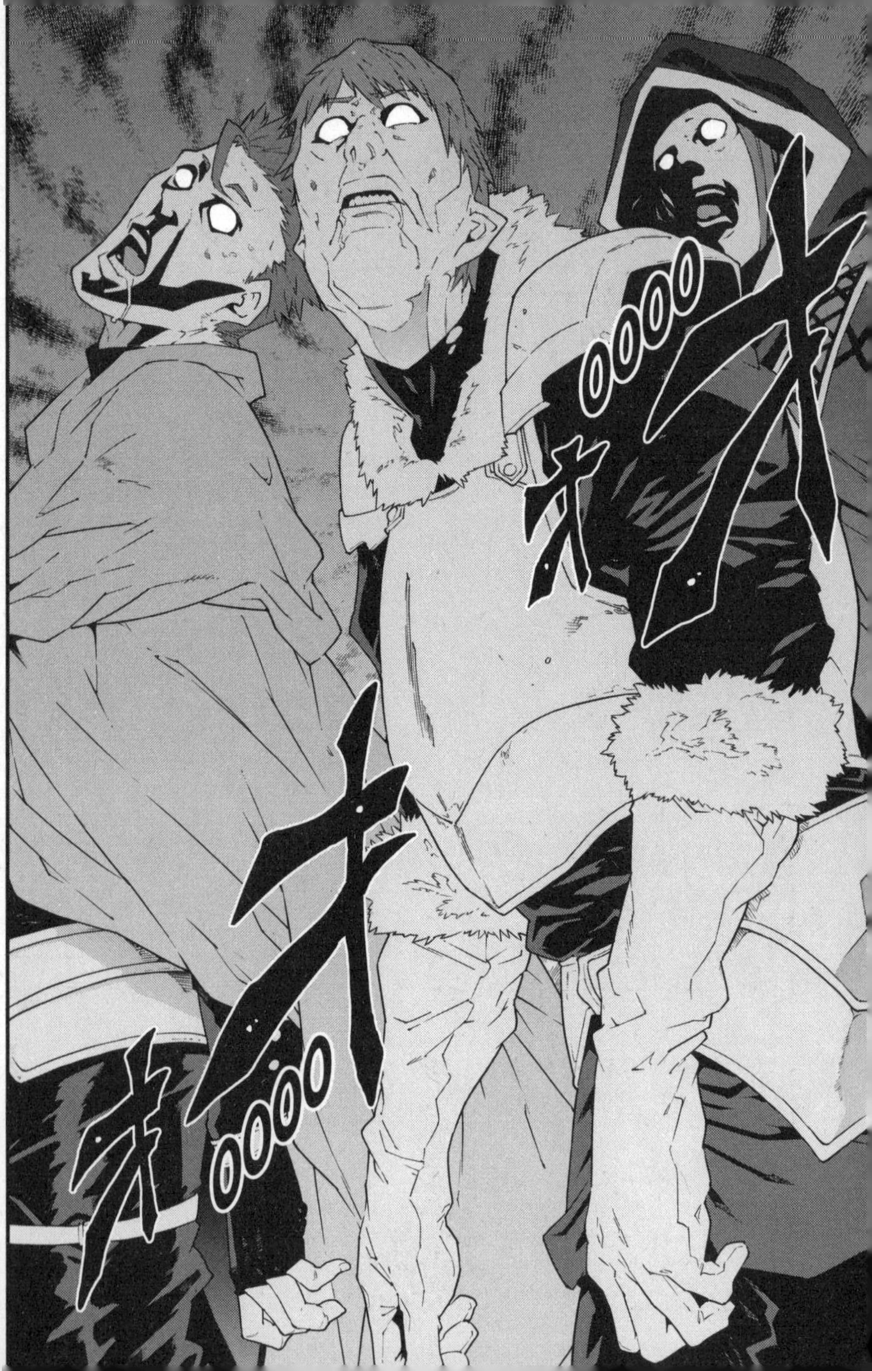
オオoooo
オオoooo

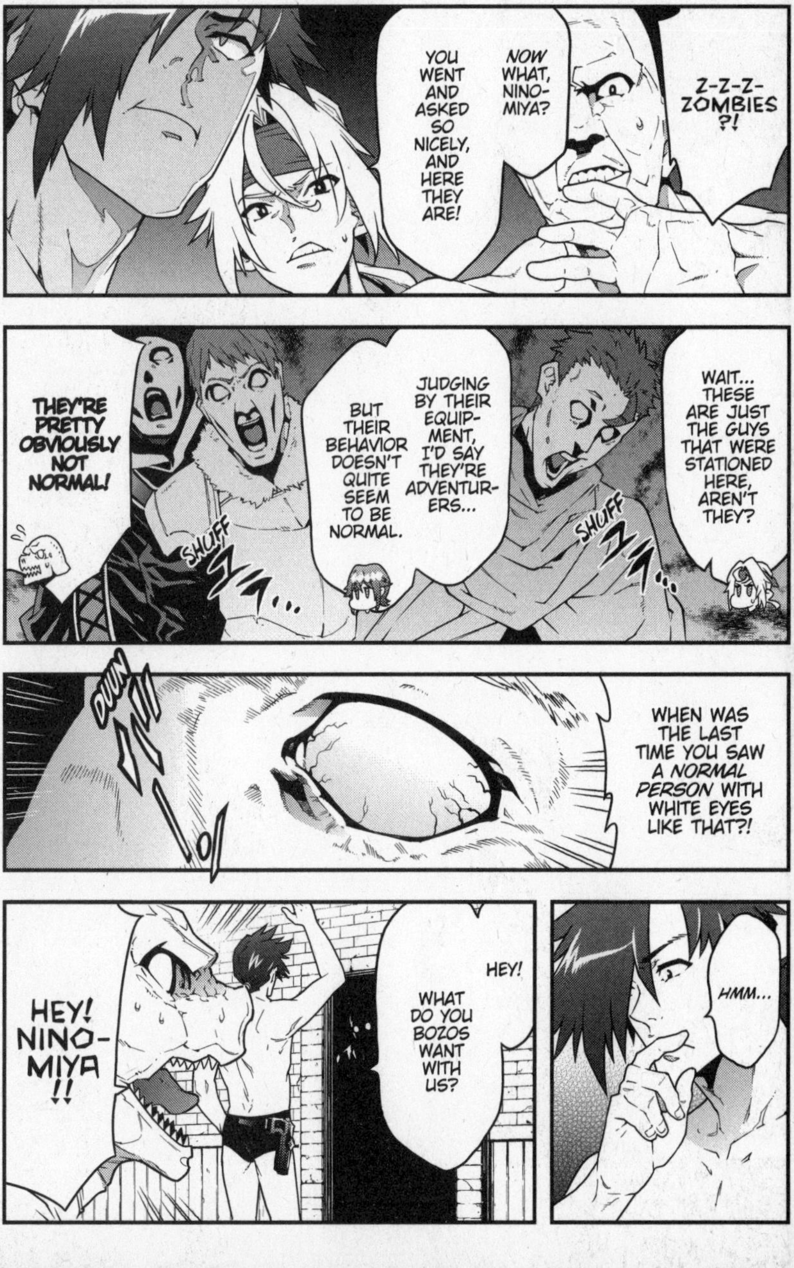
Z-Z-Z-ZOMBIES?!
NOW WHAT, NINO-MIYA?
YOU WENT AND ASKED SO NICELY, AND HERE THEY ARE!
WAIT... THESE ARE JUST THE GUYS THAT WERE STATIONED HERE, AREN'T THEY?
SHUFF
JUDGING BY THEIR EQUIP-MENT, I'D SAY THEY'RE ADVENTUR-ERS...
BUT THEIR BEHAVIOR DOESN'T QUITE SEEM TO BE NORMAL.
SHUFF
THEY'RE PRETTY OBVIOUSLY NOT NORMAL!
WHEN WAS THE LAST TIME YOU SAW A NORMAL PERSON WITH WHITE EYES LIKE THAT?!
DUUN
HMM...
HEY!
WHAT DO YOU BOZOS WANT WITH US?
HEY! NINO-MIYA!!

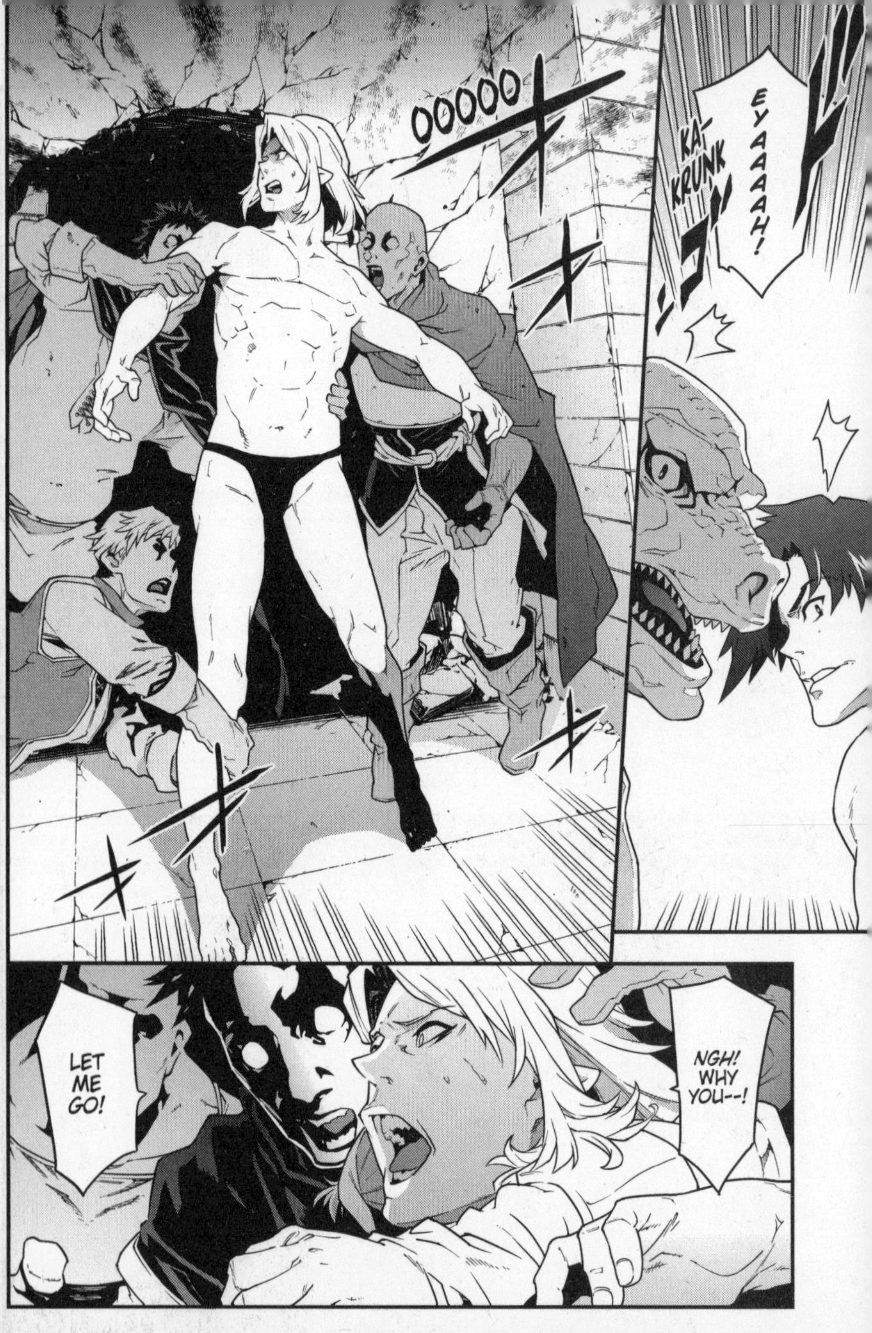
EYAAAAAH!
KA-KRUNK
OOOOO
NGH! WHY YOU--!
LET ME GO!

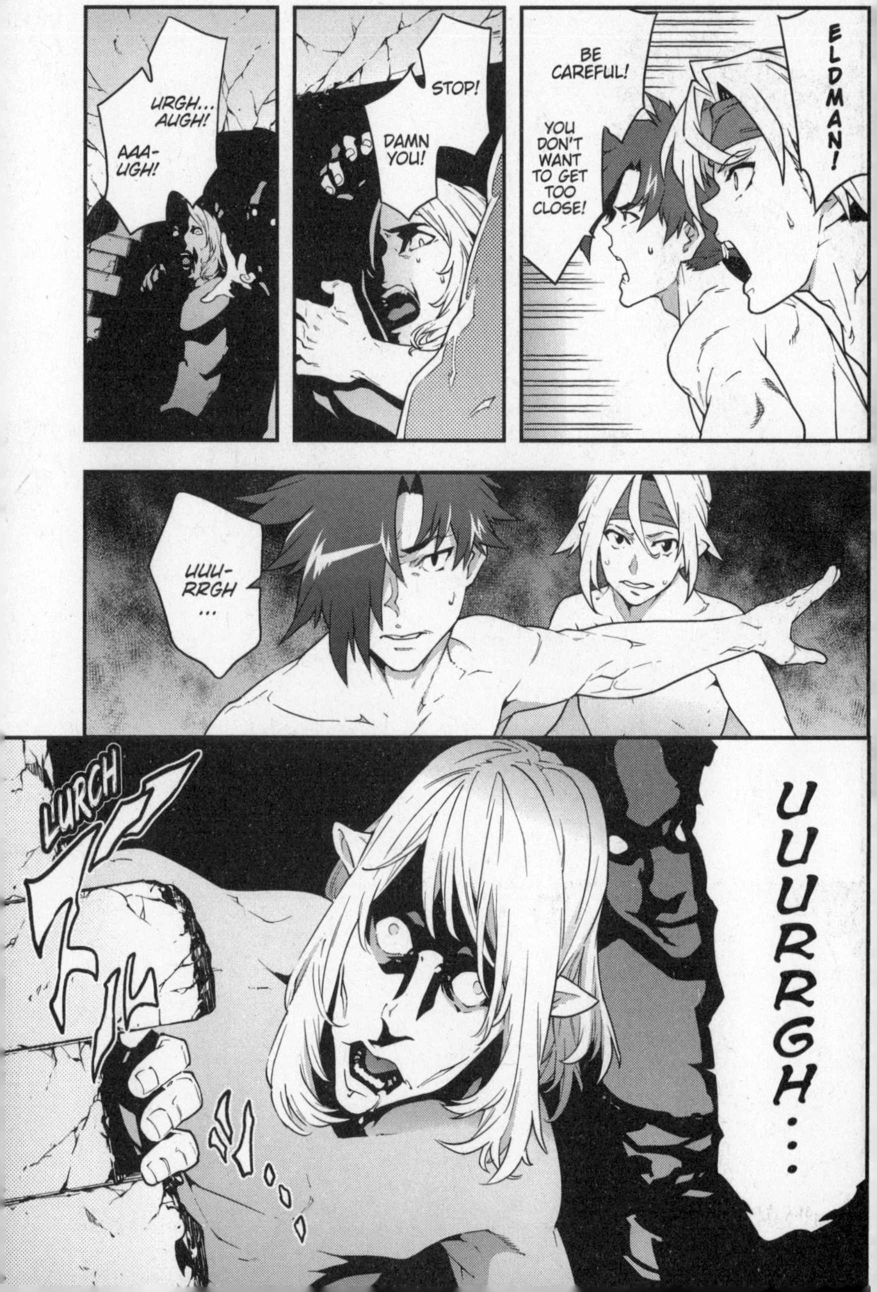
ELDMAN!
BE CAREFUL!
YOU DON'T WANT TO GET TOO CLOSE!
STOP!
DAMN YOU!
URGH... AUGH!
AAA-UGH!
UUU-RRGH...
UUURRGH...
LURCH

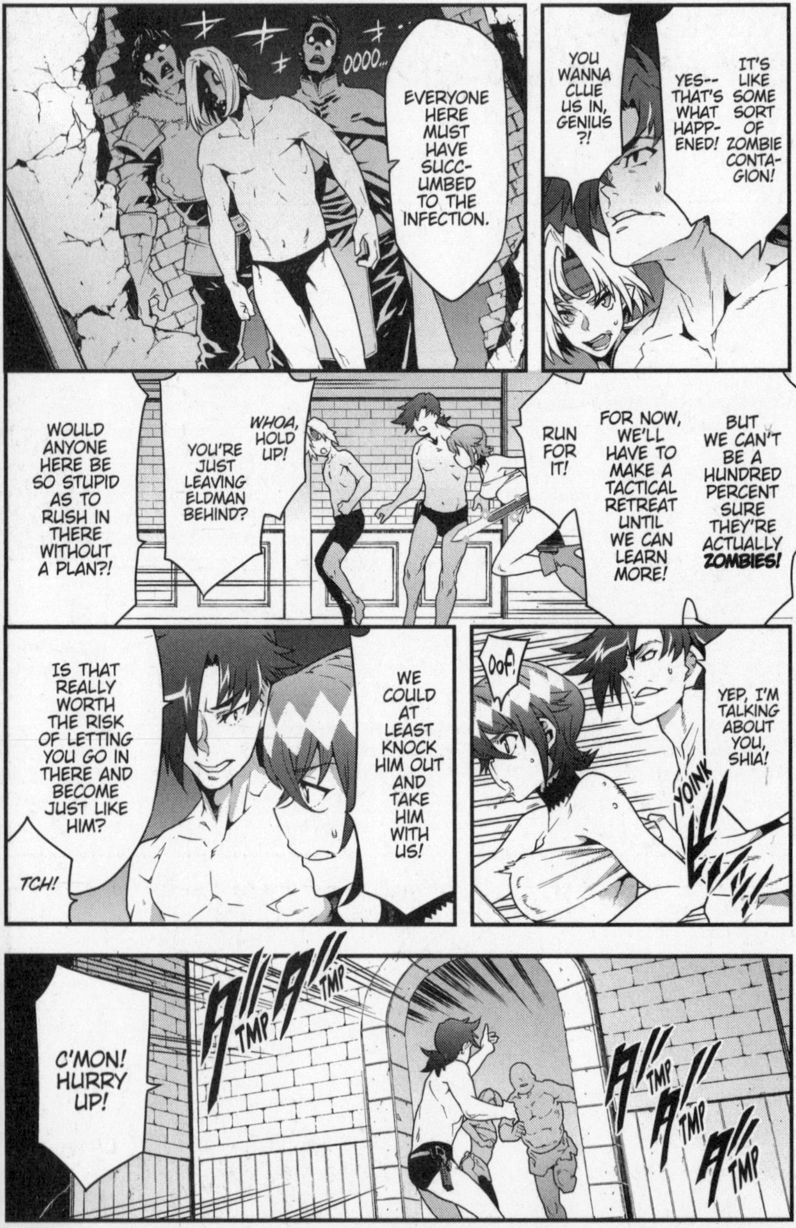
IT'S LIKE SOME SORT OF ZOMBIE CONTAGION!
YES-- THAT'S WHAT HAPP-ENED!
YOU WANNA CLUE US IN, GENIUS?!
OOOO...
EVERYONE HERE MUST HAVE SUCC-UMBED TO THE INFECTION.
BUT WE CAN'T BE A HUNDRED PERCENT SURE THEY'RE ACTUALLY **ZOMBIES!**
FOR NOW, WE'LL HAVE TO MAKE A TACTICAL RETREAT UNTIL WE CAN LEARN MORE!
RUN FOR IT!
WHOA, HOLD UP!
YOU'RE JUST LEAVING ELDMAN BEHIND?
WOULD ANYONE HERE BE SO STUPID AS TO RUSH IN THERE WITHOUT A PLAN?!
YEP, I'M TALKING ABOUT YOU, SHIA!
Oof!
YOINK
WE COULD AT LEAST KNOCK HIM OUT AND TAKE HIM WITH US!
IS THAT REALLY WORTH THE RISK OF LETTING YOU GO IN THERE AND BECOME JUST LIKE HIM?
TCH!
TMP
TMP
TMP
TMP
TMP
TMP
C'MON! HURRY UP!

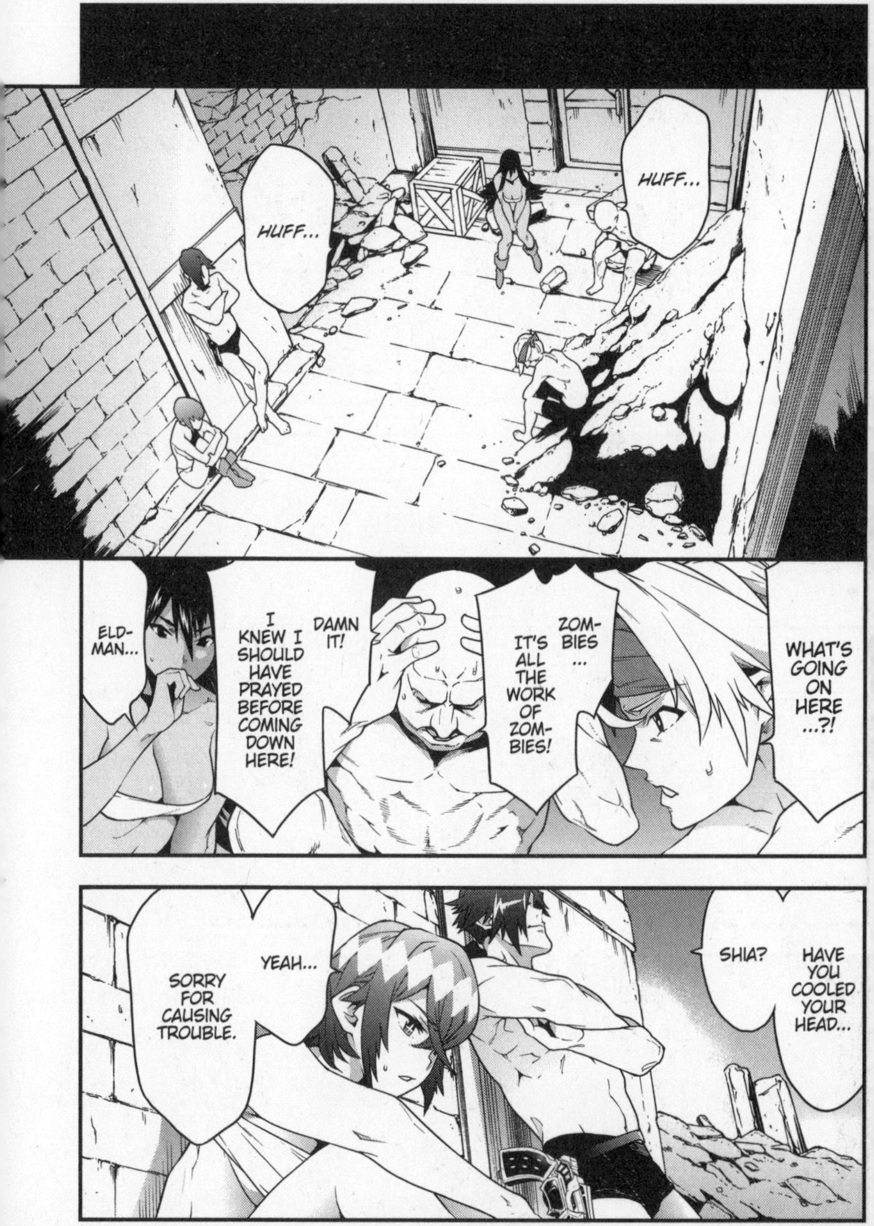
HUFF...
HUFF...
WHAT'S GOING ON HERE ...?!
ZOMBIES ...
IT'S ALL THE WORK OF ZOMBIES!
DAMN IT!
I KNEW I SHOULD HAVE PRAYED BEFORE COMING DOWN HERE!
ELDMAN...
SHIA?
HAVE YOU COOLED YOUR HEAD...
YEAH...
SORRY FOR CAUSING TROUBLE.

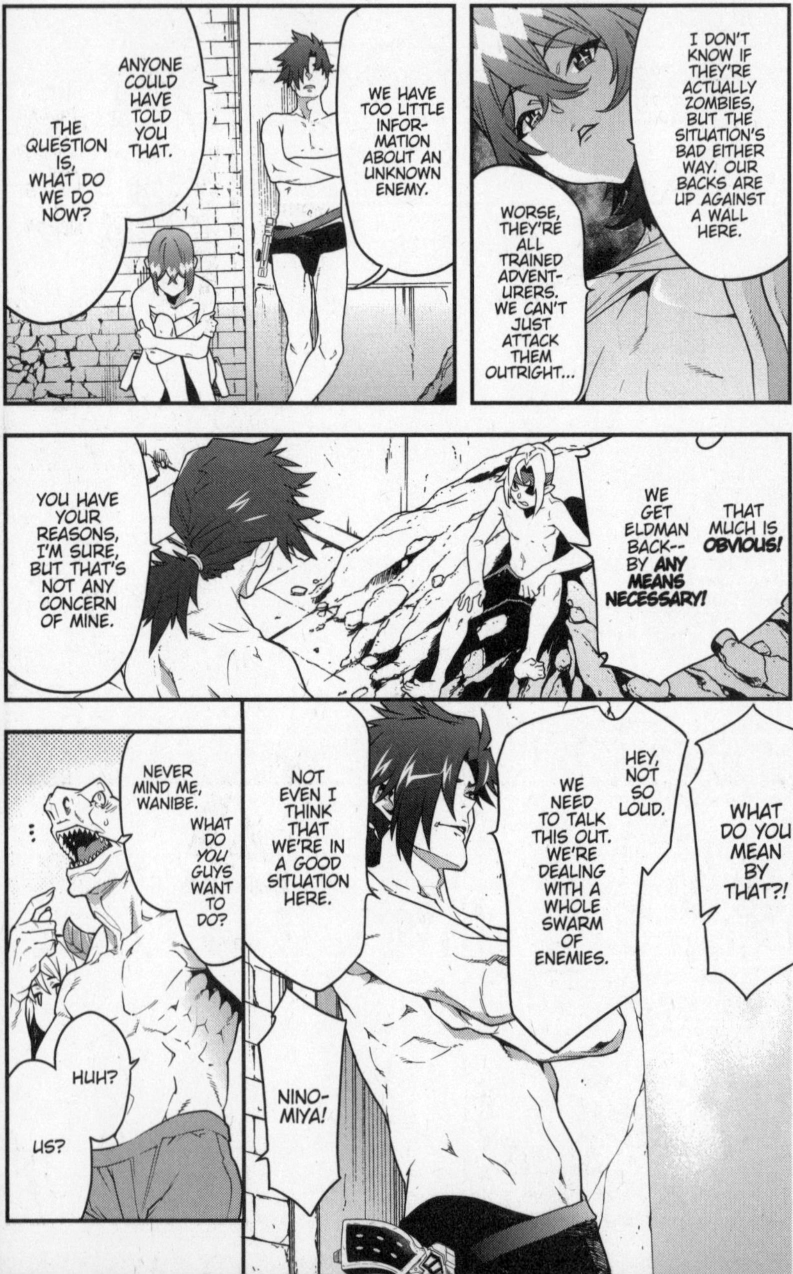
I DON'T KNOW IF THEY'RE ACTUALLY ZOMBIES, BUT THE SITUATION'S BAD EITHER WAY. OUR BACKS ARE UP AGAINST A WALL HERE.
WORSE, THEY'RE ALL TRAINED ADVENTURERS. WE CAN'T JUST ATTACK THEM OUTRIGHT...
WE HAVE TOO LITTLE INFORMATION ABOUT AN UNKNOWN ENEMY.
ANYONE COULD HAVE TOLD YOU THAT.
THE QUESTION IS, WHAT DO WE DO NOW?
THAT MUCH IS **OBVIOUS!**
WE GET ELDMAN BACK-- BY **ANY MEANS NECESSARY!**
YOU HAVE YOUR REASONS, I'M SURE, BUT THAT'S NOT ANY CONCERN OF MINE.
WHAT DO YOU MEAN BY THAT?!
HEY, NOT SO LOUD.
WE NEED TO TALK THIS OUT. WE'RE DEALING WITH A WHOLE SWARM OF ENEMIES.
NOT EVEN I THINK THAT WE'RE IN A GOOD SITUATION HERE.
NINOMIYA!
NEVER MIND ME, WANIBE.
WHAT DO *YOU* GUYS WANT TO DO?
...
HUH?
US?

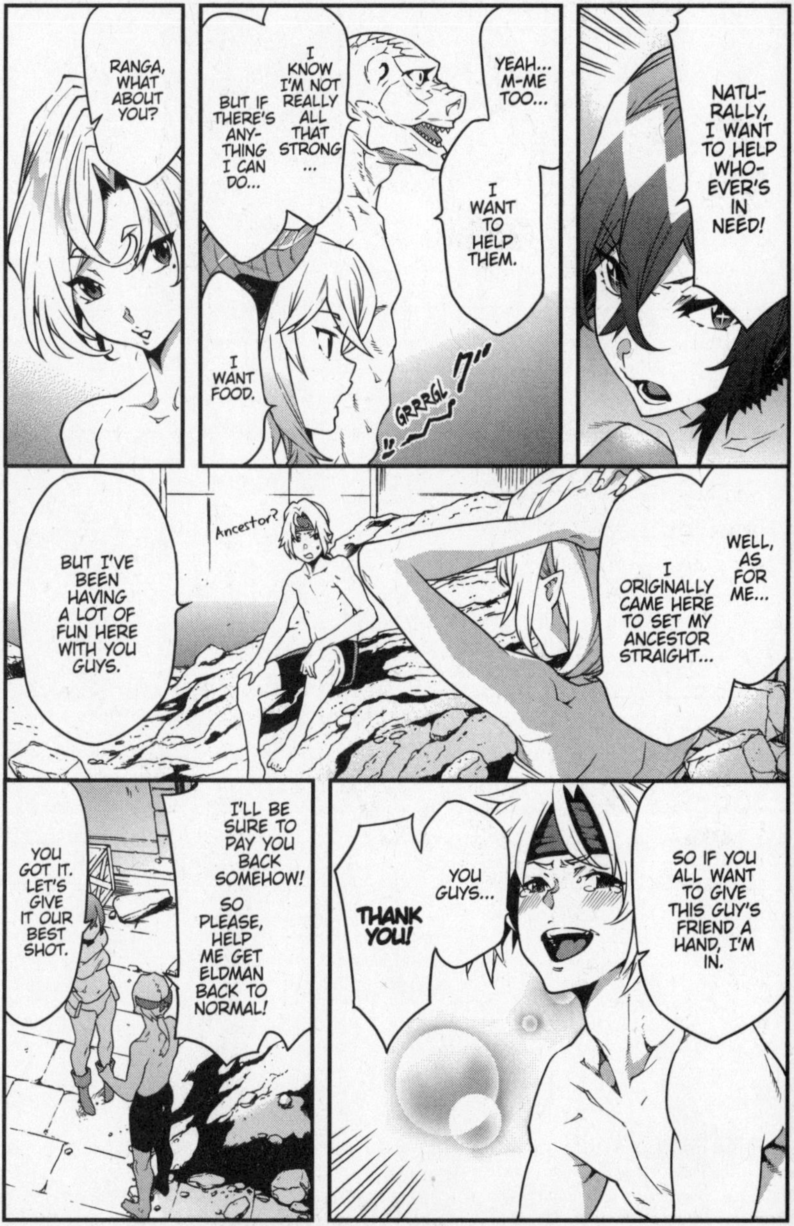
NATURALLY, I WANT TO HELP WHOEVER'S IN NEED!
YEAH... M-ME TOO...
I WANT TO HELP THEM.
I KNOW I'M NOT REALLY ALL THAT STRONG...
BUT IF THERE'S ANYTHING I CAN DO...
I WANT FOOD.
GRRRGL
!!
RANGA, WHAT ABOUT YOU?
WELL, AS FOR ME...
I ORIGINALLY CAME HERE TO SET MY ANCESTOR STRAIGHT...
Ancestor?
BUT I'VE BEEN HAVING A LOT OF FUN HERE WITH YOU GUYS.
SO IF YOU ALL WANT TO GIVE THIS GUY'S FRIEND A HAND, I'M IN.
YOU GUYS...
THANK YOU!
I'LL BE SURE TO PAY YOU BACK SOMEHOW!
SO PLEASE, HELP ME GET ELDMAN BACK TO NORMAL!
YOU GOT IT. LET'S GIVE IT OUR BEST SHOT.

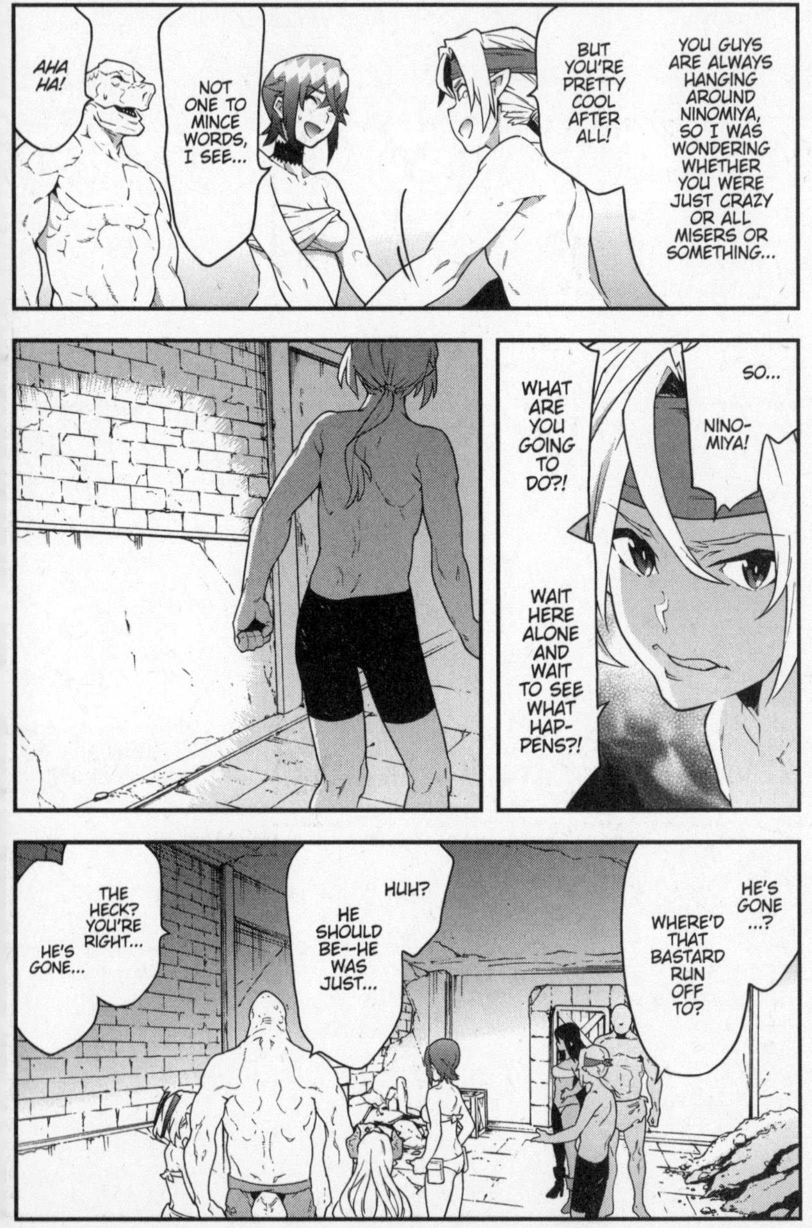
YOU GUYS ARE ALWAYS HANGING AROUND NINOMIYA, SO I WAS WONDERING WHETHER YOU WERE JUST CRAZY OR ALL MISERS OR SOMETHING...
BUT YOU'RE PRETTY COOL AFTER ALL!
NOT ONE TO MINCE WORDS, I SEE...
AHA HA!
SO...
NINOMIYA!
WHAT ARE YOU GOING TO DO?!
WAIT HERE ALONE AND WAIT TO SEE WHAT HAPPENS?!
HE'S GONE ...?
WHERE'D THAT BASTARD RUN OFF TO?
HUH?
HE SHOULD BE--HE WAS JUST...
THE HECK? YOU'RE RIGHT...
HE'S GONE...

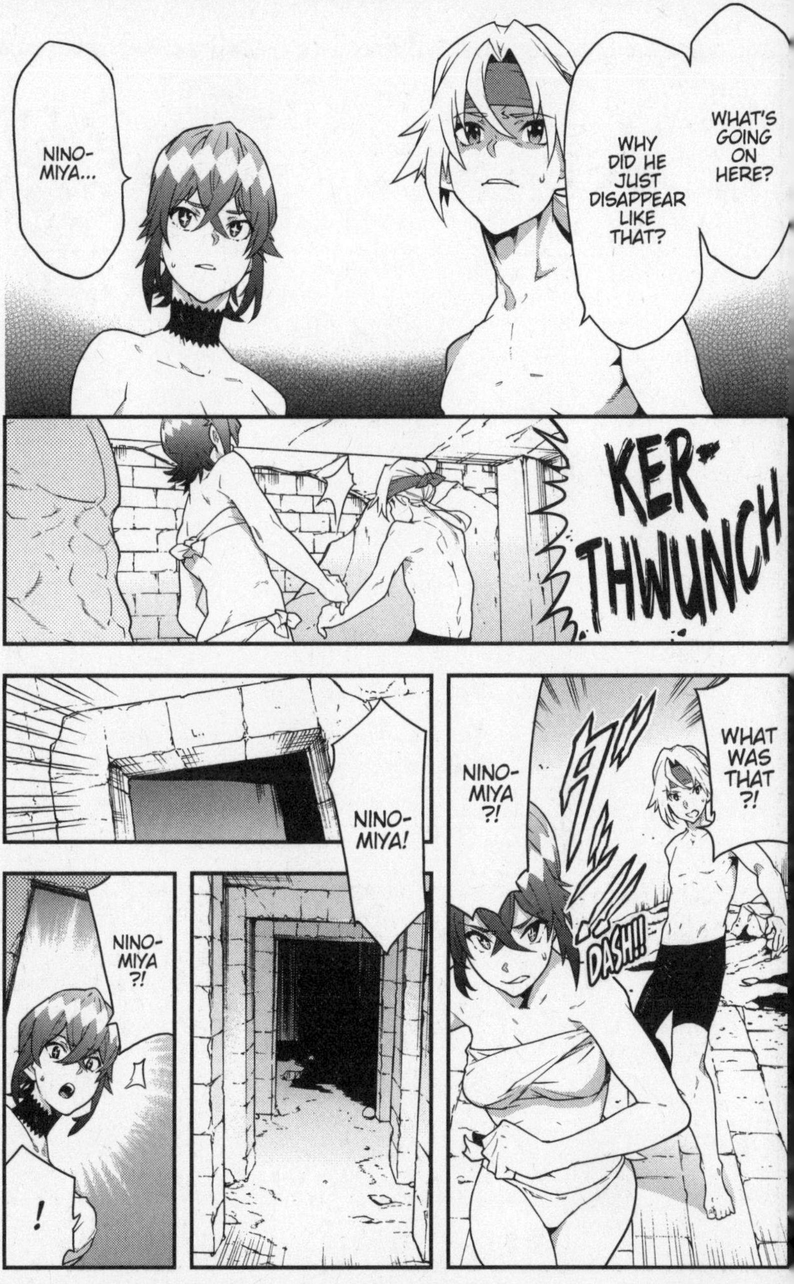
WHAT'S GOING ON HERE?
WHY DID HE JUST DISAPPEAR LIKE THAT?
NINO-MIYA...
KER-THWUNCH
WHAT WAS THAT?!
NINO-MIYA?!
DASH!!
NINO-MIYA!
NINO-MIYA?!
!
!

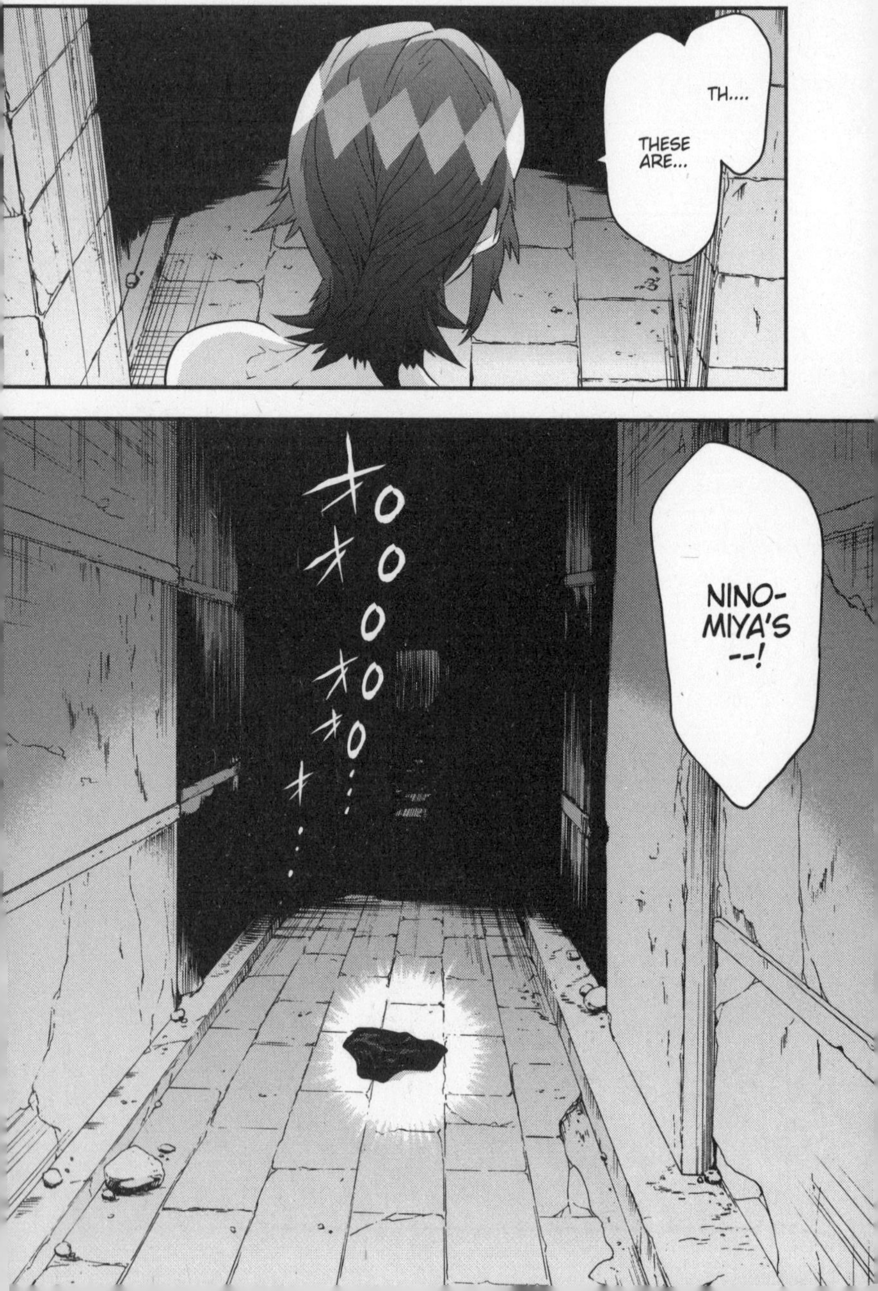
TH....
THESE ARE...
NINO-MIYA'S --!

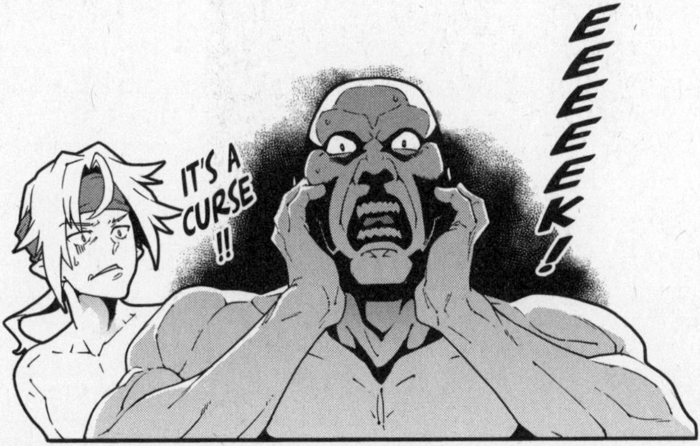
EEEEEEK!
IT'S A CURSE!!

THE DUNGEON OF
BLACK COMPANY

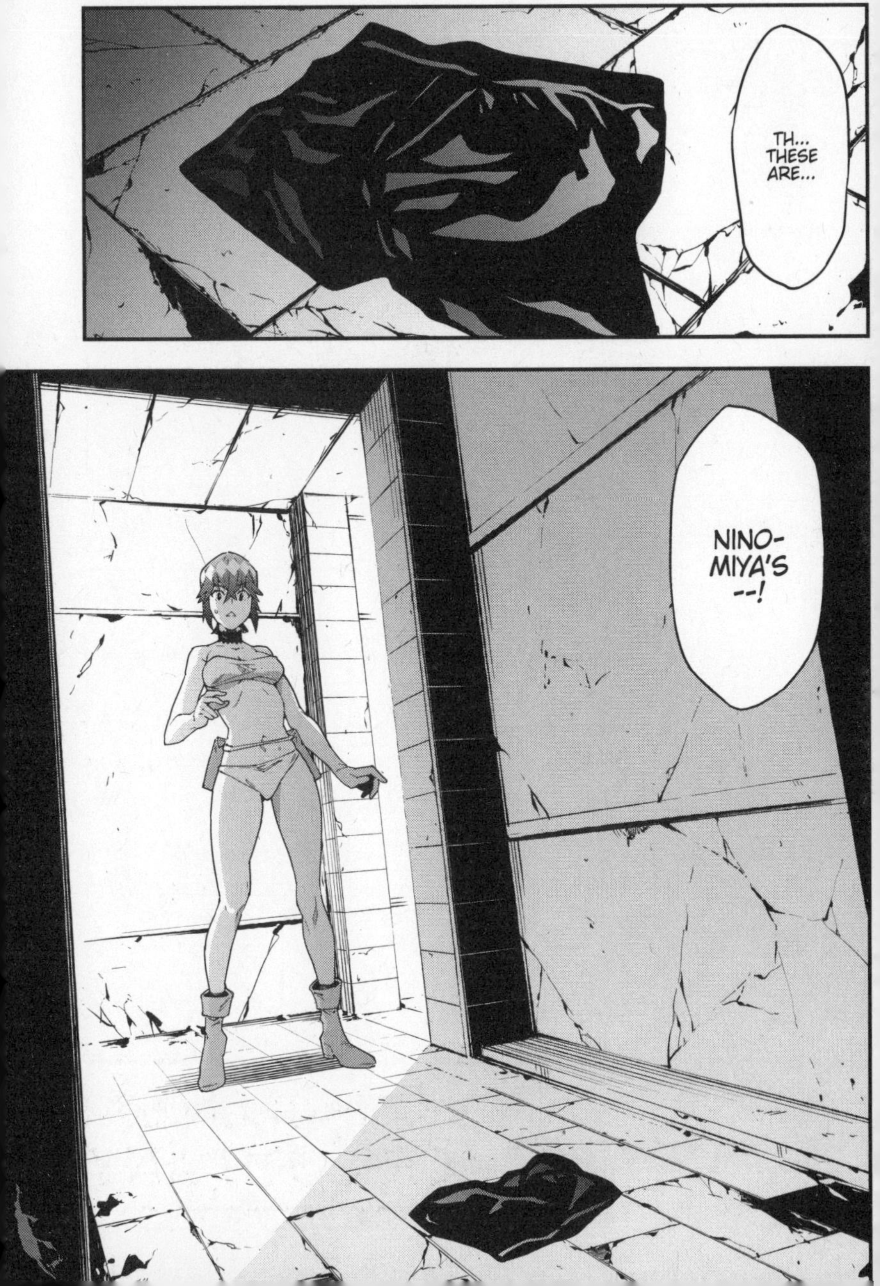
TH... THESE ARE...
NINO-MIYA'S --!

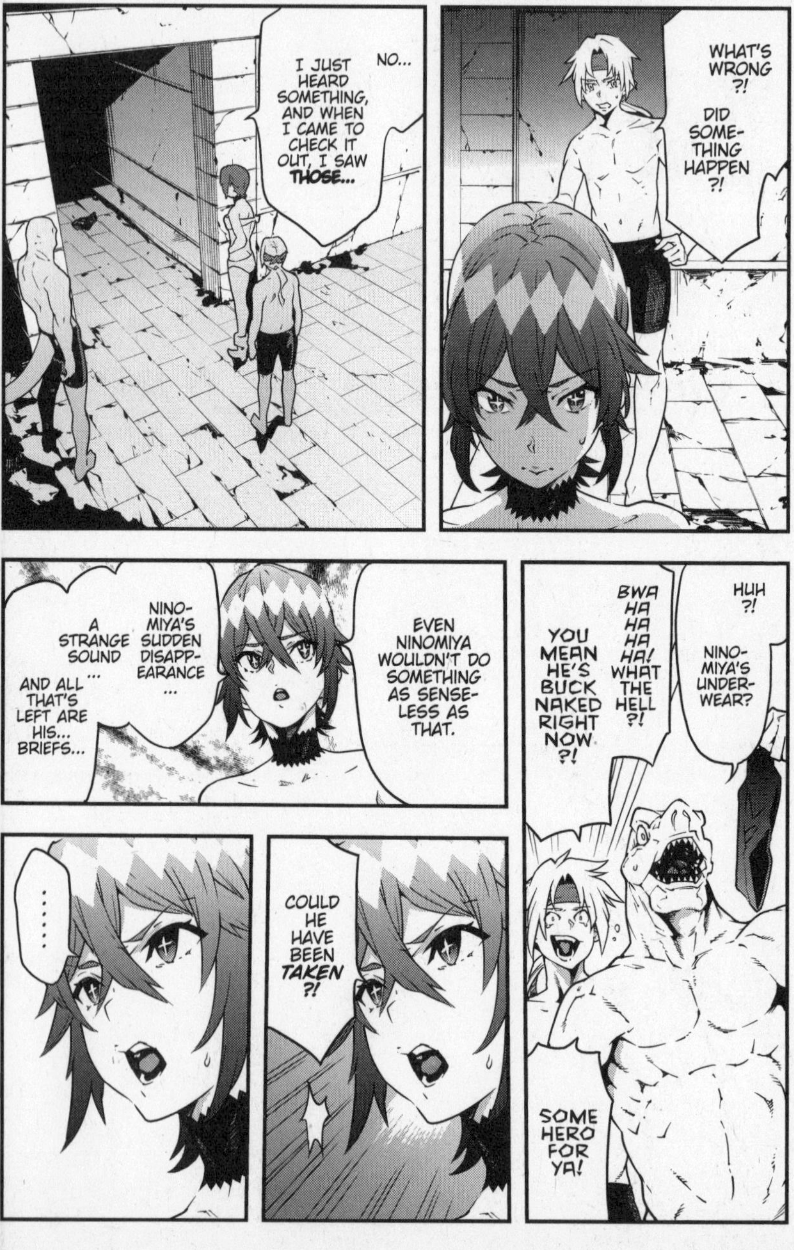
WHAT'S WRONG?!
DID SOMETHING HAPPEN?!
NO...
I JUST HEARD SOMETHING, AND WHEN I CAME TO CHECK IT OUT, I SAW **THOSE...**
HUH?!
NINOMIYA'S UNDERWEAR?
BWA HA HA HA HA! WHAT THE HELL?!
YOU MEAN HE'S BUCK NAKED RIGHT NOW?!
SOME HERO FOR YA!
EVEN NINOMIYA WOULDN'T DO SOMETHING AS SENSELESS AS THAT.
NINOMIYA'S SUDDEN DISAPPEARANCE...
A STRANGE SOUND...
AND ALL THAT'S LEFT ARE HIS... BRIEFS...
COULD HE HAVE BEEN *TAKEN*?!
......

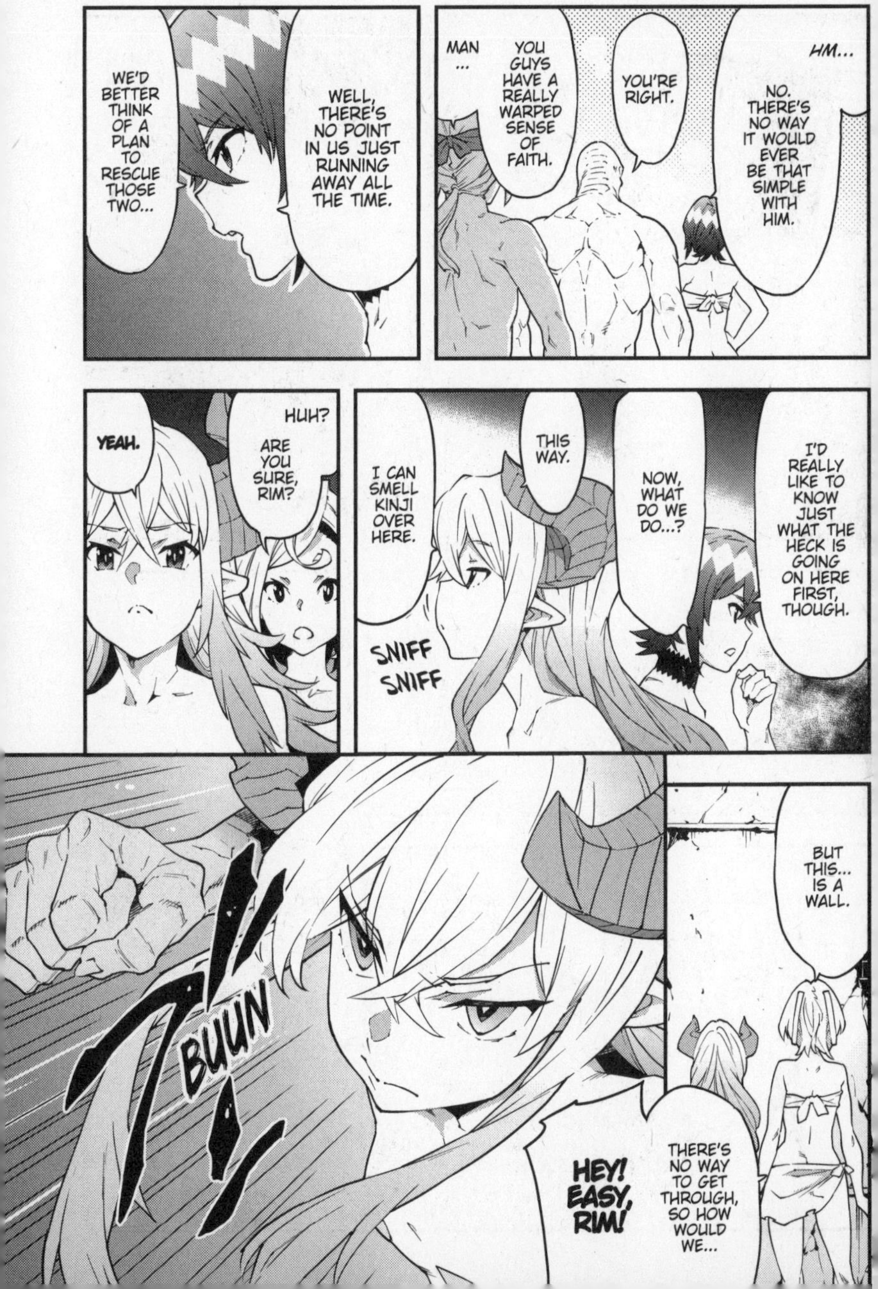
HM...
NO. THERE'S NO WAY IT WOULD EVER BE THAT SIMPLE WITH HIM.
YOU'RE RIGHT.
YOU GUYS HAVE A REALLY WARPED SENSE OF FAITH.
MAN ...
WELL, THERE'S NO POINT IN US JUST RUNNING AWAY ALL THE TIME.
WE'D BETTER THINK OF A PLAN TO RESCUE THOSE TWO...
I'D REALLY LIKE TO KNOW JUST WHAT THE HECK IS GOING ON HERE FIRST, THOUGH.
NOW, WHAT DO WE DO...?
THIS WAY.
I CAN SMELL KINJI OVER HERE.
SNIFF SNIFF
HUH? ARE YOU SURE, RIM?
YEAH.
BUT THIS... IS A WALL.
THERE'S NO WAY TO GET THROUGH, SO HOW WOULD WE...
HEY! EASY, RIM!
BUUN

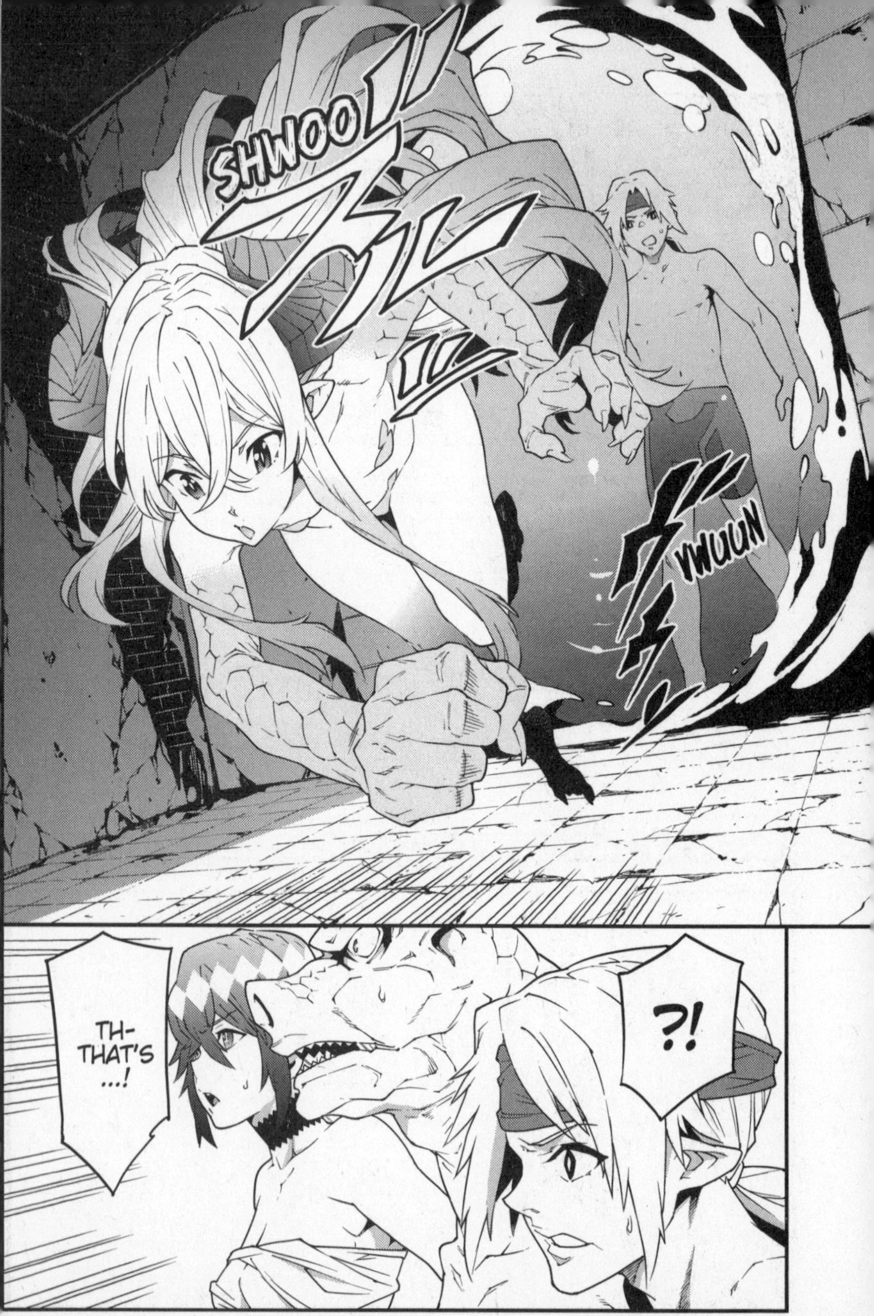
SHWOO
VWUUN
?!
TH-THAT'S ...!

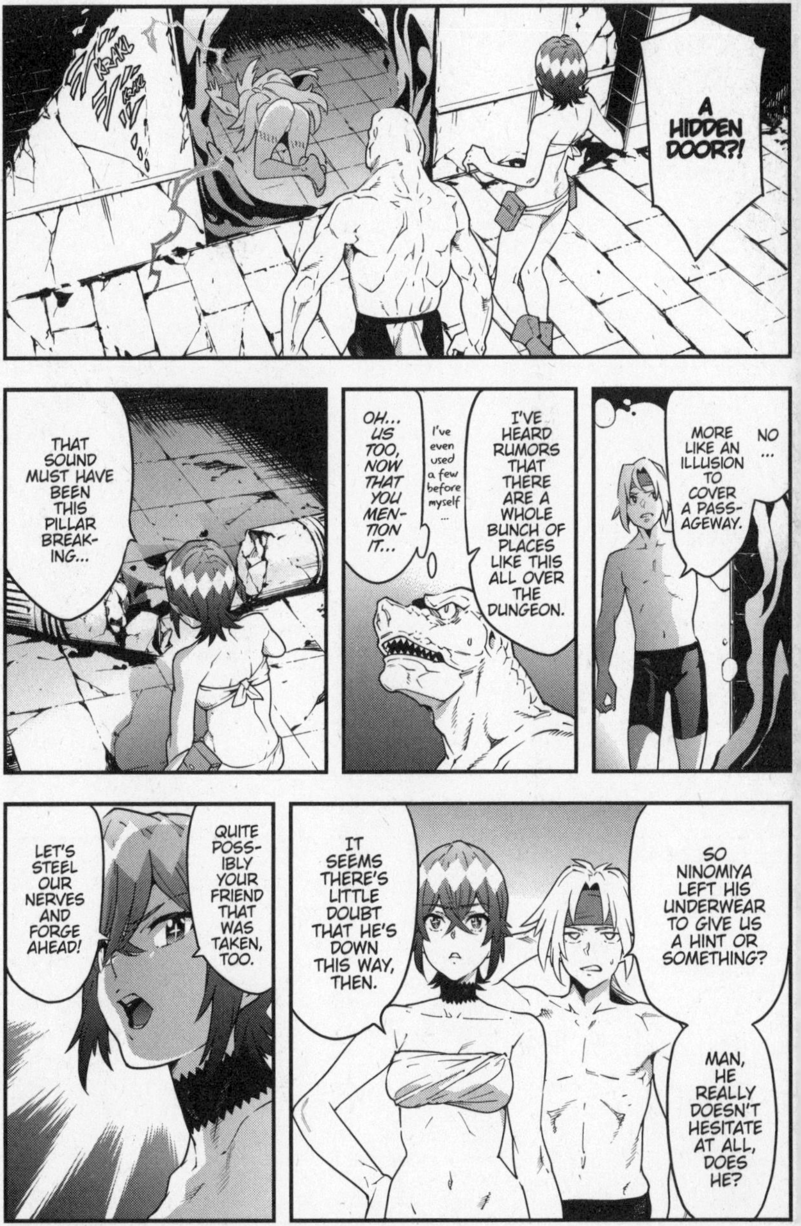
A HIDDEN DOOR?!
KRAKL
KRAKL
NO...
MORE LIKE AN ILLUSION TO COVER A PASSAGEWAY.
I'VE HEARD RUMORS THAT THERE ARE A WHOLE BUNCH OF PLACES LIKE THIS ALL OVER THE DUNGEON.
I've even used a few before myself...
OH... US TOO, NOW THAT YOU MENTION IT...
THAT SOUND MUST HAVE BEEN THIS PILLAR BREAKING...
SO NINOMIYA LEFT HIS UNDERWEAR TO GIVE US A HINT OR SOMETHING?
IT SEEMS THERE'S LITTLE DOUBT THAT HE'S DOWN THIS WAY, THEN.
MAN, HE REALLY DOESN'T HESITATE AT ALL, DOES HE?
QUITE POSSIBLY YOUR FRIEND THAT WAS TAKEN, TOO.
LET'S STEEL OUR NERVES AND FORGE AHEAD!

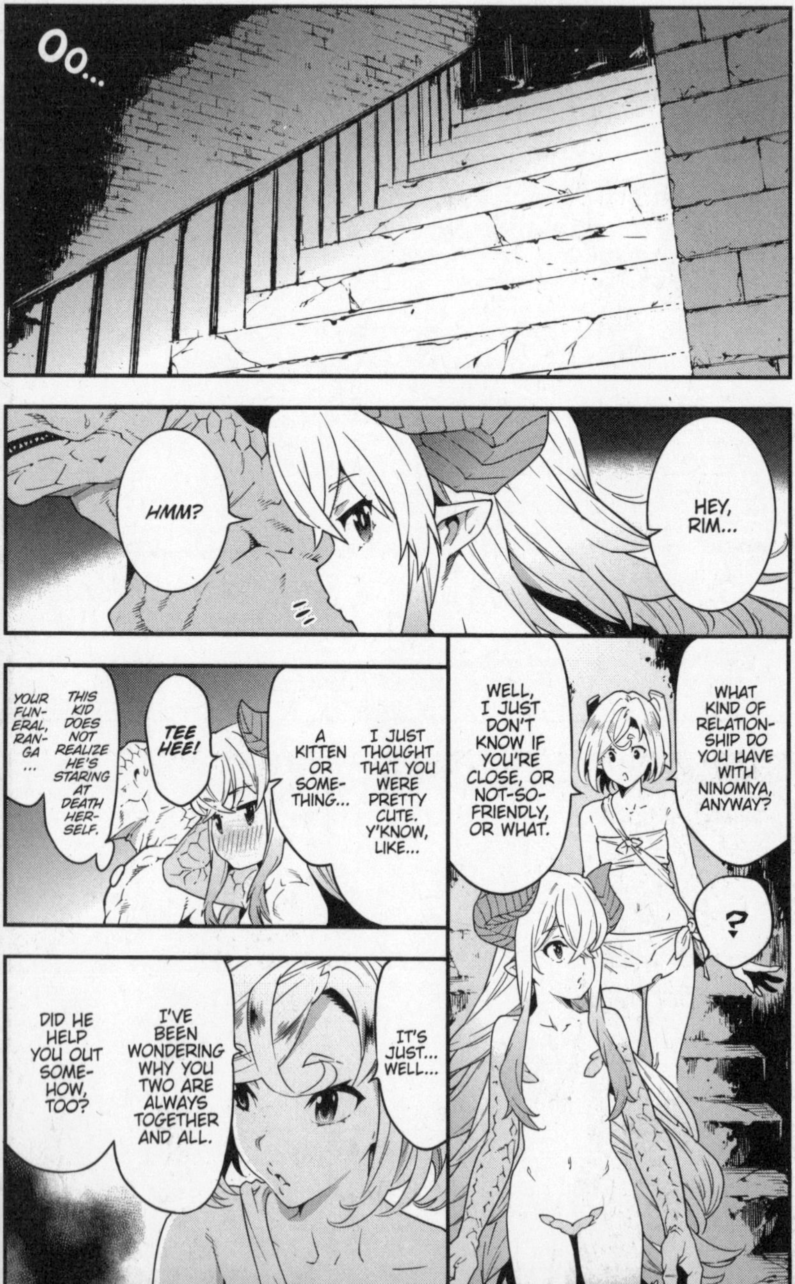
OO...
HEY, RIM...
HMM?
WHAT KIND OF RELATIONSHIP DO YOU HAVE WITH NINOMIYA, ANYWAY?
WELL, I JUST DON'T KNOW IF YOU'RE CLOSE, OR NOT-SO-FRIENDLY, OR WHAT.
?
I JUST THOUGHT THAT YOU WERE PRETTY CUTE. Y'KNOW, LIKE...
A KITTEN OR SOMETHING...
TEE HEE!
THIS KID DOES NOT REALIZE HE'S STARING AT DEATH HERSELF.
YOUR FUNERAL, RANGA...
IT'S JUST... WELL...
I'VE BEEN WONDERING WHY YOU TWO ARE ALWAYS TOGETHER AND ALL.
DID HE HELP YOU OUT SOMEHOW, TOO?

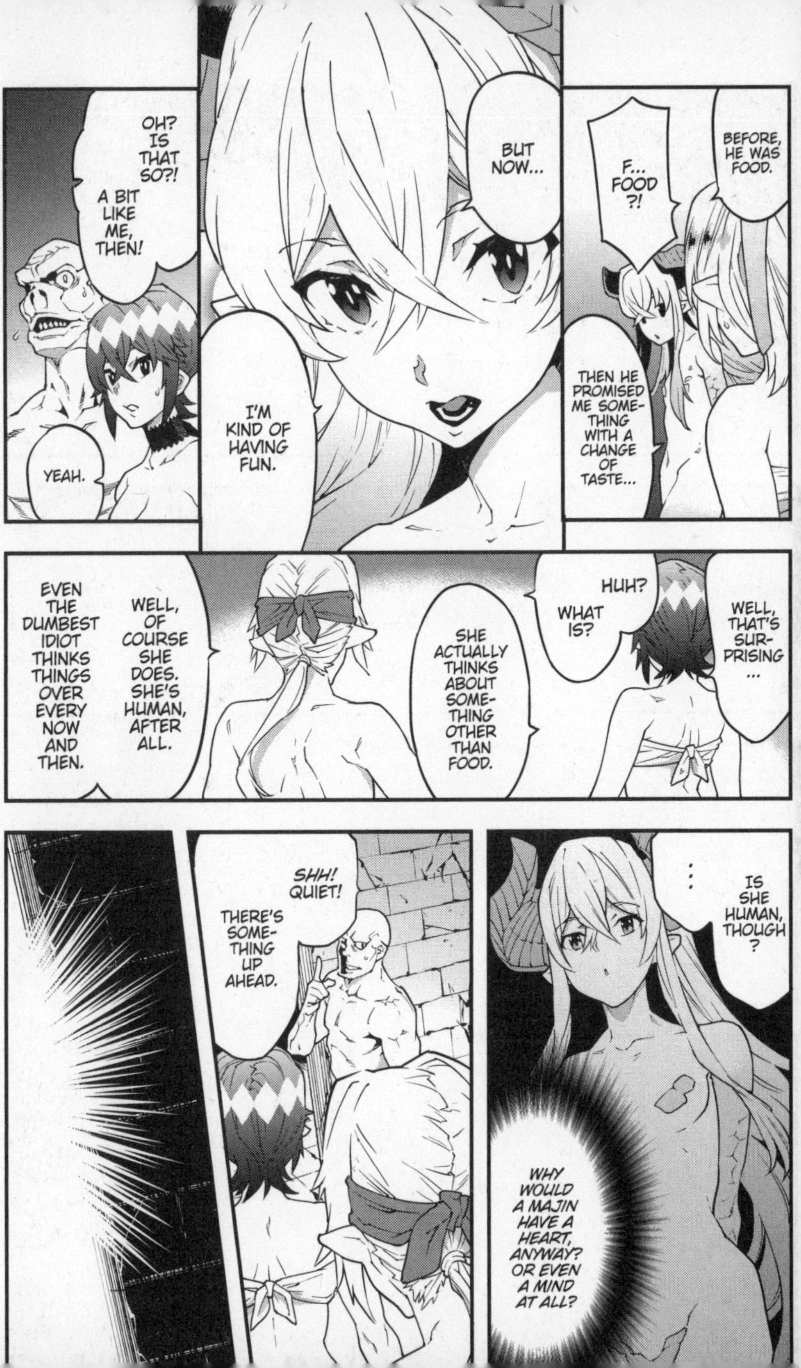
BEFORE, HE WAS FOOD.
F... FOOD?!
THEN HE PROMISED ME SOMETHING WITH A CHANGE OF TASTE...
BUT NOW...
I'M KIND OF HAVING FUN.
OH? IS THAT SO?!
A BIT LIKE ME, THEN!
YEAH.
WELL, THAT'S SURPRISING...
HUH?
WHAT IS?
SHE ACTUALLY THINKS ABOUT SOMETHING OTHER THAN FOOD.
WELL, OF COURSE SHE DOES. SHE'S HUMAN, AFTER ALL.
EVEN THE DUMBEST IDIOT THINKS THINGS OVER EVERY NOW AND THEN.
IS SHE HUMAN, THOUGH?
...
WHY WOULD A MAJIN HAVE A HEART, ANYWAY? OR EVEN A MIND AT ALL?
SHH! QUIET!
THERE'S SOMETHING UP AHEAD.

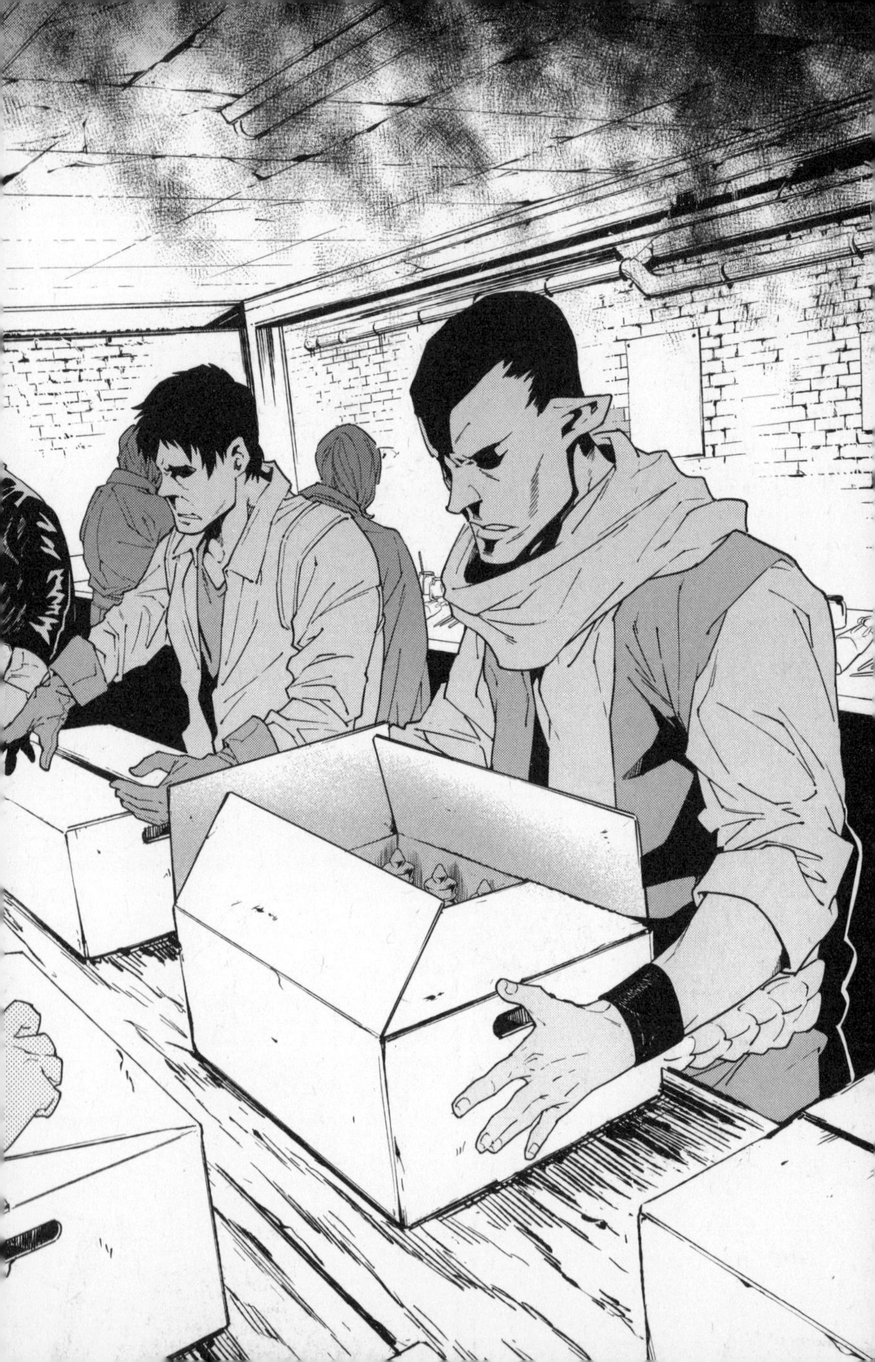

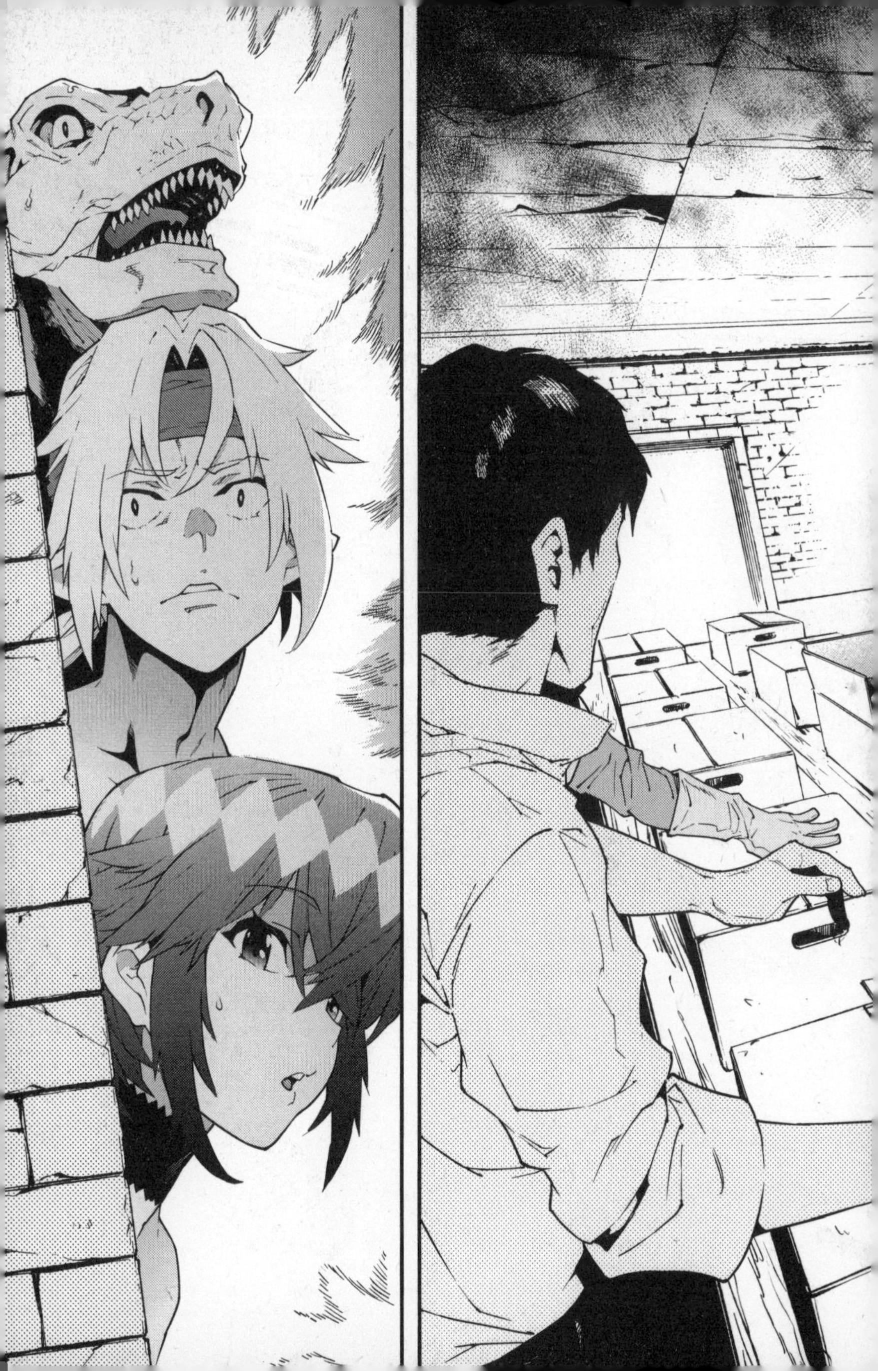

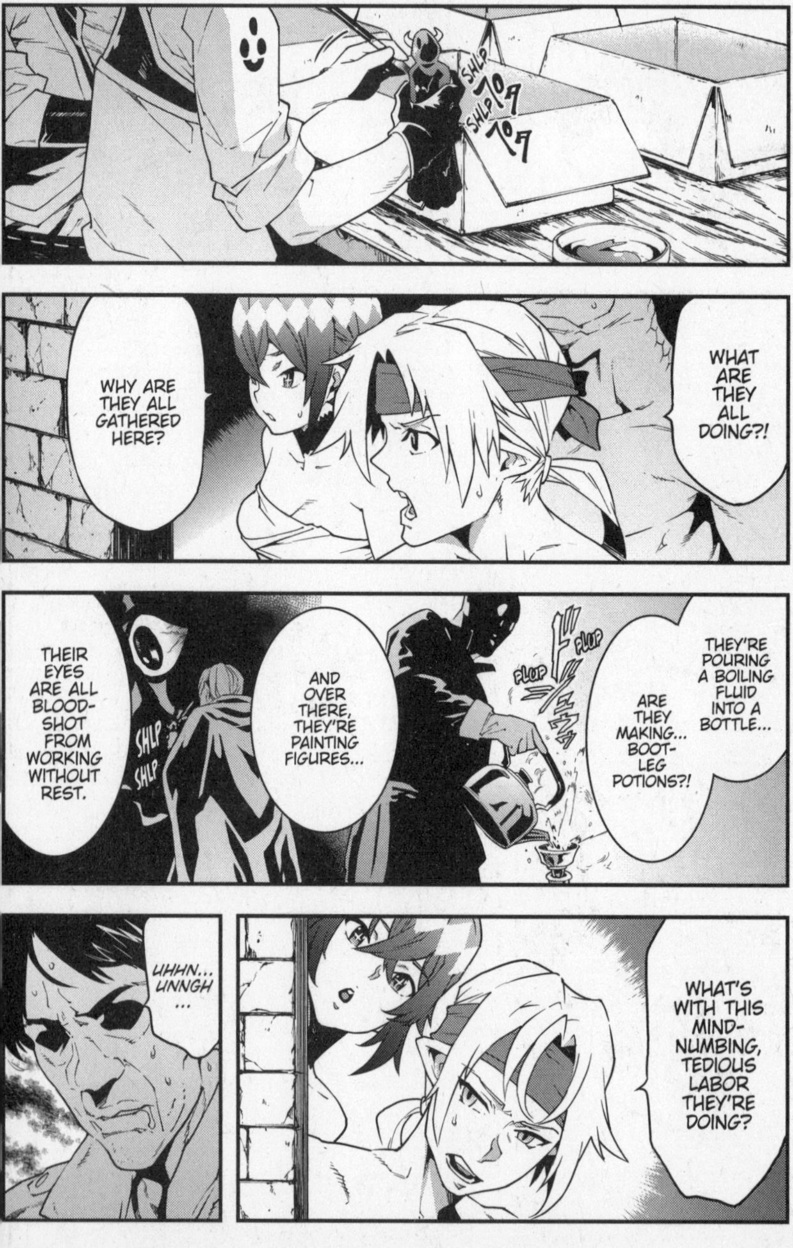
SHLP
SHLP
WHAT ARE THEY ALL DOING?!
WHY ARE THEY ALL GATHERED HERE?
THEY'RE POURING A BOILING FLUID INTO A BOTTLE...
ARE THEY MAKING... BOOT-LEG POTIONS?!
PLUP
PLUP
AND OVER THERE, THEY'RE PAINTING FIGURES...
SHLP
SHLP
THEIR EYES ARE ALL BLOOD-SHOT FROM WORKING WITHOUT REST.
WHAT'S WITH THIS MIND-NUMBING, TEDIOUS LABOR THEY'RE DOING?
UHHN... UNNGH...

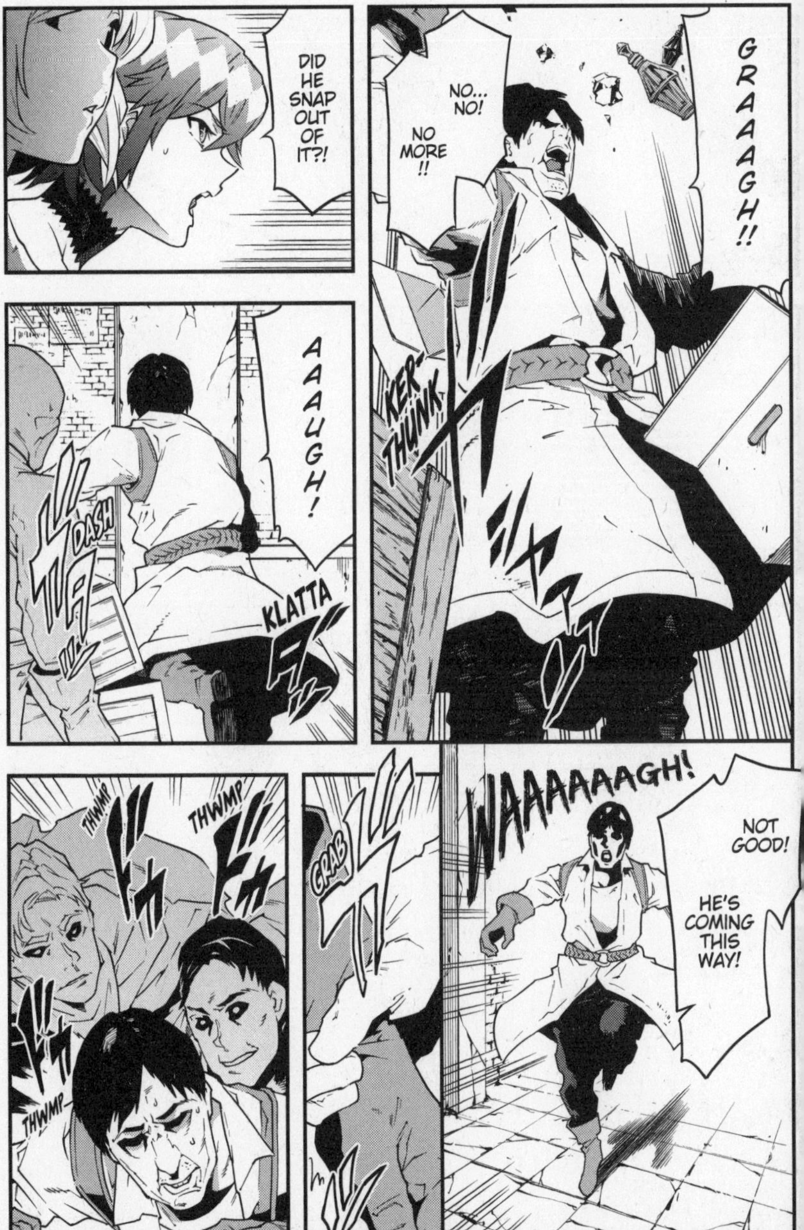
GRAAAAGH!!
NO... NO!
NO MORE!!
KER-THUNK
DID HE SNAP OUT OF IT?!
AAAAUGH!
DASH
KLATTA
WAAAAAAGH!
NOT GOOD!
HE'S COMING THIS WAY!
GRAB
THWMP
THWMP
THWMP

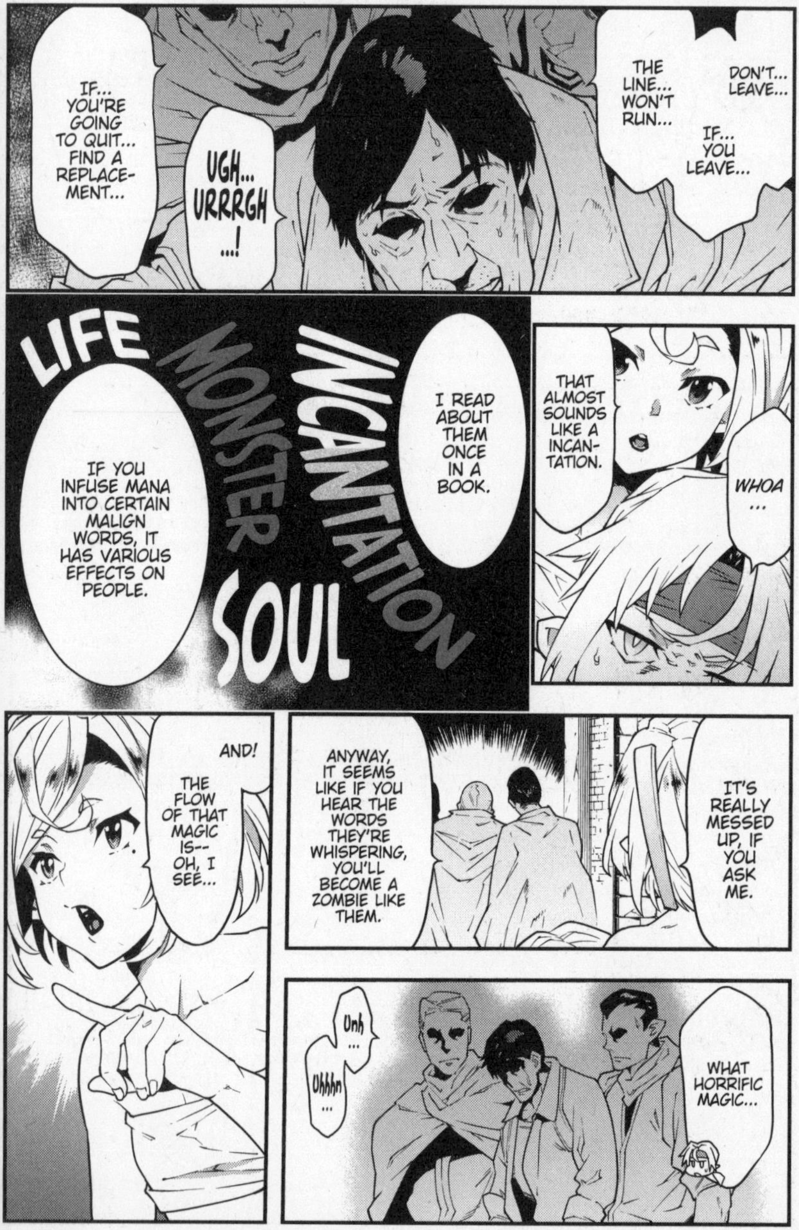
DON'T... LEAVE...
THE LINE... WON'T RUN...
IF... YOU LEAVE...
UGH... URRRGH ...!
IF... YOU'RE GOING TO QUIT... FIND A REPLACE-MENT...
WHOA ...
THAT ALMOST SOUNDS LIKE A INCAN-TATION.
I READ ABOUT THEM ONCE IN A BOOK.
INCANTATION
MONSTER
LIFE
SOUL
IF YOU INFUSE MANA INTO CERTAIN MALIGN WORDS, IT HAS VARIOUS EFFECTS ON PEOPLE.
IT'S REALLY MESSED UP, IF YOU ASK ME.
ANYWAY, IT SEEMS LIKE IF YOU HEAR THE WORDS THEY'RE WHISPERING, YOU'LL BECOME A ZOMBIE LIKE THEM.
WHAT HORRIFIC MAGIC...
Unh ...
Uhhhn ...
AND!
THE FLOW OF THAT MAGIC IS-- OH, I SEE...

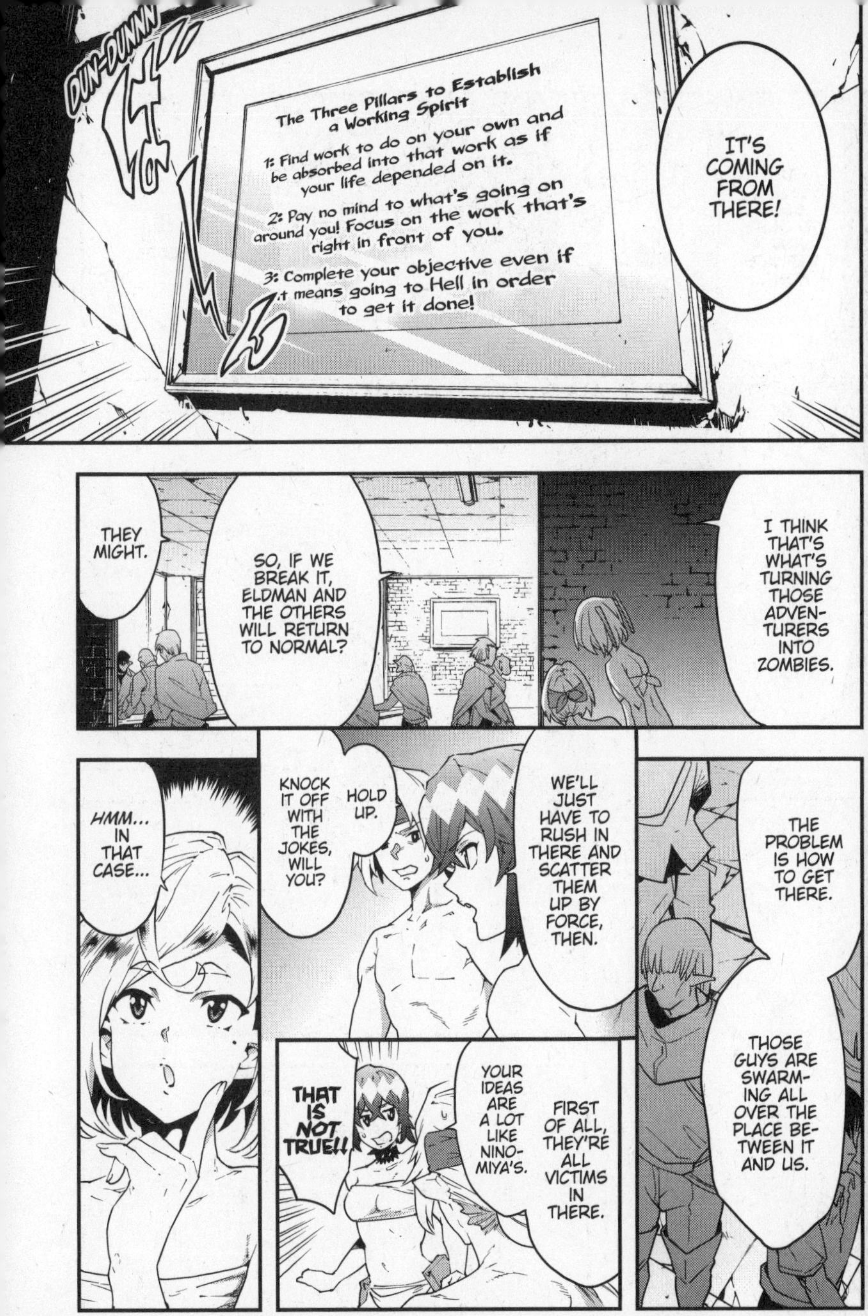
IT'S COMING FROM THERE!
The Three Pillars to Establish a Working Spirit
1: Find work to do on your own and be absorbed into that work as if your life depended on it.
2: Pay no mind to what's going on around you! Focus on the work that's right in front of you.
3: Complete your objective even if it means going to Hell in order to get it done!
DUN-DUNNN
I THINK THAT'S WHAT'S TURNING THOSE ADVEN-TURERS INTO ZOMBIES.
SO, IF WE BREAK IT, ELDMAN AND THE OTHERS WILL RETURN TO NORMAL?
THEY MIGHT.
THE PROBLEM IS HOW TO GET THERE.
THOSE GUYS ARE SWARM-ING ALL OVER THE PLACE BE-TWEEN IT AND US.
WE'LL JUST HAVE TO RUSH IN THERE AND SCATTER THEM UP BY FORCE, THEN.
HOLD UP.
KNOCK IT OFF WITH THE JOKES, WILL YOU?
FIRST OF ALL, THEY'RE ALL VICTIMS IN THERE.
YOUR IDEAS ARE A LOT LIKE NINO-MIYA'S.
THAT IS NOT TRUE!!
HMM... IN THAT CASE...

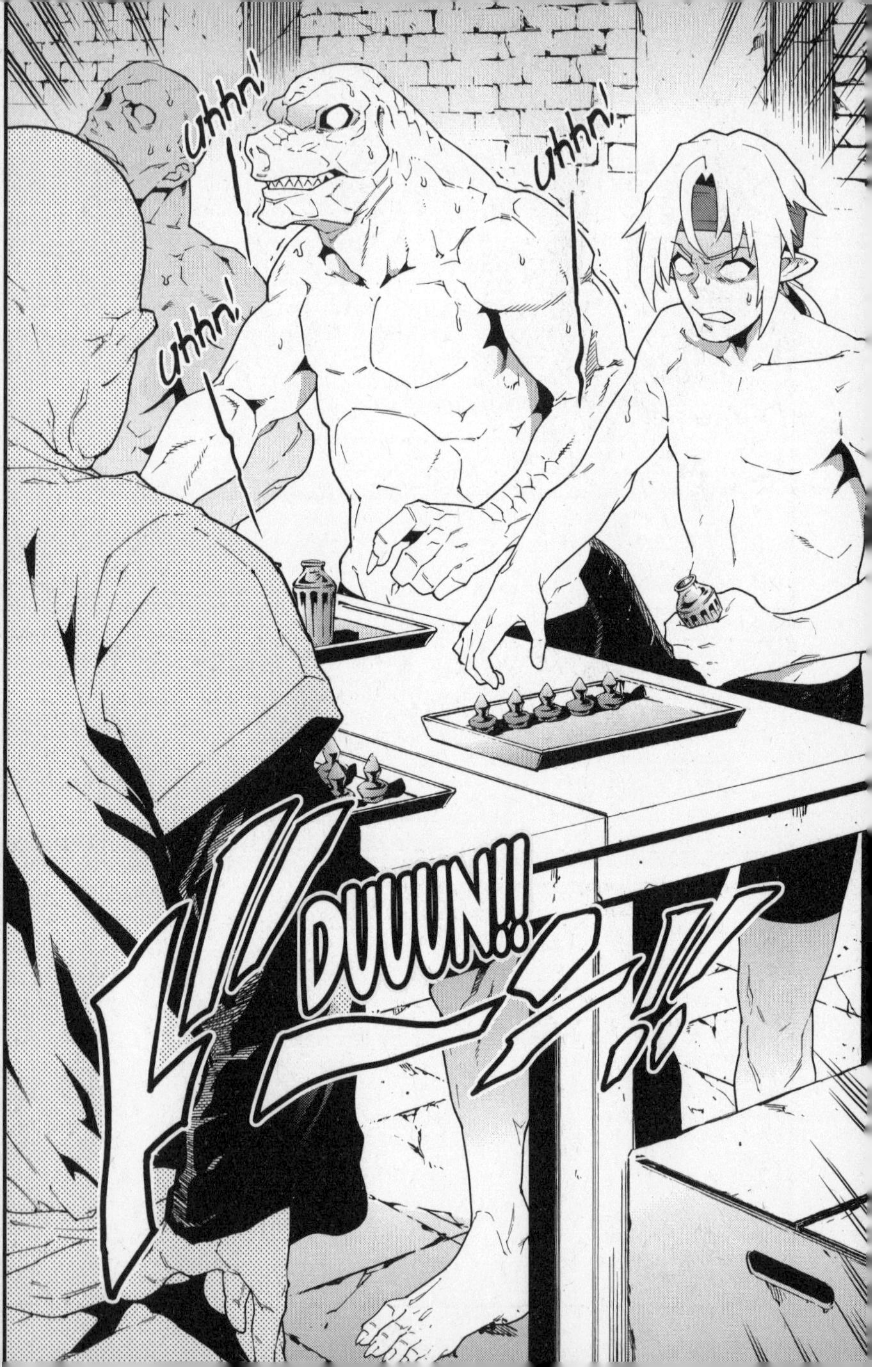
uhhn!
uhhn!
uhhn!
DUUUN!!

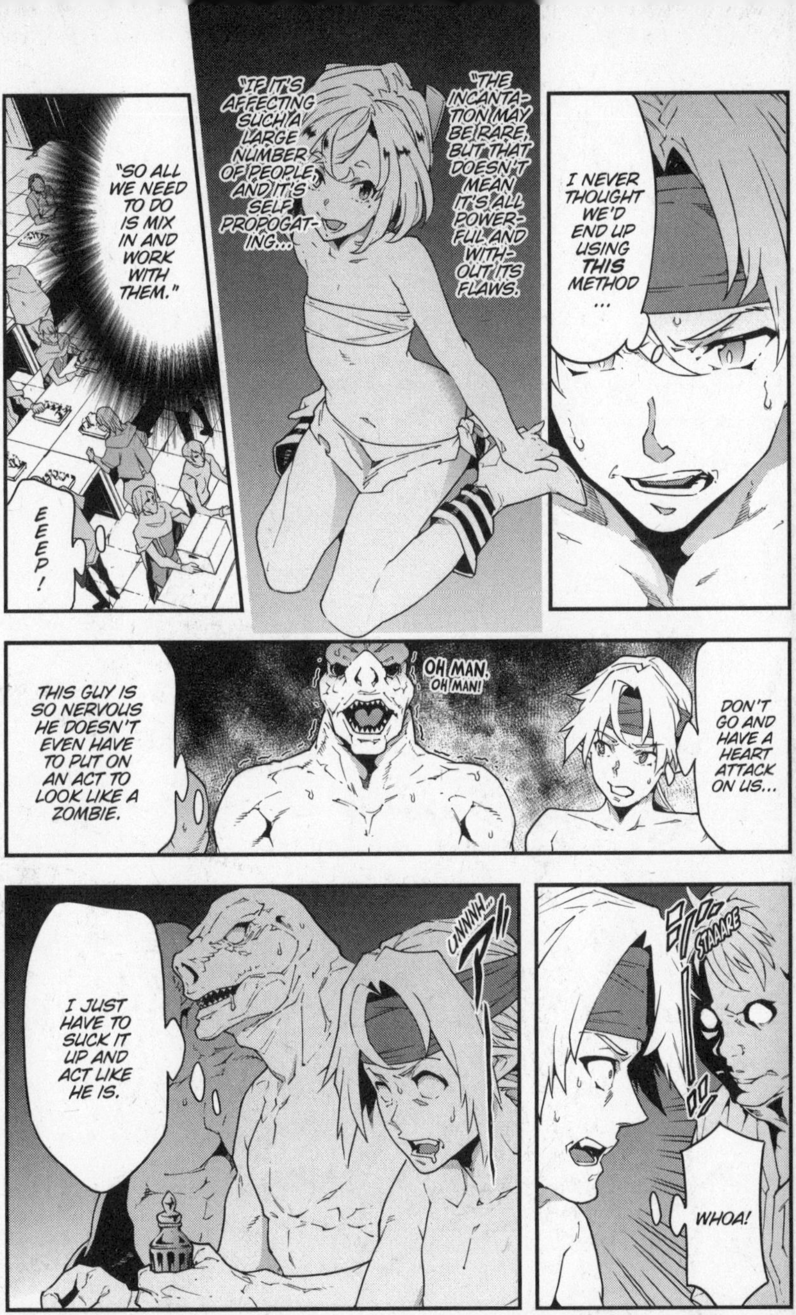
I NEVER THOUGHT WE'D END UP USING THIS METHOD ...
"THE INCANTATION MAY BE RARE, BUT THAT DOESN'T MEAN IT'S ALL POWERFUL AND WITHOUT ITS FLAWS.
"IF IT'S AFFECTING SUCH A LARGE NUMBER OF PEOPLE AND IT'S SELF PROPOGATING...
"SO ALL WE NEED TO DO IS MIX IN AND WORK WITH THEM."
EEEP!
DON'T GO AND HAVE A HEART ATTACK ON US...
OH MAN, OH MAN!
THIS GUY IS SO NERVOUS HE DOESN'T EVEN HAVE TO PUT ON AN ACT TO LOOK LIKE A ZOMBIE.
STAAARE
WHOA!
UNNNH...
I JUST HAVE TO SUCK IT UP AND ACT LIKE HE IS.

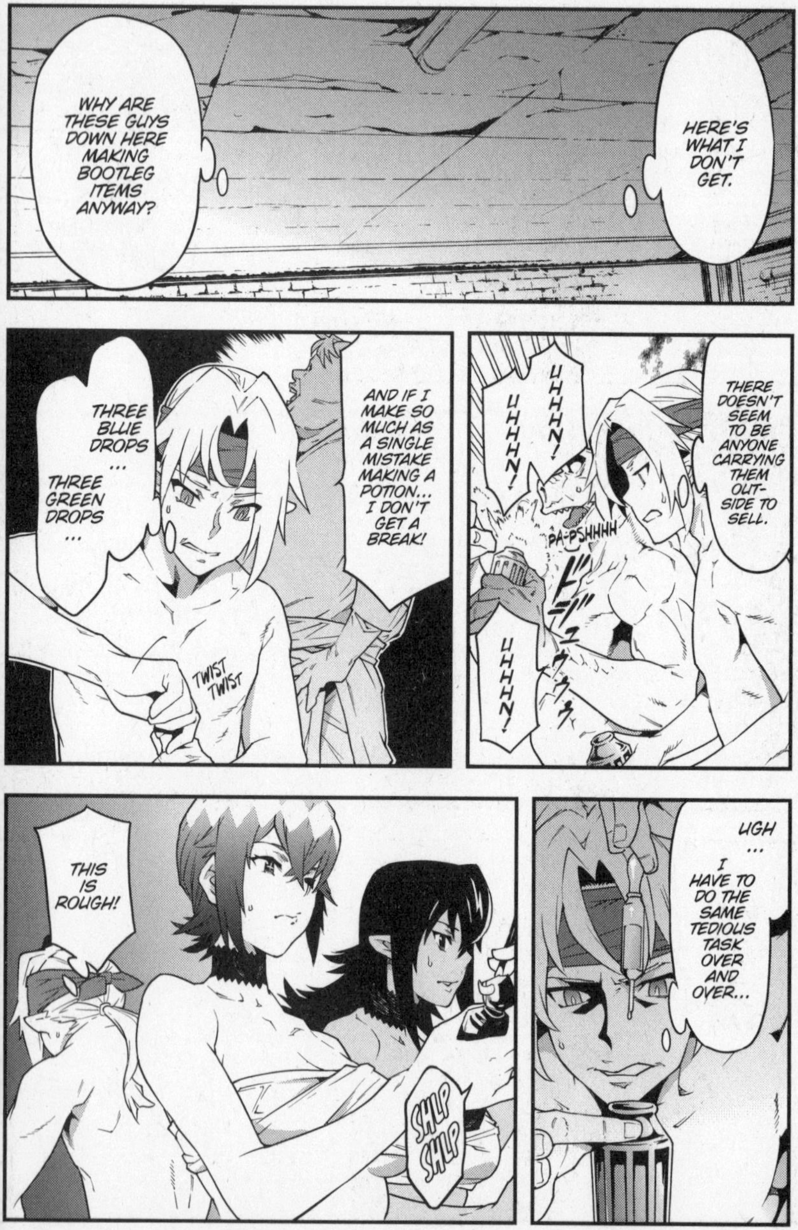
HERE'S WHAT I DON'T GET.
WHY ARE THESE GUYS DOWN HERE MAKING BOOTLEG ITEMS ANYWAY?
THERE DOESN'T SEEM TO BE ANYONE CARRYING THEM OUT-SIDE TO SELL.
UHHHN!
PA-PSHHHH
UHHHN!
UHHHN!
AND IF I MAKE SO MUCH AS A SINGLE MISTAKE MAKING A POTION... I DON'T GET A BREAK!
THREE BLUE DROPS... THREE GREEN DROPS...
TWIST TWIST
UGH... I HAVE TO DO THE SAME TEDIOUS TASK OVER AND OVER...
THIS IS ROUGH!
SHLP SHLP

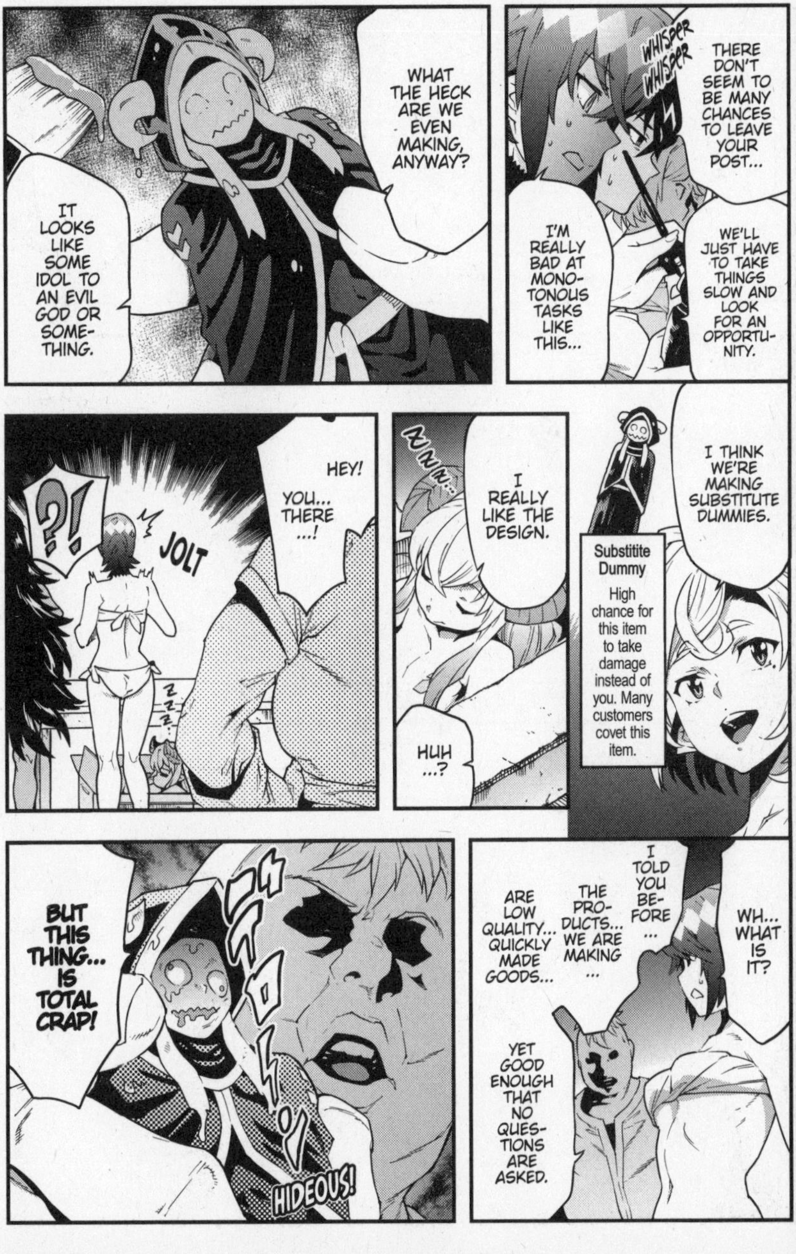
WHISPER WHISPER
THERE DON'T SEEM TO BE MANY CHANCES TO LEAVE YOUR POST...
WE'LL JUST HAVE TO TAKE THINGS SLOW AND LOOK FOR AN OPPORTUNITY.
I'M REALLY BAD AT MONOTONOUS TASKS LIKE THIS...
WHAT THE HECK ARE WE EVEN MAKING, ANYWAY?
IT LOOKS LIKE SOME IDOL TO AN EVIL GOD OR SOMETHING.
I THINK WE'RE MAKING SUBSTITUTE DUMMIES.
Substitite Dummy
High chance for this item to take damage instead of you. Many customers covet this item.
ZZZ...
I REALLY LIKE THE DESIGN.
HUH ...?
HEY!
YOU... THERE ...!
?!
JOLT
ZZZ
WH... WHAT IS IT?
I TOLD YOU BEFORE ...
THE PRODUCTS... WE ARE MAKING ...
ARE LOW QUALITY... QUICKLY MADE GOODS...
YET GOOD ENOUGH THAT NO QUESTIONS ARE ASKED.
BUT THIS THING... IS TOTAL CRAP!
HIDEOUS!

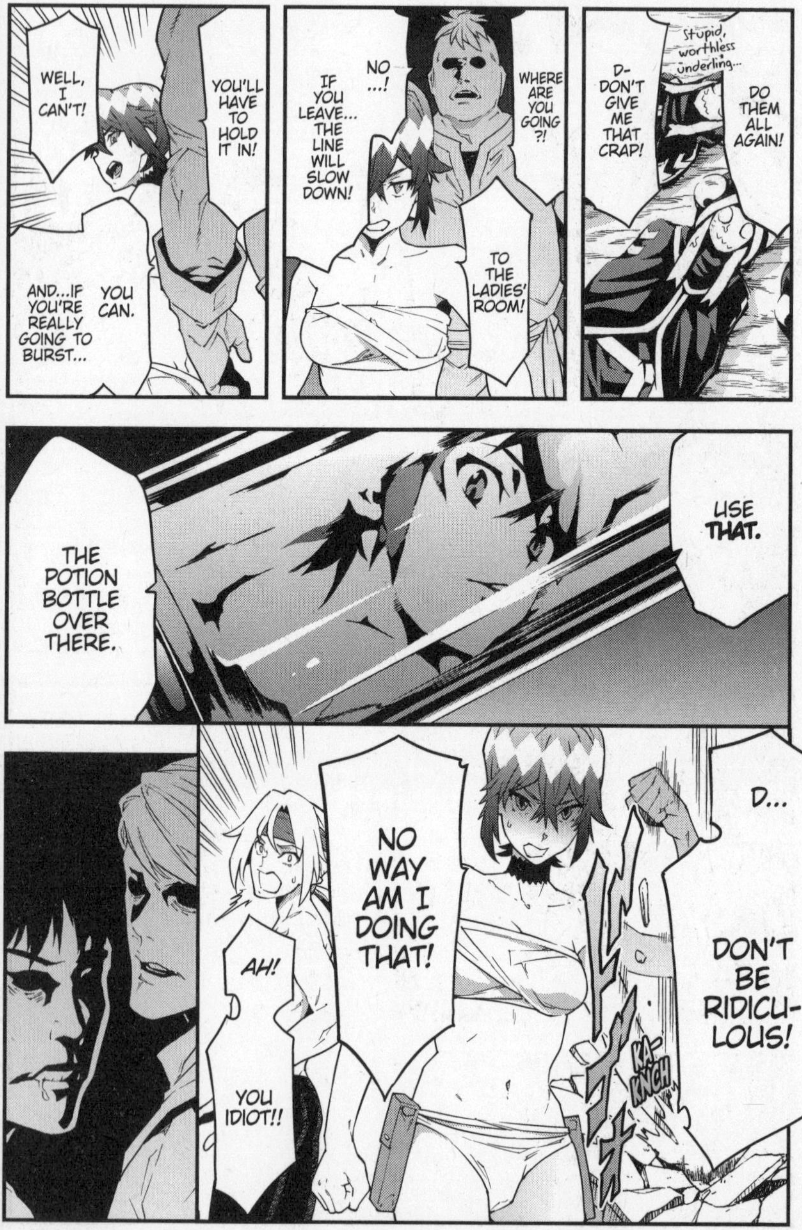
DO THEM ALL AGAIN!
Stupid, worthless underling...
D-DON'T GIVE ME THAT CRAP!
WHERE ARE YOU GOING?!
TO THE LADIES' ROOM!
NO...!
IF YOU LEAVE... THE LINE WILL SLOW DOWN!
YOU'LL HAVE TO HOLD IT IN!
WELL, I CAN'T!
YOU CAN.
AND...IF YOU'RE REALLY GOING TO BURST...
THE POTION BOTTLE OVER THERE.
USE THAT.
D...
DON'T BE RIDICU-LOUS!
KA-KNCH
NO WAY AM I DOING THAT!
AH!
YOU IDIOT!!

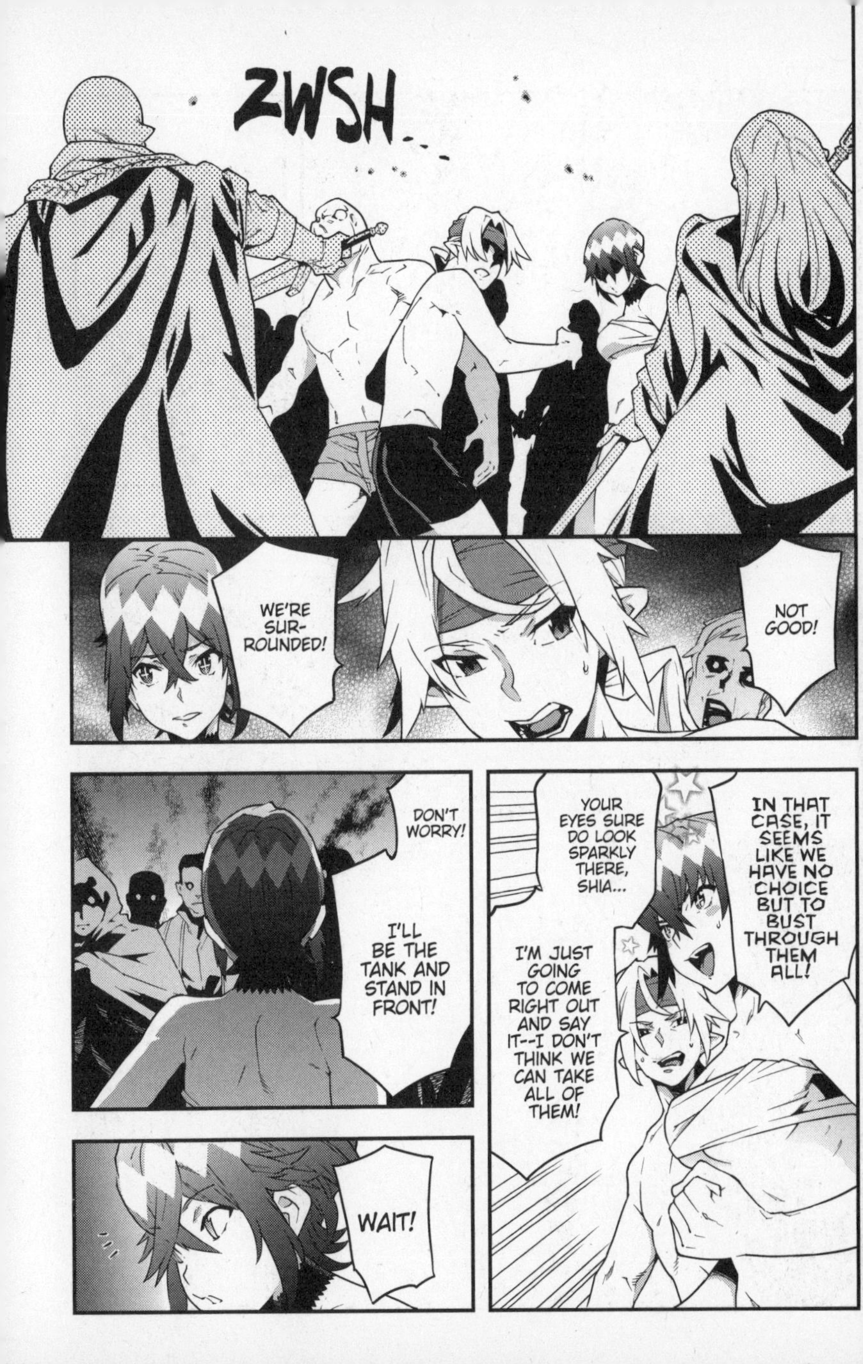
ZWSH
NOT GOOD!
WE'RE SUR-ROUNDED!
IN THAT CASE, IT SEEMS LIKE WE HAVE NO CHOICE BUT TO BUST THROUGH THEM ALL!
YOUR EYES SURE DO LOOK SPARKLY THERE, SHIA...
I'M JUST GOING TO COME RIGHT OUT AND SAY IT--I DON'T THINK WE CAN TAKE ALL OF THEM!
DON'T WORRY!
I'LL BE THE TANK AND STAND IN FRONT!
WAIT!

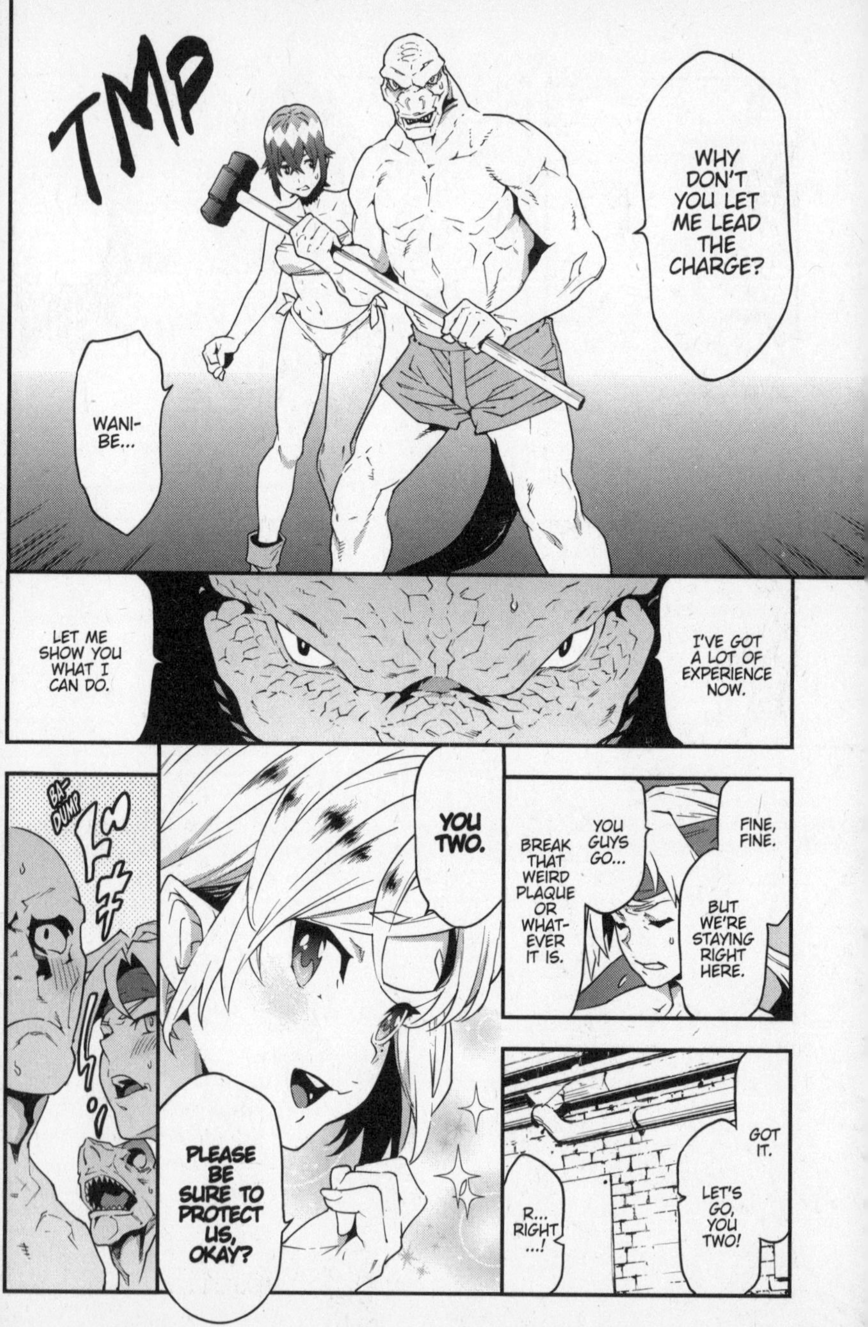
WHY DON'T YOU LET ME LEAD THE CHARGE?
TMP
WANI-BE...
I'VE GOT A LOT OF EXPERIENCE NOW.
LET ME SHOW YOU WHAT I CAN DO.
FINE, FINE.
BUT WE'RE STAYING RIGHT HERE.
YOU GUYS GO...
BREAK THAT WEIRD PLAQUE OR WHATEVER IT IS.
GOT IT.
LET'S GO, YOU TWO!
R... RIGHT ...!
YOU TWO.
PLEASE BE SURE TO PROTECT US, OKAY?
BA-DUMP

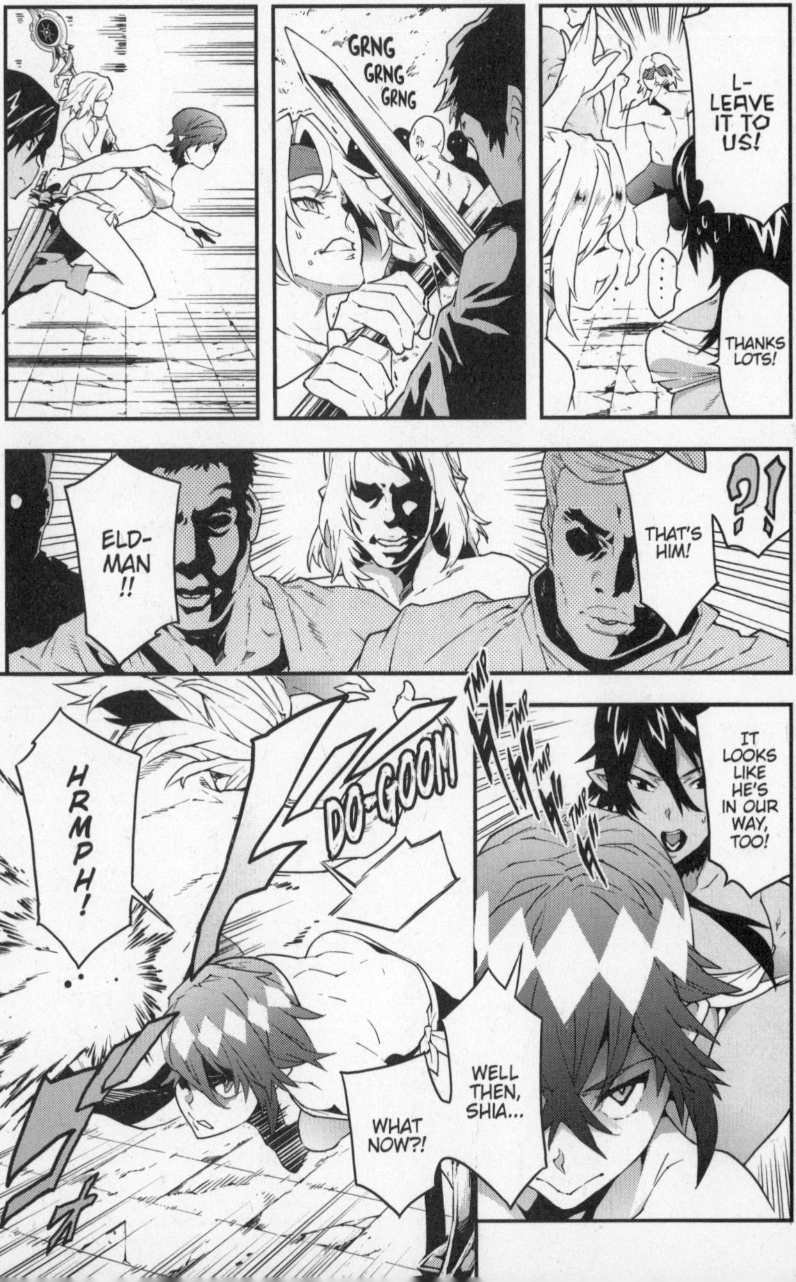
L- LEAVE IT TO US!
......
THANKS LOTS!
GRNG GRNG GRNG
?!
THAT'S HIM!
ELD-MAN!!
IT LOOKS LIKE HE'S IN OUR WAY, TOO!
TMP TMP TMP TMP
WELL THEN, SHIA...
DO-GOOM
HRMPH!
WHAT NOW?!

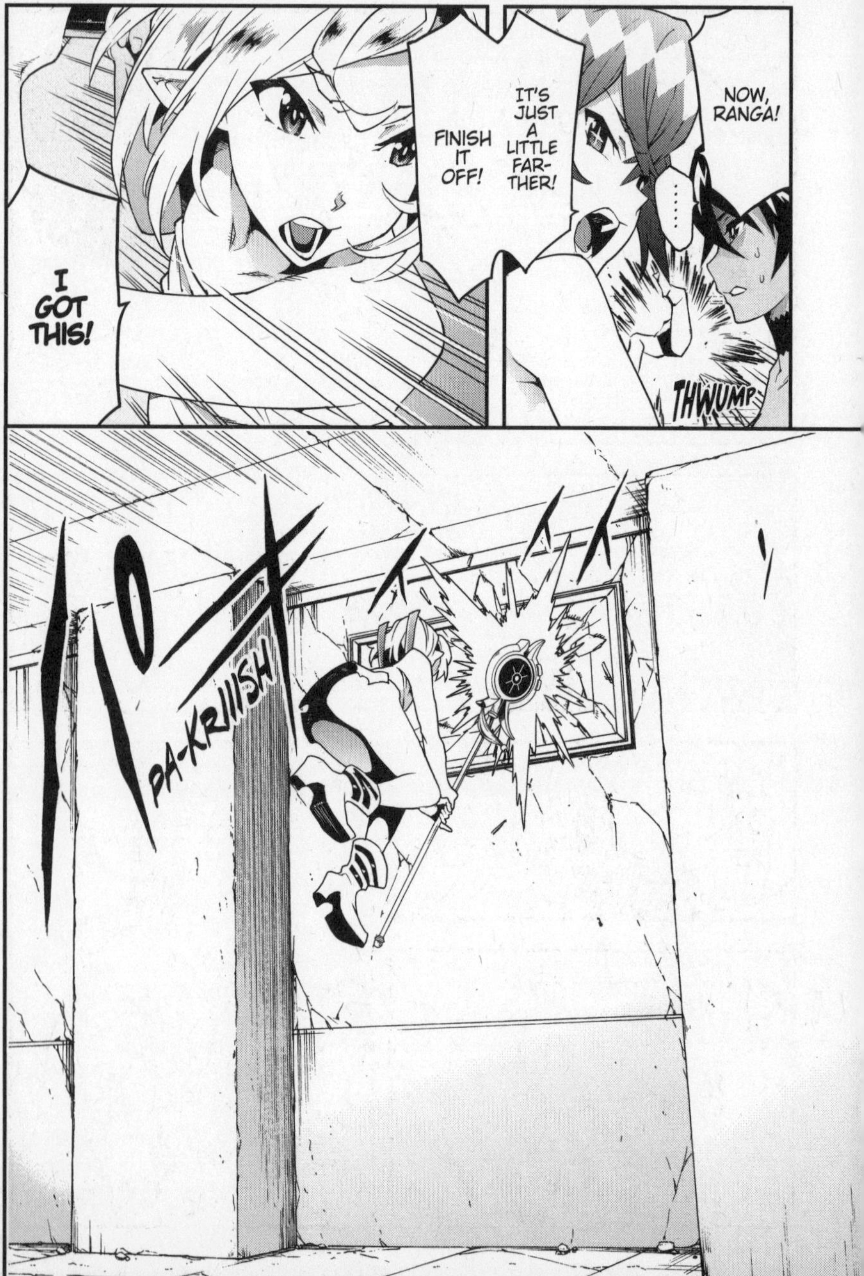
NOW, RANGA!
IT'S JUST A LITTLE FAR-THER!
THWUMP
FINISH IT OFF!
I GOT THIS!
PA-KRIIISH

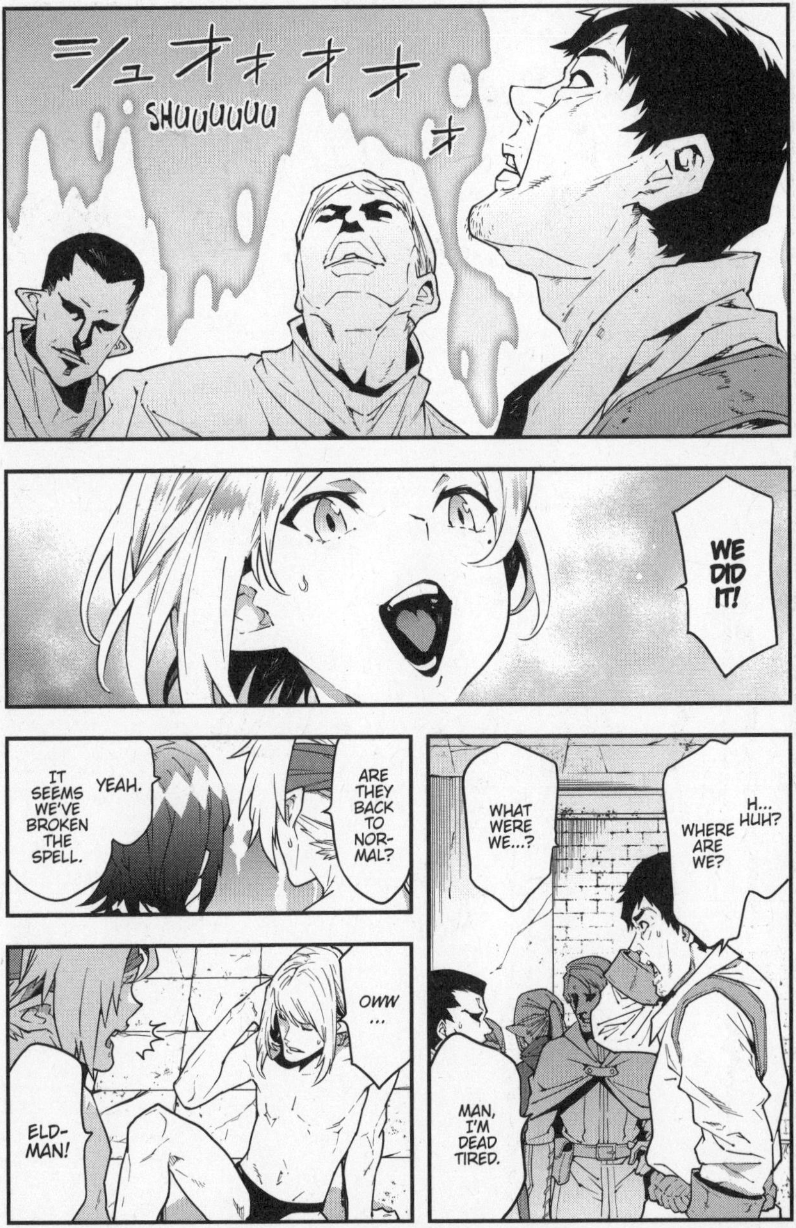
シュオォオオオ
SHUUUUUU
WE DID IT!
H... HUH?
WHERE ARE WE?
WHAT WERE WE...?
MAN, I'M DEAD TIRED.
ARE THEY BACK TO NORMAL?
YEAH.
IT SEEMS WE'VE BROKEN THE SPELL.
OWW...
ELDMAN!

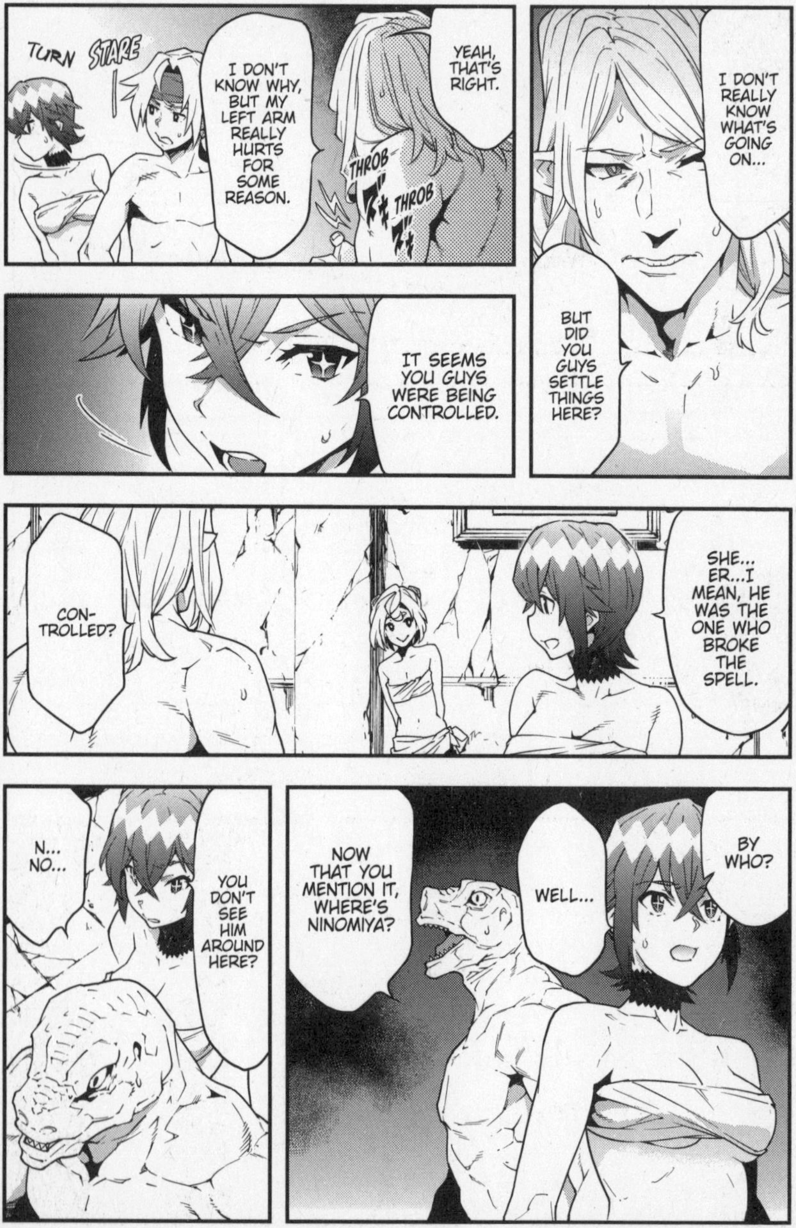
I DON'T REALLY KNOW WHAT'S GOING ON...
BUT DID YOU GUYS SETTLE THINGS HERE?
YEAH, THAT'S RIGHT.
THROB THROB
I DON'T KNOW WHY, BUT MY LEFT ARM REALLY HURTS FOR SOME REASON.
STARE
TURN
IT SEEMS YOU GUYS WERE BEING CONTROLLED.
SHE... ER...I MEAN, HE WAS THE ONE WHO BROKE THE SPELL.
CON-TROLLED?
BY WHO?
WELL...
NOW THAT YOU MENTION IT, WHERE'S NINOMIYA?
YOU DON'T SEE HIM AROUND HERE?
N... NO...

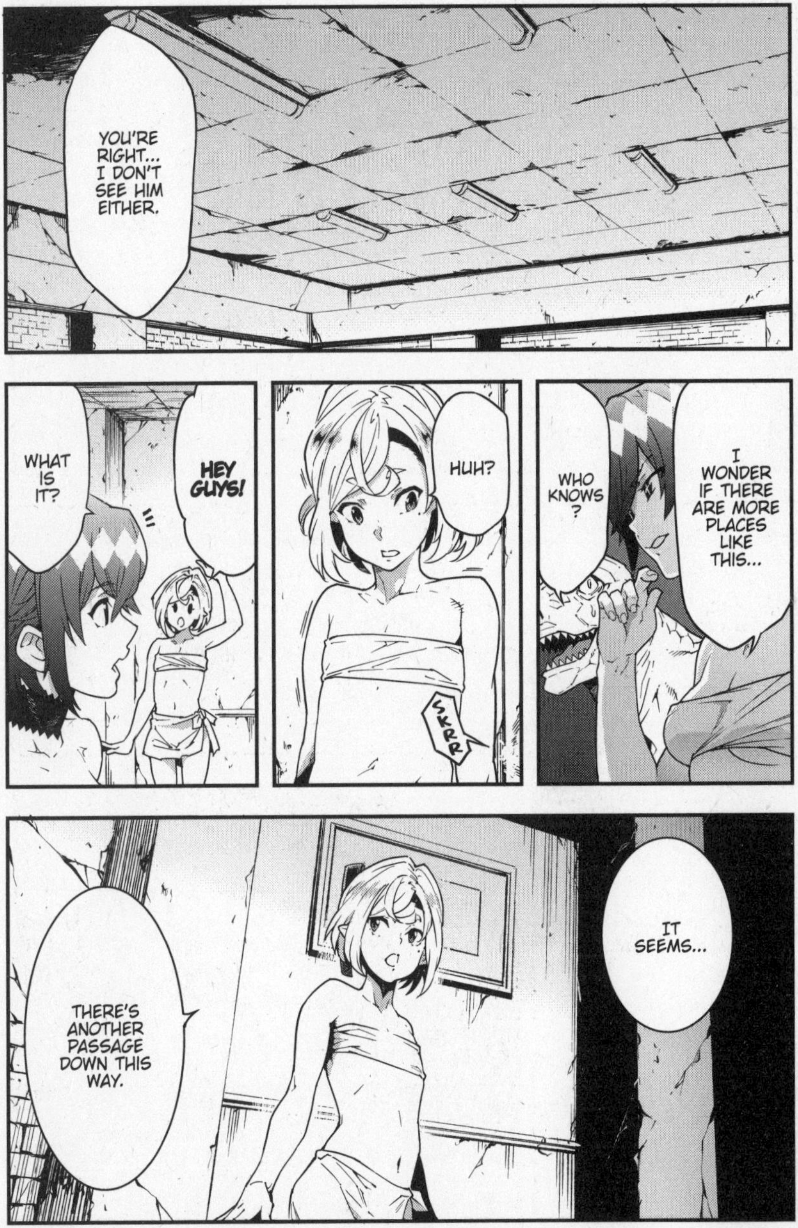
YOU'RE RIGHT... I DON'T SEE HIM EITHER.
I WONDER IF THERE ARE MORE PLACES LIKE THIS...
WHO KNOWS?
HUH?
SKRR
HEY GUYS!
WHAT IS IT?
IT SEEMS...
THERE'S ANOTHER PASSAGE DOWN THIS WAY.

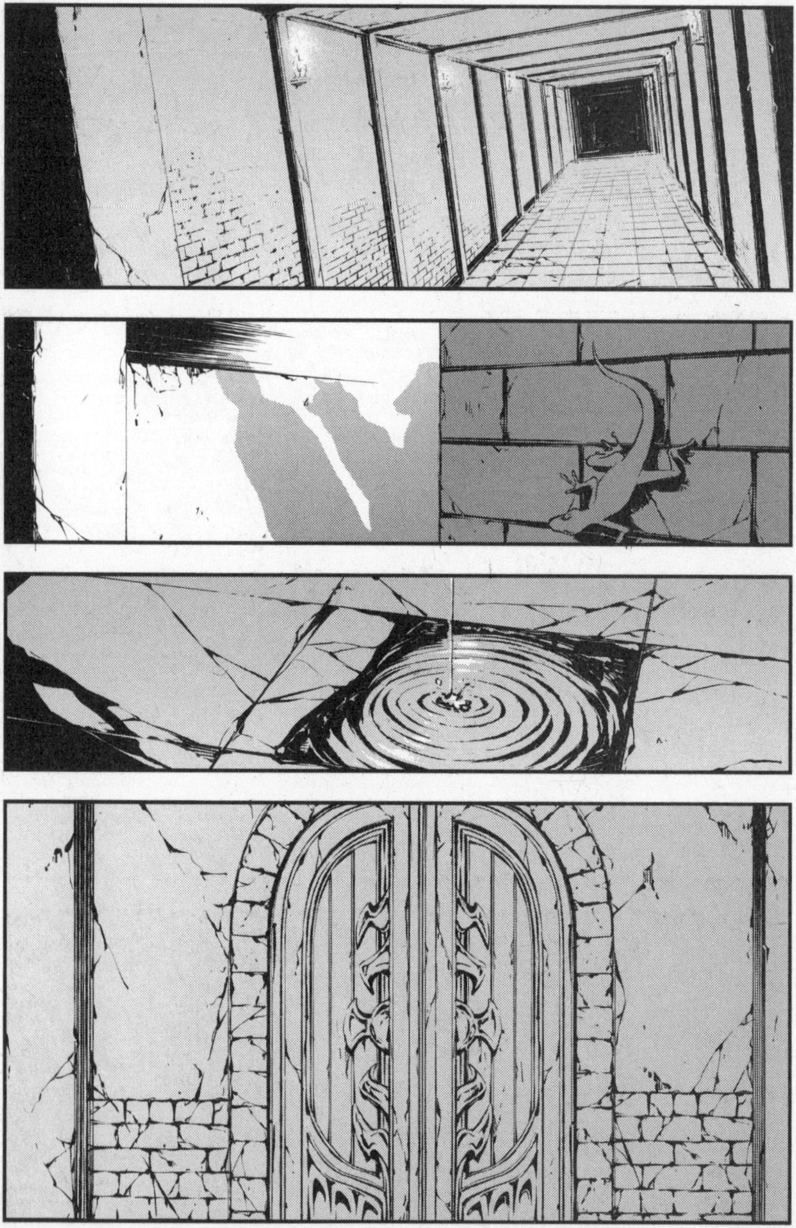

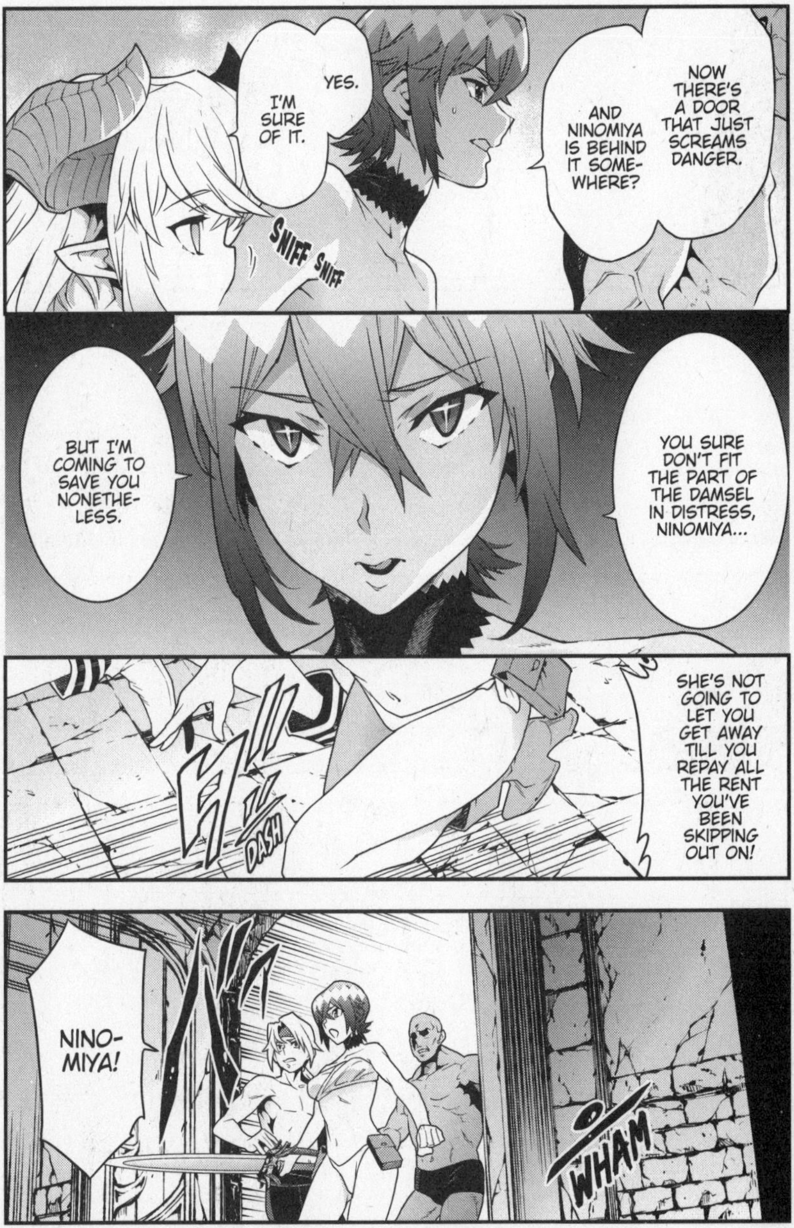
NOW THERE'S A DOOR THAT JUST SCREAMS DANGER.
AND NINOMIYA IS BEHIND IT SOME-WHERE?
YES.
I'M SURE OF IT.
SNIFF SNIFF
YOU SURE DON'T FIT THE PART OF THE DAMSEL IN DISTRESS, NINOMIYA...
BUT I'M COMING TO SAVE YOU NONETHE-LESS.
SHE'S NOT GOING TO LET YOU GET AWAY TILL YOU REPAY ALL THE RENT YOU'VE BEEN SKIPPING OUT ON!
DASH
WHAM
NINO-MIYA!

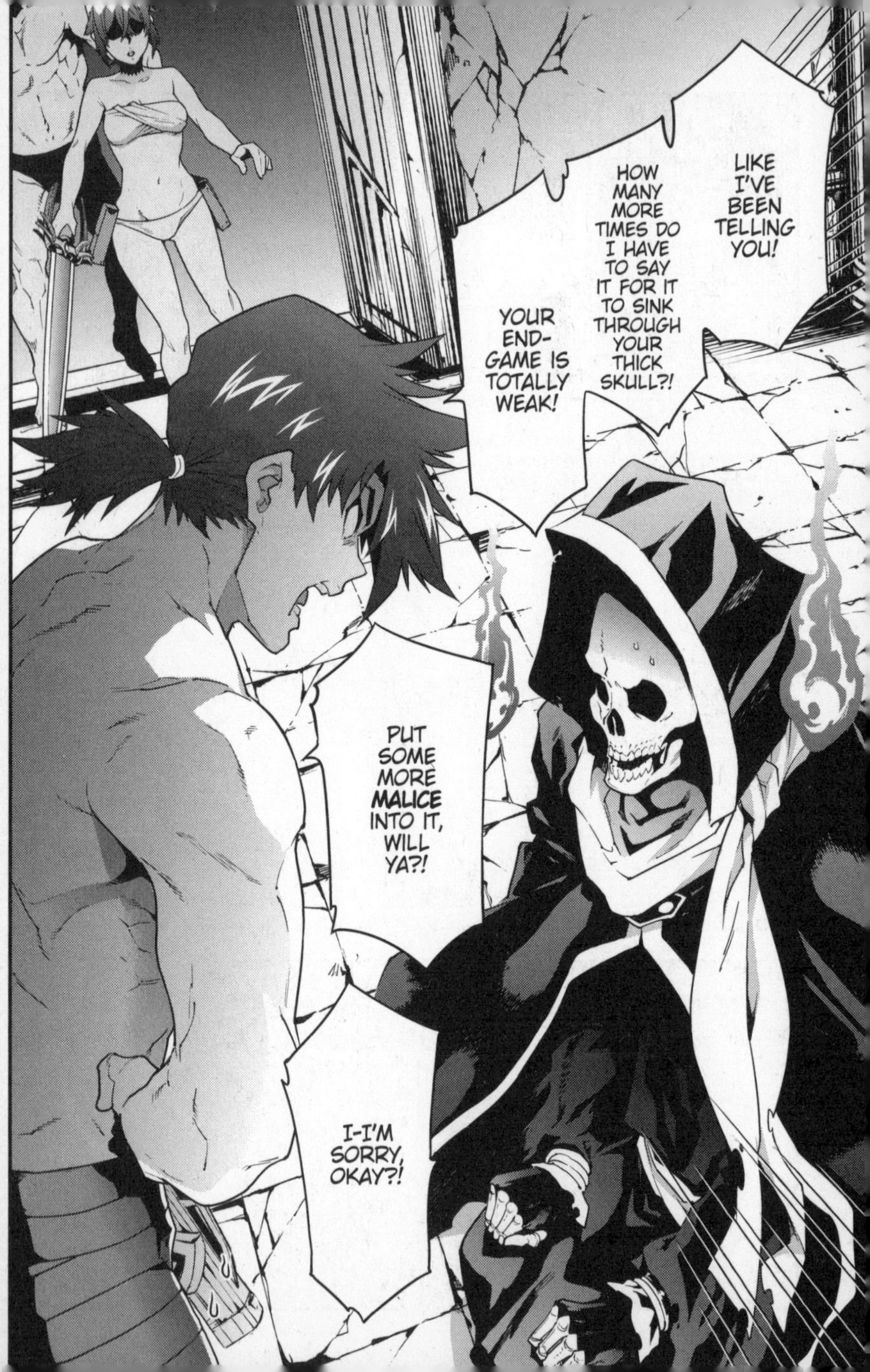
LIKE I'VE BEEN TELLING YOU!
HOW MANY MORE TIMES DO I HAVE TO SAY IT FOR IT TO SINK THROUGH YOUR THICK SKULL?!
YOUR END-GAME IS TOTALLY WEAK!
PUT SOME MORE **MALICE** INTO IT, WILL YA?!
I-I'M SORRY, OKAY?!

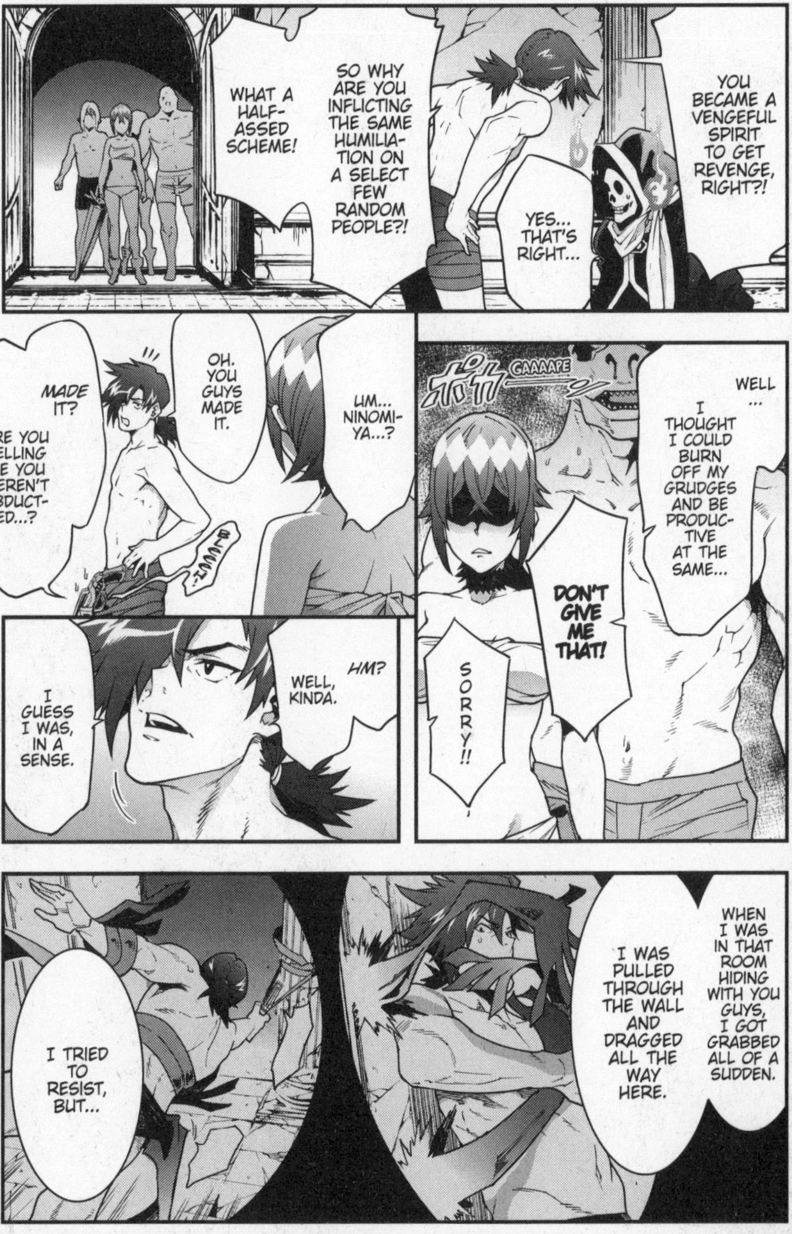
YOU BECAME A VENGEFUL SPIRIT TO GET REVENGE, RIGHT?!
YES... THAT'S RIGHT...
SO WHY ARE YOU INFLICTING THE SAME HUMILIATION ON A SELECT FEW RANDOM PEOPLE?!
WHAT A HALF-ASSED SCHEME!
WELL ... I THOUGHT I COULD BURN OFF MY GRUDGES AND BE PRODUCTIVE AT THE SAME...
GAAAAPE
DON'T GIVE ME THAT!
SORRY!!
UM... NINOMIYA...?
OH. YOU GUYS MADE IT.
MADE IT?
ARE YOU TELLING ME YOU WEREN'T ABDUCTED...?
HM?
WELL, KINDA.
I GUESS I WAS, IN A SENSE.
WHEN I WAS IN THAT ROOM HIDING WITH YOU GUYS, I GOT GRABBED ALL OF A SUDDEN.
I WAS PULLED THROUGH THE WALL AND DRAGGED ALL THE WAY HERE.
I TRIED TO RESIST, BUT...

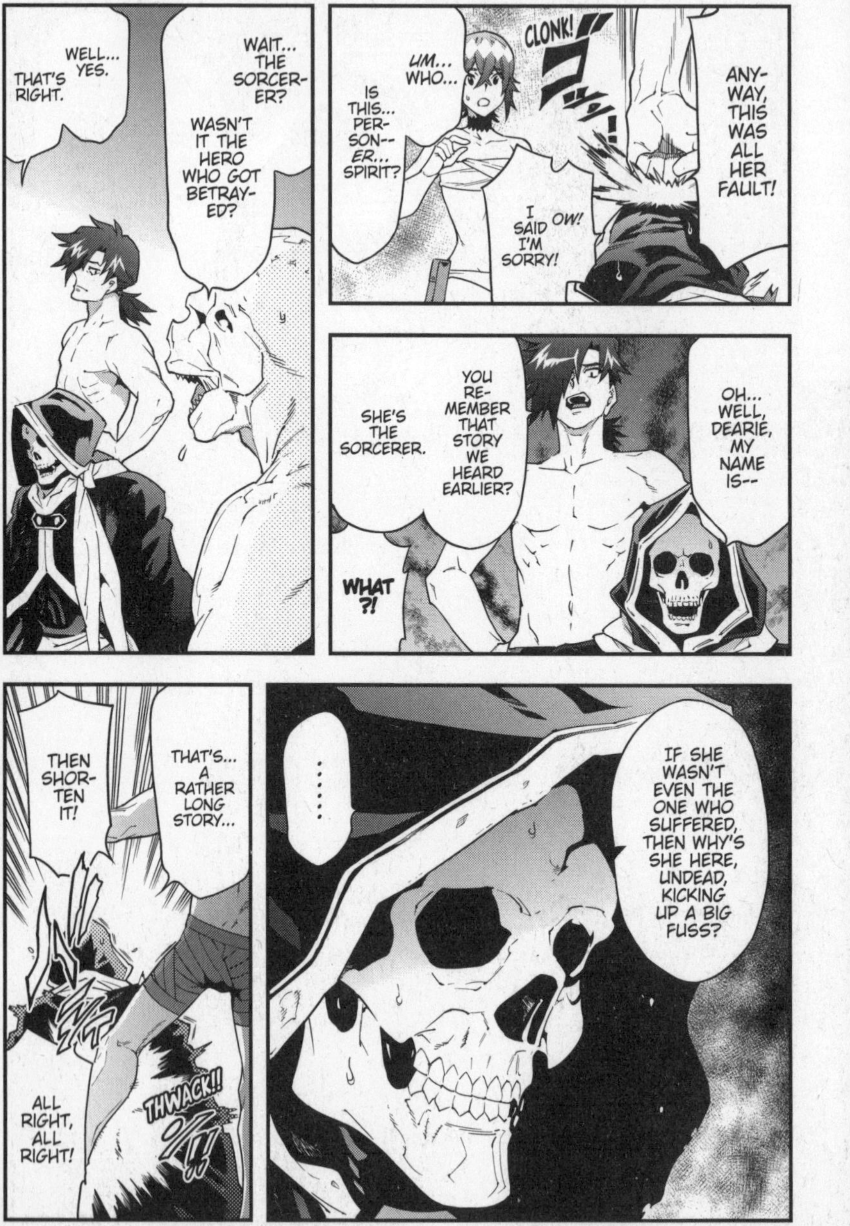
ANYWAY, THIS WAS ALL HER FAULT!
CLONK!
UM... WHO...
IS THIS... PERSON--ER... SPIRIT?
I SAID I'M SORRY!
OW!
OH... WELL, DEARIE, MY NAME IS--
YOU REMEMBER THAT STORY WE HEARD EARLIER?
SHE'S THE SORCERER.
WHAT?!
WAIT... THE SORCERER?
WASN'T IT THE HERO WHO GOT BETRAYED?
WELL... YES.
THAT'S RIGHT.
IF SHE WASN'T EVEN THE ONE WHO SUFFERED, THEN WHY'S SHE HERE, UNDEAD, KICKING UP A BIG FUSS?
......
THAT'S... A RATHER LONG STORY...
THEN SHORTEN IT!
THWACK!!
ALL RIGHT, ALL RIGHT!

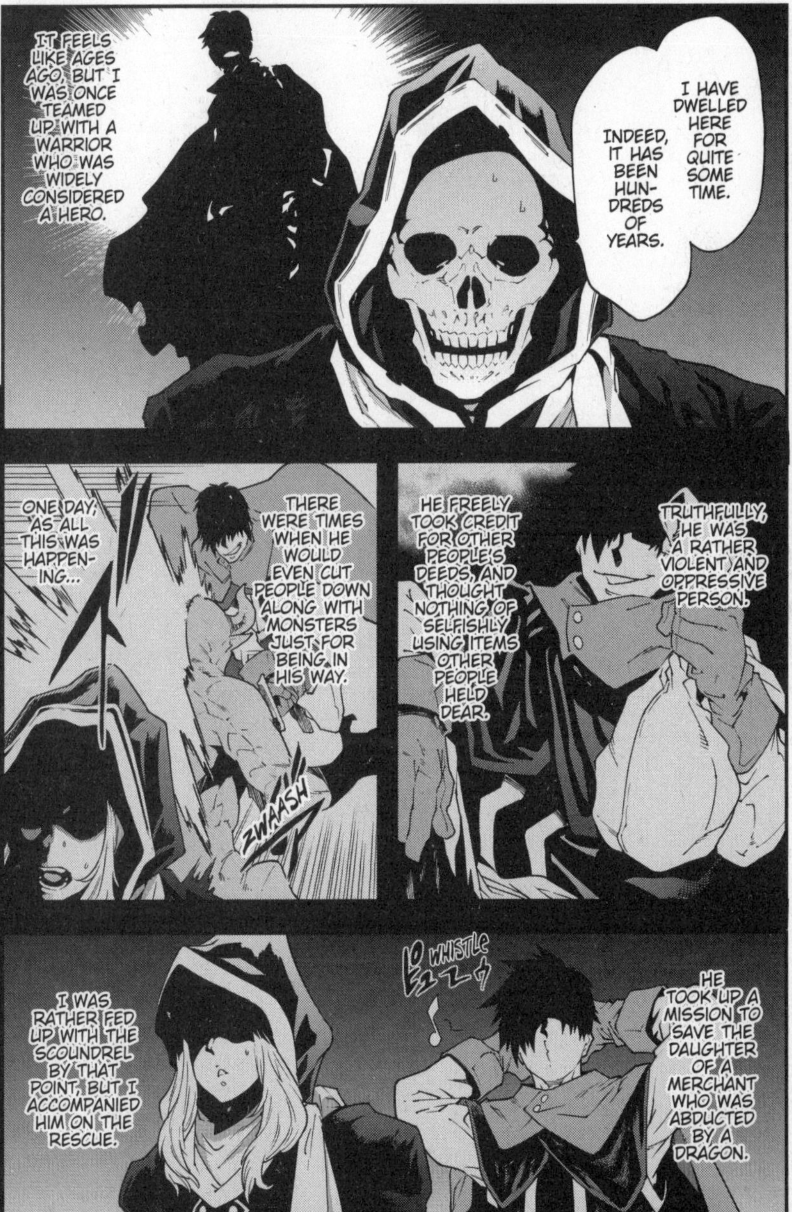
I HAVE DWELLED HERE FOR QUITE SOME TIME.
INDEED, IT HAS BEEN HUNDREDS OF YEARS.
IT FEELS LIKE AGES AGO, BUT I WAS ONCE TEAMED UP WITH A WARRIOR WHO WAS WIDELY CONSIDERED A HERO.
TRUTHFULLY, HE WAS A RATHER VIOLENT AND OPPRESSIVE PERSON.
HE FREELY TOOK CREDIT FOR OTHER PEOPLE'S DEEDS, AND THOUGHT NOTHING OF SELFISHLY USING ITEMS OTHER PEOPLE HELD DEAR.
THERE WERE TIMES WHEN HE WOULD EVEN CUT PEOPLE DOWN ALONG WITH MONSTERS JUST FOR BEING IN HIS WAY.
ZWAASH
ONE DAY, AS ALL THIS WAS HAPPENING...
HE TOOK UP A MISSION TO SAVE THE DAUGHTER OF A MERCHANT WHO WAS ABDUCTED BY A DRAGON.
WHISTLE
I WAS RATHER FED UP WITH THE SCOUNDREL BY THAT POINT, BUT I ACCOMPANIED HIM ON THE RESCUE.

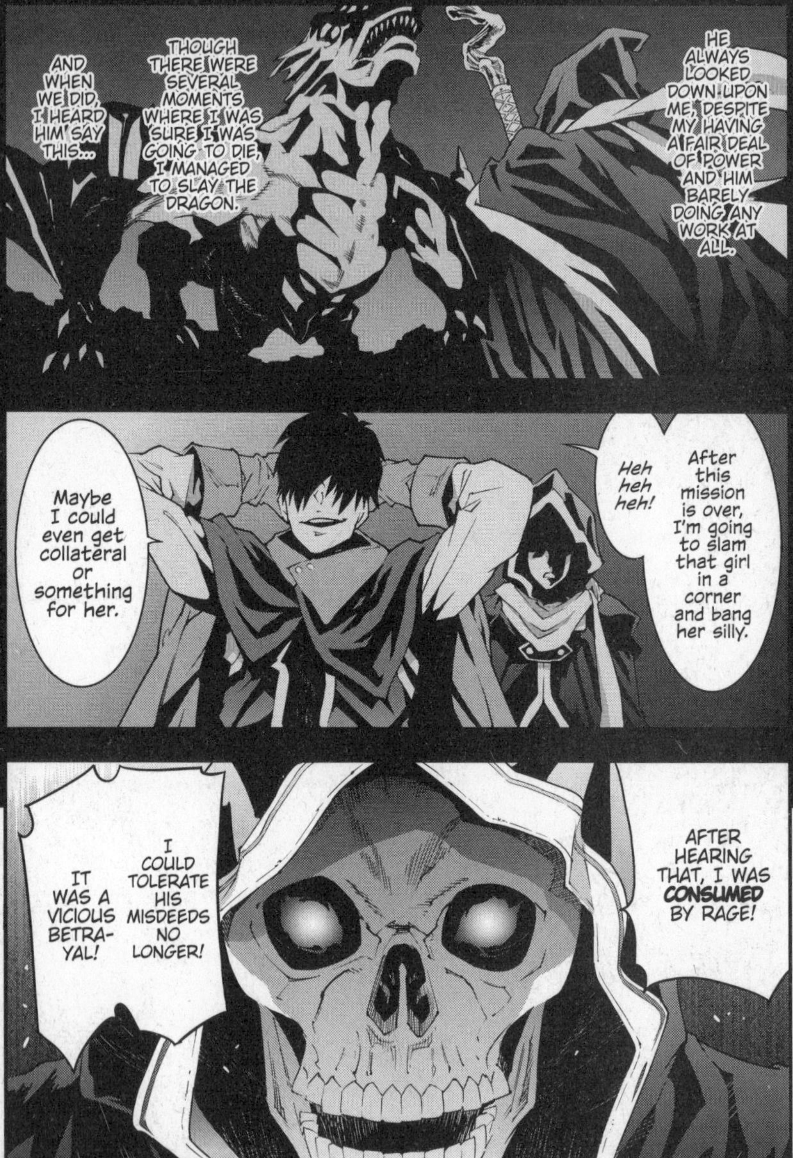
HE ALWAYS LOOKED DOWN UPON ME, DESPITE MY HAVING A FAIR DEAL OF POWER AND HIM BARELY DOING ANY WORK AT ALL.
THOUGH THERE WERE SEVERAL MOMENTS WHERE I WAS SURE I WAS GOING TO DIE, I MANAGED TO SLAY THE DRAGON.
AND WHEN WE DID, I HEARD HIM SAY THIS...
After this mission is over, I'm going to slam that girl in a corner and bang her silly.
Heh heh heh!
Maybe I could even get collateral or something for her.
AFTER HEARING THAT, I WAS CONSUMED BY RAGE!
I COULD TOLERATE HIS MISDEEDS NO LONGER!
IT WAS A VICIOUS BETRAYAL!

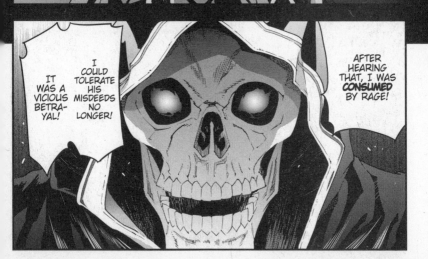

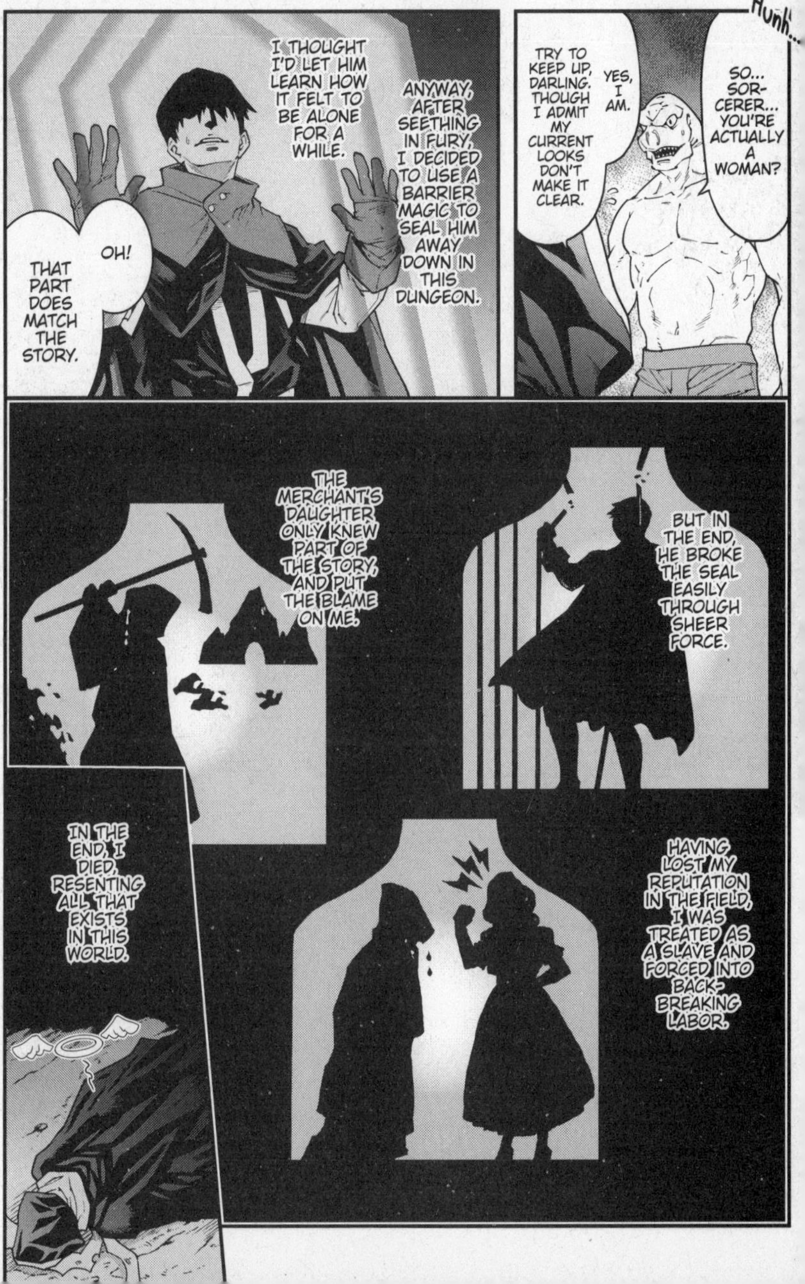
Hunh...
SO... SORCERER... YOU'RE ACTUALLY A WOMAN?
YES, I AM.
TRY TO KEEP UP, DARLING. THOUGH I ADMIT MY CURRENT LOOKS DON'T MAKE IT CLEAR.
ANYWAY, AFTER SEETHING IN FURY, I DECIDED TO USE A BARRIER MAGIC TO SEAL HIM AWAY DOWN IN THIS DUNGEON.
I THOUGHT I'D LET HIM LEARN HOW IT FELT TO BE ALONE FOR A WHILE.
OH!
THAT PART DOES MATCH THE STORY.
BUT IN THE END, HE BROKE THE SEAL EASILY THROUGH SHEER FORCE.
THE MERCHANT'S DAUGHTER ONLY KNEW PART OF THE STORY, AND PUT THE BLAME ON ME.
HAVING LOST MY REPUTATION IN THE FIELD, I WAS TREATED AS A SLAVE AND FORCED INTO BACK-BREAKING LABOR.
IN THE END, I DIED, RESENTING ALL THAT EXISTS IN THIS WORLD.

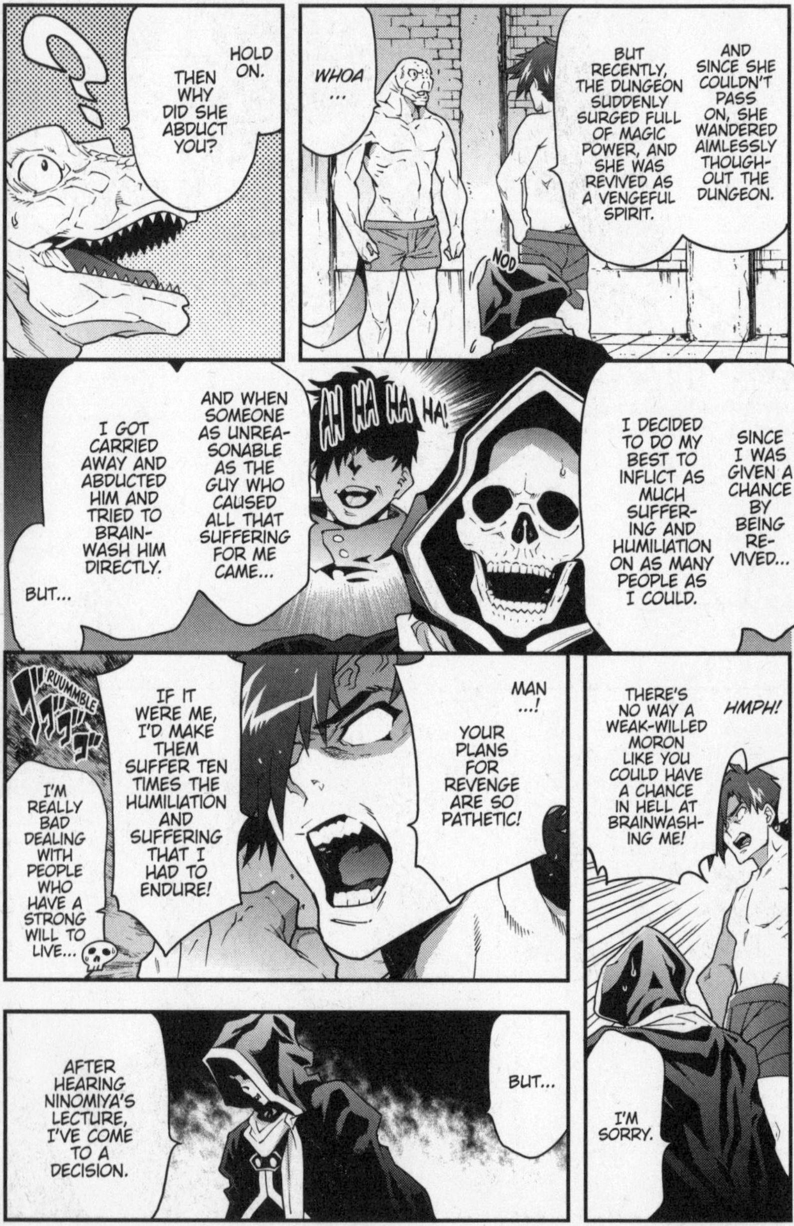
AND SINCE SHE COULDN'T PASS ON, SHE WANDERED AIMLESSLY THOUGH-OUT THE DUNGEON.
BUT RECENTLY, THE DUNGEON SUDDENLY SURGED FULL OF MAGIC POWER, AND SHE WAS REVIVED AS A VENGEFUL SPIRIT.
WHOA...
NOD
HOLD ON.
THEN WHY DID SHE ABDUCT YOU?
W... WELL...
SINCE I WAS GIVEN A CHANCE BY BEING RE-VIVED...
I DECIDED TO DO MY BEST TO INFLICT AS MUCH SUFFER-ING AND HUMILIATION ON AS MANY PEOPLE AS I COULD.
AH HA HA HA!
AND WHEN SOMEONE AS UNREA-SONABLE AS THE GUY WHO CAUSED ALL THAT SUFFERING FOR ME CAME...
I GOT CARRIED AWAY AND ABDUCTED HIM AND TRIED TO BRAIN-WASH HIM DIRECTLY.
BUT...
HMPH!
THERE'S NO WAY A WEAK-WILLED MORON LIKE YOU COULD HAVE A CHANCE IN HELL AT BRAINWASH-ING ME!
I'M SORRY.
MAN...!
YOUR PLANS FOR REVENGE ARE SO PATHETIC!
IF IT WERE ME, I'D MAKE THEM SUFFER TEN TIMES THE HUMILIATION AND SUFFERING THAT I HAD TO ENDURE!
RUUMMBLE
I'M REALLY BAD DEALING WITH PEOPLE WHO HAVE A STRONG WILL TO LIVE...
BUT...
AFTER HEARING NINOMIYA'S LECTURE, I'VE COME TO A DECISION.

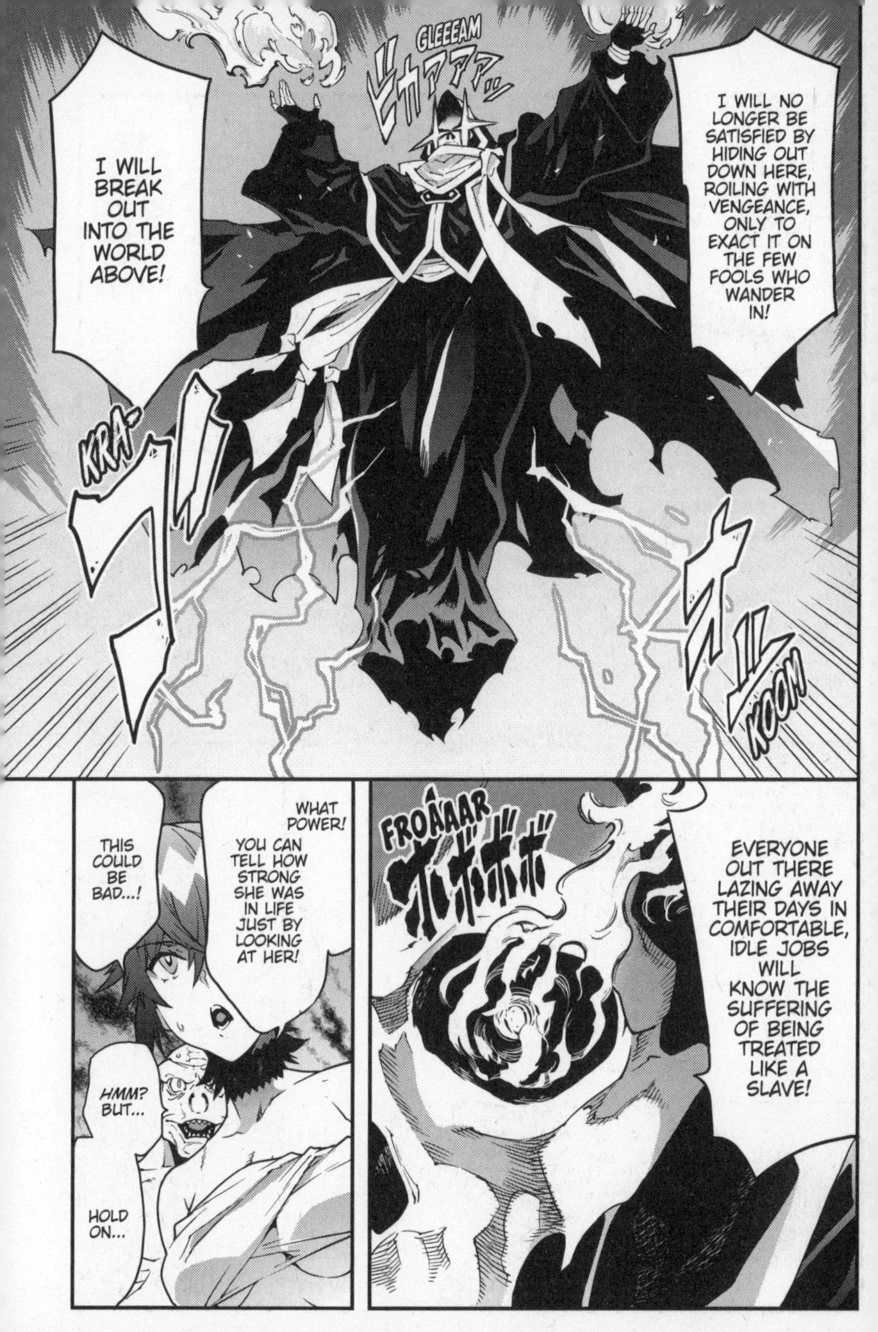
GLEEEAM
I WILL NO LONGER BE SATISFIED BY HIDING OUT DOWN HERE, ROILING WITH VENGEANCE, ONLY TO EXACT IT ON THE FEW FOOLS WHO WANDER IN!
I WILL BREAK OUT INTO THE WORLD ABOVE!
KRA-
KOOM
FROÂAAR
EVERYONE OUT THERE LAZING AWAY THEIR DAYS IN COMFORTABLE, IDLE JOBS WILL KNOW THE SUFFERING OF BEING TREATED LIKE A SLAVE!
WHAT POWER!
YOU CAN TELL HOW STRONG SHE WAS IN LIFE JUST BY LOOKING AT HER!
THIS COULD BE BAD...!
HMM? BUT...
HOLD ON...

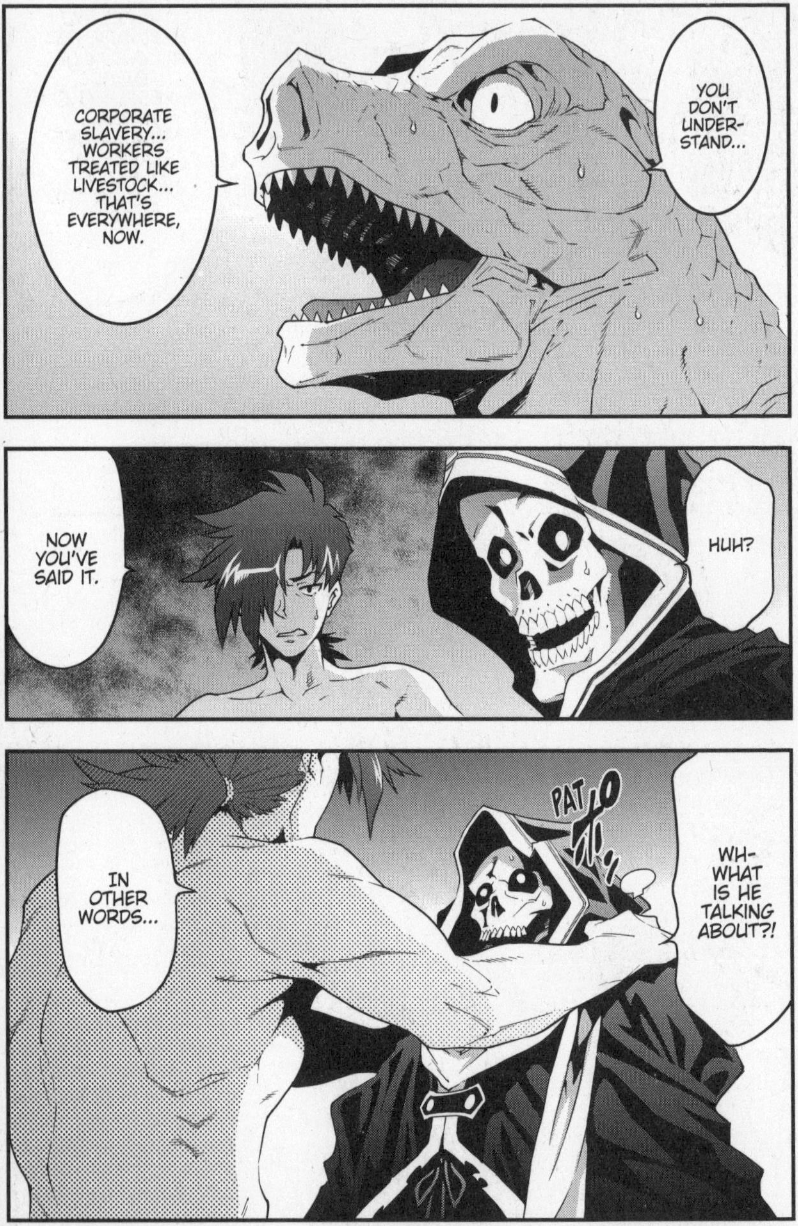
YOU DON'T UNDER- STAND...
CORPORATE SLAVERY... WORKERS TREATED LIKE LIVESTOCK... THAT'S EVERYWHERE, NOW.
HUH?
NOW YOU'VE SAID IT.
WH- WHAT IS HE TALKING ABOUT?!
PAT
IN OTHER WORDS...

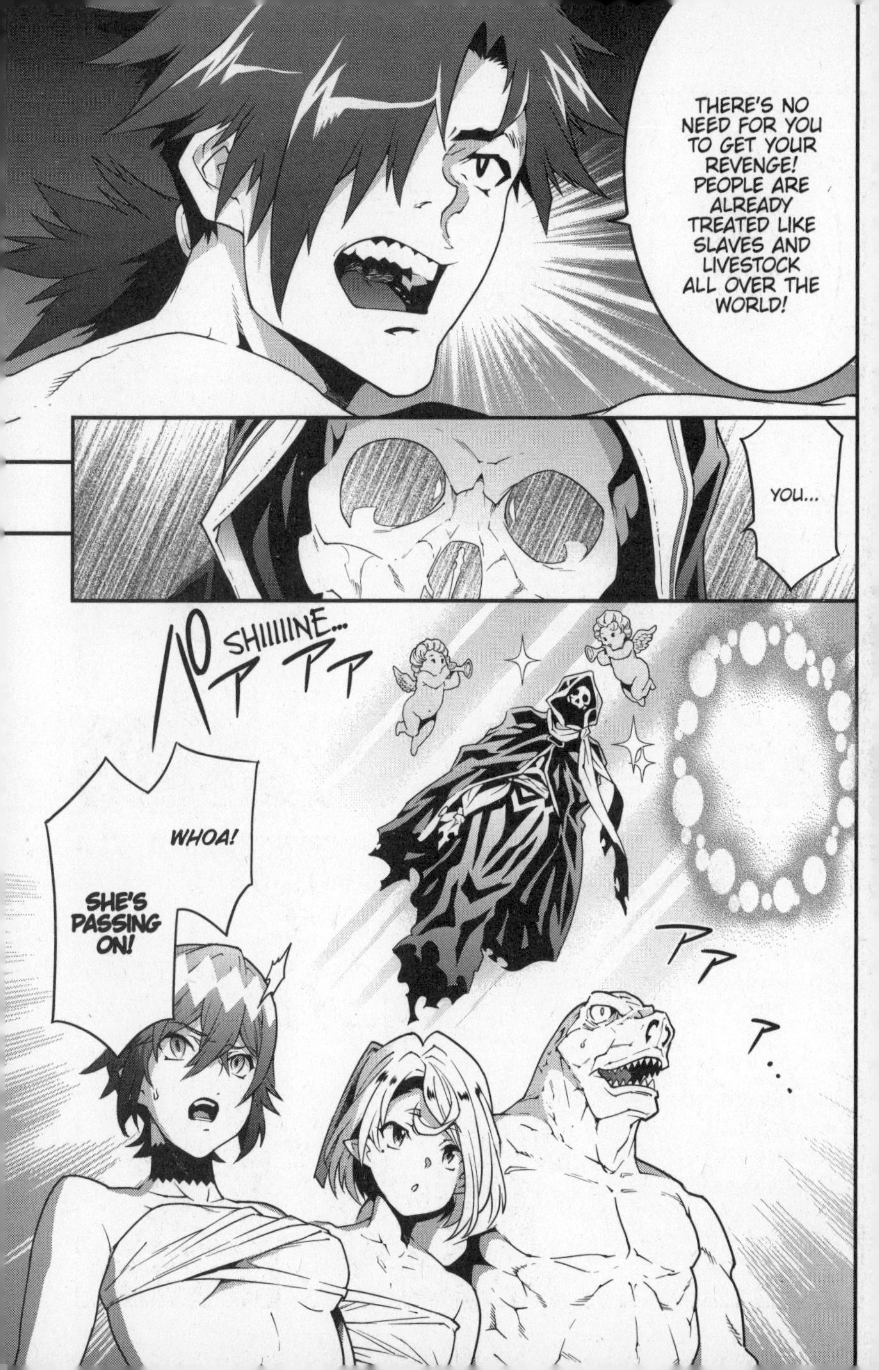
THERE'S NO NEED FOR YOU TO GET YOUR REVENGE! PEOPLE ARE ALREADY TREATED LIKE SLAVES AND LIVESTOCK ALL OVER THE WORLD!
YOU...
SHIIIIINE...
WHOA!
SHE'S PASSING ON!

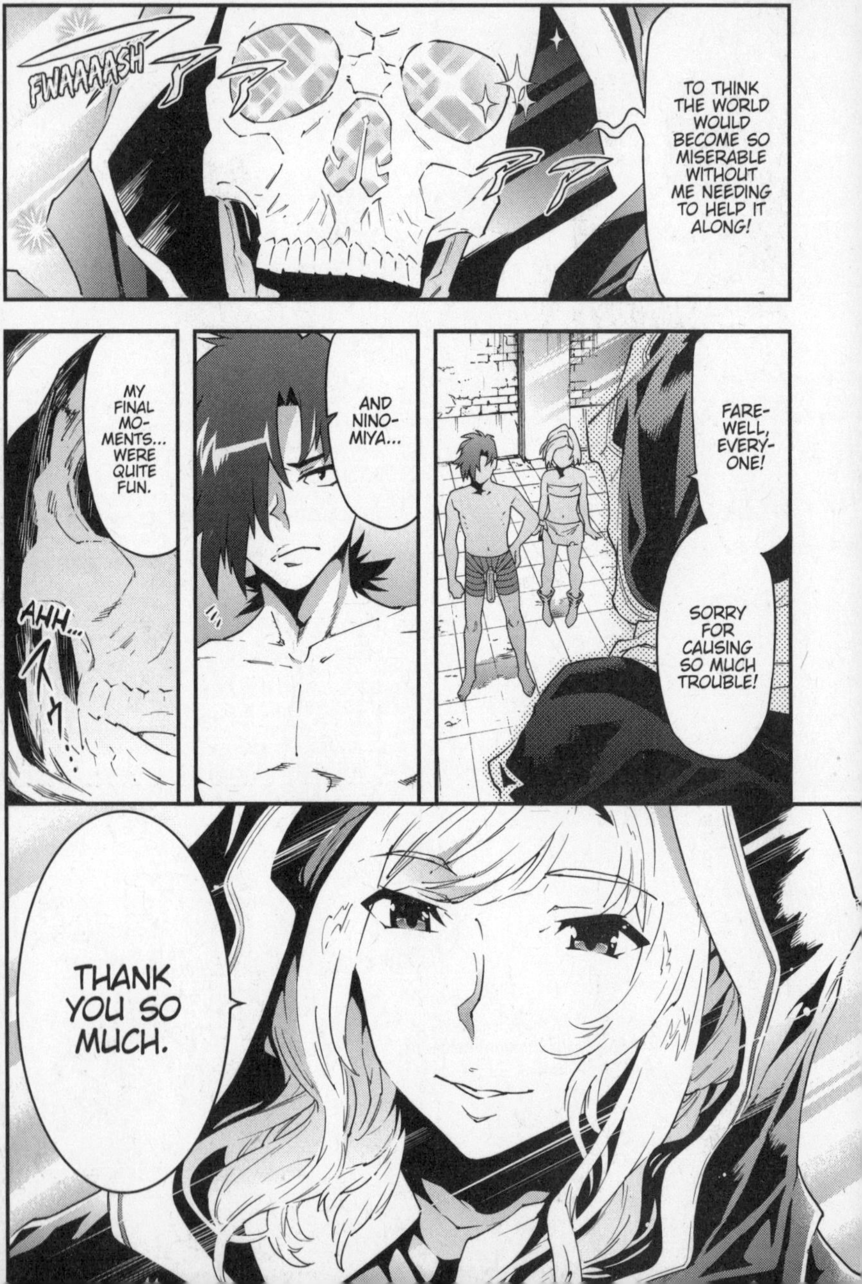
TO THINK THE WORLD WOULD BECOME SO MISERABLE WITHOUT ME NEEDING TO HELP IT ALONG!
FWAAAASH
FARE-WELL, EVERY-ONE!
SORRY FOR CAUSING SO MUCH TROUBLE!
AND NINO-MIYA...
MY FINAL MO-MENTS... WERE QUITE FUN.
AHH...
THANK YOU SO MUCH.

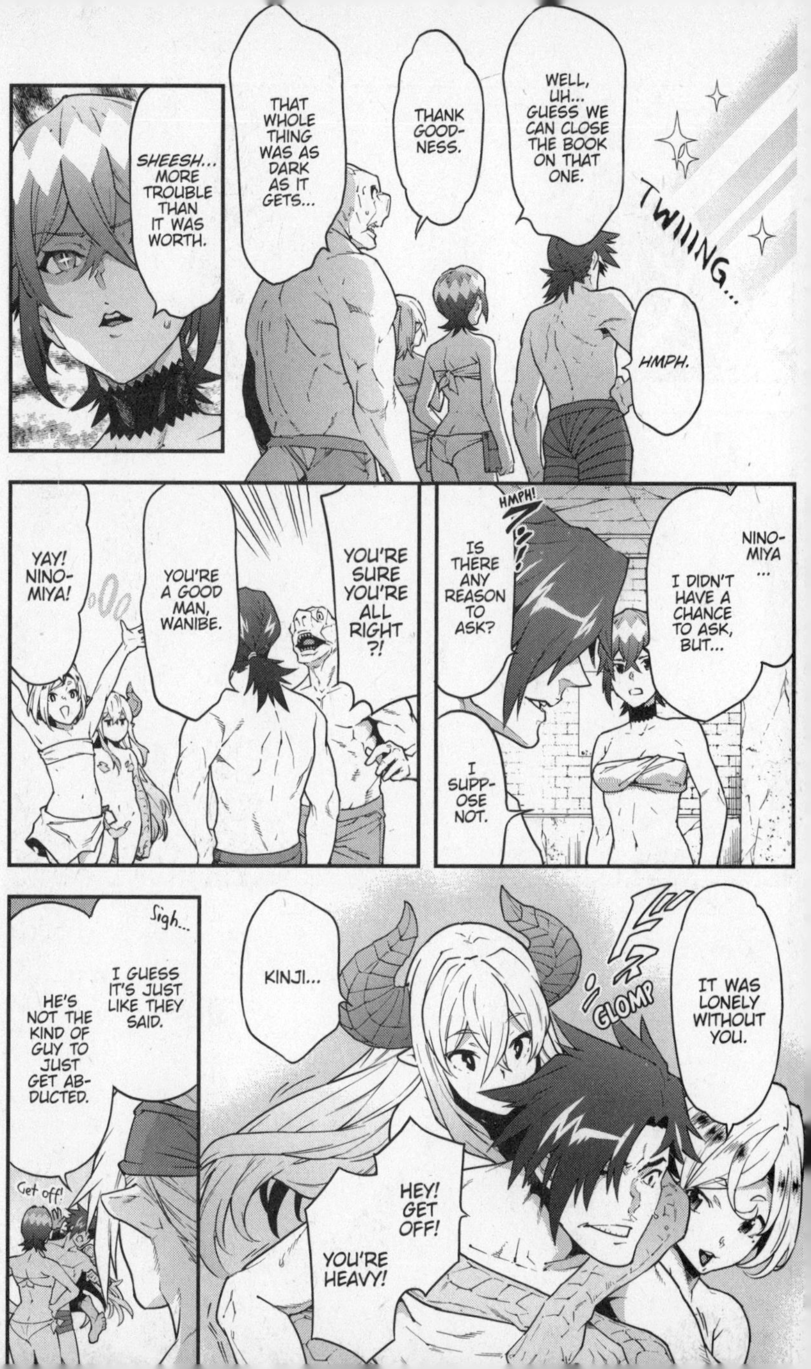
WELL, UH... GUESS WE CAN CLOSE THE BOOK ON THAT ONE.
TWIIING...
THANK GOODNESS.
THAT WHOLE THING WAS AS DARK AS IT GETS...
HMPH.
SHEESH... MORE TROUBLE THAN IT WAS WORTH.
NINOMIYA... I DIDN'T HAVE A CHANCE TO ASK, BUT...
HMPH!
IS THERE ANY REASON TO ASK?
I SUPPOSE NOT.
YOU'RE SURE YOU'RE ALL RIGHT?!
YOU'RE A GOOD MAN, WANIBE.
YAY! NINOMIYA!
IT WAS LONELY WITHOUT YOU.
GLOMP
KINJI...
HEY! GET OFF!
YOU'RE HEAVY!
Sigh...
I GUESS IT'S JUST LIKE THEY SAID.
HE'S NOT THE KIND OF GUY TO JUST GET ABDUCTED.
Get off!

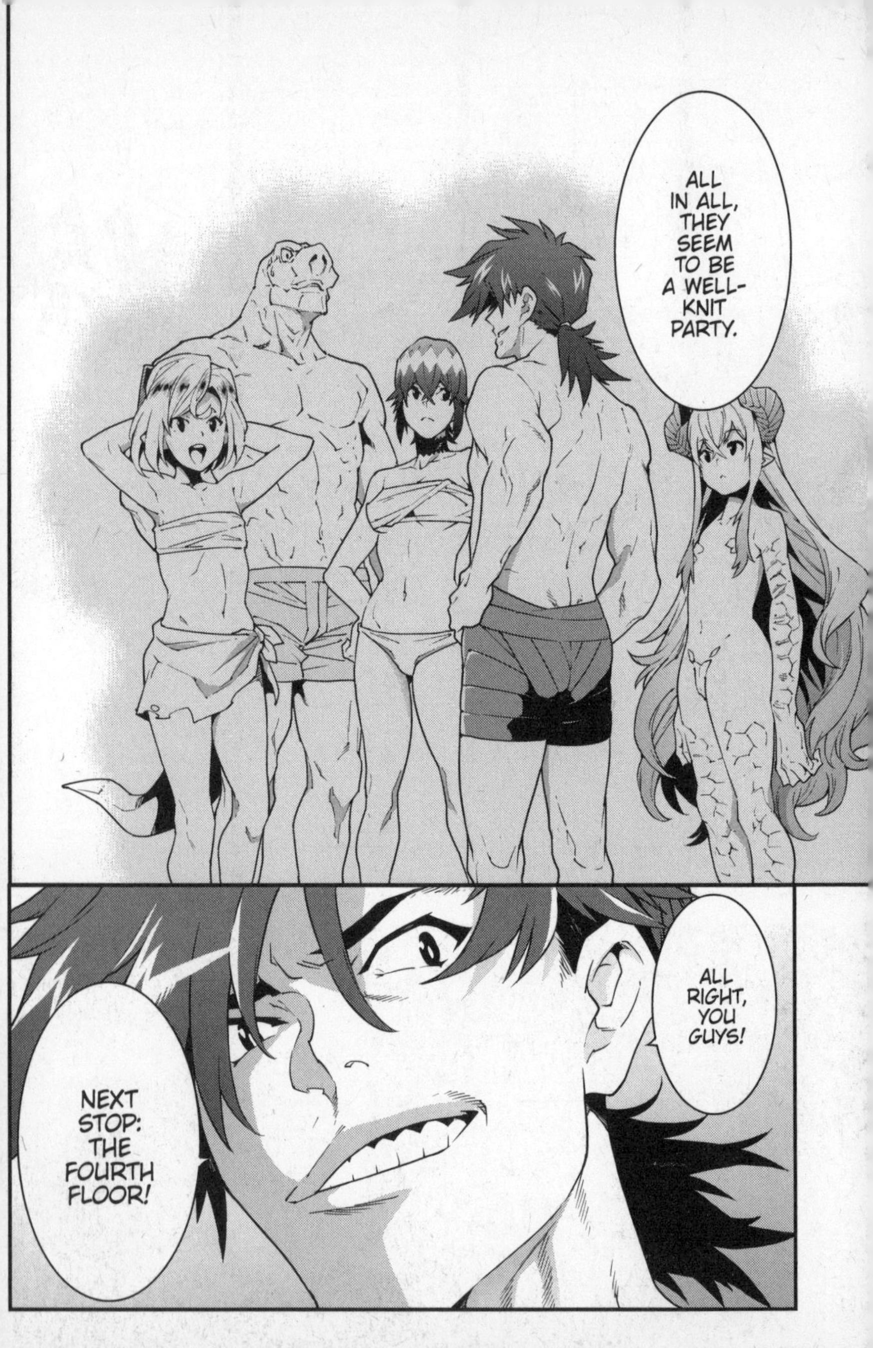
ALL IN ALL, THEY SEEM TO BE A WELL-KNIT PARTY.
ALL RIGHT, YOU GUYS!
NEXT STOP: THE FOURTH FLOOR!

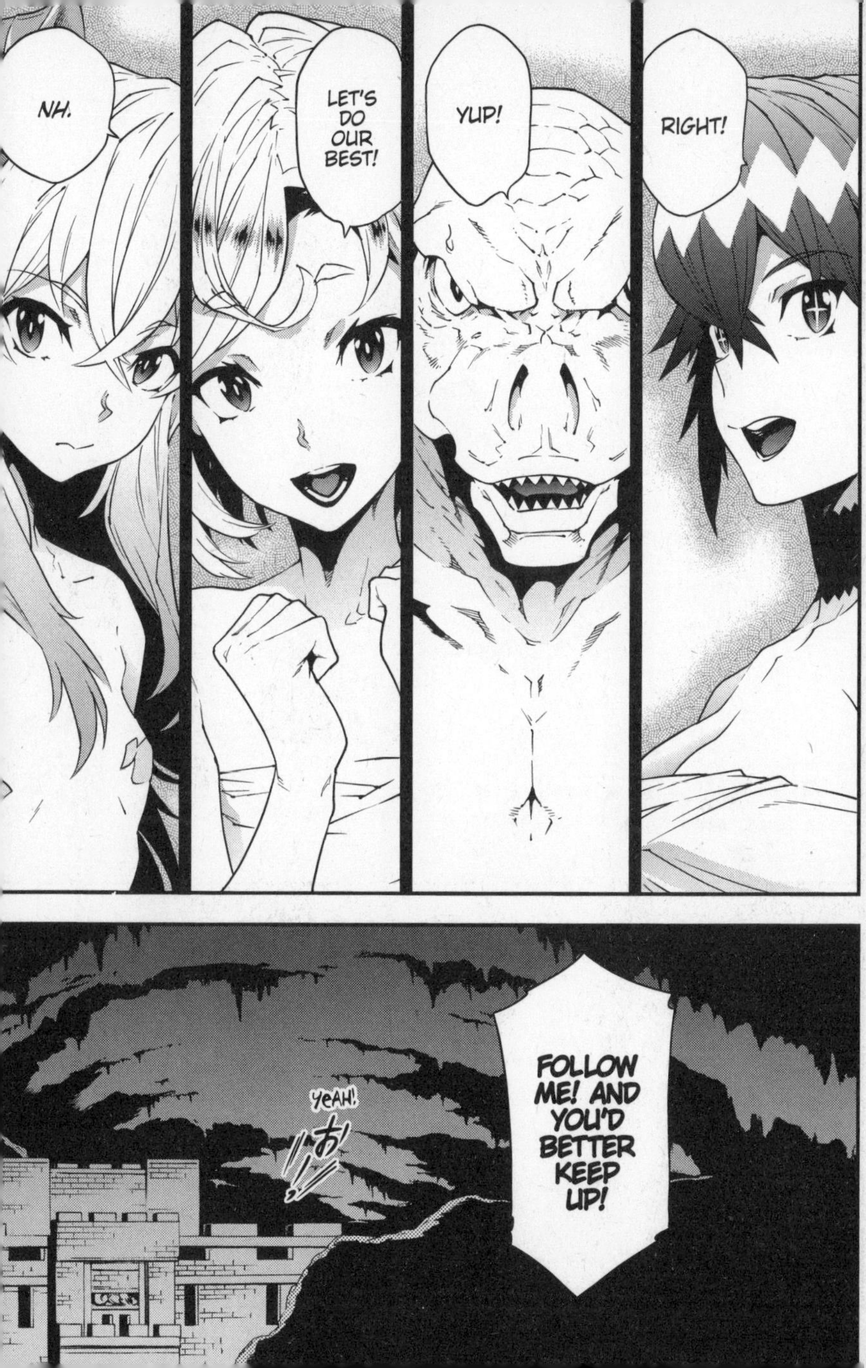
RIGHT!
YUP!
LET'S DO OUR BEST!
NH.
FOLLOW ME! AND YOU'D BETTER KEEP UP!
yeAH!
お!!

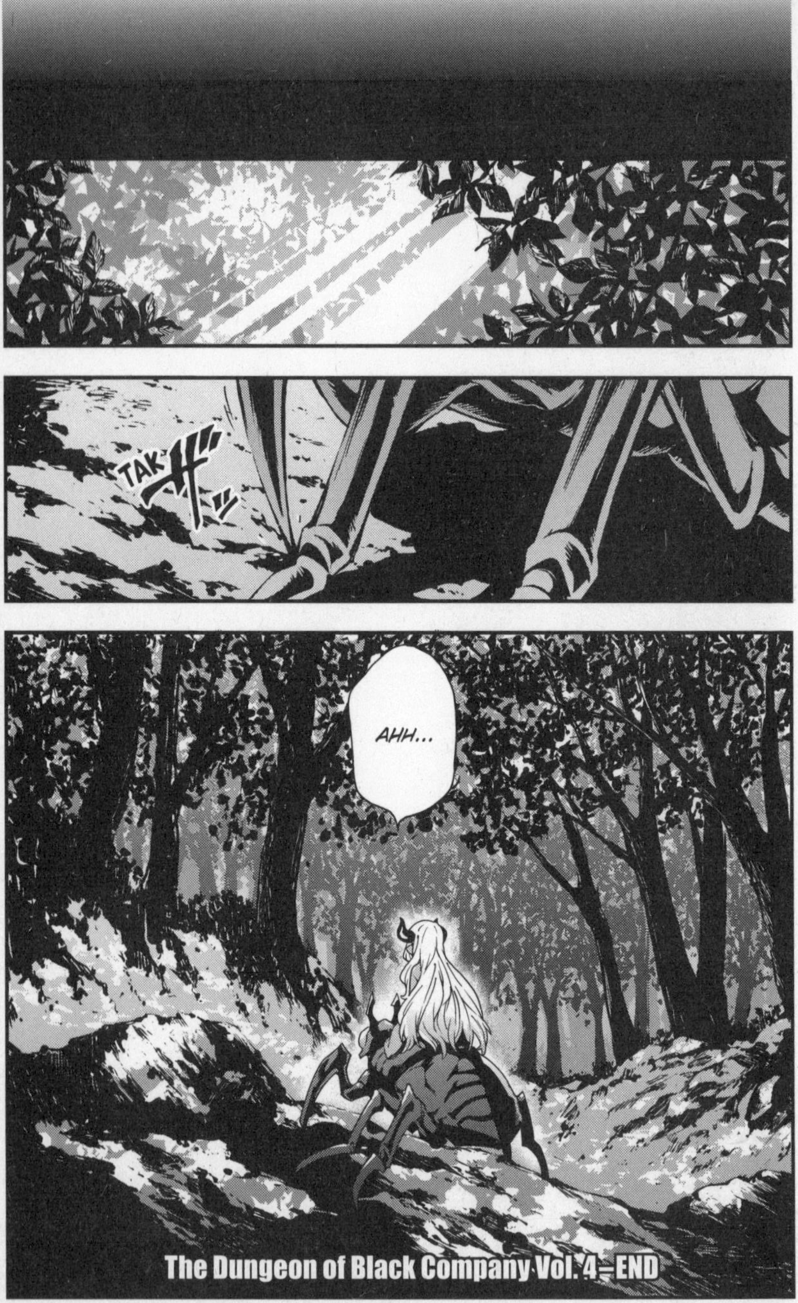
TAK
AHH...
The Dungeon of Black Company Vol. 4—END